CISM COURSES AND LECTURES

The series presents lecture notes, monographs, edited works and proceedings in the field of Mechanics, Engineering, Computer Science and Applied Mathematics.
Purpose of the series is to make known in the international scientific and technical community results obtained in some of the activities organized by CISM, the International Centre for Mechanical Sciences.

CISM COURSES AND LECTURES

INTERNATIONAL CENTRE FOR MECHANICAL SCIENCES

COURSES AND LECTURES - No. 407

UM99
USER MODELING

PROCEEDINGS OF THE
SEVENTH INTERNATIONAL CONFERENCE

BANFF, CANADA
JUNE 20 - 24, 1999

EDITED BY

JUDY KAY
UNIVERSITY OF SYDNEY

Springer-Verlag Wien GmbH

This volume contains 413 illustrations

ISBN 978-3-211-83151-9   ISBN 978-3-7091-2490-1 (eBook)
DOI 10.1007/978-3-7091-2490-1
© 1999 by Springer-Verlag Wien
Originally published by CISM, Udine in 1999.
SPIN 10731116

In order to make this volume available as economically and as
rapidly as possible the authors' typescripts have been
reproduced in their original forms. This method unfortunately
has its typographical limitations but it is hoped that they in no
way distract the reader.

ISSN 1091-2789 User Modeling Inc.

Preface

User modelling is the essential element of systems which adapt to the individual. With increasing use of computers, by wider and more diverse user populations, there is an increasing need for user-adapted systems. This demand fuels the research into the various aspects of user modelling, from the internal management of the user model to the many issues associated with driving and deploying user-adaptation.

User modelling is an inherently multi-disciplinary community. This is a natural development from research models based upon increasing specialisation. Although specialisation enables researchers to acquire depth in their particular technical area, it also produces serious problems when the goal is to produce user-adapted systems. Within each of several specialised communities, researchers have been developing theories and techniques for user-adaptation. The specialist model of research makes it difficult to achieve cross-fertilisation between these communities. In the past, this had led to near-disjoint literatures for the several research communities concerned with user modelling.

The User Modelling Conferences have played an important role in bringing together researchers from communities like AI and Education, Computational Linguistics, Intelligent User Interfaces, Information Retrieval and Database Systems. When each of these communities build systems which can adapt to the individual user, they must deal with the issues of representation of the user model, its acquisition and maintenance as well as the challenges of applying the user model to the tasks of adaptation. Finally, researchers building user-adapted systems have a common need to evaluate the effectiveness of the adaptation in those systems.

Equally, the user modelling conferences draw researchers from the communities which develop theory, techniques and tools which are important for the various elements underlying the user modelling enterprise. These include planning, machine learning and other forms of knowledge acquisition, knowledge representation, adaptive hypertext, adaptive presentation and multi-media, privacy and security management as well as broader areas such as education, psychology and information sciences. In principle, these researchers might tackle the problems from within their own specialised communities. However, they stand to gain by learning from each other.

This Seventh User Modelling Conference was held at Banff, Canada, 20-24th June, 1999. The conference series began with the small 1986 workshop in Maria Laach, Germany. The User Modelling Conferences have now become the primary conference forum for sharing user modelling research outcomes. Many of its best papers will provide foundations for the archival and more substantial papers that appear in the community's journal, User Modeling and User-Adapted Interaction.

In the current volume we see more than a coming together of researchers from other communities. Increasingly, the papers build upon the multi-disciplinary body of research that is becoming a foundation for the building of systems which provide user-adapted interaction.

It is customary to report the national origins of papers submitted for conferences. This is becoming an increasingly complex task as we see greater internationalisation. There were 103 submissions for the main technical programme, with 6 papers jointly written by authors located in different countries. In all 20 countries were represented. Also interesting is the large number of papers jointly written by authors who cross the educational and commercial areas, as reflected in their electronic mail address domain names.

The largest single group of submissions came from the USA with 33 papers, the next largest group coming from Germany with 18. Canada, our conference host country, produced 9 papers, closely followed by the United Kingdom with 8. Countries with at least three submissions were Australia, France, Ireland, Italy, Japan, Netherlands and Spain. The remainder of papers came from Brazil, China, Greece, Malaysia, Mexico, Portugal, the Russian Federation, Sweden and Tunisia.

The reviewing processes followed the established high standards for user modelling conferences with at least two and usually three reviews for each paper. The final technical programme has:

— twenty-seven full papers;
— ten short poster-papers;
— titles and authors of the 18 posters which will be presented at the conference's poster sessions where they, in addition to the short poster-papers, will serve as foundations for discussion of promising on-going work;
— eight Doctoral Symposium abstracts;
— contributions from the invited speakers, Alan Biermann, Gerhard Fischer, Pat Langely, Gerhard Weber - and the invited panel of speakers who report on large scale and national projects of significance for user modelling, Tak-Wai Chan, Alfred Kobsa, Gordon McCalla and Riichiro Mizoguchi.

There are many ways to view user modelling. Moreover, many papers involve various aspects of user modelling research. Any linear organisation of papers must take one view of the discipline to define the categories of papers and then categorise each paper into a single category. This volume is organised on the basis of the major tasks of user modelling in user-adapted systems. Taking the user's point of view, the purposes of user modelling are twofold:

— improve the system capacity to understand the user;
— assist the system's adaptation of its actions to the user.

These aspects constitute the first two collections of papers in this volume. Just a little further from the user are the essential task of constructing the user model. Again, taking the user's point of view we distinguish two cases, those where the construction is primarily

— unobtrusive, meaning that it should not make demands of the user;
— explicit, because it is achieved by interacting directly with the user.

Finally, we have the papers which present theory, techniques and tools for managing the user model. These generally involve issues more distant from the user since they are hidden in the design processes for the software that will manage the user modelling. We distinguish two categories:

— representation of the user model;
— aspects of implementation support.

Following the main collection of full papers, is the set of five contributions which have been nominated as finalists for the two prizes. The *Kluwer Academic Publishers' Distinguished Research Paper Award* will be announced at the conference for the paper in this set that earns the highest ranking from a carefully selected panel of experts. The *HumanIT Distinguished Application Paper Award* will also be announced at the conference and will be similarly assessed by an expert panel which will provide a ranking for the papers, after which

HumanIT representatives will discuss the final choice of paper. These awards give the winning papers a prize of $US 500 each, provided by the sponsors, Kluwer and HumanIT.

An important part of the technical programme was the tutorials:

— *Overview of User Modelling*, presented by Anthony Jameson.
— *Evaluating the Effectiveness of User Models by Experiments*, presented by David Chin and Martha Crosby.

Also valuable for forming future research were the workshops:

— *Machine Learning for User Modelling* organised by Mathias Bauer, Piotr Gmytrasiewicz and Wolfgang Pohl.
— *Adaptive Systems and User Modelling on the World Wide Web* organised by Peter Brusilovsky, Paul De Bra and Alfred Kobsa.
— *Attitude, Personality and Emotions in User-Adapted Interaction* organised by Fiorella de Rosis.
— *Standards for Learner Modelling* organised by Brad Goodman Frank Linton and James Schoening.

This conference represents a huge investment of effort from many people. It has been wonderful to be part of the large team which has worked for many months to ensure the success of the many aspects of the conference. A large part of the work in creating the technical programme was carried by the Programme Committee. The Programme Committee continued the tradition of detailed and high quality reviews. Several authors commented, quite justifiably, that reviews they received were very helpful and greatly appreciated even where the paper was not accepted. They also assisted with the many other tasks associated with defining the invited speaker programme and award papers. The Programme Committee is:

Jim Greer	Eric Horvitz	Helen Pain
Judy Kay	Anthony Jameson	Fiorella de Rosis
Peter Brusilovsky	Bonnie John	John Self
Sandra Carberry	Alfred Kobsa	Costas Stephanidis
Tak-Wai Chan	Diane Litman	Carlo Tasso
David Chin	Robert Mislevy	Gerrit van der Veer
Mary Czerwinski	Cécile Paris	Wolfgang Wahlster
Kristina Höök	Gordon McCalla	Geoffrey Webb
Gerhard Fischer	Riichiro Mizoguchi	Ingrid Zukerman
Brad Goodman	Reinhard Oppermann	

We also thank the additional reviewers:

Taro Adachi, Leila Alem, Joseph Beck, Marco Cavalho, Rogerio de Paula, Hal Eden, Andy Gorman, Dr Ikeda, Dr Kinshuk, Jürgen Koenemann, Bob Kummerfeld, Maria Milosavljevic, Rafael Morales, Jonathan Ostwald, Leysia Palen, Wolfgang Pohl, Eric Scharff, Gerry Stahl, Mia Stern, Christoph Thomas, Shari Trewin and Yunwen Ye.

The Doctoral Symposium co-chairs were Fiorella de Rosis and Linda Strachan. They were supported by the following members of their committee:

Helen Gigley, Floriana Grasso, Eric Horvitz, Kristina Höök, Alfred Kobsa, Gordon McCalla, Cecile Paris, Thomas Rist, Julita Vassileva and Ingrid Zukerman.

Particular thanks to Helen Gigley and the Office of Naval Research, USA for providing financial support for graduate students. This has been extremely important for ensuring that these students can participate in the conference, and in particular in the Doctoral Symposium which enables current research leaders to nurture the next generation of user modelling researchers.

We are grateful to the University of Sydney for supporting the management of the papers, reviewing processes and production of the final copy for the proceedings. Management of the reviewing process was greatly assisted by Bob Kummerfeld who wrote the elegant scripts which supported the reviewers and the generation of letters to authors. The production work was largely done by Daniel Ostermeier. There was also assistance from Bob Kummerfeld, Ray Loyzaga, Greg Ryan and Josephine Spongberg.

Throughout the many months of preparation for the conference, Anthony Jameson gave generously of his time, sharing his expertise acquired as Programme Chair for UM97, providing the paper templates and instructions and acting as a sounding board at all stages of the work on the technical programme. Carlo Tasso made generous contributions towards the publication of the proceedings, working with CISM, managing the time-consuming and difficult processes in the publication of the proceedings.

UM99 is jointly sponsored by the ARIES Laboratory, the University of Saskatchewan and UM Inc. UM Inc is the parent body and hosts the main web resources for the conference at http://um.org where the on-line proceedings are available. CISM sponsored these proceedings.

Finally, but critically important, we wish to acknowledge the hard work put in by the local arrangements team from the University of Saskatchewan, including

Julita Vassileva	Local Arrangements Chair
Gina Koehn	Conference Treasurer
Vive Kumar	Demonstration Coordinator
Seth Shacter and Ralph Deters	Technical Support

We also thank the many students assisting with the registration desk and other conference details, including: Jeff Bowes, Lori Kettel, Chaya Mudgal, Carina Ong-Scutchings, Judi Thomson, Mike Winter, and Juan-Diego Zapata.

Jim Greer, University of Saskatchewan, Canada   General Chair
Judy Kay, University of Sydney, Australia   Programme Chair

CONTENTS

MANAGING USER MODELS:
ARCHITECTURES AND REPRESENTATIONS 189

AWARD NOMINEE PAPERS 233

USER MODELS TO ASSIST SYSTEM UNDERSTANDING THE USER

Understanding Subjectivity:
An Interactionist View

Nadia Bianchi-Berthouze[1]*, Luc Berthouze[1] and Toshikazu Kato[1,2]

[1] Intelligent Systems Division, Electrotechnical Laboratory, Japan
[2] Department of Industrial and System Engineering, Chuo University, Tokyo, Japan
{bianchi,berthouz,kato}etl.go.jp

Abstract. User modeling is traditionally about constructing an explicit representation of the user. We argue against such approach because it overlooks the real nature of the human brain: plasticity and absence of monolithic control. Instead, we suggest to focus not on the modeling of the primary mechanism that explains a user's response but on the mechanisms through which technology can mediate as complex information as subjective responses. Indeed the only way two persons can reach mutual understanding over such responses is social interaction.

We propose a novel architecture based on three main components: (1) an elaborate sensory(-motor) apparatus, (2) a dynamical memory and (3) an active interface with turn-taking capability. It supports the interactive emergence of a common symbolic language through which user and system can share subjective responses over visual perceptions. We assert that while the "user model" is not explicitly constructed, it reveals in the interactive dialog between the user and the machine.

1 Introduction

Technologically-mediated information retrieval has been extensively studied recently and several systems have been made available that can successfully retrieve information based on its content (Niblack et al., 1996; Li et al., 1998; Del-Bimbo et al., 1998). The retrieval of information based on subjective requests (Kato, 1996a) has also been addressed, mainly using psychological profiles or other user models (Lee and Harada, 1998; Kitajima and Don-Han, 1998). Indeed, it is commonly accepted that modeling a user can help optimizing the coupling "user-machine", by eliminating the dissonance between natural human capability and the demands of technologically mediated activity (Gorayska et al., 1997). This is all the more relevant if one is to deal with as complex and non-explicit information as subjective or emotive response (e.g. retrieving a sad image). However, it is important to specify the nature of such user-model.

As defined by the call for paper of this conference, a user model would be an *explicit representation* of *properties* of a particular user. In this paper, we wish to argue against this definition. Our discussion is two-fold: about the *explicit* nature of the user model and about its target.

---

* The research presented in this paper was partially supported by the Science and Technology Agency of Japan, the Ministry of Education, the Ministry of Trade and Industry of Japan and the European Community.

Explicit nature of the user model: We argue that such characteristic implies an *explicit* human cognition as a basis for the design and, hence overlooks the main characteristic of the brain, namely, its continuous adaptation through processes both physical and cognitive[1]. Our claim is supported by evidence (also reported in Brooks et al. (1998)) from cognitive science and neuroscience which we summarize next.

- Human cognition doesn't rely on monolithic internal models: Such models only derive from naive models based on subjective observation and introspection and biases from common computational metaphors (Brooks, 1991). Modern understanding of cognitive science and neuroscience refutes those assumptions. Not only humans tend to minimize their internal representation of the world but those representations can even be not mutually consistent (Ballard et al., 1995). For example, in the phenomena of blind sight, cortically blind patients can discriminate different visual stimuli, but report seeing nothing (Weiskrantz, 1986). This inconsistency would not be a feature of a single central model of visual space. Humans tend to only represent what is immediately relevant from the environment, and those representations do not have full access to one another.
- Human cognition doesn't have monolithic control... but instead relies on competitive processes. Studies of split brain patients, such as the one of Gazzaniga and Ledoux (1978) show the existence of multiple independent control systems (separate halves of the subject's brain independently act appropriately even if one side falsely explained the choice of the other).
- Human cognition is not a general purpose processing system: It can be proficient in a particular set of skills, at the expense of other skills. A good example is the Stroop effect (Stroop, 1935). When presented with a list of words written in a variety of colors, performance in a color recognition and articulation task is dependent on the semantic content of the words. The task is very difficult if names of colors are printed in non corresponding colors. This experiment demonstrates the specialized nature of human computational processes and interactions.

Such evidences force us to look for alternative attributes of human cognition when attempting to construct user models. We will suggest in this paper that (social) interaction, embodiment and multi-modal integration form a valid set, if only the right target is chosen for the user model.

Target of the user model: When dealing with emotive/subjective responses, which *properties* of the user should be modeled ? The (embodied) ability to have subjective experience ? i.e. an explicit user model would then consist in modeling the full sensorimotor apparatus of the subject. Or the cognitive process by which the user makes use of concepts like "emotion" ? But that would not be possible if one considers our previous arguments on the absence of monolithic internal models and control. In this paper, we fully subscribe to the view of Frijda and Swagerman (1987) which suggest to undertake a functionalist approach to emotion/subjectivity (and hence to its possible model). *What is important in the phenomena that make one use concepts like "emotion" is not primarily subjective experience.* We shall not model the properties of the user's subjectivity because *subjective experience is not what invests those concepts with relevance, either for the*

---

[1] Designing a technology that feels good and is comfortable to use is not user modeling but merely facilitating the user adaptation to the designed system, and not his/her adaptation to the task at hand

experiencing subject or for others who make emotion ascriptions. What counts is action or, more generally, the relationship between subject and environment and the subject's readiness to modify or not to modify that relationship. The same holds for the relationship between the subject and his internal objects, his thoughts, goals [...]. Who cares about this own feelings when they have no consequence, of wanting to approach or avoid or get rid of, be it with regard to external objects or objects of thought ? What is interesting in emotion is some relationship to behavior or behavioral intent.

If this is accepted, it is then appropriate to consider that *emotive response* and subjectivity might exist and be functional in an artificial system and *it is not meaningless to disregard the question of whether that disposition does or does not have the shape of "experience", for the presence of which, criteria have yet to be devised* (Frijda and Swagerman, 1987).

User model as emergent structure of interaction: To summarize our stance, let's suppose now a system endowed with some sensorimotor apparatus, not necessarily anthropomorphic but sufficiently complex, and capable of recalling such experience, then, such system would be able of having its own "emotive/subjective response", although not necessarily the same as the user might experience or even desire. Our definition of "user model" relies on the existence of a mechanism through which the system is able to share emotional responses with the user, in such a way that both actors could reach mutual understanding. It is in this "mutual understanding" that lays our user model, though in a purely implicit form.

2   The Proposed Architecture

The above discussion casts strong constraints on the design of the architecture in term of interactive process. Human-human interaction however proves valuable as an example of interactive dynamics for sharing as complex information as emotive responses. The support of interaction include symbols (words) naturally but also postures, joint visual attention, use of metaphors or examples... Importantly, there is no explicit mapping from one actor to the other one of what one or another symbol might "mean" because the meaning of which, is grounded in the experience of the subject, sensorimotor (multisensorial body experience) on the one hand and shaped by other factors such as cultural background, character, state of mind (Saracevic et al., 1997) on the other hand.

Hence we suggest that user and system develop their own symbolic language, where a symbol ("pearl" for example) is understood as an instantiation by the subject (user or system) of his/her/its sensorimotor experience associated with the *qualia* of this symbol, i.e. (in the case of "pearl") the coldness of the material, the brightness of light reflexions, etc... This development of a specific language can also be found in humans, who tend to develop vocabulary/interactive patterns specifically suited to their counterpart (mother-child, husband-wife, nurse-elderly patient interaction ...). In human-human communication though, both actors generally share similar sensorimotor experience by virtue of their similar body. Such similarity is difficult to simulate in computer systems because they are generally disembodied, unless a Virtual Reality based system is considered (Biocca, 1997) or unless they are embedded in some physical body (Sato, 1996; Maetama et al., 1998). Fortunately human visual perception provides us with the possibility to embed motoric activity in a disembodied system by modeling human ability to shift gaze when perceiving its environment. In the next paragraphs, we describe our experimental framework and its three main components : (1) a sensorimotor apparatus, (2) a dynamical memory and (3) an active interface (see main blocks in Figure 1). We will discuss the structure of each component along with the overall integration.

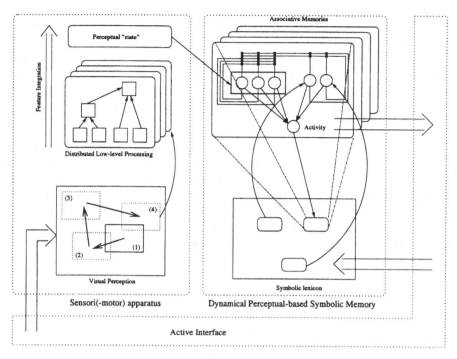

Figure 1. The proposed architecture: It shows the three main components of the system: (1) A sensorimotor apparatus performing distributed low-level processing and integrating it into a "perceptual state", (2) a distributed network of dynamical associative memories, each of which storing various sensorimotor experiences associated to a symbol of the lexicon and (3) an active interface which externalizes the internal states to the user and reciprocally allows the user to externalize his/her own internal states.

2.1   Sensori(-motor) apparatus

Observations made on human visual perception show that eyes move and successively fixate at the most informative parts of the image. It is a visuo-motor behavior that provides us with a sensorimotor basis on which to anchor the symbols that will be used by the system and the user to interact.

The sensori(-motor) apparatus runs as follows. Suppose the system attends to a specific area of an image. Our algorithm first performs a primary transformation of the image into a "retinal image" at the fixation point. The transformation provides a decrease in resolution from the center to the periphery, that simulates the decrease in resolution from the fovea to the retinal periphery in the cortical map of the retina. The retinal image is then fed to two parallel processing modules:

- A module for primary feature detection which performs a function similar to the primary visual cortex. Proposed by Rybak et al. (1998), this module is a dedicated neural architecture based on interacting neurons with orientationally selective receptive fields that extracts two types of edges, *basic edges* located at the fixation point and *context edges* located at specific positions in the retinal image. Those *context edges* are used to determine the next point of fixation (details are available in the paper mentioned above).

- An array of low-level operators processes the retinal image, after transformation in HSB (Hue, Saturation and Brightness) color coordinate system, and characterizes information such as color distribution, brightness, edges orientation (Kirsh, 1971), homogeneity (i.e. number of dominant gray-tone transitions), contrast (i.e.a mount of local variations) following algorithms proposed by Haralick et al. (1973). This information, combined with the motoric activity corresponding to the current scan-path, is used to incrementally construct the "perceptual state" (a sensorimotor pattern).

2.2 Symbolic lexicon and dynamical memory

The lexicon is interactively constructed and updated, each new symbol being initially given by the user at run-time, when labeling his/her emotive response to an image. A symbol is characterized by its label (which can be, as in our example of Figure 2, an ordinary "word" but taken as a string and not as a meaning) and by the associative memory which is associated to it as shown in Figure 1. Symbols do not have explicit connections to each other, as we discussed in (Bianchi-Berthouze et al., 1998). Instead, we suggest with this architecture that dynamical relations be constructed that would reflect apparent (externalized) relations while not making hypothesis on their real existence.

The associative memory is constructed on the basis of a Hopfield network (Hopfield, 1982). Before describing our specific implementation, we will briefly introduce the rationale for using such network. Hopfield networks are a class of neural networks fully connected, based on Hebbian rule (Hebb, 1991) which follow a stochastic dynamics of the state. The justifying fundamental principle is that nervous systems tend to look for stable states, attractors in their state space. Neighbor states tend to get close to a stable state so that (1) errors can be corrected and (2) states can be recalled even with incomplete stimulation. In other words, such network is like a memory which can be addressed by its content: a state that has been memorized can be retrieved by stabilization of the network, if it has been stimulated by a suitable part of this state. During the network's evolution towards a stable state, an energy function tends to a local minimum. In term of dynamics, this means a fixed point corresponding to one of the stored patterns is recalled by one input stimulus in a steady state. For our application though, it is desirable that more than *one* fixed point be recalled if the system is to be capable of giving examples for example or provide the user with views on his internal states. In classical Hopfield networks, this is not possible because of the lack of a mechanism erasing a fixed point once it is reached, and the lack of a mechanism that would enable the system to leave a fixed point by climbing the potential wall [2]. Tsuda et al. (1987) suggested that enlarging the basin of attraction (by an algorithm of unlearning) would increase the accessibility of attractors. In other words, it is possible, by breaking the stability of a recalled state, to reach successive recall of stored memories.

Our implementation is as follows: a single layer of neurons, with connections as described in Figure 1. The left group of neurons is corresponds to the "perceptual state" described in the

---

[2] The purpose of a Hopfield network is not to find the optimum but reasonable solutions.

previous section. This left group is fully connected. The aim of this structure is to categorize perceptual states associated to the current symbol into stable states (or attractors). The effective recognition of a perceptual state by the memory (i.e. the energy function falling into a local minimum) is fed to an *activity* neuron. The right group of neurons in each memory correspond to the activity of all other symbols of the lexicon, as evaluated at the current computing cycle. This provides us with the mechanism for dynamical learning/adapting/recalling of apparent connections between symbols.

2.3 Active interface

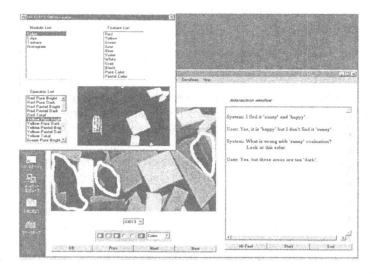

Figure 2. Snapshot of the system: The system utilizes its sensory-motor system to externalize its perception and provide the user with a view on its internal processes. The user can use this view (selecting areas on the image (in white in the image)) to externalize why his/her emotive response conflicts with the one of the system.

The main obstacle to the interactivist view is and has been the rigidity and the predominance of the machine as an actor in the user-machine dialogue. Even when human interaction is required, *the intrusion of human knowledge is somewhat peripheral: systems are still machine-centered* (Tanguy, 1997). Instead the focus should be put on user-centered design (Bianchi et al., 1996) where the user is at the center of a supportive systems, i.e. sensitive to (and actively using) the cognitive abilities as well as the affective characteristics of the user. Lee and Harada (1998) identify three cognitive processes through which humans respond to visual perceptions: shape (which we generalize in this paper to visual characteristics), metaphor and memory. Those processes, the implementation of which has been described earlier in the paper, must be fully embedded in the interface so that the user can intervene, both functionally and structurally in the system.

At the current stage of implementation, this activity of monitoring and evaluation typically involves three patterns of interaction, triggered either by a user input given in the form of a sentence in natural language or a visual example, or by the system self externalization. In the next paragraphs, we describe these interaction patterns.

Creation of a new symbol: It follows a sketch similar to the one shown in Figure 3. It doesn't simply consist in adding a new symbol but also in evaluating the instantaneous relationships of the symbol to be created with existing symbols by stimulating all memories and retrieving activated symbols. It is a mean to close the loop with the user by sharing information, turn-taking initiative etc... The user might agree/disagree with the system's evaluation and, if he wishes so, engages in another interactive pattern (as described in next paragraph). Note that he might as well ignore the system's evaluation and instead provides the system with other images for which his emotive response best matches the newly created symbol.

User: This is a *happy* image !
System: *Happy* ?
(1. processes the picture with his sensori-motor apparatus,
(2a. feds the perceptual state into all associative memories and let the networks relax. If one (at least) network stabilizes, takes the initiative to tell the user about corresponding symbols (see ??th interactive pattern).
System: I find it *light* and *refreshing*.
(2b. looks for *happy* in symbolic lexicon and doesn't find it.
(3. creates symbol *happy*, its associated memory and starts learning with current image as learning set.
System: I've never heard of *happy* images. Why don't you show me other *happy* images ?

Figure 3. The system selects and displays an image in the workspace. The user introduces a new *symbol*.

Reinforcement and specialization of existing symbols: Whereas the reinforcement of positively evaluated response is straightforward, the specialization of existing symbols is delicate because it raises the issue of how the system should handle what might be considered as inconsistencies from the user side whereas it is simply that the user, because of external factors, unconsciously focussed on another aspect of his/her perception. Handling such inconsistency in a rigorous manner would break the ability of the system to handle the variability issue we have evocated in introduction. Instead, we suggest user and system rely on a process of *externalization*. In daily life, such process can take various forms, from conversation, written texts, sketch and memos, to simply physical "records" of actions taken in the world. As mentioned by Miyake (1997), *externalized records are useful because they serve as sharable and concretely manipulable objects for constructive collaboration*. So, instead of simply reflecting in the internal process the overall evaluation by the user, the system should help the user keep record of such externalization, reflect upon them for making changes and restore them when necessary. Hence, the active interface provides the user with a view on its internal processes so that the user can projects his own internal processes onto them (or conversely, projects his response onto the system's internal process).

Even though an externalized record sheds light on the system internal processes, it does not necessarily pertain to the user's previous evaluation. Hence, previous evaluations should not necessarily be unlearned. Rather, we must reflect instantaneous inconsistency as local perturbation and let the dynamics of the system finds its own stable states. This dynamical systems view is reflected by the fourth point of Figure 4. The inconsistency is only reflected by the inhibition of the activity neuron corresponding to the symbol relevant to the externalized perceptual state. A previous evaluation is not unlearned. However, it is likely that in further interaction, as described in the next paragraph, the system would come up with its own internal inconsistency or variability: two symbols being excited while mutually excluded.

System: I find it *light* and *refreshing*.
User: Yes, it is *refreshing* but I don't find it *light*.
(1. Reinforces current perceptual state in memory associated to *refreshing*.
(2. Recalls other perceptual states associated with *light* symbol. Browses the database of images, processes them and selects a set of images whose properties match *light* symbol. Calls for user evaluation.
System: What is wrong with *light* evaluation ? This image is similar to those ones, isn't it ?
User (who selects an area in the image): Yes, but this area is too *dense* and ....
(3. Processes the area selected by user and extracts perceptual state.
(4. Creates a symbol *dense* and start memory learning on extracted perceptual state, inhibiting activity neuron corresponding to symbol *light*.

Figure 4. User and system's evaluation of the image differs (continuation of previous dialog). The user tries to externalize his/her perception.

User: How about this picture ?
(1. processes the picture with his sensori-motor apparatus,
(2. feds the perceptual state into all associative memories and let the networks relax. For all networks in a stable state, list associated symbol and related symbols (i.e. symbols for which the corresponding activity neuron, in the recalled state is excited).
(3. Checks possible inconsistencies such as inhibition of symbol otherwise excited.
(4. For each inhibitory connection, processes image, in a top-down fashion, to detect area best matching associated recalled perceptual state. Attempts to externalize internal processes to user.
System: This image is *refreshing*. Don't you think so ?
System: But I'm confused about something. Do you find this image *dense* ? or do you find it *light* ?

Figure 5. System came up with seemingly internal inconsistency. It asks for user guidance.

Externalization of the system's internal processes: We view internal inconsistencies, such as shown in Figure 5, as branching points in the interactive dynamics: the user might ignore, correct or propose alternatives. It makes the existence of "fixed point" or "trivial attractor" in the interactive dynamics unlikely. In further work, we wish to formally study the importance of this mechanism in the overall dynamics.

3 Conclusion

Retrieving information based on its content has been quite successfully investigated because computer systems are well suited to extensive search in database of explicit information. However, when retrieval involves the subjectivity of the user, the system needs to construct a model of the user so that both actors share a common support of interaction. We argued that, in light of evidences in neuroscience and cognitive science, the user model to be constructed cannot be explicit because human brain doesn't have monolithic control and internal models. What might be a *sad* image at a given time might not be so in a different context. Or content might be influencing the user's emotive response by way of *unconscious learning* (Kato, 1996b). Instead, the constructed model should mainly rely on **interaction** because what matters is not the primary subjective experience but *action*, i.e. the relationship between subject and environment and the subject's readiness to modify or not to modify that relationship. If we assume a system with a sufficiently complex **sensorimotor apparatus**, such system will be capable of own emotive responses if it is provided with mechanisms to share such information with a user. Those two elements (in bold in the text) ground our experimental framework. We propose a novel architecture endowed with (1) a sensori-motor apparatus constituted (at this stage) by the ability of the system to change its focus of attention and extracts information about the nature of the image; (2) a set of dynamical sensorimotor memories that associate symbols (one support of the interaction) with the sensorimotor experiences and supports the successive recall of past experience) and (3) an active interface allowing multi-modal interaction with the user through the use of symbols, example or processus of externalization of the system's internal processes.

A true cooperation (an interactive process) can emerge, not necessarily achieving a flawless performance but effectively supporting the transmission between each actor of complex, non-explicit information. We believe this approach provides an alternative to classical understanding of user modeling as well as human-machine interaction in general. It integrates true dialog and each actor of the dialog is re-centered based on his/her/its particular cognitive and physical properties and let adapt through interaction.

References

Ballard, D., Hayhoe, M., and Pelz, J. (1995). Memory representations in natural tasks. *Journal of Cognitive Neuroscience* 66–80.

Bianchi-Berthouze, N., Berthouze, L., and Kato, T. (1998). Towards a comprehensive integration of subjective parameters in database browsing. In Kambayashi, Y., Makinouchi, A., Uemura, S., Tanaka, K., and Masunaga, Y., eds., *Advanced Database Systems for Integration of Media and User Environments*, 227–232. World Scientific: Singapore.

Bianchi, N., Mussio, P., Padula, M., and Rinaldi, G. R. (1996). Multimedia document management: An anthropocentric approach. *Information Processing and Management* 32(3):287–304.

Biocca, F. (1997). The cyborg's dilemma: Embodiment in virtual environments. In Marsh, J., Nehaniv, C., and Gorayska, B., eds., *Cognitive Technology*, 12–26. IEEE Computer Society.

Brooks, R. A., Brezeal, C., Marjanovic, M., Scassellati, B., and Williamson, M. M. (1998). The cog project: Building a humanoid robot. In *Proceedings of the First International Workshop on Humanoid and Human Friendly Robotics, Tsukuba, Japan*, 1–36.

Brooks, R. (1991). Intelligence without reason. *Artificial Intelligence Journal* 47:139–160.

Del-Bimbo, A., Mugnaini, M., Pala, P., and Turco, F. (1998). Visual querying by color perceptive regions. *Pattern Recognition* 31(9):1241–1253.

Frijda, N. H., and Swagerman, J. (1987). Can computers feel ? theory and design of an emotional system. *Cognition and Emotion* 1(3):235–257.

Gazzaniga, M. S., and Ledoux, J. E. (1978). *The Integrated Mind*. New York: Plenum Press.

Gorayska, B., Marsh, J., and Mey, J. L. (1997). Putting the horse before the cart: Formulating and exploring methods for studying cognitive technology. In Marsh, J., Nehaniv, C., and Gorayska, B., eds., *Cognitive Technology*, 2–9. IEEE Computer Society.

Haralick, R. M., Shanmugan, K., and Dinstein, I. (1973). Texture features for image classification. *IEEE Transactions Systems, Man and Cybernetics* 3:610–621.

Hebb, D. O. (1991). *The Made-Up Minds: A Constructivist Approach to Artificial Intelligence*. Cambridge, MA: MIT Press.

Hopfield, J. J. (1982). Neural networks and physical systems with emergent collective computational abilities. In *Proceedings of the National Academy of Sciences, USA*, volume 81, 3088–3092.

Kato, T. (1996a). Cognitive user interface to cyber space database: – human media technology for global information infrastructure –. In *Proceedings of the International Symposium on Cooperative Database Systems for Advanced Applications, Kyoto, Japan*, 184–190.

Kato, T. (1996b). Implicit aspects of human learning and memory. In *Proceedings of the International Workshop on Robot and Human Communication, RoMan'96, Tsukuba, Japan*, 9–15. IEEE Press.

Kirsh, R. (1971). Computer determination of the constituent structure of biomedical images. *Computers and Biomedical Research* 4(3):315–328.

Kitajima, M., and Don-Han, K. (1998). Communicating kansei design concept via artifacts: A cognitive scientific approach. In *Proceedings of the International Workshop on Robot and Human Communication, RoMan'98, Hakamatsu, Japan*, 321–326. IEEE Press.

Lee, S., and Harada, A. (1998). A design approach by objective and subjective evaluation of kansei information. In *Proceedings of the International Workshop on Robot and Human Communication, RoMan'98, Hakamatsu, Japan*, 327–332. IEEE Press.

Li, Z., Zaiane, O. R., and Yan, B. (1998). C-bird: Content-based image retrieval from digital libraries using illumination invariance and recognition kernel. In Wagner, R. R., ed., *Proceedings of the Ninth International Workshop on Database and Expert Systems Applications, Vienna, Austria*, 361–366. IEEE Computer Society Press.

Maetama, S., Yuta, S., and Harada, A. (1998). Mobile robot in the remote museum for modeling the evaluation structure of kansei. In *Proceedings of the International Workshop on Robot and Human Communication, RoMan'98, Hakamatsu, Japan*, 315–320. IEEE Press.

Miyake, N. (1997). Making internal process external for constructive collaboration. In Marsh, J., Nehaniv, C., and Gorayska, B., eds., *Cognitive Technology*, 119–123. IEEE Computer Society.

Niblack, W., Barber, R., Equitz, W., Flickner, M., Glasman, E., Petkovic, D., Yanker, P., Faloutsos, C., and Taubin, G. (1996). The qbic project: Querying images by content using color, texture and shape. Technical Report Research Report 9203, IBM Research Division.

Rybak, I. A., Gusakova, V. I., Golovan, A. V., Podladchikova, L. N., and Shevtsova, N. A. (1998). A model of attention-guided visual perception and recognition. *Vision Research* 38:2387–2400.

Saracevic, T., Spink, A., and Wu, M. (1997). Users and intermediaries in information retrieval: What are they talking about. In Jameson, A., Paris, C., and Tasso, C., eds., *User Modeling: Proceedings of the Sixth International Conference, UM'97, Sardinia*, 43–54. Springer Wien New York.

Sato, T. (1996). Expressive robot with touching behavior. Private communication.

Stroop, J. R. (1935). Studies of interference in serial verbal reactions. *Journal of Experimental Psychology* 18:643–662.

Tanguy, L. (1997). Computer-aided language processing. In Marsh, J., Nehaniv, C., and Gorayska, B., eds., *Cognitive Technology*, 136–145. IEEE Computer Society.

Tsuda, I., Koerner, E., and Shimizu, H. (1987). Memory dynamics in asynchronous neural networks. *Progress of Theoretical Physics* 78(1):51–71.

Weiskrantz, L. (1986). *Blindsight: A Case Study and Implications*. Oxford: Clarendon Press.

The Application of User Modeling Techniques to Reason about the Human Contribution to Major Accidents

C.W. Johnson

Department of Computing Science, University of Glasgow, Glasgow, Scotland.
http://www.dcs.gla.ac.uk/~johnson

Abstract. Accident reports are important documents for the development of many interactive systems. They are a primary mechanism by which designers and regulators learn about human 'error' and systems 'failure'. These documents do, however, suffer from a number of limitations. In particular, it can be difficult for readers to trace the ways in which particular individuals are influenced by, and in turn help to influence, their colleagues' behavior. This paper argues that user modeling techniques can help to improve our understanding of operator interaction in the lead-up to accidents and incidents. This argument is illustrated by a "near miss" that occurred when two Air Traffic Controllers failed to coordinate the arrival and departure of aircraft at Heathrow Airport on the 27th August 1997.

1 Introduction

Human intervention has played a critical role in the causes of many major accidents. The officers and crew of the Herald of Free Enterprise set to sea with their bow doors open (Sheen, 1987). The pilot and co-pilot throttled back their one working engine rather than the engine that had failed prior to the Kegworth air crash (AAIB, 1990). The workers at the Bhopal chemical plant pumped Methyl-isocyanate into a leaking tank (Morehouse and Subamaniam, 1986). In all of these accidents, users failed to predict the consequences of their actions because they could not gain an accurate indication about the state of their system. This raises two questions for the design of safety-critical, interactive systems. First, can we help operators to gain a more accurate impression of the state of their application? Second, can we then help users to make better predictions about the effects of their actions based upon an improved view of their application? This paper uses a near-miss incident to illustrate the importance of such situation awareness and anticipatory control for the design of safety-critical, interactive systems.

1.1 The Heathrow Case Study

The case study in this paper centres on the actions of two Air Traffic Controllers at Heathrow Airport in the United Kingdom during August 1997 (Air Accident Investiation Branch, 1997). One was responsible for marshalling arrivals whilst their colleague supervised departures. The Air Departures Controller was also undergoing training and was, therefore, being overseen by a

Mentor. This incident is appropriate because the incident typifies the complex communication failures that can occur between teams of users operating a number of inter-dependent control systems. It also illustrates the profound impact that particular expectations can have upon users' decision making behaviour. A Boeing 737 (SAB603) was attempting to land on Runway 27 Left (27L) when poor weather conditions forced the crew to initiate a missed approach. The Air Arrivals Controller was informed of this and they, in turn, informed the Air Departures Controller. This was standard procedure because the Arrivals Controller would have to alert SAB603 of any departing aircraft that might cause a hazard as they prepared for another landing. The Departures controller alerted their colleague that there was another flight, AFR813, about to depart. They also confirmed that this aircraft would be turned to the right. The Air Arrivals Controller, therefore, requested that SAB603 also turn right to maximise the separation from AFR813. On hearing this, the Mentor who was overseeing the Departures Controller, alerted the Arrivals Controller that another Boeing 757, BAW818, was also departing. The Arrivals Controller immediately ordered SAB603 to turn left while the Departures Controller ordered BAW818 to turn right. According to the Instrument Flight Rules applicable at Heathrow there should have been either 1,000 feet vertical separation or 2.5 nautical miles of horizontal separation between the aircraft. Subsequent calculations revealed that the minimum separation was 200 feet vertically and 0.16 nautical miles of horizontal separation.

1.2 User Modelling and Epistemic Logics

A number of user modelling techniques might be recruited to analyse the situation awareness problems described in the previous section. For example, SOAR provides automated means of analysing the operations interaction with their system. It can, however, be difficult to characterise the Controller's tasks in terms of problem solving activities. The maximisation of throughput and the maintenance of minimum separation criteria form part of several more complex co-ordination tasks. Other user modelling techniques, such as Interacting Cognitive Subsystems (ICS) (Barnard, 1985) and Executive-Process/Interactive Control (EPIC) (Kieras, Wood and Meyer, 1998), can be applied to focus more narrowly on the psychological precursors of the Controllers' interactions. Alternatively, it is possible to recruit stochastic models to represent and reason about the impact of risk and utility on individual decision making (Johnson, 1995a). Unfortunately, a number of problems frustrate these approaches to accident analysis. The limited evidence that is available after a major disaster can prevent investigators from developing detailed psychological models of the individuals that were involved in an accident. The AAIB only provides brief biographies and limited psychological `profiles' of individual operators. Given this lack of detail, it is almost impossible for analysts to accurately identify the precursors of problems such as high workload. It is, therefore, important to identify some 'coarse grained' means of representing and reasoning about these cognitive factors that are described in accident reports. The following pages, therefore, exploit epistemic logics.

Epistemology, or the study of knowledge, has a history stretching back to the Ancient Greeks (Fagin, Halpern, Moses and Vardi 1995, Barwise and Perry, 1983). This work has produced a number of logics that can be used to represent changes in an individual's knowledge over time. Epistemic logics have a number of attractions for accident analysis. In particular, it is possible to build more complex user models out of epistemic formulae. For example, each of the cognitive systems in the ICS approach contains an epistemic subsystem. The rest of this paper, therefore, demonstrates that epistemic logics can capture the cognitive observations that are embedded within the AAIB report

2   First Order Logic and Accident Investigations

Logic can be used to represent and reason about the flow of events leading to major incidents. The first stage in this approach is to model the agents and objects that were involved in the accident. For instance, the runways and air traffic control information systems are classified as inanimate objects. Agents include the Air Traffic Controllers as well as the Mentor. One of the benefits of this approach is that analysts can represent both agents and objects at different levels of abstraction. For instance, it is not always necessary to model all of the individuals involved in an accident. In our case study, the accident report does not distinguish between the individual officers onboard SAB 603, AFR 813 and BAW 818. For instance, the following proposition states that the crew of SAB 603 missed their approach to runway 27L.

$$miss\_approach(sab603, 27L). \tag{1}$$

It is also possible to specify what a particular individual or group of individuals should do under such circumstances. For instance, the "missed approach procedure for aircraft approaching any of the East/West runways at Heathrow, published in the UK Aeronautical Information Publication was for aircraft to climb straight ahead to 3,000 feet..." (AAIB, 1998).

$$miss\_approach(Plane, Runway) \land east\_west(Runway) \Rightarrow climb(Plane, 3000). \tag{2}$$

This formalistion process is important because proof techniques can be applied to determine whether or not the crew responded appropriately given the context of operation. For example, the following rule states that if we know P and that if P is true then Q is true then it is safe to conclude Q:

$$P, \ P \Rightarrow Q \ \vdash \ Q \tag{3}$$

In the context of the previous discussion, we can apply this inference rule to assess whether or not the crew of SAB 603 correctly followed the missed approach procedure. In order to do this, we must first determine whether the antecedent, P, of the implication actually holds. In other words, did the aircraft miss its approach and was 27L an East-West runway. We already know from formula [1] that the aircraft missed its approach. It is also possible to confirm that 27L was an West-East runway (AAIB, 1998). It is, therefore, possible to conclude that the crew did satisfy the relevant operating procedures of [2] when they climbed to 3,000 feet: "they complied with the laid down procedure which was to 'Climb straight ahead to 3,000 feet then as directed by the Air Traffic Control'" (AAIB, 1998). This might seem relatively obvious, however, if further enquiries revealed that 27L was not an East-West runway then the procedures of [2] need not have applied and, in turn, the crews actions may not have been appropriate.

As mentioned, logic can be used to focus in upon critical incidents in the course of an accident. For instance, it is important that the Arrivals Officer informs the Departures Officer if an aircraft misses its approach because the aircraft could cross the flight paths of aircraft that are departing from another runway. The following formulae not only illustrates how this requirement can be represented, it also shows how logic can explicitly represent implicit assumptions about an operator's behaviour. In this case, we specify that the Arrivals officer must first observe the missed approach if they are to warn their colleague:

$$miss\_approach(Plane, Runway) \wedge confirm(atc\_arrivals, Plane, missed\_approach) \Rightarrow$$
$$inform\_miss\_approach(atc\_arrivals, atc\_departures, Plane, Runway). \qquad [4]$$

We can again check to determine whether these antecedents did, indeed, hold during the case study incident. We already know from [1] that the approach was missed and we know that "Air Arrivals had seen the aircraft going around and had acknowledged the manoeuvre by radio to the crew" (AAIB, 1998):

$$confirm(atc\_arrivals, sab603, missed\_approach) \qquad [5]$$

Given this series of behavioural requirements on the operators, it is possible to reconstruct the ways in which events unfolded during the particular incident as follows:

$$miss\_approach(SAB603, 27l) \wedge confirm(atc\_arrivals, sab603, missed\_approach) \Rightarrow$$
$$inform\_miss\_approach(atc\_arrivals, atc\_departures, sab603, 27l).$$

(Instantiation of SAB603 for Plane and 27l for Runway in [4])   [6]

$$inform\_miss\_approach(atc\_arrivals, atc\_departures, sab603, 27l).$$

(Modus ponens, application of [3] to [6] given [1] and [5])   [7]

This line of reasoning leads to yet further requirements on the operators; "Air Arrivals and Air Departures are to co-ordinate with each other to establish separation between the "go-around (aircraft)" and any conflicting departing traffic" (AAIB, 1998). The following clause focuses on the Departures Officer and specifies that if anyone informs them of a missed approach then they must check for any conflicts with other aircraft. Additional clauses can be added to such formulae to represent subsequent instructions to alter the height or direction of those aircraft:

$$inform\_miss\_approach(Anyone, atc\_departures, Plane, Runway) \Rightarrow$$
$$conflicting\_traffic(atc\_departures, Plane, Runway, Conflicts) \qquad [8].$$

As before, we can apply the reasoning techniques of first order logic to formalise the changing requirements that must be satisfied by the operators of safety critical control systems:

inform_miss_approach(atc_arrivals, atc_departures, sab603, 271) $\Rightarrow$
conflicting_traffic(atc_departures, sab603, 271, baw818).   [9]

inform_miss_approach(atc_arrivals, atc_departures, sab603, 271) $\Rightarrow$
conflicting_traffic(atc_departures, sab603, 271, afr813).   [10]

(Instantiation of atc_arrivals for Anyone, sab603 for Plane, 271 for Runway etc in [8])

conflicting_traffic(sab603, 271, baw818) $\wedge$ conflicting_traffic(sab603, 271, afr813).

(Modus ponens, application of [3] to [9] given [8])   [11]

This final inference brings us to the heart of the accident because it captures the assumption that both BAW 818 and AFR 813 were in potential conflict with the revised flight path of SAB 603. Unfortunately, the MATS regulations cited earlier rely upon a subjective definition of what constitutes conflicting departing traffic. "However, the actions of the Air Departures was based on the supposition that Air Arrivals would turn SAB 603 to the left. She did not consider that BAW 818 was a confliction and therefore did not inform Air Arrivals of its departure" (AAIB, 1998). Unfortunately, if we want to represent and reason about such differences in the knowledge and beliefs of agents we must move beyond the relatively simple first order logics used in the previous formulae to higher order, epistemic logics.

3   Epistemic Logics and User Modelling in Accident Investigations

The Air Departures Controller did not consider that BAW 818 was in potential conflict with SAB 603 as it missed its approach. This can be represented by the following negation:

not(conflicting _traffic(sab603, 271, baw818))   [12]

From a logic perspective, this leads to a contradiction because we have already stated in [11] that both BAW 818 and AFR 813 were, in fact, in conflict with SAB 603. We cannot in first order logic allow the same fact to be both true and not true at the same time:

conflicting _traffic(sab603, 271, baw818) $\wedge$ not conflicting _traffic(sab603, 271, baw818)

($\wedge$ introduction, [12] and [11])   [13]

Epistemic logics provide means of avoiding such contradictions. For example, we can introduce a modal operator to express the fact that the ATC Departures Officer knows that BAW 818 does not conflict with SAB 603:

$Kn_{atc\_departures}$(not conflicting_traffic(sab603, 271, baw818)).   [14]

This does not lead to a contradiction. It is perfectly possible for other operators, such as the Arrivals Officer, to believe that BAW 818 does conflict with the going around aircraft at the same time that the Departure Officer knows that it does not create a conflict:

$$Kn_{atc\_departures}(\text{not conflicting\_traffic}(sab603, 271, baw818)) \wedge$$
$$Kn_{atc\_arrivals}(\text{conflicting\_traffic}(sab603, 271, baw818)) \qquad [15]$$

The semantics of the Kn operator is introduced in Appendix A. In contrast the remainder of this section goes on to apply this notation to represent and reason about the causes of the communications failures that led to the near miss at Heathrow Airport. This relatively simple notational extension opens up a range of user modelling techniques. For instance, it is also possible to reason about an individual's knowledge of the information that is available to their colleagues. In our case study, it can be argued that the Departure Officer did not know whether or not the Arrivals Officer knew about BAW 818:

$$\text{not } Kn_{atc\_departures} (Kn_{atc\_arrivals}(\text{conflicting\_traffic}(sab603, 271, baw818))) \wedge$$
$$\text{not } Kn_{atc\_departures} (Kn_{atc\_arrivals}(\text{not conflicting\_traffic}(sab603, 271, baw818))) \qquad [16]$$

The previous clause illustrates the use of epistemics to reason about an individual's view of their colleague's knowledge. It is also possible to reason more generally at the level of "common knowledge". These shared assumptions often lie at the heart of major accidents. They, typically, cause problems for operators in one of two ways. Firstly, the knowledge may not be available to all of the members in a group. Secondly, the shared information may be incorrect. This is particularly dangerous because users seldom challenge common knowledge when they rely upon the understanding of their colleagues. In order to represent this form of knowledge we must first define the group which shares the knowledge:

$$atc\_officers = \{ atc\_arrivals, atc\_departures, departures\_mentor \} \qquad [17]$$

An epistemic operator E_{group} can then be used to state that everyone in a group knows that a certain proposition is true. As before the semantics for this and the other epistemic operators are provided in Appendix A. This operator is particularly useful for our case study because the Departure Officer's decision not to communicate with the Arrival Officer about BAW 818 was partly justified by a belief that SAB 603 would be turned to the left. "the Mentor stated that he had never previously witnessed a missed approach from Runway 271 being turned right. The assumption was therefore made that SAB 603 would be turned left away from the departure runway and Air Departures, acting on this expectation failed to inform Air Arrivals of the second departure i.e., BAW 818 since she perceived the main requirement at the time as dealing with AFR 813":

$$E_{atc\_officers}(\text{alter\_course}(atc\_arrivals, sab\_603, left)) \qquad [18]$$

The previous clause states that all ATC officers know that SAB 603 is requested to alter course to the left. However, the previous quotations indicate an even stronger assumption in which not only did the officers know that SAB 603 would be turned to the left but that they assumed that the others in the group knew this. The stronger C_{group} operator can be used to capture this assumption:

$$C_{atc\_officers}(alter\_course(atc\_arrivals, sab\_603, left))$$ [19]

Unfortunately, neither clause [18] nor clause [19] capture the true state of operator knowledge in the lead up to the incident. The Arrivals Officer did not share the same set of assumptions as either the Departure Officer or their mentor. They chose to turn SAB 603 to the right rather than to the left. The following section looks at the reasons for this decision.

4   Epistemic Logics and the Causes of Operator Error

The near miss stemmed from the Arrival Officer's decision to alter the course of SAB 603 to the right. This decision went against normal procedure but was based upon a desire to increase the separation between SAB 603 and AFR 813. "Air Arrivals decided to turn SAB603 right because he considered that a left turn would have been a possible confliction to the 'Midhurst' departure (AFR 813) and a right turn would cause less disruption as he was not aware of the 'Brookmans Park' departure" (AAIB, 1998):

$$Kn_{atc\_arrivals} (conflicting\_traffic(sab603, 271, afr813) \wedge$$
$$not\ Kn_{atc\_arrivals} (conflicting\_traffic(sab603, 271, baw818)) \Rightarrow$$
$$alter\_course(atc\_arrivals, sab\_603, right)$$ [20]

The previous clause illustrates how the decision to turn the aircraft to the right was based both on the controller's knowledge of AFR813 and their ignorance of BAW818. This analysis was confirmed, with hindsight, by the subsequent investigation. "Air Arrivals stated, however, that had he known about BA 818, he would have turned the missed approach aircraft left in the manner anticipated by his colleagues":

$$Kn_{atc\_arrivals} (conflicting\_traffic(sab603, 271, baw818)) \Rightarrow$$
$$alter\_course(atc\_arrivals, sab\_603, left)$$ [21]

None of this, of course, explains why the Departure's Controller decided not to inform their colleague about BAW818. "The assumption was therefore made that SAB 603 would be turned left away from the departure runway and Air Departures, acting on this expectation failed to inform Air Arrivals of the second departure i.e., BAW 818":

$$alter\_course(atc\_arrivals, sab\_603, left) \Rightarrow$$
$$Kn_{atc\_departures}(not\ conflicting\_traffic(sab603, 271, baw818))$$ [22]

Clauses [21] and [22] illustrate how epistemic logic helps to focus on the communication problems that lies at the heart of our case study. If the Arrivals Officer had known about the conflict with BAW 818 then they would have routed SAB 603 to the left. The Departures Officer did not inform them of the potential conflict because if SAB 603 had been routed to the left then there would have been no conflict.

Our approach is limited in the sense that it focuses on knowledge requirements during interaction with safety-critical interfaces. We have not attempted to represent the physiological factors that contribute to many major accidents. Elsewhere we have described how logic can be used to reason about the physical layout of complex working environments (Johnson, 1996). Future work intends to build on this to represent the ways in which operators must integrate computer-based tasks with more general, physical activities in safety-critical systems. This can be achieved by using epistemics to represent and reason about components of more general user models such as EPIC and ICS that both account for physiological aspects of interaction. For instance, epistemic logics can express the propositional and implicational information that is represented in the ICS model (Busse and Johnson, 1998). The intention would be to provide a concrete syntax and vocabulary for analysing the sorts of information and knowledge that might be held within these subsystems during particular traces of interaction.

5 Conclusion

This paper has argued that operators often make incorrect assumptions about the information that is known to their colleagues. This, in turn, can prevent them from correctly anticipating the future behaviour of other workers. Although this is a serious problem, it does not always threaten safety. Users can initiate repair activities by asking colleagues about their knowledge and intentions at regular intervals during interaction. Safety can, however, be jeopardised if operators forget or consider it unnecessary to verify their understanding of their colleagues' view of the situation.

This argument has been illustrated by a case study in which the Air Traffic Controllers at Heathrow Airport failed to ensure adequate separation between two aircraft. The case study illustrated the complexity that arises when using natural language to discuss the recursive nature of shared knowledge. We quickly begin to talk about an individual's knowledge of another individual's knowledge. Epistemic logics provide a means of addressing this complexity because they provide a clear and coherent language in which to reason about both individual and shared knowledge. Using this notation, it was possible to identify the mutual dependency that led to the incident in the first place. This dependency prevented each of the operators from gaining an accurate impression of the information that was known to the other. This can be summarised as follows: if the Arrivals Officer had known about the conflict with BAW 818 then they would have routed SAB 603 to the left. The Departures Officer did not inform the Arrivals Officer of the potential conflict because if SAB 603 had been routed to the left then there would have been no conflict.

This work represents a first step towards a more detailed understanding of the errors that arise when groups of individuals must share their knowledge to improve a collective "situation awareness". Much remains to be done. We have already argued that epistemic logics must be integrated with more general user modelling techniques. The great weakness, and also the great strength, of this notation is that it focuses upon a specific aspect of interaction. This makes it appropriate for accidents that stem from communications problems, such as those mentioned above. It is far less appropriate for accidents that involve perceptual or physiological problems. However, the importance of this focus should not be underestimated. The Air Accident Investigation Branch (1998) concluded "An important element of Air Traffic Control is communication. It is not altogether surprising, therefore, that communication breakdown occurs or that it should figure so prominently in the occurrence of incidents. The issue is to understand why communication fails and what can be done to prevent such failure in the future or, at least, to mitigate its effects". User modelling provides tools to improve our understanding of these failures. Without such tools, many incidents will continue to be classified as simple instances of operator 'error'.

Acknowledgements

Thanks go to the members of the Glasgow Interactive Systems Group (GIST) and to the Formal Methods and Theory Group in Glasgow University. This work is supported by the UK Engineering and Physical Sciences Research Council, grants GR/JO7686, GR/K69148 and GR/K55040.

6 Appendix A: Semantics of the Epistemic Logic

In formal terms, the Kn operator relies upon a Kripke Semantics which is represented by the following tuple: $(S, \pi, K_1,...,K_n)$. S is a set of states or possible worlds. π is an interpretation function that associates the values true or false with primitive propositions in each state. Therefore, we can apply $\pi(s)(p)$ to determine whether or not the proposition p is true in state s. In contrast, K_i is a binary relation between states. It is used to denote whether an agent i believes a state to be possible from the information that they have in the current state. We can define the truth of a proposition inductively as follows:

$(M, s) \models p$ (for a primitive proposition p) iff $\pi(s)(p)$ = true
$(M, s) \models p \wedge q$ iff $(M, s) \models p$ and $(M, s) \models q$
$(M, s) \models$ not p iff $(M, s) \not\models p$
$(M, s) \models Kn_i p$ iff $(M, t) \models p$ for all t such that $(s, t) \in Kn_i$

The final case illustrates how an agent i knows a proposition p to be true in a state s if p is true in all states that i considers to be possible from s. In passing it should be mentioned that Kn is an equivalence relation and is based on the initial epistemic model introduced by Fagin, Halpern, Moses and Vardi (1995).

The semantics of common knowledge can be introduced as follows for E_{group} (read as 'everyone knows'), C_{group} ('everyone knows that everyone knows...') and D_{group} ('information is shared amongst the group'):

$(M, s) \models E_{group} p$ iff $(M, s) \models Kn_i$ forall i in $group$
$(M, s) \models C_{group} p$ iff $(M, s) \models E_{group\ i}$ forall i in $group$
$(M, s) \models D_{group} p$ iff $(M, s) \models p$ forall t such that (s, t) in $\cap_{i\ in\ group} Kn_i$

The final definition illustrates how a proposition p is known amongst a group by removing all of the worlds that either agent considers to be impossible. What remains is the intersection of their knowledge. This models the situation where one or more agents could communicate to achieve a better understanding than would have otherwise been possible.

References

Air Accidents Investigations Branch, Department of Transport. Report On The Accident To Boeing 737-400 G-OBME Near Kegworth, Leicestershire on 8th January 1989, number 4/90, Her Majesty's Stationery Office. London, United Kingdom, 1990

Air Accident Investigation Branch, Report on the Incident near London Heathrow Airport on 27 August 1997, Aircraft Incident Report Number 5/98, Her Majesty's Stationery Office, London, 1998.

P. Barnard, Interacting Cognitive Subsystems: A Psycholinguistic Approach to Short Term Memory. In A. Ellis (ed) Progress in the Psychology of Language, Lawrence Erlbaum Associates, Hove, United Kingdom, 197-258, 1985.

J. Barwise and J. Perry. *Situations And Attitudes.* Bradford Books, Cambridge, United States of America 1983.

D. Busse and C.W. Johnson, Modelling Human Error within a Cognitive Theoretical Framework. In F.E. Ritter and R.M. Young (eds.) The Second European Conference on Cognitive Modelling, Nottingham University Press, 90-97, 1998.

R. Fagin, J. Halpern, Y. Moses, and M. Vardi. *Reasoning About Knowledge.* MIT Press, Boston, United States of America 1995.

C.W. Johnson, *A Probabilistic Logic For The Development of Safety-Critical Interactive Systems.* International Journal of Man-Machine Systems, 39(2):333-351, 1993.

C.W. Johnson, *The Formal Analysis Of Human-Computer Interaction During Accident Investigations.* In G. Cockton, S.W. Draper and G.R.S. Weir, editors, People And Computers IX, 285-300. Cambridge University Press, Cambridge, 1994.

C.W. Johnson, *The Application of Petri Nets to Represent and Reason about Human Factors Problems During Accident Analyses* In P. Palanque and R. Bastide, editors, The Specification And Verification Of Interactive Systems, 93-112, Springer Verlag, Berlin, 1995.

C.W. Johnson, *Decision theory and Safety-Critical Interfaces.* In K. Nordby, P.H. Helmersen, D. Gilmore and S. Arensen (eds.) Interact '95, 127-132, Chapman Hall, London, United Kingdom, 1995a.

C.W. Johnson, Impact of Working Environment upon Human-Machine Dialogues: A Formal Logic for the Integrated Specification of Physical and Cognitive Ergonomic Constraints on User Interface Design. Ergonomics (39)3:512-530, 1996.

D. Kieras, S.D. Wood, D.E. Meyer, Predictive Engineering Models based on the EPIC Architecture for Multimodal High Performance Human Computer Interaction Tasks. To appear in ACM Transactions on Human Computer interaction, 1998.

W. Morehouse and M.A. Subamaniam, The Bhopal Tragedy. Technical Report. Council for International and Public Affairs, New York, United States of America, 1986.

D. Norman, *The 'Problem' With Automation : Inappropriate Feedback And Interaction Not Over-automation.* In D.E. Broadbent and J. Reason and A. Baddeley (eds.), Human Factors In Hazardous Situations, 137-145, Clarendon Press, Oxford, United Kingdom, 1990.

J. Reason, *Managing the Risks of Organisational Accidents*, Ashgate, Aldershot, United Kingdom, 1997.

Sheen, Formal Investigation into the Sinking of the mv Herald of Free Enterprise, UK Department of Transport, Report of court 8074, Her Majesty's Stationery Office, 1987.

Using Plan Recognition in Human-Computer Collaboration

Neal Lesh[1], Charles Rich[1] and Candace L. Sidner[2] *
{lesh, rich}@merl.com, csidner@lotus.com

[1] MERL–A Mitsubishi Electric Research Laboratory
[2] Lotus Development Corporation

Abstract. Human-computer collaboration provides a practical and useful application for plan recognition techniques. We describe a plan recognition algorithm which is tractable by virtue of exploiting properties of the collaborative setting, namely: the focus of attention, the use of partially elaborated hierarchical plans, and the possibility of asking for clarification. We demonstrate how the addition of our plan recognition algorithm to an implemented collaborative system reduces the amount of communication required from the user.

1 Introduction

An important trend in recent work on human-computer interaction and user modeling has been to view human-computer interaction as a kind of *collaboration* (e.g, Ferguson and Allen, 1998, Guinn, 1996, Rich and Sidner, 1998, Rickel and Johnson, 1998). In this approach, the human user and the computer (often personified as an "agent") coordinate their actions toward achieving shared goals. A common setting for collaboration, illustrated in Figure 1(a), and which is the focus of this paper, is when two participants can both communicate with each other and observe each other's actions on some shared artifact.

Successful collaboration requires the participants to have substantial mutual understanding of their shared goals and the actions intended to achieve them (these are part of what Grosz and Sidner (1990) call the *SharedPlan*). One way to maintain this mutual understanding is through verbal communication—the participants can explicitly discuss each goal and the method they propose to achieve it. However, it is often more efficient and natural to convey intentions by performing actions. For example, if two people are attempting to get into their locked car and one picks up a brick, the other can infer that the proposed plan is for the first person to smash a window, reach in, and unlock the door. *Plan recognition* (e.g., Carberry, 1990, Kautz and Allen, 1986) is the term generally given to the process of inferring intentions from actions.

Although plan recognition is a well-known feature of human collaboration, it has proven difficult to incorporate into practical human-computer collaboration systems due to its inherent intractability in the general case (see Section 2.1). In this work, we describe how to exploit properties of the collaborative setting in order to make plan recognition practical. Specifically, the properties we exploit are: the focus of attention, the use of partially elaborated hierarchical plans, and the possibility of asking for clarification.

We demonstrate our approach in the context of an implemented collaborative system for email. Section 1.1 below presents two example sessions with this system. Section 2 describes the

---

* Thanks to Jeff Rickel for his insightful comments on an earlier draft of this paper.

underlying plan recognition and discourse interpretation algorithms in detail. We then discuss
related work and conclude.

1.1   Collagen Email Example

Collagen (Rich and Sidner, 1998) is an application-independent collaboration manager based on
the SharedPlan theory of task-oriented collaborative discourse (e.g., Lochbaum, 1998). We are
currently experimenting with Collagen in several different application areas, including air travel
(see Grosz and Kraus, 1996,Rich and Sidner, 1998) and email.

Figure 1(b) shows how the abstract setting for human-computer collaboration in Figure 1(a) is
instantiated using Collagen in the email domain. The large window in Figure 1(b) is the graphical
interface to the email part of Lotus eSuite™; this is the "shared artifact" of the collaboration. The
two smaller, overlapping windows in the corners of Figure 1(b) are the agent's and user's *home
windows*, through which they communicate with each other.

For an application-independent tool like Collagen, a key step in building a collaborative agent
is to develop a detailed task model for the domain. Based on empirical study of people working
on email, Sidner and colleagues have formalized the task structure of this domain in terms of
high-level goals, such as "working on email", lower-level goals, such as "filling in a message,"
and primitive actions corresponding to individual clicks on the eSuite interface.

Without Plan Recognition. Let us look first at the left column of Figure 1(c), which shows how
Collagen functions without plan recognition. In the first part of this session (lines 1–8) the user
has the initiative. Notice how the user laboriously announces each goal before performing a
primitive action which contributes to achieving it. Without plan recognition, this is the only way
to maintain the mutual understanding necessary for successful collaboration.

A simple example of collaboration occurs after the user returns from a long lunch (line 9).
At this point, the user's earlier intentional state is not immediately evident from the state of the
graphical interface, which would show only a browser window (resulting from clicking on a
URL in the message being read) with the email window behind or below it. Based on the user's
earlier announcement of goals, however, the agent has constructed a SharedPlan, which it can
communicate back to the user (lines 11–16) to help him reorient to what he was doing and what
is expected next.[1]

The user now continues as before, announcing his subgoals as he goes, until line 27, when
he declares that he is done with the goal of filling in the new message started in line 19. The
agent uses this as an opportunity to suggest some expected actions (line 28), one of which the
user requests the agent to perform (lines 29–30).

With Plan Recognition. The right column of Figure 1(c) shows the same task as the left column,
but with our plan recognition algorithm incorporated into Collagen. Notice that, unlike the previous example, the user in this session is not required to announce each goal and subgoal before
performing a primitive act (i.e., lines 3, 5, 7, 17, 18, and 20 are missing). Nevertheless, as we see
in lines 11–16, the agent constructs the same SharedPlan as before.

Plan recognition does not, however, totally eliminate the need for communication about intentions. In particular, collaborators must ask for clarification when there is ambiguity regarding

---

[1] The agent's communication in lines 11–16 derives from a more general capability in Collagen for maintaining what is called a *segmented interaction history*—see Rich and Sidner (1998).

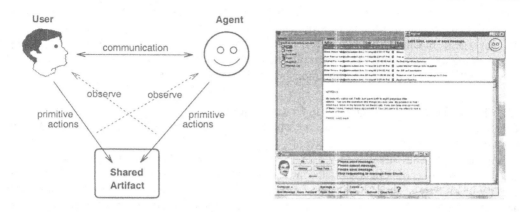

(a) A setting for human-computer collaboration.   (b) Graphical interface for email collaboration.

without plan recognition   *with plan recognition*

```
1   USER:   "Let's work on email."              USER:   "Let's work on email."
2   AGENT:  "You have 5 unread messages."       AGENT:  "You have 5 unread messages."
3   USER:   "Let's read a message."
4   USER:   <Select message from Chuck>         USER:   <Select message from Chuck>
5   USER:   "Let's read message in its own window."
6   USER:   <Open message>                      USER:   <Open message>
7   USER:   "Let's do something using message."
8   USER:   <Visit http://foo.bar.com>          USER:   <Visit http://foo.bar.com>
9           ...long lunch...                             ...long lunch...
10  USER:   "What was I doing?"                  USER:   "What was I doing?"
11  AGENT:  "Working on email.                   AGENT:  "Working on email.
12              Reading message from Chuck.                  Reading message from Chuck.
13               Reading message in its own window.            Reading message in its own ...
14              Done something using message.                Done something using message.
15               <Visit http://foo.bar.com>                   <Visit http://foo.bar.com>
16              Expecting to react to message."              Expecting to react to message."
17  USER:   "Let's react to message."
18  USER:   "Let's send email."
19  USER:   <Start new message>                  USER:   <Start new message>
20  USER:   "Let's fill in message."
21  USER:   <Address message to Dan>             USER:   <Address message to Dan>
22                                               AGENT:  "Why you sending email to Dan?
23                                                           (a) reacting to msg from Chuck
24                                                           (b) as a new goal "
25                                               USER:   "I'm reacting to msg from Chuck."
26          ...additional editing actions...             ...additional editing actions...
27  USER:   "Done filling in message."           USER:   "Done filling in message."
28  AGENT:  "Let's send, cancel or save msg."    AGENT:  "Let's send, cancel or save msg."
29  USER:   "Please save message."               USER:   "Please save message."
30  AGENT:  <Save message>                       AGENT:  <Save message>
```

Key: "utterance"   <primitive action>

(c) Collagen email session with and without plan recognition.

Figure 1.

how to interpret some given actions. For example, the user's actions in lines 19 and 21 are consistent with two possible intentions: by sending a message to Dan, the user may either be reacting to the message from Chuck (for example, if Chuck suggested sending email to Dan) or be starting a new, unrelated email goal. The agent interrupts the user at line 22 to resolve this ambiguity.[2] Section 2.2 discusses strategies for composing clarification questions.

1.2   The Role of Plan Recognition in Collaboration

This section previews the main points presented in the remainder of the paper, abstracted away from the details of the example above.

According to SharedPlan theory, a key component of the mental state of each participant in a collaboration is a set of beliefs about the mutually believed goals and actions to be performed, and about the mutually believed capabilities, intentions, and commitments of each participant. Each participant updates this set of beliefs, called the *SharedPlan*, based in part on communication with and observation of the other participants. Each participant also knows a set of methods, called *recipes*, for decomposing goals into subgoals.

Generally speaking, the role of plan recognition in this framework is as follows: Suppose one participant, e.g., the software agent, observes another participant, e.g., the user, perform an action A. The agent invokes plan recognition to determine the set of possible extensions to its current SharedPlan which are consistent with its recipe knowledge and include the user performing A. If there is exactly one possible such extension, the agent adopts this extension as its new SharedPlan; otherwise, it may ask a clarification question. A similar story can be told if the user does not actually perform A, but only proposes doing A (as in, "Let's do A").

We exploit three properties of the collaborative setting to make this use of plan recognition tractable. The first property is the *focus of attention*. When the user says, "Let's work on email," he is not only proposing a certain action be performed, he is also establishing a new context which restricts the interpretation of future utterances and actions. The full implications of focus of attention are beyond the scope of this paper (see Grosz and Sidner, 1990); in this work we use the weaker notion of the "focus act[3]" to limit the search required for plan recognition.

A second property of collaboration we exploit is that the processes of developing, communicating about, and executing plans are interleaved. Consequently, both the input and output of the plan recognizer are partially elaborated hierarchical plans. Unlike the "classical" definition of plan recognition (e.g., Kautz and Allen, 1986), which requires reasoning over complete and correct plans, our recognizer is only required to incrementally extend a given plan.

Third, it is quite natural during collaboration to ask for clarification, either because of inherent ambiguity, or simply because the computation required to understand an observed or mentioned action is beyond a participant's abilities. We use clarification to ensure that the number of actions the plan recognizer must interpret will always be small.

2   Algorithms

This section presents our plan recognizer and describes how it is used in discourse interpretation. We begin by adopting a straightforward formalization of actions, plans, and recipes.

---

[2] If the agent knows that the message to Dan is in reaction to the message from Chuck, it can, for example, be more helpful a week later when the user asks, "Did I ever react to the message from Chuck?"

[3] The focus act is what is called the "discourse segment purpose" in SharedPlan theory (see Lochbaum, 1998). The theory also specifies the rules by which discourse segments (contexts) are pushed and popped.

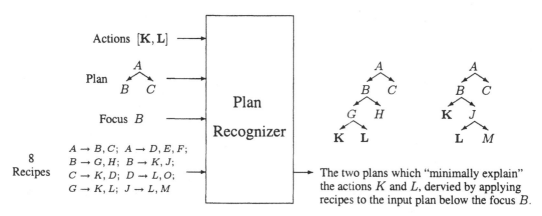

Figure 2. Simple example of inputs and outputs of plan recognition for collaboration

Let $\mathcal{ACT}$ be a set of actions which includes primitive actions, $\mathcal{PRIM} \subseteq \mathcal{ACT}$, and "top level" actions, $\mathcal{TOP} \subseteq \mathcal{ACT}$, which might be done for no other purpose than themselves. Primitive actions can be executed directly, while non-primitive (abstract) actions are achieved indirectly by achieving other actions. We assume a predicate DONE?(A) which returns true if A has been achieved or executed. In our implementation, each action also has an associated type, parameters, timestamp, and so on; but will not need to explicitly refer to these here.

Beliefs concerning hierarchical goal decomposition (such as found in a SharedPlan) are formalized as a tuple $\langle \mathcal{A}, \mathcal{E}, \mathcal{C} \rangle$, which we will simply call a "plan," where $\mathcal{A}$ is a set of actions, $\mathcal{E}$ is a set of directed acyclic edges on $\mathcal{A}$, where the edge $A_i \to A_j$ means that A_j is a step in achieving A_i, and where $\mathcal{C}$ is a set of constraints. $\mathcal{C}$ may include temporal ordering between actions in $\mathcal{A}$, as well as other logical relations among their parameters.[4] As shown in Figure 2, plans can be viewed as trees (with an associated set of constraints, not shown in diagrams).

For plan $P = \langle \mathcal{A}, \mathcal{E}, \mathcal{C} \rangle$, we define $A_i \in P$ to mean $A_i \in \mathcal{A}$. Let CONSISTENT?(P) be a predicate which determines whether $\mathcal{C}$ is satisfiable; and REPLACE(P, A_1, A_2) be a function which returns the (possibly inconsistent) plan resulting from replacing action A_1 with action A_2 in $\mathcal{A}$, $\mathcal{E}$, and $\mathcal{C}$.

Recipes are methods for decomposing non-primitive actions into subgoals. We represent recipes as functions that map an action to a plan that achieves the action. Let $\mathcal{RECIPE}$ be a set of recipes, where each recipe R_k is a function from a non-primitive action A_i to a plan $\langle \mathcal{A}', \mathcal{E}', \mathcal{C}' \rangle$, where A_i is in $\mathcal{A}'$ and for every $A_j \neq A_i$ in $\mathcal{A}'$ there is an edge $A_i \to A_j$ in $\mathcal{E}'$ i.e., the A_j are the *steps* in recipe R_k for achieving A_i.[5] For convenience, we define a function EXTEND(P, R_k, A_i), which returns the plan $\langle \mathcal{A} \cup \mathcal{A}', \mathcal{E} \cup \mathcal{E}', \mathcal{C} \cup \mathcal{C}' \rangle$.

2.1 Plan Recognition

As shown in Figure 2, the inputs to our plan recognizer are a sequence of actions $[A_1, ..., A_n]$, a plan $P = \langle \mathcal{A}, \mathcal{E}, \mathcal{C} \rangle$, a focus action $f \in P$, and a recipe library $\mathcal{R} \subseteq \mathcal{RECIPE}$. The output

---

[4] As shown in line 16 of Figure 1(c), our implementation allows recipes with optional steps, but for simplicity we do not include this feature in our formulation here.

[5] R_k may return the plan $\langle \{A_i\}, \emptyset, \emptyset \rangle$ if it is not applicable to A_i.

(a) Plan recognition.   (b) Focus, ambiguity and clarification.

RECOGNIZE($[A_1, .., A_n], P, f, \mathcal{R}$) $\equiv$

$\mathcal{EXPL} \leftarrow \emptyset, \mathcal{Q} \leftarrow \emptyset$

if $P = \langle \emptyset, \emptyset, \emptyset \rangle$

  foreach $T_i \in \mathcal{TOP}$

    add $\langle [A_1, .., A_n], \langle \{T_i\}, \emptyset, \emptyset \rangle, T_i \rangle$ to $\mathcal{Q}$

else foreach $g_i \in \text{FRINGE}(P, f)$

  add $\langle [A_1, .., A_n], P, g_i \rangle$ to $\mathcal{Q}$

until $\mathcal{Q} = \emptyset$

  remove $\langle [A'_1, .., A'_{n'}], P', act \rangle$ from $\mathcal{Q}$

  $P'' \leftarrow \text{REPLACE}(P', act, A'_1)$

  if CONSISTENT?(P'')

    if $n' = 1$ add P'' to $\mathcal{EXPL}$

    else foreach $g_i \in \text{FRINGE}(P'', f)$

      add $\langle [A'_2, .., A'_{n'}], P'', g_i \rangle$ to $\mathcal{Q}$

  if $act \notin \mathcal{PRIM}$

    foreach recipe $R_k \in \mathcal{R}$

      $P''' \leftarrow \text{EXTEND}(P', R_k, act)$

      foreach s_j, where $act \rightarrow s_j \in P'''$

        add $\langle [A'_1, .., A'_{n'}], P''', s_j \rangle$ to $\mathcal{Q}$

return $\mathcal{EXPL}$

$plan \leftarrow \langle \emptyset, \emptyset, \emptyset \rangle, focus \leftarrow null, acts \leftarrow [\,]$

repeat

  wait for next input action A_i,

  if DONE?(root of $plan$)

    $plan \leftarrow \langle \emptyset, \emptyset, \emptyset \rangle, focus \leftarrow null$

  add A_i to $acts$

  pick $\leftarrow null$

  $\mathcal{EXPL} \leftarrow \text{RECOGNIZE}(acts, plan, focus, \mathcal{R})$

  if $\mathcal{EXPL} = \emptyset$

    set $focus$ to root of $plan$

    $\mathcal{EXPL} \leftarrow \text{RECOGNIZE}(acts, plan, focus, \mathcal{R})$

  if $|\mathcal{EXPL}| = 1$

    remove $pick$ from $\mathcal{EXPL}$

  else if $\mathcal{EXPL} = \emptyset$ or $|acts| > MaxWait$

    $pick \leftarrow \text{CLARIFY}(\mathcal{EXPL})$

  if $pick \neq null$

  $plan \leftarrow pick$

  $focus \leftarrow \text{UDATEFOCUS}(plan, A_i)$

  $acts \leftarrow [\,]$

Figure 3. Pseudo-code for algorithms.

of the recognizer is a (possibly empty) set of extensions of P which "minimally explain" the input actions by applying recipes "below" the focus. More formally, each output plan, $P' = \langle \mathcal{A}', \mathcal{E}', \mathcal{C}' \rangle$, has the following properties:

1. $\{A_1, ..., A_n\} \subseteq \mathcal{A}'$,
2. every action in $(\mathcal{A}' - \mathcal{A})$ is reachable in $\mathcal{E}'$ from f,
3. P' can be derived from P by a composition of calls to EXTEND($..., R_k, ...$), where $R_k \in \mathcal{R}$, and REPLACE($..., ..., A_k$), where $A_k \in \{A_1, ..., A_n\}$, and
4. no smaller plan $\langle \mathcal{A}'', \mathcal{E}'', \mathcal{C}'' \rangle$, and $\mathcal{A}'' \subseteq \mathcal{A}', E'' \subseteq E', C'' \subseteq C'$, satisfies these properties.

Figure 3(a) shows pseudo-code for a simple plan recognizer that performs an exhaustive search of all possible ways of extending the input plan to explain the input actions. To understand the search space, consider how the input plan might be extended to include the first input action A_1. To explain A_1, the recognizer must apply some sequence of recipes $R_1, ..., R_k$ to the input plan P and then replace an action in the resulting plan with A_1.[6] The first recipe R_1 must be applied to a non-primitive action g_o in plan P that has not yet been expanded. Additionally, g_o must be beneath the focus act f in the subgoal structure of P. The function FRINGE(P, f) returns the set of actions in P reachable from f which are leaves of the plan tree and are not DONE?.

After applying recipe R_1 to an action g_o on the fringe of P, the recognizer only considers applying a second recipe, R_2, to g_o's subgoals, i.e., the steps added by R_1. This is justified because a plan can never be *minimally* extended to explain one action by applying recipes to

---

[6] The recipe sequence can have length zero, i.e., we replace an action already in the plan with A_1.

multiple actions in the original plan. Similarly, the recognizer need only consider applying recipe R_3 to steps added by R_2 and, generally, only considers applying R_i to the steps added by R_{i-1}. It follows that the size of the search space to explain one action is bounded by $F(R \times S)^L$, where S is the maximum number of steps in a recipe, R is the maximum number of recipes applicable to an action, F is the number of actions on the fringe of P, and L is the length of the longest sequence of recipes $R_1, ..., R_L$ the algorithm must consider.[7]

When the recognizer finds a plan P' which explains A_1 but there are more input actions to explain, it repeats the entire process to find all ways of extending P' to also explain action A_2, and so on until it has found all plans that minimally explain every input action. Since the algorithm recurses for each input action, its worst-case complexity is $O((F'(R \times S)^L)^N)$, where F' is the maximum fringe size at any point and N is the number of input actions. .

How does this compare to the general case? In the general case, the recognizer needs to search the entire plan space, because its output plans must contain no non-primitive steps that have not been decomposed. Let d be the depth of the deepest possible plan. Note that $d \geq L$, because if L recipes can be applied to explain a single action, then there must be a plan of at least depth L. The total number of plans that have to be searched is then $O((R^S)^d)$. Thus if the number of input actions is small, the collaborative plan recognition problem is significantly more tractable than the general plan recognition problem. We guarantee that the number of input actions will be small with a policy that asks for clarification whenever the number of unexplained actions a threshold (described in next section).

2.2 Focus, Ambiguity and Clarification

We now discuss how to incorporate plan recognition into a collaborative agent (summarized in Figure 3(b)). It is beyond the scope of this paper to present the full SharedPlan discourse interpretation algorithm Lochbaum (1998) used in Collagen. Instead, we concentrate on the role of the focus of attention and what to do when the recognizer returns multiple explanations.[8]

First, consider the focus of attention. In natural dialogue, people use context to help understand otherwise ambiguous statements. People do not typically even think about all possible interpretations of a potentially ambiguous phrase, such as "Let's save it", if there is an obvious interpretation that makes sense given what was just said. Analogously, we use the focus act to restrict the search space of our plan recognizer. Only if the recognizer fails to find any explanations using the current focus do we expand the context; we do so by setting the focus to the root of the current plan and calling the recognizer again. The function UPDATEFOCUS($plan, act$) in Figure 3(b) returns act if act is not DONE?; otherwise act's nearest ancestor in the plan that is not DONE?. Thus, the focus is in general set at the lowest-level goal which is not yet achieved, but includes the last observed or mentioned act.

Of course, the focus of attention does not guarantee a unique explanation. When ambiguity arises, we choose between two options: either wait or ask for clarification. A reason to wait is that

---

[7] In general, there might not be a bound on L due to cycles in the recipe set. In practice, we halt search whenever a cycle is encountered. For simplicity, here we assume that the recipe library is acyclic (as in Kautz and Allen, 1986).

[8] There are also strategies in Collagen, not described here, for when the recognizer returns no explanations as well as methods for clarification of ambiguity between starting a new top level goal vs. working on optional steps of the current recipe.

future actions might resolve the ambiguity. A reason to ask now is that a collaborative system can be much more helpful when it knows what the user is doing. We believe it will be very difficult, in general, to compute the precise utility of asking for clarification. Instead, we use a simple heuristic: we ask for clarification as soon as there are $MaxWait$ or more unexplained actions, where $MaxWait$ is a small integer, currently set to 2.

We now briefly discuss how to manage a clarification sub-dialogue. Our collaborative agent first asks the user about the purpose of his most recent action, such as in lines 22–24 in Figure 1(c). If ambiguity remains, the agent then asks about the purpose of other actions in the user's plan which would disambiguate intermediate recipes. In general the agent can pursue a variety of clarification strategies, including potentially lengthy dialogues in which the agent asks the user many simple questions, brief dialogues which require the user to choose a possible explanation from the agent's current hypotheses, and a mixture of the two. At present, our agent engages in the potentially lengthy dialogues, but we intend to expand its repertoire to include other strategies.

2.3 Preliminary Evaluation

We have implemented the plan recognizer described above and integrated it into Collagen. The addition of plan recognition significantly reduced the amount of communication required of the user in typical scenarios. Our subjective impression was that this lead to a much more natural collaboration, because the eliminated utterances were those that seemed most unnatural to a human.

In an initial attempt to quantify the impact of plan recognition, we have run some randomized experiments in the Lotus eSuite™ email domain. This recipe library contains 31 recipes, 32 primitive actions, and 19 non-primitive actions. In each trial, we randomly instantiated a plan and simulated a user executing it. Without recognition, the user must communicate every non-primitive action (goal) in the current plan. With recognition, our simulated user never volunteers information; it only performs primitive actions and answers clarification questions from the agent. Based on 100 random samples, we found that, without recognition, the user has to communicate, on average, about 4.4 times per plan. With recognition (and $MaxWait = 2$) the user only has to answer, on average, about 1.2 clarification questions per plan. The recognizer took an average of .94 CPU seconds to process each action. These results, however, convey only a general sense of how plan recognition can enhance collaboration, since the performance of the recognizer is very sensitive to the structure of the recipe library.

3   Related Work

The dominant framework for plan recognition research has been "keyhole" recognition, in which the observed actor is unaware of or indifferent to the observer (e.g.,Kautz and Allen, 1986). Our recognizer takes two inputs that a keyhole recognizer does not: a partially elaborated plan and a focus act. These additional inputs simplify the plan recognition task because the recognizer must only extend the input plan, by applying recipes below the focus, just enough to explain the input actions. In the collaborative setting, the role of plan recognition is not to cleverly deduce an actor's plan, but rather to allow collaborators to communicate more naturally and efficiently.

In the proliferation of recent work on plan recognition, researchers have addressed various limitations of the keyhole framework. We now discuss a variety of these approaches and illustrate how their settings and resulting techniques differ from our own.

Vilain (1990) presented a plan recognizer that runs in polynomial time. However, it only recognizes top level goals which is not sufficient for our purposes, and can only achieve polynomial time if the steps in the recipes are totally ordered, which is too restrictive for our domains. We believe Vilain's or other's fast recognition algorithms could be adapted to our formulation.

Lochbaum (1991) presented a plan recognition algorithm based on the SharedPlan model of collaboration. Her plan recognizer does not chain recipes together, as our does, and thus performs only "one level deep" recognition. It does, however, make use of a wider range of relations by which actions contribute to goals than we do.

Plan recognition has also been studied within a collaborative setting in which each participant works on their own plan but pools information and coordinates actions with others (e.g., Guinn, 1996, Smith et al., 1992). In particular, this work explores the opportunity for plan recognition when a participant announces that one of their goals has failed.

Our work is close in spirit to research on plan recognition for cooperative dialogues. Our use of context to narrow the scope of plan recognition resembles Carberry's (1990) focusing heuristics. Much work on cooperative response generation addresses the listener's need to know only enough of the speaker's plan to answer her questions adequately (e.g., Ardissono and Sestero, 1996). In contrast, we concentrate on a collaborative setting in which a joint plan is maintained by all collaborators and there is a shared artifact that all participants can interact with. A related distinction concerns ambiguity. The primary source of ambiguity in the cooperative response generation work resides in determining the user's top level goal (e.g., does the student want to take the course for credit or as an audit— see Lambert and Carberry (1991)). In our work, ambiguity arises because there are multiple ways of connecting actions to known higher level goals.

A variety of strategies for reducing ambiguity for plan recognition have been proposed. These include adopting the worst possible explanation for the observer in adversarial settings (e.g., Tambe and Rosenbloom, 1995), and assuming the observed person is doing what a expert system would suggest in a medical assistance domain (e.g., Gertner and Webber, 1996). In our collaborative setting, we use the focus of attention to reduce ambiguity, but failing this, we believe it often best just to ask the person what they are doing.

Probabilistic approaches to plan recognition (e.g., Bauer et al., 1993) would likely be effective and beneficial in the context of collaboration. However, we do not believe that probabilistic reasoning will eliminate either ambiguity or the need for clarification in human-computer collaboration because both seem fundamental to human-human collaboration.

Previous work has considered how to recognize the plans of someone who is performing more than one task at a time (e.g., Kautz and Allen, 1986, Lesh and Etzioni, 1995). We believe that in a collaborative setting, working on many tasks in parallel requires a great deal of communication and thus extending Collagen to handle simultaneous tasks primarily requires extensions to the discourse interpretation rather than the plan recognition component.

Plan recognition has often been proposed for improving user interfaces or to facilitate intelligent user help (e.g., Goodman and Litman, 1990, Lesh and Etzioni, 1995). Typically, the computer watches the user "over the shoulder" and jumps in with advice or assistance when the recognizer deduces the user's goals (e.g., Wilensky et al., 1988). This approach does not view human-computer interaction as collaboration, in which all participants are committed to maintaining mutual understanding of the common goals. Instead, it makes the (to us) implausible assumption that it is possible to infer the user's goals and plans by observing only primitive interface actions and to choose appropriate assistance without any mutual understanding.

4   Conclusion

Human-computer collaboration is a fruitful application for plan recognition because all participants are committed to maintaining a mutual understanding of the goals and actions to be performed. The question isn't whether the software agent will know the user's plan, but how the
agent and the user can best communicate their intentions to each other. We have shown that plan
recognition can allow more efficient and natural communication between collaborators, and can
do so with relatively modest computation effort.

References

Ardissono, L., and Sestero, D. (1996). Using dynamic user models in the recognition of the plans of the
    user. In *User Modeling and User Adapted Interaction*, volume 2, 157–190.

Bauer, M., Biundo, S., Dengler, D., Kohler, J., and G., P. (1993). PHI–a logic-based tool for intelligent
    help systems. In *Proc. 13th Int. Joint Conf. AI.*

Carberry, S. (1990). Incorporating default inferences into plan recognition. In *Proc. 8th Nat. Conf. AI*,
    volume 1, 471–8.

Ferguson, G., and Allen, J. (1998). Trips: An integrated intelligent problem-solving assistant. In *Proc.
    15th Nat. Conf. AI*, 567–572.

Gertner, A., and Webber, B. (1996). A bias towards relevance: Recognizing plans where goal minimization
    fails. In *Proc. 13th Nat. Conf. AI*, 1133–1138.

Goodman, B., and Litman, D. (1990). Plan recognition for intelligent interfaces. In *Proc. 6th IEEE Conf.
    AI Applications.*

Grosz, B. J., and Kraus, S. (1996). Collaborative plans for complex group action. *Artificial Intelligence*
    86(2):269–357.

Grosz, B. J., and Sidner. C. L. (1990). Plans for discourse. In Cohen, P. R., Morgan, J. L., and Pollack,
    M. E., eds., *Intentions and Communication*. Cambridge, MA: MIT Press. 417–444.

Guinn, C. I. (1996). Mechanisms for dynamically changing initiative in human-computer collaborative
    discourse. In *Human Interaction with Complex Systems Symposium.*

Kautz, H., and Allen, J. (1986). Generalized plan recognition. In *Proc. 5th Nat. Conf. AI*, 32–37.

Lambert, L., and Carberry, S. (1991). A tripartite plan-based model of dialogue. In *Proc. 29th Annual
    Meeting of the ACL*, 47–54.

Lesh, N., and Etzioni, O. (1995). A sound and fast goal recognizer. In *Proc. 14th Int. Joint Conf. AI*,
    1704–1710.

Lochbaum, K. E. (1991). An algorithm for plan recognition in collaborative discourse. In *Proc. 29th
    Annual Meeting of the ACL.*

Lochbaum, K. E. (1998). A collaborative planning model of intentional structure. *Computational Linguis-
    tics* 24(4).

Rich, C., and Sidner, C. (1998). COLLAGEN: A collaboration manager for software interface agents.
    User Modeling and User-Adapted Interaction 8(3/4):315–350.

Rickel, J., and Johnson, W. L. (1998). Animated agents for procedural training in virtual reality: Perception,
    cognition, and motor control. *to appear in Applied Artificial Intelligence.*

Smith, R. W., Hipp, D. R., and Biermann, A. W. (1992). A dialog control algorithm and its performance.
    In *Third Conference on Applied Natural Language Processing.*

Tambe, M., and Rosenbloom, P. (1995). RESC: An approach for real-time, dynamic agent-tracking. In
    Proc. 14th Int. Joint Conf. AI, 103–110.

Vilain, M. (1990). Getting serious about parsing plans: A grammatical analysis of plan recognition. In
    Proc. 8th Nat. Conf. AI, 190–197.

Wilensky, R., Chin, D., Luria, M., Martin, J., Mayfield, J., and Wu, D. (1988). The Berkeley UNIX
    Consultant project. *Computational Linguistics* 14(4):35–84.

USER MODELS DRIVE ADAPTATION OF SYSTEM ACTIONS

Tailoring the Interaction With Users in Electronic Shops*

Liliana Ardissono and Anna Goy

Dipartimento di Informatica, Università di Torino
C.so Svizzera 185; 10149 Torino, Italy
E-mail: {liliana, goy}@di.unito.it

Abstract. We describe the user modeling and personalization techniques adopted in SETA, a shell supporting the construction of adaptive Web stores which customize the interactions with users, suggesting the items best fitting their needs, and adapting the description of the store catalog to their preferences and expertise. SETA uses stereotypical information to handle the user models and applies personalization rules to dynamically generate the hypertextual pages presenting products: the system adapts the graphical aspect, length and terminology used in the descriptions to the user's receptivity, expertise and interests. Moreover, it maintains a profile associated to each person the goods are selected for, to provide multiple criteria for the selection of items, tailored to the beneficiaries' preferences.

1 Introduction

With the expansion of Internet, tools have been built to help vendors to set up Web stores, building the store databases and managing the order processing and payment transactions. These tools typically do not focus on issues like the personalization of the interaction with the customers. However, Web stores are characterized by two main features:

- Since they are accessed by heterogeneous users, they should satisfy different preferences in the suggestion of goods; this ability requires filtering capabilities, to identify the items suited to the specific customer. So, these stores are close to the applications in the information filtering area, where several recommender systems have been developed to exploit user models in the personalized selection of items (e.g., Popp and Lödel, 1996, Karunanithi and Alspector, 1997, Raskutti et al., 1997).
- Since they are hypermedia systems, they should meet the users' interaction needs. Benyon (1993) explains that users differ in many parameters, like status, expertise and preferences, which should be taken into account to improve the usability of systems. For instance, to increase the flexibility of the interactions, the product descriptions should be tailored to the users' expertise and interests (e.g., Milosavljevic and Oberlander, 1998), and the users' preferences on interaction media should be accounted for (e.g., Joerding, 1998, Fink et al., 1997).

* This work is developed in the project "Servizi Telematici Adattativi" (http://www.di.unito.it/~seta), carried on at the Dipartimento di Informatica of the University of Torino within the national initiative "Cantieri Multimediali", granted by Telecom Italia. We are grateful to L. Console, L. Lesmo, C. Simone and P. Torasso for having contributed to this work with suggestions and fruitful discussions. Many thanks to G. Petrone and C. Barbero who have developed the SETA system together with us.

The issue of tailoring information to the user has been deeply analyzed in the flexible hypermedia research, where a major distinction was made between personalizing the navigation task and the description of the information items to be presented (Brusilovsky, 1996). Some researchers, like Calvi (1997), have focused on the dynamic adaptation of the hypertextual structure to users with different backgrounds. Others, like Milosavljevic et al. (1996) and Hirst et al. (1997), have focused on the dynamic generation of text tailored to the system's user. However, an analysis of the electronic sales reveals other issues to be faced in an on-line store: e.g., the user should be assisted while browsing the catalog and selecting items to purchase; the system should keep track of her actions, to remember which items she has analyzed, and other data useful to identify her real needs. On top of this, the product description should be planned to highlight the information most important to the user, so that she can easily compare products and decide which one to buy; finally, the properties having the greatest impact on her might be highlighted to convince her to buy the items (e.g., Jameson et al., 1995).

Various techniques have been used to select interesting items in environments where heterogeneous information sources are exploited, or little information is available about the user's needs (e.g., Ackerman et al., 1997, ACM, 1997). We believe that, while those techniques are suited to deal with large-scale applications, such as information retrieval on the Web, virtual stores can benefit from the presence of motivated users[1] and a constrained information space. Products can be carefully defined and classified, so that the search task is performed in the presence of significant information about the hyperspace nodes. For these reasons, we believe that knowledge-intensive approaches, where detailed user profiles are built and items and descriptions are selected on the basis of a deep evaluation of the user's needs, are promising in the development of Web stores.

In this paper, we describe the user modeling and personalization techniques adopted in SETA, a tool for building adaptive Web stores which tailor the interactions to their customers' features, possibly suggesting the items which best fit their preferences. SETA is a virtual store shell and can be instantiated on a new sales domain by configuring the knowledge bases and the databases containing the domain-dependent information; our current prototype works on the telecommunication domain (selling phones, faxes and similar products). In the development of this Web store, we have focused on issues related to the adaptive provision of information, leaving apart the adaptability of the interface: we have considered the customization of the presentation style, the selection of the product information to provide, and the selection of items to recommend. In the following sections, we describe the portion of SETA handling the personalization of the interaction; Ardissono et al. (1999b) provides a description of the overall system architecture.

2   Management of the User Models

The user models are handled by a User Modeling Component (UMC). During a session, the direct user may choose items for herself and for other people. The UMC builds a direct user model to tailor the product presentation and the selection of goods to her needs; moreover, it creates a user model for each third person for whom she selects goods: the beneficiaries' models are used to suggest the goods suited to the persons they are selected for, if different from the direct user.

---

[1] They are looking for items to buy and, if they want to be helped, we can assume that they are willing to cooperate with the system and provide information about themselves.

The user models are initialized by retrieving the users' records from a Users DB. New customers are asked to fill in a form where the classification information is asked; then, the UMC initializes their models by exploiting stereotypical information.[2] The UMC retrieves the domain-dependent knowledge about users from a Stereotype KB, which contains a hierarchical taxonomy of stereotypes clustering the properties of homogeneous customer groups. The user features to be modeled in a specific sales domain are defined at the store configuration time: when a new virtual store is created, the Stereotype KB can be defined using a dedicated configuration tool, which also generates a template, used to create the user models during the interactions. The Stereotype KB may contain the description of multiple market segmentations, called "stereotype families". A family describes the features characteristic of the customer classes (stereotypes) belonging to it. The stereotype families represent orthogonal segmentations of the population and describe customers under different viewpoints; for example, for our prototype we have defined three families concerning the users' domain expertise, life style and destination use of the items to purchase (we distinguish home and business use, involving different preferences towards product properties). The stereotype families exploit (partially overlapping) classificatory data, but make predictions on different user preferences and personality traits. Each user is classified independently in each family and the stereotypical predictions are merged to initialize her user model.

The representation formalism of the user models includes a descriptive and a predictive part. The *descriptive part* stores the data explicitly asked to the user to classify her in the stereotypical user classes, and the information about the user's needs. The *predictive part* contains the information about the user's features inferred by the system, by exploiting stereotypical information.

In our prototype, the *classification data* are the user's personal data (age, gender, job, education level); however, when configuring the Stereotype KB of a new store, different user features might be selected for that sales domain (e.g., preferred colors and sports). In general, user *needs* may regard very different product features. However, as a first step to enable their recognition, we have associated needs only to the the functionalities offered by products (e.g., the transmission of voice is a possible user need and is the main functionality offered by phones). As a simplifying assumption, we currently suppose that the user is aware of her own high-level needs and can identify the generic product categories satisfying them (e.g., she knows that she needs a phone, although she may need help to select the specific item to purchase); so, needs are information that the system explicitly elicits from the user at the beginning of the interaction.

The *predictive part* of a user model concerns personality traits and preferences. The *personality traits* are used to tailor the descriptions to the user and include the receptivity (i.e. amount of information she is able to acquire), domain expertise, technical interest and interest for aesthetic information. The *preferences* represent the user's attitudes towards product properties (e.g., ease of use) and are used to suggest the items suited to her.[3] Following the formalism introduced in Torasso and Console (1989), personality traits and preferences are represented as parameters structured as follows (the personality traits have no importance slot):

Parameter Name; Importance;
Values: <Value, Probability> pairs;

---

[2] Recent developments of our system include the use of dynamic user modeling techniques, not described here, to update the user models on the basis of the user's behavior and product selections.

[3] We consider preferences as more general than the functionalities needed by the user. For instance, the user may have a generic preference for easy-to-use products.

The *Importance* slot takes values in the range [0..1] and represents the importance of the property to the user. Each *<Value, Probability>* pair contains a linguistic value that the parameter can take, and the probability that the user prefers that value for the product property. The probabilities associated to the linguistic values of a parameter are normalized and sum up to 1. For example, a user's preference towards the products "ease of use" might be:

> *Ease of use; Importance: 1;*
> *Values: <low, 0.0>, <medium, 0.3>, <high, 0.7>.*

This means that (the system believes that) the user considers the ease of use extremely important; moreover, she prefers very easy to use products with probability 0.7 (*high:* 0.7), average complexity products with probability 0.3, and she does not prefer complex products (*low:* 0.0).

2.1 Classification of Users

A stereotype *classification part* contains the data used to evaluate the probability that the user belongs to the represented customer class; we call this number *matching degree*, since it is calculated in a non-strictly probabilistic way (see below).[4] Each classification datum has an *Importance* slot and a list of *<Value, Probability>* pairs. The first slot describes the importance of the datum to the classification (i.e. how strongly it influences the evaluation of the user's degree of matching with the stereotype). The *<Value, Probability>* pairs represent the conditional probabilities that the user belongs to the stereotype, given the linguistic value of the datum.

To classify the user in a stereotype S, the UMC matches her data on the stereotype classification data; then, it combines the results, to obtain her matching degree with S. Let's consider two classification data, A and B (e.g., age and job), their importance, Imp_A and Imp_B, and their *<Value, Probability>* pairs: $\{<a_1, p_{a_1}>, ..., <a_m, p_{a_m}>\}, \{<b_1, p_{b_1}>, ..., <b_n, p_{b_n}>\}$. Suppose that the values for a user are a_i and b_j (e.g., she is a young teacher). The UMC first filters the conditional probabilities of the classification data to take into account their importance: if a datum is important, it should fully influence the task; if it is irrelevant, it should not (the neutral value is 1, see below). We used the following filtering function to modify the probability provided by a single classification datum (datum A), and obtain its matching score ($score_A$):

$$score_A = Imp_A * p_{a_i} + (1 - Imp_A). \qquad \text{(i)}$$

This formula raises the contribution to the classification provided by less important data, while it leaves that of important data unchanged: e.g., the score of the totally irrelevant data is 1, independent of the value of p_{a_i}; instead, if $Imp_A = 1$, then $score_A = p_{a_i}$.

The user's degree of matching with S is evaluated by applying the following function (Lesmo et al., 1985) to the scores computed for the classification data:

$$Match(score_A, score_B) = score_A * score_B / (score_A + score_B - score_A * score_B) \quad \text{(ii)}$$

For instance, if $score_A = 0.6$, $score_B = 0.9$, and A and B were the only classificatory data of S, the user's degree of matching with S would be 0.562. Function (ii) evaluates the fuzzy AND of the classification data, by combining their scores in a multiplicative way, and can be incrementally evaluated.[5]

---

[4] The main deviation from probability theory is due to the use of the importance of data: this factor is exploited to provide the store designer with an intuitive mechanism to tune the influence of data on the classification process, without requiring that she masters probabilistic concepts.

[5] Other functions have been used to compute the fuzzy AND: e.g., the product of the evidence of the ANDed conditions, or their minimum evidence. Function (ii) takes greater values than the product, which

2.2 Prediction of User Features

A stereotype *predictive part* makes predictions on the user's personality traits and preferences: each prediction has an *Importance* slot, representing an estimate of how important the preference is to the user, and a list of $<Value, Probability>$ pairs (predictions on personality traits have no importance). These are the conditional probabilities of the linguistic values for the datum, given that the user belongs to the stereotype.

The UMC initializes each personality trait and preference in the user model by merging the stereotypical predictions on its linguistic values (stereotypes in different families produce non overlapping predictions). The merge is obtained as the weighted sum of the probabilities suggested by each stereotype (the weights are the user's degree of matching with the stereotype). For instance, consider the "Domain Expertise" family and the preference towards the products "ease of use". If the user classification has produced the following matching degrees: Novice (0.7), Intermediate (0.2), Expert (0.1), and the stereotypes predict:

Novice: Importance: 1; <low, 0>, <medium, 0.3>, <high, 0.7>;
Intermediate: Importance: 0.8; <low, 0.1>, <medium, 0.6>, <high, 0.3>;
Expert: Importance: 0.5; <low, 0.3>, <medium, 0.4>, <high, 0.3>;

then the prediction on the importance of the preference, and that on its *"low"* value are:

Importance: $0.7*1+0.2*1+0.1*0.5 = 0.95.$; *low:* $0.7*0+0.2*0.1+0.1*0.3 = 0.05.$[6]
The weighted sum allows the best matching stereotypes to influence the predictions in a stronger way; moreover, if different stereotypes make similar predictions, they enforce each other.

3 Suggestion of Goods to the User

The information about the items sold in the store is maintained in a Products DB, where they are grouped in product classes (e.g., phones, faxes). When the items to suggest have to be displayed, a module, the Product Extractor, retrieves from the Products DB the records of the items matching the user's query (e.g., the phone models available in the store). Then, it ranks and sorts them, depending on how close they match the preferences in the beneficiary's user model. In this way, the items can be presented showing the most interesting ones first. The matching between the beneficiary's preferences and the properties of items is possible because their records contain information about features and *properties* (e.g., ease of use), and the properties correspond to the preferences specified in the user models. An item record stores, for each property, the linguistic value fitting the item; e.g., the "Super Slim" phone is described as follows:

Features:
   code: SuperSlim;
   price: LIT. 59000;
   color: black;
Properties:
   quality: high;
   ease of use: medium;

---

is influenced by the number of conjuncts to evaluate. Moreover, (ii) is more precise than the minimum, which takes into account the worst-matching feature and ignores the other classification conditions.

[6] After these assignments, the values are normalized so that they sum up to 1 and can be interpreted as probabilities again.

The Product Extractor gets from the UMC the preferences of the beneficiary of the goods. Then, it ranks each item by evaluating how close its properties match such preferences. To this extent, the Product Extractor exploits the same formulae described in Section 2.1 for the classification of users: an item suited to the user should match all her important preferences, possibly ignoring irrelevant mismatching properties; moreover, if an item mismatches an extremely important user preference, it should not be recommended at all. So, the user preferences are used as classification conditions for evaluating the overall matching degree of the item and are combined, again, in a fuzzy AND. First, given the property values of the item and the importance of such properties to the beneficiary (importance of the preference in the user model), the formula (i) is applied to neutralize the impact of irrelevant (mismatching) properties (raising their contribution to 1). Then, the filtered scores are inputed to the formula (ii) to obtain the overall score of the item.

4   Personalization of the Presentation

In SETA, a Personalization Agent dynamically generates the HTML code for the hypertextual pages to display during the interaction with the user. This module applies some personalization strategies to customize the pages, varying their contents and layout on the basis of the user's features (stored in the user model) and of the characteristics of the information to provide. The information sources used by the Personalization Agent include:

- The type of page to produce; e.g., a form, a page presenting a product / item, and so forth.
- The product / item to be presented, and the information about it. This information is stored in the Product Taxonomy (a knowledge base keeping the conceptual representation of the product classes), and in the Products DB, containing the specific data about items.
- The internal structure of the catalog, used to decide which hypertextual links to include (e.g., links to more specific products). This structure corresponds to the organization of products in the Product Taxonomy.
- The interaction context keeping the user's selections and a memory of which products and pages she has already seen.[7]
- The user's personality traits, used to select the information to provide and the technicality of the descriptions.
- A set of personalization rules, used to decide how to customize the pages on the basis of the contents of the user model.

The dynamic generation of pages and the fact that their contents are retrieved from declarative knowledge sources represent a step forward with respect to previous approaches, like that of Popp and Lödel (1996), where multiple static versions of the catalog exist and the system selects the one to display. In fact, in our approach, the pages may be adapted to the user's needs at the granularity level of the product features; moreover, the configurability of the system is enhanced.

The Personalization Agent generates different pages (choosing different layouts, colors, etc.) depending on the user's "backgrounds" (such as age and job); moreover, it produces different product descriptions, tailoring the selection of content to the user's interests and receptivity, and basing the selection of the linguistic form on her domain expertise.

---

[7] This context is maintained by the Dialog Manager, a component of the system we will not describe.

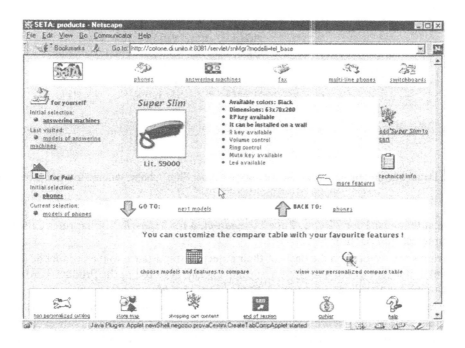

Figure 1. A page generated by our system presenting the "Super Slim" phone to an expert user.

Figure 1 shows a presentation page describing the "Super Slim" phone. In the leftmost portion of the page the system displays the user's selections and enables her to switch among them. The central area describes the functionalities and features offered by the product and is tailored to the user's interests, expertise level (showing detailed and technical descriptions) and receptivity (many features of phones are described). Below this area, there is the bar containing the links to the more specific/generic products in the Product Taxonomy View ("GO TO", "BACK TO"). The topmost bar provides the links to the main product categories available in the store, while the bar at the bottom of the page contains the general control buttons (e.g., "EXIT" button and link to the site map). Figure 2 focuses on the description of the same item, but it has been produced for a non-expert user; as it can be noticed, in this case fewer features are listed; moreover, the sentences displayed are simpler and more intuitive than those in Figure 1.

The Personalization Agent exploits a set of production rules to customize the portion of the hypertextual pages describing the features of products and items: it first selects the features to describe, by ranking their relevance on the basis of the user's interests and their intrinsic importance to the product description. Then, it plans the overall appearance of the Web page. Since its decisions have to be taken on the basis of criteria concerning different factors (e.g., user characteristics and information about products, etc.) a separate set of rules is applied to take each decision and the final result is obtained by combining the various contributions.

1) A first set of rules rates each product feature on the basis of the user's interests: for instance, a rule takes into account the user's technical interest (TI) and assigns the following scores to all

- Available colors: Black
- Dimensions: 63x70x200
- You can modify the ring type and its volume
- You can control the volume of the hands-free speakerphone
- A mute key is available to put on hold a call

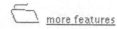

Figure 2. Detail of a presentation page describing the "Super Slim" phone, tailored to a non-expert user.

the technical features: 1 for TI=*low*, 2 for TI=*medium*, 3 for TI=*high*. Similar rules exist for the aesthetic interest, and so forth.

2) A rule ranks the features on the basis of their objective importance to the product description: this information is part of the description of products and is stored in the Product Taxonomy (it can take the following values: 1 for *low*, 2 for *medium*, 3 for *high* importance).

The estimates produced by the rules are weighted, to tune their influence to the evaluation of the overall score of the features: in our prototype, the weights are set to 1; however, the store designer may appropriately configure them, depending on whether the user's interests, or the objective importance of features should influence the evaluation most (she can also set them to 0, to neutralize the impact of the information to the evaluation task). This aspect is especially relevant in electronic sales applications, where there are typically data about products that have to be communicated to the customer, independently of her interests. The application of the rules in 1) and 2) produces a list of product features, partitioned in groups of equally scored elements. At this point, those to show to the user are selected.

3) A rule sets the number of information items that can be displayed in the same page, on the basis of the user's receptivity. This number enables the Personalization Agent to identify the portion of the feature list to show; the rest of the list is made available by introducing a "more information" link. Given the total number of features in the ordered list (n), and the user's receptivity (*low*, *medium*, or *high*, represented by r), the rule works as follows:

If $Receptivity = r$ then number of features to show $= x \pm \delta$;

In the formula, the value of x is a function of r and is retrieved from a correspondence table defined on the basis of the results of psychological studies about cognitive load. The δ variable represents a "tolerance factor", used to cut the feature list in a flexible way: if the value of x falls inside a group of features having the same score, an arbitrary decision should be taken to identify the features to show and those to exclude; δ enables the system to extend or restrict the number of features to show. For instance, let's assume that the user's receptivity is high and x takes value x_0; if the number of equally ranked features exceeding x_0 is greater then δ, then the group containing these features is hidden; otherwise, it is shown.

4) Finally, a rule selects the appropriate linguistic form for each feature, on the basis of the user's domain expertise. The linguistic descriptions are generated by exploiting templates, whose slots are filled by linguistic expressions corresponding to the feature values extracted from the records of items in the Products DB. A difficulty level is associated to each template (basically

depending on its technicality) and matched with the user's domain expertise level. In this way, the appropriate descriptions can be selected for the user: if the user's expertise is low, very simple descriptions, suited to a novice user, are used; if her expertise is high, the Personalization Agent includes concise and technical descriptions.

The final HTML code is generated by choosing the appropriate display settings (the font size, the color, and other special markers), on the basis of the scores associated to the features (e.g., some features in the Figures 1 and 2 are bold faced). As shown in Figure 1, the system also offers facilities to ask for more information about goods; for instance, the user can create comparative tables on the fly, by selecting the goods to examine and the features (and properties) which she would like to consider, therefore avoiding the examination of huge, precompiled structures, which compare all the items of a product category with respect to all their features.

5   Conclusions

We have described the user modeling and personalization techniques exploited in SETA, a shell supporting the construction of adaptive Web stores. The system demonstrates how advanced AI technologies can be applied in the electronic sales area, where two goals have to be merged: on one side the interaction needs to be user-friendly and personalized, and this task requires the application of techniques developed in the user modeling, knowledge representation and human-computer interaction research areas. On the other hand, on-line stores are real-world applications; so, the AI methods have to be embedded into robust and usable prototypes, which impose in many aspects a pragmatic approach to the development of systems.

Our system maintains a detailed user model where information about the user's preferences and needs is stored. This model is initialized by means of stereotypical information and it is exploited to dynamically generate Web pages tailored to the user: the system customizes the description of products, varying their length, terminology, and graphical appearance on the basis of the (direct) user's expertise, interests and receptivity. Moreover, the system maintains a model associated to each person the user is selecting goods for; so, the user's selections may be supported by suggesting the items most suited to their beneficiary, taking into account that the beneficiary's needs may be different from those of the direct user. The system can be configured on specific sales domains and the knowledge used to describe products and handle the user models can be configured by the store designer, by means of appropriate configuration tools.

For the moment, we have tested our prototype and tuned it on the basis of the suggestions collected from a restricted number of users (including psychologists and computer science experts), who have helped us to improve the interface and the interaction mode. A field trial is necessary to test the system on real users. As future work, we would like to increase the system's initiative: e.g., during an interaction, the system should interact more frequently with the user, asking her whether she would prefer items with slightly different characteristics (Linden et al., 1997); moreover, the system should promptly react to the user's behavior, exploiting her interests to promote specific products (Greer et al., 1996). We feel that reactive planning approaches, as that of de Carolis (1998), could be very effective to this task.

Our system is a Three Tier Application Architecture written in Java and based on the JavaSoft Java Web Server 1.1; see (Ardissono et al., 1999b, Ardissono et al., 1999a) for details.

References

Ackerman, M., Billsus, D., Gaffney, S., Hettich, S., Khoo, G., Kim, D., Klefstad, R., Lowe, C., Ludeman, A., Muramatzu, J., Omori, K., Pazzani, M., Semler, D., Starr, B., and Yap, P. (1997). Learning probabilistic user profiles. *AI Magazine* Summer:47–55.

ACM (1997). Recommender systems. *Communications of the ACM* 40(3).

Ardissono, L., Barbero, C., Goy, A., and Petrone, G. (1999a). An agent architecture for personalized web stores. To appear on *Proceedings of the Third International Conference on Autonomous Agents*.

Ardissono, L., Goy, A., Meo, R., Petrone, G., Console, L., Lesmo, L., Simone, C., and Torasso, P. (1999b). A configurable system for the construction of adaptive virtual stores. To appear on the *World Wide Web journal*.

Benyon, D. (1993). Adaptive systems: a solution to usability problems. *User Modeling and User-Adapted Interaction* 3:65–87.

Brusilovsky, P. (1996). Methods and techniques of adaptive hypermedia. *User Modeling and User-Adapted Interaction* 5(2-3):87–129.

Calvi, L. (1997). Multifunctional (hyper)books: a cognitive perspective (on the user's side). In *Proceedings of the workshop "Adaptive Systems and User Modeling on the World Wide Web*, 23–30.

de Carolis, B. D. (1998). Introducing reactivity in adaptive hypertext generation. In *Proceedings of the Thirteenth European Conference on Artificial Intelligence*.

Fink, J., Kobsa, A., and Nill, A. (1997). Adaptable and adaptive information access for all users, including disabled and the elderly. In *Proceedings of the Sixth Conference on User Modeling*, 171–173.

Greer, J., MacKenzie, M., and Koehn, G. (1996). User models for coercion, persuasion and sales. Research Report 96-1, ARIES Laboratory, Department of Computer Science, University of Saskatchewan.

Hirst, G., DiMarco, C., Hovy, E., and Parsons, K. (1997). Authoring and generating health-education documents that are tailored to the needs of the individual patient. In *Proceedings of the Sixth Conference on User Modeling*, 107–118.

Jameson, A., Shafer, R., Simons, J., and Weis, T. (1995). Adaptive provision of evaluation-oriented information: tasks and techniques. In *Proceedings of the Fourteenth International Joint Conference on Artificial Intelligence*, 1886–1893.

Joerding, T. (1998). Intelligent multimedia presentations in the web: Fun without annoyance. In *Proceedings of the Seventh World Wide Web Conference*.

Karunanithi, N., and Alspector, J. (1997). Feature-based and clique-based user models for movie selection: a comparative study. *User Modeling and User-Adapted Interaction* 7:279–304.

Lesmo, L., Saitta, L., and Torasso, P. (1985). Evidence combination in expert systems. *International Journal of Man-Machine Studies* 22:307–326.

Linden, G., Hanks, S., and Lesh, N. (1997). Interactive assessment of user preference models: The automated travel assistant). In *Proceedings of the Sixth Conference on User Modeling*, 67–78.

Milosavljevic, M., and Oberlander, J. (1998). Dynamic hypertext catalogues: Helping users to help themselves. In *Proceedings of the Ninth ACM Conference on Hypertext and Hypermedia*.

Milosavljevic, M., Tulloch, A., and Dale, R. (1996). Text generation in a dynamic hypertext environment. In *Proceedings of the Nineteenth Australasian Computer Science Conference*, 417–426.

Popp, H., and Lödel, D. (1996). Fuzzy techniques and user modeling in sales assistants. *User Modeling and User-Adapted Interaction* 5:349–370.

Raskutti, B., Beitz, A., and Ward, B. (1997). A feature-based approach to recommending selections based on past preferences. *User Modeling and User-Adapted Interaction* 7:179–218.

Torasso, P., and Console, L. (1989). *Diagnostic Problem Solving*. North Oxford Academic.

User-Tailored Plan Generation

Detlef Küpper, Alfred Kobsa

GMD FIT, German Nat'l Research Center for Information Technology, D-53754 St. Augustin, Germany

Abstract. The output of advice-giving systems can be regarded as plans to be executed by the user. Such plans are fairly useless if the user is not capable of executing some of the involved plan steps, or if he does not know them. We propose a two-phase process of user-tailored plan generation and plan presentation to produce advice that enables a user to reach his goals. This paper reports the first phase, the generation of a plan under the constraints of the user's capabilities. The capabilities are represented as a hierarchy of plan concepts. System assumptions about user capabilities form a part of the user model, but are separate from assumptions about the user's knowledge, goals etc. With this representation, we can re-use the techniques for collecting assumptions about the user's conceptual knowledge for inferring his capabilities as well. We show an example of plan generation for users with different capabilities.

1 Introduction

Adapting system responses to users is a central area of user modeling. However, the question of whether or not such responses really enable a user to reach his goals did not receive much attention so far. For advice-giving systems like online help and assistance systems this is however a crucial issue. We take the view that advice for a user is a proposed plan that the user should execute. The user must understand the system's advice and must be capable of executing the plan in order to reach the intended goals. We propose a two-phase process for creating such advice. The first phase generates a plan according to the user's capabilities. This plan is then the starting point for the second phase which creates a presentation of that plan taking the user's knowledge into account. Our approach to the problem of user-tailored plan generation will be illustrated within the context of a help system for a typical computerized office environment. There we assume a heterogeneous network of computers with different operating systems and users with various capabilities.

This paper describes the first phase in generating a user-tailored plan. We first describe the extent to which AI research on plan generation considers user-tailored planning. Then we define the notion of capabilities as we use it in this approach and discuss how a user model may represent such capabilities. We employ the user modeling shell system BGP-MS[1] (Kobsa and Pohl, 1995) to represent user models and demonstrate example user models for five different users. The partial order planner UCPOP (Penberthy and Weld, 1992) then generates plans for an example goal, taking the capabilities of these users into account.

---

[1] We use a slightly extended version of release 2.2. It provides means for the definition of new modalities and allows stereotypes for all defined modalities (Pohl and Höhle, 1997).

2 Planning

In the field of user modeling, plan processing mainly deals with plan libraries for plan recognition (e.g. Carberry, 1990, Kautz, 1991, Bauer, 1996). Only very few help systems generate plans (e.g., Breuker, 1990), however not user-specific ones. Plan libraries are assumed to contain all meaningful plans in an application domain. This approach, however, does not scale up very well when a large number of possible plans must be considered, or when plans have many variants. Unfortunately the number of potential plans increases exponentially with the number of tools that an agent may use.

Plan libraries also presume that the domain remains fairly static so that changes in the plan libraries do not occur very often. We therefore prefer plan generation (planning) over plan libraries, even though it is computationally expensive (Bylander, 1991, Erol et al., 1995). A static plan library approach even seems meaningless for user-tailored planning since it must not only contain plans for every possible goal but also plan variants for each possible combination of relevant user capabilities.

For an assessment of whether or not AI planning might extend to plan generation for a user, we take a short look at its main ideas. Planning means searching for a sequence of plan steps - the *solution* or the *plan* - that achieves the *goal* by executing the plan steps in a required order provided that the execution begins in a *start situation*. A plan step is an instance of a plan operator; it is defined by its precondition and its effect. Planning systems require goals, situations, preconditions and effects to be described by a restricted first order logic expression - usually a conjunction of literals. Even though today's view of plan *generation* is quite different[2], the following description may still give a rough idea of what happens when a plan is being *executed*. Executing a plan step in a situation *s* changes the situation by adding all literals of the step's effect and deleting all literals of *s* that contradict them. A plan step may only be executed in a situation that fulfills its precondition. We may imagine that reaching the goal by executing a plan means changing the start situation step by step until we finish with the last step in an end situation that fulfills the goal. A correct plan guarantees the precondition of each step to hold just before its execution.

Clearly a traditional planning process presumes the acting agent to be capable of executing all plan steps - otherwise the execution of the plan would fail. The fixed set of operators that the planner uses for generating plans defines the *activity potential* of the agent. For an artificial agent like a robot, this set is defined by the functional interface of the agent. We may likewise think of modeling the activity potential of users by sets of plan operators.

An example of one such operator is *open a file with text processor of type X* (open-file-tpx). We describe it with the syntax of the planner UCPOP:

```
(:operator open-file-tpx
 :parameters   (?app ?f)
 :precondition (and (tpx-file ?f) (local-fs-object ?f)
                    (tpx ?app) (launched ?app))
 :effect       (active ?app ?f))
```

---

[2] See e.g. (Russell and Norvig, 1995) for an overview of planning, (McDermott and Hendler, 1995) for an overview of the evolution of the view of planning, and (Weld, 1994) for extensions of precondition and effect descriptions and their consequences.

The meaning of this expression is that the agent may execute the operator if there is a local file (local-fs-object) that is appropriate for text processor X (tpx-file) and a launched text processor of type X (launched ∧ tpx). After the execution of this operator, this file is the active file of that text processor. Names of variables are marked by the prefix "?".

This example directly leads to the question of what is an adequate level of abstraction for this set of all operators. Here we have to distinguish between plan presentation and plan generation. The central task of plan presentation is to choose a level of abstraction that does not exhibit redundant and possibly misleading details, but on the other hand provides sufficient information enabling the user to recognize the intended plan (see, e.g. Young, 1996). In the field of plan generation, hierarchical task network (HTN) planning (Sacerdoti, 1977, Erol et al., 1994) deal with abstraction. They exploit several levels of abstraction for improving the efficiency of the planning process. At the end of the day, however, a plan must include all details because otherwise correctness cannot be guaranteed. This means that plan generation has to use the most detailed operators. But what *most detailed operators* means differs between the users, due to the different level of system's knowledge about users (see chapter 5 for an example).

3 Users' Abilities and Knowledge

The user's activity potential in a domain is mainly determined by his abilities and his authorization. The ability to climb stairs or to hit a special key combination on a computer keyboard are examples of the former. While normal users are able to perform such actions, some handicaps may prevent people from carrying them out. Examples of actions that usually depend on authorization are: *reading mail* (the user needs, e.g., an account), *open a ftp connection* (e.g., the user needs to pass a firewall), *printing on an expensive printer* (e.g., the user needs an account).

For plan generation, it makes no difference *why* a user is assumed to be capable of some action. We may define plan operators for all kinds of actions a user is capable of. This leads to a definition of the term *activity potential* of a user for the purpose of our approach:

> The *activity potential* of a user is the set of plan operators that the user is in principle able and authorized to execute.

The proviso *in principle* has been added since we also consider plan operators that users currently cannot execute due to lack of knowledge or due to unfulfilled preconditions. The above definition may be extended to arbitrary agents by replacing 'user' with 'agent'.

Some terminological remarks: Several researchers distinguish between the user's knowledge (which must be true) and his beliefs (which may be wrong). Since we do not need an explicit representation of this distinction we employ the terms interchangeably. Also, we will use the shorter term *capabilities* as a synonym for activity potential in the remainder of this paper. This should not be confused with *inferential capabilities* of users, which are investigated in text planning (e.g. Horacek, 1997, Zukerman and McConachy, 1993).

It is important to note that the user's capabilities should not be mixed up with the user's beliefs about plans. In our system, we strictly separate (system assumptions about) the user's capabilities from (system assumptions about) his beliefs - especially his beliefs about plan operators. Most real-world actions require both. For instance, users may not know how to reboot a DOS-PC, even if they are physically capable of hitting the famous key combination. On the other hand, some users, such as those who are handicapped, may not be able to hit these keys even when they have the required knowledge.

This separation of users' beliefs from their capabilities is not very common in AI systems. This is not surprising since a distinction is not really necessary in their application domains. Planning systems, for instance, usually generate plans for robots, and not for people. The capabilities of robots are determined by their functional interface. Therefore, the commands they accept as an input define exactly what they can do. A separation of beliefs (whatever this might be for a robot) from capabilities makes no sense when planning for robots. The same holds true for plan recognition systems that recognize user plans based on their actions. Such systems only see those actions that the user both knows and is able to perform.

In contrast, advice-giving systems that want to enable users to reach their goals do need to separate capabilities and knowledge. Lack of knowledge is far less critical than lack of capabilities since it can be overcome by instruction. This leads to the two-phase process for advice generation mentioned above. The first phase generates a plan from the operators of the user's activity potential, disregarding any assumptions about the user's beliefs. The presentation phase then generates an explanation of those plan steps that are unknown to the user. If we were to restrict plan generation to those operators only that are both in the user's activity potential *and* known by him, we would find less plans and specifically lose the opportunity of explaining plan steps to the user which he is capable to perform. The benefit of such help systems would be rather limited.

Although this paper does not deal with plan presentation, we should note that this two-phase process is not unidirectional. For instance, if a candidate plan generated in the first phase requires lengthy explanations in the presentation phase because many plan steps are unknown to the user, the presentation component may request the generation of an alternative plan.

Our model presumes easily changeable beliefs of the user, while his capabilities are assumed to be constant. We assume that the capabilities of a user do not change during the interaction with the system, nor during the execution of an advised plan. However this does not mean that the system's assumptions about the user's capabilities cannot change. In our system, updating the *assumptions* about the user's capabilities is done by the same techniques as updating assumptions about the user's beliefs.

4 Representation of concepts and plans

The user's beliefs about domain concepts form a significant part of his knowledge. Many user models represent this as an abstraction hierarchy of concepts with a terminological knowledge representation system (e.g., Sleeman, 1985, McCoy, 1989, Sarner and Carberry, 1992, Kobsa et al., 1994). In our system, we use SB-ONE (Kobsa, 1991) for this purpose, which forms part of the user modeling shell BGP-MS. SB-ONE fits loosely into the KL-ONE-paradigm (Brachman and Schmolze, 1985). With this approach a concept may be defined by its superconcepts and its attribute descriptions, i.e. its relations to other concepts (these relations are called *roles*). We adopt this approach for also representing beliefs about plan operators in conceptual abstraction hierarchies since we want to exploit the rich research experience in this area (e.g., for explaining concepts to the users and gathering conceptual knowledge of the user) and also take advantage of the inferential services of terminological representation systems (e.g., inferences over subsumption and disjointness relationships).

The same arguments hold true for assumptions about the user's capabilities. Therefore we represent capabilities and beliefs in a uniform way. We call the terminological representation of a plan operator a *plan concept.*

Some representations of plans in abstraction hierarchies disregard preconditions and effects (Kautz, 1991, Weida, and Litman, 1992). While this is often sufficient for the purposes of plan recognition, it is insufficient for the generation and explanation of plans. This view is also found in (Devanbu and Litman, 1996). We extend their approach to provide plan operators with variables. This leads to a different view of what preconditions and effects are. Devanbu and Litman model them as situations (sets of predicates that are expected to be true). We model preconditions as objects that are needed before, and effects as objects that are available after the execution of plan operators. We represent the relation of these objects to their plan concepts by roles with a number restriction of exactly one. Properties of the objects are represented by value restrictions on these roles, and relations between the objects are expressed by role-value-maps. Since plan operators change properties, we cannot use identical objects for preconditions and effects. Therefore we distinguish between object descriptions for preconditions and for effects.

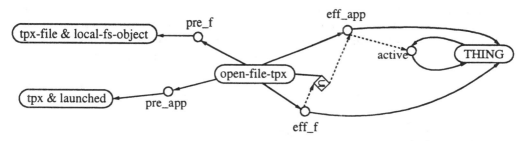

Figure 1. Terminological representation of the operator open-file-tpx in SB-ONE.

Figure 1 shows the terminological representation of the operator open-file-tpx in SB-ONE. The roles pre_app and pre_f specify that this plan concept needs two objects as preconditions: one of type tpx that is launched (a text processor of type X), and one that satisfies the conditions of a local-fs-object and a tpx-file (a local file that is appropriate for text processor X). The effects of the plan concept are expressed by roles eff_app and eff_f, and a role-value-map eff_f $\subseteq$ eff_app ∘ active. They specify that the execution of the plan does not introduce additional type constraints on the objects since the chosen type is the most general concept THING. A relation *active* between the two objects is however introduced which expresses that the active document of the application will be identical to the document that becomes opened by open-file-tpx.

5 Structure of a User Model with Capabilities

In this section we present a representation for all ingredients of our model, namely knowledge about plan operators and their abstraction hierarchies, system assumptions about users' capabilities and beliefs, and stereotypes that contain default assumptions about certain user subgroups. The partition approach (Cohen, 1978), which is supported by BGP-MS, is an elegant means for distinguishing between capabilities and beliefs in the user model representation.

We will use an example that includes the following agents:

Oscar   a member of staff, a typical user of office programs
Trixie   a guest who is a typical Unix user
Nick   a skilled student
Theo   a less skilled student
Sue   a person that is not well known to the system

Figure 2 shows the structure of all system assumptions about the beliefs of the users, of belief stereotypes and the system's beliefs about the domain. Rectangles denote partitions. The labels outside of partitions are partition names. All partition names in this figure end with "B", which marks them as belief partitions. For instance, the partition SBSueB contains the system's beliefs (i.e., assumptions) about Sue's beliefs. Partitions that are not leaves are stereotype partitions that are labeled with their names and the suffix "B". The labels within rectangles are abbreviations of plan concept names that belong to the respective partition (for reasons of simplicity we only show plan concepts). The arrows between partitions express an inheritance relation between two partitions (in the opposite direction of the arrow). Inherited concepts are not shown, i.e., although SBOscarB is empty the system assumes Oscar to know the concepts app-print, user-get, launch and open-file-tpx. The abbreviations of plan concept names mean the following: app-print (print the file that is active in an application), user-get (user gets an object), launch (an

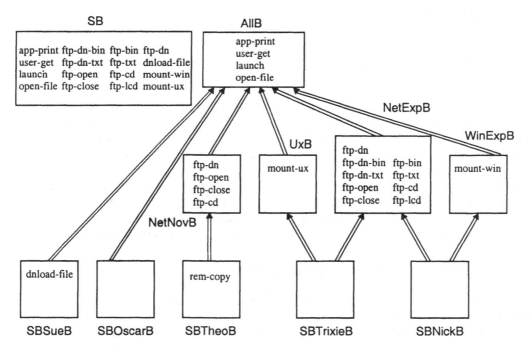

Figure 2. Structure of the *belief part* of the example user model.

application), **open-file-tpx** (open a file with text processor of type X), **ftp-download-file-bin** (download file with ftp in binary mode), **ftp-download-file-txt** (the same in text mode), **ftp-open** (open ftp connection), **ftp-close**, **ftp-bin** (change ftp-mode to binary), **ftp-txt** (change ftp-mode to text), **ftp-cd** (change remote directory of ftp), **ftp-lcd** (change local directory of ftp), **ftp-download-file** (download file with ftp disregarding file type), **download-file** (abstract download of a file), **mount-win** (mounting a directory with windows), **mount-ux** (the same with Unix), **remote-copy** (copy from or to a different host).

The example shows the assumed beliefs of the mentioned agents and several stereotypes for beliefs about different aspects of computer know-how in the areas of operating systems and networking. Partition **SBTheoB** contains beliefs that the system does not share. Agent **Theo** is assumed to believe in the existence of plan concept *remote-copy* that allows arbitrary copy operations from other computers. The system does not hold this belief.

The next figure shows the system's assumptions about the agents' capabilities. All labels of capability partitions have the suffix "C". As we separate the assumptions about capabilities of users from their beliefs, we also need a separate set of stereotypes for capabilities.

While the belief stereotypes of our example represent assumptions about typical beliefs of certain user subgroups, the corresponding capability stereotypes represent typical permissions in the example domain. Staff members have unlimited permissions, guest staff have no access to the Internet (via ftp), and students have no access to other computers of the local network (via mount).

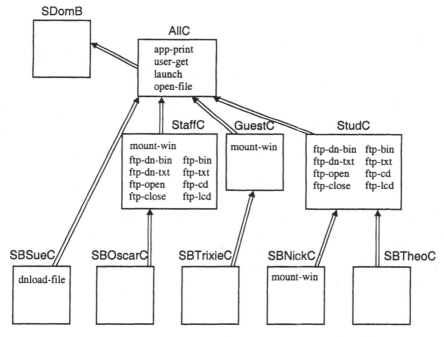

Figure 3. Structure of the *capability part* of the example user model.

SDomB is a special partition that contains the system's beliefs[3] about domain concepts (i.e. any concept that is not a plan concept). We do not show any contents of SDomB because we restrict the figures to plan concepts, as mentioned above.

6 Planning for Users - an Example

This chapter explains how the two different models of users' capabilities and beliefs influence the generation of a user-tailored plan. The example goal is:

> The user wants to have a printout of the file xy.doc that is located on the remote host konstanz. More precisely, he wants to have a new paper document that shows the contents of that file.

Note that this rather simple goal requires two different tools: a text processor and a ftp-program (or some mounting-tool). This is beyond the scope of usual help systems and even help assistants.

Let constants F-KN-xy-doc denote the file in question, and USER the user. Then we may write this goal in Predicate Logic:

$\exists$ *info*   fso-contents(F-KN-xy-doc, *info*) $\land$ paperdoc(Dx) $\land$ pd-contents(Dx, *info*) $\land$ has(USER, Dx)

The same expression according to the UCPOP syntax:

```
(exists (fso-contents F-KN-xy-doc ?info)
        (and (paperdoc Dx) (pd-contents Dx ?info)
             (has USER Dx)))
```

Assume further that constant *Dx* does not denote any object of the domain before the execution of the plan, i.e., free (Dx) is true while p (Dx) is false for any other predicate p[4]. After the execution, the goal expression requires Dx to denote a paper document, i.e., paperdoc (Dx) is true.

With the nomenclature of the last chapter, the user must use a text processor of type X to print the file. This requires the file to be located in the local file system of the user's computer. Depending on the capabilities of the different users and on whether or not konstanz exports the relevant directory, the goal may be achieved by downloading the file (via ftp, or in an arbitrary way for Sue) or by mounting an appropriate directory of host konstanz. The results of the plan generation are shown in Table 1.

Except for Trixie, all users can in principle reach the goal in both situations. For plans in italics, at least one plan step is unknown to the user according to the user model. In this case, the user needs an explanation of the steps in question or the planner has to generate an alternative plan. Note that this is the fact even for Theo who knows ftp-download but not the required and more special ftp-download-bin. This must be distinguished from Sue's plan. The system cannot go into details (i.e., refine the plan) because it does not know how Sue can perform the download.

Note that in our example it is impossible to generate a common plan that would work for all users.

---

[3] SDomB is a direct super partition of SB. For clarity, we omitted it in figure 2.

[4] We omit a full presentation of the extensive representation of the start situation, which contains all facts in the situation (like that F-KN-xy-doc is a tpx-file, is located in directory /home/otto/docs on host konstanz, etc.). A complete description is available from *http://zeus.gmd.de/~kuepper/UM99/*.

Table 1. The results of the plan generation.

User	Directory is exported	Directory is *not* exported
Oscar	*mount*	*ftp*
Trixie	*mount*	fails
Nick	mount	ftp
Theo	*ftp*	*ftp*
Sue	download	download

where	stands for the plan
mount	launch (text processor), mount-win (appropriate directory), open-file-tpx, app-print, user-get
ftp	launch (text processor), launch (ftp program), ftp-open-connection (to computer konstanz), ftp-lcd & ftp-cd (appropriate directories), ftp-binary-mode, ftp-download-file-bin, open-file-tpx, app-print, user-get
download	launch (text processor), download-file, open-file-tpx, app-print, user-get

7 Conclusion

This paper introduced plan generation for advice-giving that considers users' capabilities and knowledge. We used a partial order planner that obtains its working set of plan operators from a user model. Modeling users' plan execution capabilities in a similar way as users' beliefs allows one to employ standard user model acquisition techniques. We demonstrated the use of stereotypes.

The strict separation of beliefs and capabilities allows for the generation of plans that include steps that are unknown to the user, rather than restricting plan generation by the user's knowledge. This separation grants advice-giving systems the option to explain unknown plan steps to the user, and leads to the next research question of generating a system response that enables a user to reach his goals in the domain. It seems promising to extend the ideas of M. Young (Young, 1996) for serving the needs of various users to fit into the approach of this work.

References

Bauer, M. (1996). Acquisition of user preferences for plan recognition. In *Proceedings of 5th International Conference on User Modeling*, Kailua-Kona, HI, 105-112.

Brachman, R., and Schmolze, J. (1985). An overview of the KL-ONE knowledge representation system. *Cognitive Science 9*:171-216.

Breuker, J., ed. (1990). *EUROHELP: Developing Intelligent Help Systems*. EC, Kopenhagen.

Bylander, T. (1991). Complexity results for planning. In *Proceedings of 12th International Joint Conference on Artificial Intelligence*, Sidney, Australia, 274-279.

Carberry, S. (1990). *Plan Recognition in Natural Language Dialogue*. MIT Press, Cambridge, MA.

Cohen, P. (1978). On knowing what to say: planning speech acts. Tech.Report 118, Department of Computer Science, University of Toronto, Canada.

Devanbu, P., and Litman, D. (1996). Taxonomic plan reasoning. *Artificial Intelligence 84*:1-35.

Erol, K., Hendler, J., and Nau, D. (1994). Semantics for hierarchical task-network planning. Tech.Report CS-TR-3239, Computer Science Dept., University of Maryland.

Erol, K., Nau, D., and Subrahmanian, V. (1995). Complexity, decidability and undecidability results for domain-independent planning. *Artificial Intelligence 76*:75-88.

Horacek, H. (1997). A model for adapting explanations to the user's likely inferences. *User Modeling and User-Adapted Interaction 7*:1-55.

Kautz, H. (1991). A formal theory of plan recognition and its implementation. In *Reasoning about Plans*, Allen, Kautz, Pelavin, and Tenenberg, eds., Kaufmann, San Mateo, CA. 69-126.

Kobsa, A. (1991). Utilizing knowledge: the components of the SB-ONE knowledge representation workbench. In *Principles of Semantic Networks*, Sowa, J., ed., Kaufmann, San Mateo, CA. 457-486.

Kobsa, A., Müller, D., and Nill, A. (1994). KN-AHS: an adaptive hypertext client of the user modeling system BGP-MS. *Proceedings of the 4th International Conference on User Modeling*, Hyannis, MA, 99-105.

Kobsa, A., and Pohl, W. (1995). The BGP-MS user modeling system. *User Modeling and User-Adapted Interaction 4*:59-106.

McCoy, K. (1989). Generating context-sensitive responses to object-related misconceptions. *Artificial Intelligence 41*:157-195.

McDermott, D., and Hendler, J. (1995). Planning: what it is, what it could be. *Artificial Intelligence 76*:1-16.

Penberthy, J., and Weld, D. (1992). UCPOP: A sound, complete, partial order planner for ADL. In *Principles of Knowledge Representation and Reasoning - Proceedings of the 3rd International Conference KR'92*, Cambridge, MA, 103-114.

Pohl, W., and Höhle, J. (1997). Mechanisms for flexible representation and use of knowledge in user modeling shell systems. In *User Modeling: Proceedings of the 6th International Conference, UM97*, Chia Laguna, Italy, 403-414.

Russell, S., and Norvig, P. (1995). *Artificial Intelligence: A Modern Approach*. Prentice Hall, Upper Saddle, River, NJ.

Sacerdoti, E. (1977). *A Structure for Plans and Behavior*. Elsevier/North-Holland, Amsterdam, London, New York.

Sarner, M., and Carberry, S. (1992). Generating tailored definitions using a multifaceted user model. *User Modeling and User-Adapted Interaction 2*:181-210.

Sleeman, D. (1985). UMFE: A user modelling front-end subsystem. *International Journal of Man-Machine Studies 23*:71-88.

Weida, R., and Litman, D. (1992). Terminological reasoning with constraint networks and an application to plan recognition. In *Principles of Knowledge Representation and Reasoning - Proceedings of the 3rd International Conference KR'92*, Cambridge, MA, 282-293.

Weld, D. (1994). An introduction to least commitment planning. *AI Magazine 4*:27-61.

Young, M. (1996). Using plan reasoning in the generation of plan descriptions. In *Proceedings of 13th National Conference on Artificial Intelligence*, Portland, OR, 1075-1080.

Zukerman, I., and McConachy, R. (1993). Generating concise discourse that addresses a user's inferences. In *Proceedings of 13th International Joint Conference on Artificial Intelligence*, Chambery, France, 1202-1207.

Empirically Evaluating an Adaptable Spoken Dialogue System

Diane J. Litman[1] and Shimei Pan[2]*

[1] AT&T Labs - Research, Florham Park, NJ, USA
[2] Computer Science Department, Columbia University, New York, NY, USA

Abstract. Recent technological advances have made it possible to build real-time, interactive spoken dialogue systems for a wide variety of applications. However, when users do not respect the limitations of such systems, performance typically degrades. Although users differ with respect to their knowledge of system limitations, and although different dialogue strategies make system limitations more apparent to users, most current systems do not try to improve performance by adapting dialogue behavior to individual users. This paper presents an empirical evaluation of TOOT, an adaptable spoken dialogue system for retrieving train schedules on the web. We conduct an experiment in which 20 users carry out 4 tasks with both adaptable and non-adaptable versions of TOOT, resulting in a corpus of 80 dialogues. The values for a wide range of evaluation measures are then extracted from this corpus. Our results show that adaptable TOOT generally outperforms non-adaptable TOOT, and that the utility of adaptation depends on TOOT's initial dialogue strategies.

1 Introduction

Recent technological advances have made it possible to build real-time, interactive spoken dialogue systems for a wide variety of applications. However, due to limitations in such areas as vocabulary, grammar, and application functionality, most deployed systems can only accept a small set of natural language inputs from users. When users do not respect the limitations of spoken dialogue systems, system performance typically degrades. For example, user utterances are more likely to be rejected or misunderstood, dialogue length typically increases, and users are less likely to achieve their task goals. Although individual users differ with respect to their knowledge of system limitations (Kamm et al., 1998), and although different dialogue strategies make system limitations more apparent to users (Walker et al., 1997a; Danieli and Gerbino, 1995), current spoken dialogue systems typically do not try to adapt their dialogue strategies to individual users. A major obstacle to having a spoken dialogue system perform such adaptation dynamically is that there is currently little understanding of the type of properties that would need to be represented in a user model for this task, let alone automatically acquired during the course of a dialogue. Nevertheless, users do seem to intuitively know when and how their interactions with a spoken dialogue system could be changed, in order to improve overall system performance. This observation has led us to explore the utility of an *adaptable* spoken dialogue system, where the *user* rather than the system controls the adaptation of the system's dialogue strategies. In particular, we hypothesize that if a user can effectively adapt the system's behavior, so that the system will use the dialogue strategies that best match the user's needs at any point in a dialogue, then the overall performance of the system should improve.

---

* We thank J. Chu-Carroll, C. Kamm, D. Lewis, M. Walker, and S. Whittaker for helpful comments.

Figure 1 shows an example dialogue with an adaptable train-timetable spoken dialogue system called TOOT.[1] In this excerpt, TOOT initially uses a set of dialogue strategies often found

U1:   I'd like to go to Chicago from Baltimore on Saturday at 8 am.
T1:   Do you want to leave in the morning or in the evening?
U2:   Uh morning.
T2:   Sorry, I can't understand you. Please repeat your answer.
U3:   In the morning.
T3:   Do you want me to find the trains from Baltimore to Chicago on Saturday around 10 morning now?
U4:   No.
T4:   How may I help you?
U5:   I would like to go from Baltimore to Chicago on Saturday at 8 o'clock.
T5:   Do you want me to find the trains from Baltimore to DC on Tuesday around 11:45 am now?
U6:   No.
T6:   How may I help you?
U7:   Change strategy.
T7:   You are using the user initiative. Which initiative do you want to change to? System –
U8:   System initiative please.
T8:   You are using the no confirmation strategy. Which confirmation strategy do you want to change to?
      No confirmation, implicit confirmation, or explicit confirmation?
U9:   Implicit please.
T9:   I heard you say go to DC on Tuesday around 11:45 am.
      Do you want me to find the trains from Baltimore to DC on Tuesday around 11:45 am now?
U10: No.
T10: Which city do you want to go to?
U11: Chicago.
T11: I heard you say go to Chicago. Which city do you want to leave from?
U12: Baltimore.
T12: I heard you say leave from Baltimore. On which day of the week do you want to leave?
U13: Saturday.
T13: I heard you say leave on Saturday. What time do you want to leave?
U14: 8:00 in the morning.
T14: Sorry, I can't understand you. Please repeat your answer.
U15: 8:00 in the morning.
T15: I heard you say leave around 8:00 in the morning. Do you want me
      to find the trains from Baltimore to Chicago on Saturday around 8:00 in the morning now?
U16: Yes.

Figure 1. Example dialogue with an adaptable spoken dialogue system.

in human-human interactions. However, the strategies do not work particularly well for this user. Utterances U1 and U5 are misunderstood by TOOT, and U2 is not understood at all. Recognizing a mismatch, the user changes the strategies used by TOOT (U7 - U9). As a result, the open ended prompt that TOOT used earlier in the dialogue (T4) is now replaced with a series of specific questions (T10, T11, T12, and T13). TOOT also now highlights any potential misrecog-

---

[1] This excerpt is taken from the experimental corpus described below.

nitions by prefacing its utterances with "I heard you say ...". Earlier in the dialogue, it took 5 utterances before the user was aware that TOOT had misrecognized the "8" in U1 as "10". As a result of these changes, the dialogue proceeds more smoothly after the adaptation (e.g., TOOT's misrecognition rate is reduced), and a correct database query is soon generated (T15-U16).

In this paper, we present an evaluation of adaptability in TOOT. We conduct an experiment in which 20 novice users carry out 4 tasks with one of two versions of TOOT (*adaptable* and *non-adaptable*), resulting in a corpus of 80 dialogues. The values for a range of evaluation measures are then extracted from this corpus. Hypothesis testing shows that a variety of differences depend on the user's ability to adapt the system. A PARADISE assessment of the contribution of each evaluation measure to overall performance (Walker et al., 1997b) shows that the phenomena influenced by adaptation are also the major phenomena that significantly influence performance. Our results show that adaptable TOOT generally outperforms non-adaptable TOOT, and that the utility of adaptation depends on the initial configuration of dialogue strategies.

2 TOOT

TOOT is a voice-enabled dialogue system for accessing train schedules from the web via a telephone conversation. TOOT is implemented using a spoken dialogue system platform (Kamm et al., 1997) that combines automatic speech recognition (ASR), text-to-speech (TTS), a phone interface, and modules for specifying a dialogue manager and application functions. ASR in our platform is speaker-independent, grammar-based and supports *barge-in* (which allows users to interrupt TOOT when it is speaking, as in utterances T7 and U8 in Figure 1). The dialogue manager uses a finite state machine to control the interaction, based on the current system state and ASR results. TOOT's application functions access train schedules available at www.amtrak.com. Given a set of constraints, the functions return a table listing all matching trains in a specified temporal interval, or within an hour of a specified timepoint. This table is converted to a natural language response which can be realized by TTS through the use of templates.[2]

Depending on the user's needs during the dialogue, TOOT can use one of three dialogue strategies for managing initiative ("system", "mixed" or "user"), and one of three strategies for managing confirmation ("explicit," "implicit," or "no"). TOOT's initiative strategy specifies who has control of the dialogue, while TOOT's confirmation strategy specifies how and whether TOOT lets the user know what it just understood. In Figure 1, TOOT initially used user initiative and no confirmation, then later used system initiative and implicit confirmation. The following fragments provide additional illustrations of how dialogues vary with strategy:

System Initiative, Explicit Confirmation	*User Initiative, No Confirmation*
T: Which city do you want to go to?	T: How may I help you?
U: Chicago.	U: I want to go to Chicago from Baltimore.
T: Do you want to go to Chicago?	T: On which day of the week do you want to leave?
U: Yes.	U: I want a train at 8:00.

---

[2] The current version of TOOT uses a literal response strategy (Litman et al., 1998). Informally, if the returned table contains 1-3 trains, TOOT lists the trains; if the table contains greater than 4 trains, TOOT lists the trains 3 at a time; if the table is empty, TOOT reports that no trains satisfy the constraints. TOOT then asks the user if she wants to continue and find a new set of trains.

Although system initiative with explicit confirmation is the most cumbersome approach, it can help improve some aspects of performance for users who do not have a good understanding of the system's limitations. The use of system initiative helps reduce ASR misrecognitions and rejections (Walker et al., 1997a), by helping to keep the user's utterances within the system's vocabulary and grammar. The use of explicit confirmation helps increase the user's task success (Danieli and Gerbino, 1995), by making the user more aware of any ASR misrecognitions and making it easier for users to correct misrecognitions when they occur. On the other hand, system initiative and explicit confirmation typically increase total dialogue length (Walker et al., 1997a; Danieli and Gerbino, 1995). For users whose utterances are generally understood, other strategies might be more effective. Consider the use of user initiative with no confirmation, the most human-like approach. In user (as well as in mixed) initiative mode, TOOT can still ask the user specific questions, but can also ask open-ended questions such as "How may I help you?". Furthermore, in user (but not in mixed) initiative mode, TOOT even lets the user ignore TOOT's questions (as in the last user utterance in the example above). By allowing users to specify multiple attributes in a single utterance, and by not informing users of every potential misrecognition, this approach can lead to very short dialogues when ASR performance is not a problem.

In an earlier implementation of TOOT (as well as in other spoken dialogue systems that we have studied (Walker et al., 1997a; Kamm et al., 1998)), a set of initial dialogue strategies was assigned to the system as a default for each user, and could not be changed if inappropriate.[3] As discussed above, however, we hypothesize that we can improve TOOT's performance by dynamically adapting the choice of dialogue strategies, based on the circumstances at hand. Although one of our long-term goals is to have TOOT automatically control the adaptation process, this would require that we first solve several open research topics. For example, TOOT would need to be able to detect, in real time, dialogue situations suggesting system adaptation. As a result, our initial research has instead focused on giving users the ability to dynamically adapt TOOT's dialogue behaviors. For example, if a user's utterances are not being understood, the user could try to reduce the number of ASR rejections and misrecognitions by changing the strategies so that TOOT would take more initiative. Conversely, if a user's utterances are being correctly understood, the user could try to decrease the dialogue length by having TOOT perform less confirmations. To allow us to test whether such an adaptable system does indeed increase performance, we have created both "adaptable" and "non-adaptable" versions of TOOT. In adaptable TOOT, users are allowed to say "change strategy" at any point(s) in the dialogue. TOOT then asks the user to specify new initiative and confirmation strategies, as in utterances U7-U9 in Figure 1. In non-adaptable TOOT, the default dialogue strategies can not be changed.

3   Experimental Design

Our experiment was designed to test if adaptable TOOT performed better than non-adaptable TOOT, and whether any differences depended on TOOT's initial dialogue strategies and/or the user's task. Our design thus consisted of three factors: *adaptability*, *initial dialogue strategy*, and *task scenario*. Subjects were 20 AT&T technical summer employees not involved with the design or implementation of TOOT, who were also novice users of spoken dialogue systems in

---

[3] In particular, the previous version of TOOT always used system initiative with implicit confirmation (Litman et al., 1998).

general. 10 users were randomly assigned to *adaptable* TOOT and 10 to *non-adaptable* TOOT. For each of these groups, 5 users were randomly assigned to a version of TOOT with the initial dialogue strategies set to *system initiative* and *explicit confirmation* (SystemExplicit TOOT); the remaining 5 users were assigned to a version of TOOT with the initial dialogue strategies set to *user initiative* and *no confirmation* (UserNo TOOT). Each user performed the same 4 tasks in sequence. Our experiment yielded a corpus of 80 dialogues (2633 turns; 5.4 hours of speech).

Users used the web to read a set of experimental instructions in their office, then called TOOT from their phone. The experimental instructions consisted of a description of TOOT's functionality, hints for talking to TOOT, and links to 4 task scenarios. An example task scenario is as follows: "Try to find a train going *to* **Chicago** *from* **Baltimore** on **Saturday** at **8 o'clock am**. If you cannot find an exact match, find the one with the **closest** departure time. Please write down the **exact departure time** of the train you found as well as the **total travel time**." The instructions for adaptable TOOT also contained a brief tutorial explaining how to use "change strategy", and guidelines for doing so (e.g., " if you don't know what to do or say, try system initiative").

We collected three types of data to compute a number of measures relevant for spoken dialogue evaluation (Walker et al., 1997a). First, all dialogues were recorded. The recordings were used to calculate the total time of each dialogue (the evaluation measure **Elapsed Time**), and to (manually) count how many times per dialogue each user interrupted TOOT (**Barge Ins**).

Second, the dialogue manager's behavior on entering and exiting each state in the finite state machine was logged. This log was used to calculate the total number of **System Turns** and **User Turns**, **Timeouts** (when the user doesn't say anything within a specified time frame, TOOT provides suggestions about what to say), **Helps** (when the user says "help", TOOT provides a context-sensitive help message), **Cancels** (when the user says "cancel", TOOT undoes its previous action), and **ASR Rejections** (when the confidence level of ASR is too low, TOOT asks the user to repeat the utterance). In addition, by listening to the recordings and comparing them to the logged ASR results, we calculated the concept accuracy (intuitively, semantic interpretation accuracy) for each utterance. This was then used, in combination with ASR rejections, to compute a **Mean Recognition** score per dialogue.

Third, users filled out a web survey after each dialogue. Users specified the departure and travel times that they obtained via the dialogue. Given that there was a single correct train to be retrieved for each task scenario, this allowed us to determine whether users successfully achieved their task goal or not (**Task Success**). Users also responded to the following questionnaire:

- Was the system easy to understand? (**TTS Performance**)
- Did the system understand what you said? (**ASR Performance**)
- Was it easy to find the schedule you wanted? (**Task Ease**)
- Was the pace of interaction with the system appropriate? (**Interaction Pace**)
- Did you know what you could say at each point of the dialogue? (**User Expertise**)
- How often was the system sluggish and slow to reply to you? (**System Response**)
- Did the system work the way you expected it to? (**Expected Behavior**)
- From your current experience with using our system, do you think you'd use this regularly to access train schedules when you are away from your desk? (**Future Use**)

Each question measured a particular usability factor, e.g., **TTS Performance**. Responses ranged over *n* pre-defined values (e.g., *almost never, rarely, sometimes, often, almost always*), and were mapped to an integer in $1 \ldots 5$ (with 5 representing optimal performance). **User Satisfaction** was computed by summing each question's score, and thus ranged in value from 8 to 40.

4 Results

We use analysis of variance (ANOVA) (Cohen, 1995) to determine whether the adaptability of TOOT produces significant differences in any of the evaluation measures for our experiment. We also use the PARADISE evaluation framework (Walker et al., 1997b) to understand which of our evaluation measures best predicts overall performance in TOOT. Following PARADISE, we organize our evaluation measures along the following four performance dimensions:

- *task success*: Task Success
- *dialogue quality*: Helps, ASR Rejections, Timeouts, Mean Recognition, Barge Ins, Cancels
- *dialogue efficiency*: System Turns, User Turns, Elapsed Time
- *system usability*: User Satisfaction (based on TTS Performance, ASR Performance, Task Ease, Interaction Pace, User Expertise, System Response, Expected Behavior, Future Use)

4.1 Adaptability Effects

Recall that our mixed[4] experimental design consisted of three factors: *adaptability*, *initial dialogue strategy*, and *task scenario*. Each of our evaluation measures is analyzed using a three-way ANOVA for these three factors. The ANOVAs demonstrate a *main effect of adaptability* for the task success and system usability dimensions of performance. These main adaptability effects are independent of TOOT's initial dialogue strategy as well as of the task scenario being executed by the user. The ANOVAs also demonstrate *interaction effects of adaptability and initial dialogue strategy* for the dialogue quality and system usability performance dimensions. In contrast to the main effects, these adaptability effects are not independent of TOOT's initial dialogue strategy (i.e., the effects of adaptability and initial strategy are not additive).[5]

Table 1 summarizes the means for each evaluation measure that shows a main effect of adaptability, and that cannot be further explained by any interaction effects. The first row in the table indicates that Task Success is significantly higher for adaptable TOOT than for non-adaptable TOOT. Users successfully achieve the goals specified in the task scenario in 80% of the dialogues with adaptable TOOT, but in only 55% of the dialogues with non-adaptable TOOT. The probability $p<.03$ indicates that the difference is statistically significance (the standard upper bound for calling a result statistically significant is $p<.05$ (Cohen, 1995)). The second row indicates that with respect to User Satisfaction, users also rate adaptable TOOT more highly than non-adaptable TOOT. Recall that User Satisfaction takes all of the factors in the usability questionnaire into account. As will be discussed below, PARADISE correlates overall system performance with this measure. In sum, our ANOVAs indicate that making TOOT adaptable increases users' rates of task success as well as users' perceptions of overall system usability.

Table 2 summarizes the means for each evaluation measure that shows an interaction effect of adaptability and initial dialogue strategy. A similar pattern of interaction emerges in the first and

---

[4] *Task scenario* is between-groups and *initial dialogue strategy* and *adaptability* are within-group.

[5] Effects of *initial dialogue strategy* and *task scenario* are beyond the scope of this paper.

Table 1. Main effects of adaptability.

Measure	Non-Adaptable (n=40)	Adaptable (n=40)
Task Success (%) (p<.03)	55.00	80.00
User Satisfaction (p<.03)	26.68	31.60

Table 2. Interaction effects of adaptability and initial dialogue strategy.

	Non-Adaptable (n=40)		Adaptable (n=40)	
Measure	SystemExplicit	UserNo	SystemExplicit	UserNo
Mean Recognition (%) (p<.01)	88.44	57.94	82.55	75.85
User Expertise (p<.05)	4.69	3.01	4.45	3.85
Future Use (p<.02)	3.50	1.70	3.60	3.80

second rows of the table. When users are given the capability to adapt TOOT, Mean Recognition decreases for SystemExplicit TOOT (88.44% versus 82.55%) but increases for UserNo TOOT (57.94% versus 75.85%). Perceptions of User Expertise also decrease for adaptable SystemExplicit TOOT (4.69 versus 4.45) but increase for adaptable UserNo TOOT (3.01 versus 3.85). In contrast, Future Use is higher for adaptable TOOT than for non-adaptable TOOT, for both initial strategies. Thus, users of adaptable TOOT are more likely than users of non-adaptable TOOT to think that they would use TOOT on a regular basis. However, the increase in Future Use is smaller for SystemExplicit TOOT (3.5 to 3.6) than for UserNo TOOT (1.7 to 3.8). In sum, Table 2 indicates that differences reflecting both dialogue quality and system usability are an effect of the interaction of the adaptability of TOOT and TOOT's initial dialogue strategy. For the UserNo version of TOOT, making TOOT adaptable increases the means for all of the measures shown in Table 2. For the SystemExplicit version of TOOT, despite the Mean Recognition and User Expertise results in Table 2, users are nevertheless at least if not more likely to use adaptable System Explicit TOOT in the future. We speculate that users are willing to tolerate minor levels of particular types of performance degradations in SystemExplicit TOOT, in order to obtain the sense of control provided by adaptability. We also speculate that the utility of adaptable SystemExplicit TOOT would increase for expert users. In conjunction with Table 1, our results with novice users suggest that adaptability is an extremely useful capability to add to UserNo TOOT, and a capability that is still worth adding to SystemExplicit TOOT.

It is interesting to also examine the way in which adaptation is performed for each initial dialogue strategy. Of the 20 dialogues with adaptable SystemExplicit TOOT, 5 dialogues contained 1 adaptation and a 6th dialogue contained 2 adaptations. 3 of the 5 users adapted at least 1 dialogue, and overall, confirmation was changed more times than initiative. Of the 20 dialogues with adaptable UserNo TOOT, 10 dialogues contained 1 adaptation and an 11th dialogue contained 2 adaptations. All 5 users of UserNo TOOT adapted at least 1 dialogue. Users of UserNo TOOT changed initiative more than they changed confirmation, and also changed initiative more drastically. In conjunction with our ANOVA results, these observations lead us to speculate that adapting a poorly performing system is both more feasible and more important for novice users than adapting a reasonably performing system.

4.2 Contributors to Performance

To quantify the relative importance of our multiple evaluation measures to performance, we use the PARADISE evaluation framework to derive a performance function from our data. The PARADISE model posits that performance can be correlated with a meaningful external criterion of usability such as User Satisfaction. PARADISE then uses stepwise multiple linear regression to model User Satisfaction from measures representing the performance dimensions of task success, dialogue quality, and dialogue efficiency:

$$\text{User Satisfaction} = \sum_{i=1}^{n} w_i * \mathcal{N}(measure_i)$$

Linear regression produces coefficients (i.e., weights w_i) describing the relative contribution of predictor factors in accounting for the variance in a predicted factor. In PARADISE, the task success and dialogue cost measures are predictors, while User Satisfaction is predicted. The normalization function $\mathcal{N}$ guarantees that the coefficients directly indicate the relative contributions.

The application of PARADISE to the TOOT data shows that the most significant contributors to User Satisfaction are Mean Recognition, Task Success, and Elapsed Time, respectively. In addition, PARADISE shows that the following performance function provides the best fit to our data, accounting for 55% of the variance in User Satisfaction:[6]

User Satisfaction $= .45\mathcal{N}$(Mean Recognition) $+ .33\mathcal{N}$(Task Success) $- .14\mathcal{N}$(Elapsed Time)

Our performance function demonstrates that TOOT performance (estimated using subjective usability ratings) can be best predicted using a weighted combination of objective measures of dialogue quality, task success, and dialogue efficiency. In particular, more accurate speech recognition, more success in achieving task goals, and shorter dialogues all contribute to increasing perceived performance in TOOT.

Our performance equation helps explain the main effect of adaptability for User Satisfaction that was shown in Table 1. Recall that our ANOVAs for both Mean Recognition and Task Success showed adaptability effects (Tables 2 and 1, respectively). Our PARADISE analysis showed that these measures were also the most important measures in explaining the variance in User Satisfaction. It is thus not surprising that User Satisfaction shows an effect of adaptability, with users rating the performance of adaptable TOOT more highly than non-adaptable TOOT.

A result that was not apparent from the analysis of variance is that Elapsed Time is a performance predictor. However, the weighting of the measures in our performance function suggests that Mean Recognition and Task Success are more important measures of overall performance than Elapsed Time. These findings are consistent with our previous PARADISE evaluations, where measures of task success and dialogue quality were also the most important performance predictors (Litman et al., 1998; Walker et al., 1998; Kamm et al., 1998). Our findings draw into question a frequently made assumption in the field regarding the centrality of efficiency to performance, and like other recent work, demonstrates that there are important tradeoffs between efficiency and other performance dimensions (Danieli and Gerbino, 1995; Walker et al., 1997a).

---

[6] Linear regression assumes that predictors are not highly correlated (e.g., because correlations above .70 can affect the coefficients, deletion of redundant predictors is advised (Monge and Cappella, 1980)). There is only 1 positive correlation among our predictors (between Mean Recognition and Task Success), and it is well below .70.

5 Related Work

In the area of spoken dialogue, van Zanten (1998) has proposed a method for adapting initiative in form-filling dialogues. Whenever the system rejects a user's utterance, the system takes more initiative; whenever the user gives an over-informative answer, the system yields some initiative. While this method has the potential of being automated, the method has been neither fully implemented nor empirically evaluated. Smith (1998) has evaluated strategies for dynamically deciding whether to confirm each user utterance during a task-oriented dialogue. Simulation results suggest that context-dependent adaptation strategies can improve performance, especially when the system has greater initiative. Walker et al. (1998) and Levin and Pieraccini (1997) have used reinforcement learning to adapt dialogue behavior over time such that system performance improves. We have instead focused on optimizing performance during a single dialogue.

The empirical evaluation of an adaptive interface in a commercial software system (Strachan et al., 1997) is also similar to our work. Analysis of variance demonstrated that an adaptive interface based on minimal user modeling improved subjective user satisfaction ratings.

6 Conclusion

We have presented an empirical evaluation of adaptability in TOOT, a spoken dialogue system that retrieves train schedules from the web. Our results suggest that adaptable TOOT generally outperforms non-adaptable TOOT for novice users, and that the utility of adaptation is greater for UserNo TOOT than for SystemExplicit TOOT. By using analysis of variance to examine how a set of evaluation measures differ as a function of adaptability, we elaborate the conditions under which adaptability leads to greater performance. When users interact with adaptable rather than non-adaptable TOOT, User Satisfaction and Task Success are significantly higher. These results are independent of TOOT's initial dialogue strategy and task scenario. In contrast, Mean Recognition, User Expertise, and Future Use illustrate an interaction between initial dialogue strategy and adaptability. For SystemExplicit TOOT, the adaptable version does not outperform the non-adaptable version, or does not outperform the non-adaptable version very strongly. For UserNo TOOT, the adaptable version outperforms the non-adaptable version on all three measures.

By using PARADISE to derive a performance function from data, we show that Mean Recognition, Task Success, and Elapsed Time best predict a user's overall satisfaction with TOOT. These results help explain why adaptability in TOOT leads to overall greater performance, and allow us to make predictions about future performance. For example, we predict that a SystemImplicit strategy is likely to outperform our SystemExplicit strategy, since we expect that Mean Recognition and Task Success will remain constant but that Elapsed Time will decrease.

Currently, we are extending our results along two dimensions. First, we have made a first step towards automating the adaptation process in TOOT, by using machine learning to develop a classifier for detecting dialogues with poor speech recognition (Litman et al., 1999). (Recall that our PARADISE evaluation suggested that recognition accuracy was our best performance predictor.) We hope to use this classifier to determine the features that need to be represented in a user model, and to tell us when the user model indicates the need for adaptation. Guided by our empirical results, we can then develop an initial adaptation algorithm that takes dialogue strategy into account. For example, based on our experiment, we would like UserNo TOOT to adapt itself fairly aggressively when it recognizes that the user is having a problem. Second, the experiments reported here considered only our two most extreme initial dialogue strategy configurations. To generalize our results, we are currently experimenting with other dialogue strategies. To date we have collected 40 dialogues using a mixed initiative, implicit confirmation version of TOOT, with initial promising results. For example, user satisfaction continues to exhibit the same main effect of adaptability when our corpus is augmented with these new dialogues.

References

Cohen, P. (1995). *Empirical Methods for Artificial Intelligence*. MIT Press, Boston.

Danieli, M., and Gerbino, E. (1995). Metrics for evaluating dialogue strategies in a spoken language system. In *Proc. AAAI Spring Symposium on Empirical Methods in Discourse Interpretation and Generation*, 34–39.

Kamm, C., Narayanan, S., Dutton, D., and Ritenour, R. (1997). Evaluating spoken dialog systems for telecommunication services. In *Proc. 5th European Conf. on Speech Communication and Technology*.

Kamm, C., Litman, D., and Walker, M. (1998). From novice to expert: The effect of tutorials on user expertise with spoken dialogue systems. In *Proc. 5th International Conf. on Spoken Language Processing*, 1211–1214.

Levin, E., and Pieraccini, R. (1997). A stochastic model of computer-human interaction for learning dialogue strategies. In *Proc. 5th European Conf. on Speech Communication and Technology*.

Litman, D., Pan, S., and Walker, M. (1998). Evaluating Response Strategies in a Web-Based Spoken Dialogue Agent. In *Proc. 36th Annual Meeting of the Association for Computational Linguistics and 17th International Conf. on Computational Linguistics*, 780–786.

Litman, D., Walker, M., and Kearns, M. (1999). Automatic detection of poor speech recognition at the dialogue level. Manuscript submitted for publication.

Monge, P., and Cappella, J., eds. (1980). *Multivariate Techniques in Human Communication Research*. Academic Press, New York.

Smith, R. W. (1998). An evaluation of strategies for selectively verifying utterance meanings in spoken natural language dialog. *International Journal of Human-Computer Studies* 48:627–647.

Strachan, L., Anderson, J., Sneesby, M., and Evans, M. (1997). Pragmatic user modelling in a commercial software system. In *Proc. 6th International Conf. on User Modeling*, 189–200.

van Zanten, G. V. (1998). Adaptive mixed-initiative dialogue management. Technical Report 52, IPO, Center for Research on User-System Interaction.

Walker, M., Hindle, D., Fromer, J., Fabbrizio, G. D., and Mestel, C. (1997a). Evaluating competing agent strategies for a voice email agent. In *Proc. 5th European Conf. on Speech Communication and Technology*.

Walker, M., Litman, D., Kamm, C., and Abella, A. (1997b). PARADISE: A general framework for evaluating spoken dialogue agents. In *Proc. 35th Annual Meeting of the Association for Computational Linguistics and 8th Conf. of the European Chapter of the Association for Computational Linguistics*, 271–280.

Walker, M., Fromer, J., and Narayanan, S. (1998). Learning optimal dialogue strategies: A case study of a spoken dialogue agent for email. In *Proc. 36th Annual Meeting of the Association for Computational Linguistics and 17th International Conf. on Computational Linguistics*, 1345–1352.

CONSTRUCTING USER MODELS EXPLICITLY

User Modeling in the Design of Interactive Interface Agents

Michael Fleming and Robin Cohen*

Department of Computer Science,
University of Waterloo,
Waterloo, ON, Canada

Abstract. This paper presents a model for more interactive interface agents. This more interactive style of agents aims to increase the trust and understanding between user and agent, by allowing the agent, under certain conditions, to solicit further input from the user about his preferences and desires. With the user and agent engaging in specific clarification dialogues, the user's input is employed to adjust the agent's model of the user. Moreover, the user is provided with an ability to view this user model, under certain well defined circumstances. Since both the agent and user can take the initiative to interact, basic issues regarding mixed-initiative systems arise. These issues are addressed in our model, which also takes care to restrict the agent's interaction with the user, to avoid bothering the user unduly. We illustrate our design for more interactive interface agents by including some examples in the domain of electronic mail.

Keywords: user modeling agents, personalized and adaptive information assistants, mixed-initiative interaction

1 Overview

In recent years, the area of intelligent agents has been one of the most prevalent fields of research in the AI community. This paper deals with one specific type of agent, the interface agent, which is a program that acts as a personal assistant to a user dealing with a particular computer-based application, and which is able to "view" and act upon the application interface just as a human user might. Previous designs of interface agents can be broadly classified into two categories: autonomous agents (*e.g.*, Maes, 1994), which attempt to automate certain actions on behalf of the user, and collaborative agents (*e.g.*, Rich and Sidner, 1997), which are more equal partners with their users, working together on a joint plan and participating in a dialogue in order to determine an appropriate course of action.

We argue that there is a middle ground to be covered. Using autonomous learning interface agents as a starting point, we propose a model which makes these agents more interactive, allowing them to take the initiative to solicit further input from the user, toward improving their overall performance.

---

* This work was supported in part by the Natural Sciences and Engineering Research Council of Canada (NSERC).

2 Background

In order to develop our model, we have used as a starting point the learning interface agent architecture developed by the Software Agents group at MIT. The following is a very brief description of how these agents operate; see Maes (1994) for more detail. The MIT agents act primarily by observing their users, and by using a form of learning called memory-based reasoning (Stanfill and Waltz, 1986). For each new situation that arises, the agent computes the distance between the current state and each of the past situations it has stored in its memory, using a weighted sum of several relevant features. According to the actions taken by the user in the most similar past situations, the agent selects an action for the current situation, and calculates a corresponding confidence value (Kozierok, 1993). According to "do-it" and "tell-me" thresholds established by the user, the agent determines whether to automate an action on the user's behalf, to suggest an action, or to do nothing at all. Figure 1 shows a simplified description of these learning agents.

PRIOR TO OPERATION: The user has set the tell-me and do-it thresholds, has indicated how many past situations the agent should look at during its action selection, *etc.*

INPUT: A signal that there exists a new situation to be addressed (*e.g.*, in the e-mail domain, a new mail message arrives, the user has just finished reading a message, etc.)

OUTPUT: The agent has completed an action on the user's behalf, has suggested an action, or has decided to do nothing for the current situation.

Select action A via learning techniques and assign confidence value C.

if $C >$ do-it threshold **then**

- perform action A and add it to a list of automated actions for user to examine at his own leisure
- if user indicates that action was incorrect, ask user to adjust priority weightings for the various features which contribute to calculations

else if $C >$ tell-me threshold **then**

- suggest action A

else

- consult other agents for help, establish suggested action A' and compute new confidence value C'.
- **if** $C' >$ do-it... (as above)
- **else if** $C' >$ tell-me... (as above)
- **else** do nothing

Figure 1. High-level algorithm for the behaviour of learning interface agents

3 More Interactive Interface Agents

While the MIT design has many strong points, several shortcomings can be identified (Fleming, 1998). In particular: (i) these agents do not deal very well with situations that are somewhat ambiguous; (ii) the lack of communication between agent and user makes it difficult for a user to understand and to trust such an agent; (iii) memory-based learning can be quite slow because it may require an examination of a large number of previous situations.

We address these issues and others, by presenting a variation on the architecture of the MIT learning agents. This new model allows for an agent which is still more or less autonomous, but which recognizes opportunities for asking the user for further information, with the goal of improving the agent's overall performance. The information which is solicited then becomes part of the agent's user model, to be used in future interactions with the user. A very high level algorithm for our semi-autonomous agents is shown in Figure 2. A few major points of the algorithm are explained in this paper, illustrated for the domain of assisting users with e-mail. It is important to note that the algorithm is general enough to operate in a variety of application areas. The central decisions made are when to solicit input from the user and how to manage the agent's rule base in such a way that the user can contribute to its specification.

PRIOR TO OPERATION: The user has set the tell-me, do-it and bother thresholds, has indicated how many past situations the agent should look at during its action selection, *etc.*

INPUT: A signal that there exists a new situation to be addressed (*e.g.*, in the e-mail domain: a new mail message arrives, the user has just finished reading a message, *etc.*)

OUTPUT: The agent has completed an action on the user's behalf, has suggested an action or has communicated to the user that it can do nothing for the current situation.

  (0) Consult rule database for applicable rules previously created by the user (with or without the agent's help). If a single rule is found to apply, then use that rule. If two or more conflicting rules are found, initiate rule conflict dialogue with user. If no rules are found to apply, then proceed with step 1.

  (1) Use learning techniques to get possible actions A_1, ..., A_n

  (2) **if** choice of action A is clear[a] **then**

      (3) Compute confidence value C (as in the MIT agents – see Kozierok (1993), for example)

      (4) **if** $C >$ do-it threshold **then** perform action A and indicate that there is a proposed rule for the user to approve/reject/edit

      (5) **else if** $C >$ tell-me threshold **then** suggest action A

  (6) **else** //choice unclear because two or more actions have similar scores

      (7) **if** peer agents exist and are able to provide trustworthy advice **then** automate/suggest recommended action

      (8) **else** // choice still unclear

          (9) Compute clarification factor CF.

          (10) **if** $CF >$ user-defined bother threshold **then** initiate dialogue with user.

---

[a] The choice is considered clear if the score computed for the highest-scoring action exceeds the score of the next best choice by a constant difference threshold (say, 10%).

Figure 2. High-level algorithm for our more interactive interface agents

3.1 Ambiguous Situations

A key circumstance which suggests the value of user input is that of ambiguous situations: cases where the agent, via its learning methods, is unable to select one course of action as being a clear winner. (See steps 6-10 in the algorithm.) For example, in the e-mail domain, suppose an agent has successfully learned that all messages from David Fleming should be filed in the *David* folder and that all messages with subject "Hockey pool" should be filed in the *Hockey* folder. What will the agent do with a message from David Fleming with subject "Hockey pool"?

Suppose a message with the following feature values has just been read:

Feature	From	Cc	Date	Subject
Value	David Fleming	None	October 26	Hockey pool

Suppose also that the agent has assigned the following weights to each of the relevant fields, based on how well the current situation's value in each of those fields has typically predicted the action taken (as in Kozierok, 1993).

Feature	From	Cc	Date	Subject
Weight	0.90	0.08	0.01	0.88

Finally, suppose that the following four messages were found to be the most similar to the current situation, with the distance between the value in the current situation and the corresponding value in the past situation shown in the third row. The overall distance between two situations (shown in the fourth row) is computed by taking the sum of the products $d_i w_i$, where d_i is the distance between the values of field i and w_i is the weight assigned to field i.

Feature	From	Cc	Date	Subject
Value	David Fleming	None	October 11	Habs
Distance	0	0	0.90	0.98
$\Delta(s_{new}, s_1)$	0.8714			
Action	File under David			

Feature	From	Cc	Date	Subject
Value	David Fleming	None	October 3	Hi
Distance	0	0	0.92	1
$\Delta(s_{new}, s_2)$	0.8892			
Action	File under David			

Feature	From	Cc	Date	Subject
Value	Owen Barnhill	None	October 7	Hockey pool
Distance	1	0	0.86	0
$\Delta(s_{new}, s_3)$	0.9086			
Action	File under Hockey			

Feature	From	Cc	Date	Subject
Value	S. Fillmore	None	October 23	Hockey pool
Distance	1	0	0.90	0
$\Delta(s_{new}, s_4)$	0.9090			
Action	File under Hockey			

In such a situation, MIT's *Maxims* (Metral, 1993) e-mail agent would compute scores for each of the two candidate actions (*File under David* and *File under Hockey*), would choose the action with the higher score and would calculate a confidence value. In this case, the scores for the two actions would be very close together; the agent would choose filing the message in the *David* folder but would have a very low confidence value. As a result, this agent would likely do nothing in such a situation. It would be the responsibility of the user to realize that nothing had been done, and to perform an appropriate action himself. It is important to note that the autonomous agents (as in Maes, 1994) will not even suggest an action, if there is low confidence. A user has the responsibility of performing any required actions which are simply left unaddressed by the agent.

Our more interactive agent, on the other hand, would examine the same situation and recognize that two candidate actions have similar scores. Based on how close together the scores are, along with a number of other factors,[1] the agent will compute a *clarification factor*. This clarification factor is then compared to a user-defined *bother threshold* to determine whether or not to initiate a clarification dialogue with the user. The goal of such a dialogue is to find out which action is most appropriate in this situation and to attempt to generalize this into a rule. Possible actions are provided, along with explanations, which serve as an encapsulation of the learning algorithm which led the agent to consider these actions. These explanations essentially provide the user with an understanding of the underlying user model which the agent is proposing – they show what the agent has determined to be the user's preferences, based on past actions. An example screen is presented below:

Situation: The following message has just been read.

From	Cc	Date	Subject	...
David Fleming	None	Oct. 26	Hockey pool	...

Possible actions:

Action	Score	Explanation
File under David	2.272	In past situations in which the sender was David Fleming, the action taken was *File under David* in 95% of cases.
File under Hockey	2.201	In past situations in which the subject was ''Hockey pool'', the action taken was *File under Hockey* in 100% of cases.

Please click on the action you wish to choose, or click | Cancel | to conclude this interaction.

---

[1] These factors include how "important" the agent considers the candidate actions to be (based on the do-it thresholds (Maes, 1994) established by the user for those actions) and how often the user has been bothered recently. We omit the presentation of the actual formula in this short paper.

If the user were to choose the action *File under Hockey*, for example, the agent would proceed to propose two rules, as seen in Figure 3. The first states specifically that when the subject line is "Hockey pool" and the message sender is David Fleming, the message should be filed in the *Hockey* folder. The second rule is more general, and states that any messages with subject line "Hockey pool", regardless of the sender, should be filed in the *Hockey* folder. The user has the option of accepting or editing either of these rules, or of cancelling the interaction entirely if neither rule is appropriate. When the user approves a rule, this rule is then employed by the agent in future interactions and the agent updates the model of the user's preferred actions.

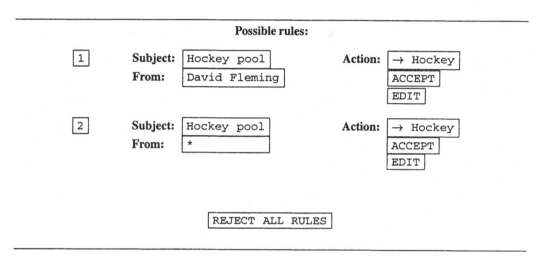

Figure 3. Agent's proposal of possible rules

Even in cases in which the user is not immediately bothered by the agent (*i.e.*, the clarification factor does *not* exceed the bother threshold), the agent can indicate that it has a question for the user without actually requiring the user to deal with it immediately. To achieve this interaction, we propose having the agent maintain a "question box" where it would store information about situations with which it could benefit from the user's help, but for which it chose not to interrupt the user immediately due to a low clarification factor. This question box would appear in the interface as a small box in the lower left corner of the screen, indicating how many questions the agent currently had. The user could choose to click on this box at his own convenience, in order to initiate dialogues of the form presented earlier.

This feature is incorporated into our model to explicitly allow both the user and the agent to initiate interactions. The user is essentially provided with an opportunity for finding out more about the proposed actions of the agent and the underlying user model which leads to these proposals, at a time which is convenient to the user.

3.2 Rule Base

Another novel aspect of our algorithm, as compared to the learning interface agents developed at MIT, is its incorporation of truly hard-and-fast rules into the agent's behaviour. An example of such a rule, from the e-mail domain, might be "If a message arrives with subject line 'Make money fast', then delete it." Rules can either be programmed by the user, or developed and proposed by the agent when it has high confidence in a prediction (as in Step 4 of Figure 2). Although the MIT group does provide "rules" for its agents, these rules are simply represented as hypothetical situations, and are treated just as though they were situations the agent had actually observed in the past. In any new situation, an agent would still have to examine each past situation in its memory and go through a series of calculations. Our proposal is for the agent to maintain an entirely separate database of rules, which can be fired immediately whenever an appropriate situation is encountered.

We believe that the incorporation of rules is a necessary addition for two main reasons: (1) it will likely speed up the agent's performance[2] in situations where it can simply apply a rule, rather than going through a series of complex calculations involved in the agent's learning algorithm; (2) because rules are more explicit and concrete than the calculations involved in learning techniques, having a separate rule base which is always available to inspect would help to provide the user with a better understanding of, more trust in, and a better sense of control over, the agent's behaviour. Our agents also allow for agent-user communication in the event of conflicts occurring in the actual rules programmed by the user (Step 0). This communication is not through natural language, but rather via dialogue boxes, menus and buttons in a graphical user interface. Fleming (1998) presents examples illustrating dialogues to address such rule conflicts.

4 Reflecting on Initiative

The design outlined in Section 3 allows for both the agent and the user to take the initiative and can therefore be classified as a mixed-initiative AI system. Allen (1994) and Burstein and McDermott (1996) identify several important issues which must be addressed when designing mixed-initiative systems, including: (i) specification of when exactly the system and user should communicate, and what that communication should look like; (ii) registration of context when one party interrupts the other; (iii) ensuring that both parties share the responsibilities involved in the task, and are fully aware of the responsibilities of each party.

For the particular application of interface agent design, our model addresses each of these issues. An algorithm is presented for determining when an agent should choose to initiate communication with the user, and details are given about the format of this interaction. Registration of context is also taken into consideration in the model. Whenever the agent interrupts the user, it must take care to set the stage for what exactly it wishes to ask the user. For instance, in the example presented earlier, the agent registers the context by establishing that the user has just finished reading a message which the agent does not know how to treat, and by providing the user with the exact features of that particular message. In our model, the agent and user share responsibilities quite well, and should always be aware of who is responsible for what tasks. Upon

---

[2] Note that, in practice, the actual gain in performance by using a rule-based approach would depend strongly on the size of the rule base and on the format used to represent rules.

encountering any new situation, it is understood that the agent will attempt to do whatever it can to perform an action for the user (or to make a suggestion) using the knowledge it has previously acquired. If it has insufficient information to do anything, it will still be able to inform the user by adding messages to the question box discussed earlier.[3]

Among other things, the agent in our model can take the initiative to clarify ambiguous situations, to ask for contradictory rules to be clarified, to propose generalizations of rules specified by the user, to propose rules when its confidence is high enough, to maintain the question box and to indicate to the user when new items have been added. The user can take the initiative to set threshold values, to react to proposed rules from the agent, to accept or reject the agent's proposed generalizations of rules, and to click on the agent's messages in the communication column or in the question box in order to initiate dialogues.

5   Discussion

This research has obvious comparisons to previous work on interface agents, which was drawn out somewhat in Sections 2 and 3. In situations where other agents (*e.g.*, Maes, 1994) would be unable to propose an action for a user (and would therefore rely on the user to act), our agents would engage in clarification, resulting in an action taken for the user. As the user communicates with the agent, a better understanding of the agent's operations is gained. Yet, there is still an opportunity for autonomy on the part of the agent, so that there is less burden on the user to "program" the agent's every move. There is also important value to mapping out the circumstances under which agent and user can take the initiative to act, as discussed in Section 4.

Our model also suggests some valuable new directions for user modeling. The user model in our kind of application is simply a record of the user's past actions (which can be surveyed at any time, to find possible patterns of similarity with the current situation), together with a critical rule base which captures the general rules the agent has developed, to characterize the user's preferences, from previous learning episodes. The clarification dialogues which are introduced essentially provide the user with the opportunity to view the system's user model and to directly propose changes to that model. Typically, user models have either been acquired implicitly (by inference) or explicitly (from some kind of interview process) and have changed on the basis of observation of the user (as discussed in Kobsa and Wahlster, 1989). The style of interaction which we have developed allows the user a more active role in the ongoing maintenance of the user model. Providing users with this role as an option, carefully administered so as not to overburden, is the best method of engaging the user, in our opinion.

Other work which has investigated the use of user models in interfaces includes Thomas and Fischer (1996). Here, a user model is maintained to assist users in browsing the Web. However, the user model is essentially acquired implicitly, on the basis of the user's actions. Our approach is somewhat more in line with that of McCalla et al. (1996), which allows users to change a case library, to influence the user model which is maintained, for applications of information filtering. In our model, the opportunities for the user to influence the agent are well specified and

---

[3]   Fleming (1998) discusses other methods for communicating with the user as well. For example, it is possible to use a separate "communication column" in the display of all e-mail messages in a mailbox, which records the current status of that message with respect to the agent's processing.

constrained to a clarification dialogue, so that both parties are aware and can build up trust and understanding between them.

Cesta and D'Aloisi (1998) have also discussed the value of mixed-initiative interaction between users and agents. Their MASMA meeting scheduler is in fact a multi-agent system, where users define and maintain their own user profile (so that this information is not learned by the agents). Then, depending on the criticality of the task, agents may interact further with users. Users are also able to control and inspect their agents, at any time. This work therefore suggests a somewhat different role for users, but reinforces the hypothesis that it is important for users to know and trust their agents.

In a similar vein, in Akoulchina and Ganascia (1997), the user is allowed to create hypothetical rules to direct the agent, which is also a part of our model. However, the user is required to make all the final decisions, so the agent has less opportunity for autonomy, compared to our agents.

For future work, in our model, it may also be useful to track which rules the agent and the user have discussed, to possibly influence the form of future communication about these rules. For application areas such as recommending Web pages (see Fleming and Cohen, 1998), it may be more critical to track previous interactions. A useful reference here is Maglio and Barrett (1997), which suggests displaying the user's past interactions in a condensed representation, to facilitate the user's understanding of the agent's user model.

In summary, we have presented a model for designing autonomous, interactive agents. These agents make an effort not to bother indiscriminately, but provide their users with a view of the user model which underlies their operation and, in so doing, offer increased reliability.

References

Akoulchina, I., and Ganascia, J.-G. (1997). Satelit-agent: An adaptive interface based on learning interface agents. In *Proceedings of the Sixth International Conference on User Modeling*, 21–32.

Allen, J. (1994). Mixed-initiative planning: Position paper. Presented at the ARPA/Rome Labs Planning Initiative Workshop. Available on the World Wide Web at http://www.cs.rochester.edu/research/trains/mip.

Burstein, M., and McDermott, D. (1996). Issues in the development of human-computer mixed-initiative planning. In Gorayska, B., and Mey, J., eds., *In Search of a Humane Interface*. Elsevier Science B.V. 285–303.

Cesta, A., and D'Aloisi, D. (1998). Mixed-initiative issues in an agent-based meeting scheduler. *User Modeling and User-Adapted Interaction (to appear)*.

Fleming, M., and Cohen, R. (1998). Interactive interface agents as recommender systems. In *Papers from the AAAI 1998 Workshop on Recommender Systems*, 42–46. AAAI Press.

Fleming, M. (1998). Designing more interactive interface agents. Master of Mathematics thesis, University of Waterloo, Waterloo, Ontario.

Kobsa, A., and Wahlster, W., eds. (1989). *User Models in Dialog Systems*. Springer-Verlag.

Kozierok, R. (1993). A learning approach to knowledge acquisition for intelligent interface agents. Master of Science thesis, Massachusetts Institute of Technology, Cambridge MA.

Maes, P. (1994). Agents that reduce work and information overload. *Communications of the ACM* 37(7):31–40.

Maglio, P., and Barrett, R. (1997). How to build modeling agents to support web searchers. In *Proceedings of the Sixth International Conference on User Modeling*, 5–16.

McCalla, G., Searwar, F., Thomson, J., Collins, J., Sun, Y., and Zhou, B. (1996). Analogical user modelling: A case study in individualized information filtering. In *Proceedings of the 5th International Conference on User Modeling*, 13–20.

Metral, M. (1993). Design of a generic learning interface agent. Bachelor of Science thesis, Massachusetts Institute of Technology, Cambridge MA.

Rich, C., and Sidner, C. (1997). Collagen: When agents collaborate with people. In *First International Conference on Autonomous Agents*, 284–291.

Stanfill, C., and Waltz, D. (1986). Toward memory-based reasoning. *Communications of the ACM* 29(12):1213–1228.

Thomas, C., and Fischer, G. (1996). Using agents to improve the usability and usefulness of the World-Wide Web. In *Proceedings of the 5th International Conference on User Modeling*, 5–12.

Modeling the Social Practices of Users in Internet Communities

Mildred L. G. Shaw and Brian R. Gaines

Knowledge Science Institute, University of Calgary, Alberta, Canada T2N 1N4

Abstract. As the Internet has become widely accessible mailing list servers are being used increasingly to support collaborative discourse in scholarly communities. The majority of these communities are open and new users may join who have met few, if any, of the other list members, and come to know them primarily through email discourse. However, new members joining the discourse of an established group may have difficulty calibrating their constructs with those of the existing members, particularly since the disciplinary background of members may not be evident and may vary widely. Major misunderstandings can arise because members use the same term with different technical meanings, or use different terms for the same construct. This article provides a framework for modeling the conceptual structures of members in an Internet community and describes web-based tools that can be used by members to develop models of the social practices of other users in the community and to calibrate their own use of terminology and constructs against those of others.

1 Introduction

Communities develop social practices (Phillips, 1977; Bloor, 1983) that make it difficult for those outside the community to understand the *language games* within it (Wittgenstein, 1958; Shotter, 1993). This is particularly problematic for those joining Internet list servers since the rationale for the discourse is often undefined, and the backgrounds of those participating is usually unclear. Scholarly communities, in particular, often use colloquial words as *aide memoires* for technical terms which are intended to evoke a highly specific context for the discourse (Roberts and Good, 1993). Members who do not know the technical term will be misled if they read it colloquially, and members who know the term in a different disciplinary context may be misled into thinking they understand the discourse when they do not. The issues of academic discourse as social practice are well-documented (Brodkey, 1987; Bourdieu, Passeron and Martin, 1994), as are the specific problems in the use of language that arise in scientific prose in different disciplines (Atran, 1990; Gross, 1990; Selzer, 1993). One way to support new members of an Internet community is to provide them with systems through which they can test their use of terms against usage representing the practice of the community.

Personal construct psychology (Kelly, 1955) offers a constructivist approach to thought and language that leads to tools that enable individuals' conceptual frameworks to be compared. Individuals are modeled as focusing on *elements* of the world and classifying them through *constructs* that make distinctions among elements in order to anticipate future distinctions. People differ in their constructions and, when communicate, they use terms for elements and constructs that may also differ, so that processes for the formation of socially shared constructions and terminology are significant, and the comparison of individual construct systems may show major differences. Kelly developed a technique called the *repertory grid* in order to elicit elements and constructs from an individual, and various analyses have been developed to derive conceptual structures from grids and to compare structures between grids and across populations (Shaw, 1979; Gaines and Shaw, 1980; Shaw, 1980). Repertory grid elicitation and analysis from experts in a domain has also been used extensively as a knowledge acquisition technique for expert systems (Shaw and Gaines, 1983; Bradshaw, Ford, Adams-Webber and Boose, 1993; Gaines and Shaw, 1993b; Gaines and Shaw, 1993a).

The repertory grid is a technique for modeling actual practice in the use of language that can be used to enable individuals to compare their practices with those prevalent in a community. We developed a system on a network of the Apple Macintosh computers called *RepGrid-Net* that allowed a special-interest group to combine email with grid elicitation and analysis in order to understand the community and find those with similar interests (Shaw and Gaines, 1991), but its use was limited to local area networks. In recent years we have ported the grid elicitation and analysis techniques to the web as *WebGrid*, a system that supports knowledge acquisition for expert system development on the Internet (Gaines and Shaw, 1997). *WebGrid* was intended primarily to introduce repertory grid techniques to new users and focused on basic capabilities. However, it rapidly came into widespread use for major research projects and interest grew in having a full range of knowledge acquisition tools available on the web. *WebGrid-II* extends *WebGrid* to provide integration with multimedia, additional data types in the grid, entailment analysis to induce rules from grid data, and an expert system inference engine to allow the rules to be tested on new cases as part of the elicitation process. *WebGrid-II* also extends the system to provide the features of RepGrid-Net as a public service on the web so that communities can incorporate conceptual modeling and comparison facilities in their web facilities on an anonymous basis without requiring any special privileges at our servers.

This article describes WebGrid-II in its application to community modeling.

2 Repertory Grid Elicitation

To show WebGrid-II in action we will use an example from an international research community undertaking intelligent manufacturing systems research that we have supported and studied as a 'society of research agents' (Gaines and Norrie, 1997). One problem for this community was the presentation of the project objectives and activities to its funding agencies. There was a common theme of 'soft' or reconfigurable systems in the technical program, but it became clear that this was inadequately explained in the project documents. In preparation for a major review meeting in June 1993 an analysis was made of the *soft machine* construct using repertory grid tools.

Six major sub-projects were used as initial elements (which the user called "systems", see Figure 1), and the ensuing repertory grid elicitation process resulted in the addition of another 10 systems, including human operators and organizational structures that provided contrasts to some aspects of the technological projects. Eleven bipolar constructs (which the user called "qualities") were elicited that provided detailed insights into the complexity of the notion of reconfigurability, and were used in presentations to the funding agencies to explain more clearly the roles of the projects and their relevance to issues of soft machinery. The resultant grid provides a record of the social practices in the use of constructs and terminology in the community and provides a referent for newcomers against which to calibrate their own conceptual systems.

We will first illustrate how such a reference grid is elicited. Figure 1 shows the initial screen of WebGrid-II.

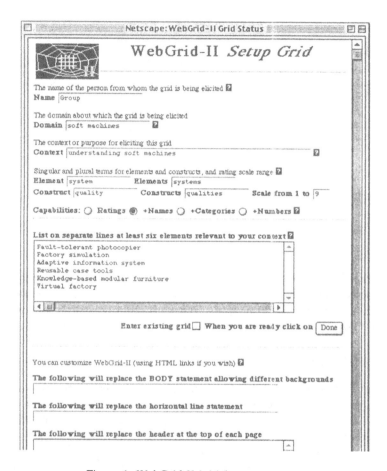

Figure 1. WebGrid-II initial setup screen.

The HTML form requests the usual data required to initiate grid elicitation: user name; domain and context; terms for elements and constructs; default rating scale; data types allowed; and a list of initial elements. It also allows the subsequent screens to be customized with an HTML specification of a header and trailer—this capability to include links to multimedia web data is also used to allow annotation, text and pictures, to be attached to elements.

When the user clicks on the "Done" button at the bottom the server processes the data and generates an HTML document resulting in the screen that allows the user to elicit a construct from a triad of elements. The user clicks on a radio button to select an element which she construes as different from the other two and enters terms characterizing the construct. When the user clicks on "Done" the server generates the screen shown on the left of Figure 2 which places a popup menu rating scale alongside each element enabling the user to rate each one along the new construct as shown on the right.

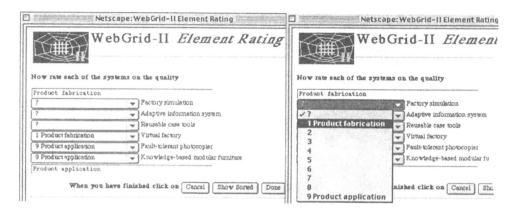

Figure 2. Rating elements on constructs.

Clicking on the "Done" button in Figure 2 sends the ratings back to the server which generates the status screen. This shows the elements and constructs entered, allowing them to be selected for deletion, editing and so on. It also offers various suggestions as how to continue the elicitation based on the data entered so far, facilities for analysis, saving the grid, and so on.

3 Repertory Grid Analysis

To show WebGrid-II in action we will use an example from an international research community undertaking intelligent manufacturing systems research that we have supported and studied as a 'society of research agents' (Gaines and Norrie, 1997). One problem for this community was the presentation of the project objectives and activities to its funding agencies. There was a common theme of 'soft' or reconfigurable systems in the technical program, but it became clear that this was inadequately explained in the project documents. In preparation for a major review meeting in June 1993 an analysis was made of the *soft machine* construct using repertory grid tools.

The repertory grid elicitation continues with the system generating more triads, suggesting that the user enters elements to break matches between constructs, and *vice versa*, and generally attempting to prompt the user into exploring all the relevant dimensions of their conceptual space. In the example being used here this process resulted in 17 elements and 12 constructs.

WebGrid-II provides various analysis tools to reflect back to the user the conceptual structure it has elicited. Figure 3 shows the output of the "Map" tool which uses the FOCUS (Shaw, 1980) algorithm to sort a grid to bring similar elements and similar constructs together. The tree diagrams on the far right show how the constructs (top) and the elements (bottom) cluster together. For example, it shows that the two most similar "qualities" are "System notes reconfiguration need—User notes reconfiguration need" and "System reconfigures itself—User reconfigures system." Three pairs of highly matched elements can be seen—two pairs at the top of the lower tree, and one pair at the bottom of the lower tree.

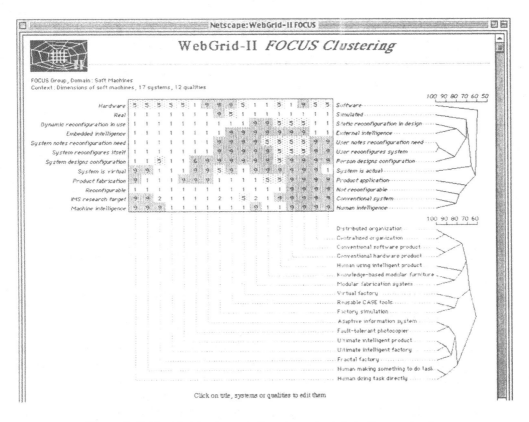

Figure 3. Grid sorted to show similar elements and similar constructs.

4 Repertory Grid Comparison

The visual analysis of repertory grids as shown in Figure 3 provides a conceptual model for a user of the relations between their elements and between their constructs which is valuable in its own right. The grid can also be used to enable other members of the community to compare their conceptual models with that embodied in this grid. WebGrid-II allows grids to be cached at the server and provides URLs for other members of the community to use the data in them for comparison purposes. The underlying theory of grid comparison has been documented elsewhere (Gaines and Shaw, 1989; Shaw and Gaines, 1989) and will be briefly reviewed here before giving some examples of comparative analysis.

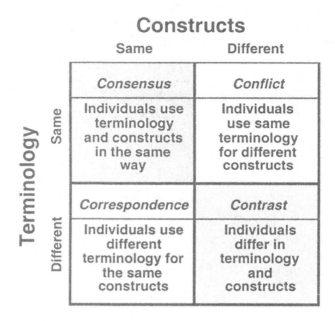

Figure 4. Consensus, conflict, correspondence and contrast in construct systems.

Figure 4 shows a two-way analysis of constructs dependent on whether two constructs make the same distinction among elements and whether they use the same terminology, leading to notions of consensus, conflict, correspondence and contrast.

The recognition of *consensual* constructs is important because it establishes a basis for communication using shared constructs and terminologies. The recognition of *conflicting* constructs establishes a basis for avoiding confusion over the labeling of differing constructs with the same terms. The recognition of *corresponding* concepts establishes a basis for mutual understanding of differing terms through the availability of common constructs. The recognition of *contrasting* constructs establishes that there are aspects of the differing knowledge about which communication and understanding may be very difficult, even though this should not lead to confusion.

Comparison of repertory grids provides a basis for recognizing consensus, correspondence, conflict and contrast in construct systems. If one member of community attempts to fill in the ratings in a grid derived from that of another member by deleting the ratings, then matches between constructs indicate consensus and major mis-matches indicate conflict. If member attempts to construe elements in a grid derived from that of another member by deleting both ratings and constructs, then a match between a construct in one grid and that in the other indicates correspondence, while lack of such a match indicates contrast.

The methodology used in WebGrid-II is to first have a new member develop their own constructs for a cached grid representing community practice with the ratings removed, and then have them fill in the representative grid with the ratings removed. The analysis of the first grid indicates correspondence and contrast (Figure 5), and that of the second grid consensus and conflict (not shown). After having calibrated their own constructs and terminology against those of the community, the new member can examine the analysis of the reference grid as shown in Figure 3. In this way a new member can situate their constructs and terminology within the social practice of the community.

The person in the community responsible for managing the use of WebGrid-II can insert script commands in the initial web page that control the initial triads used for elicitation and provide some offered constructs that prompt the users for constructs related to their personal interests or which are fundamental to the community. In this example "Relevant to my project—Irrelevant" and "Soft system—Hard system" have been inserted in the script as offered constructs.

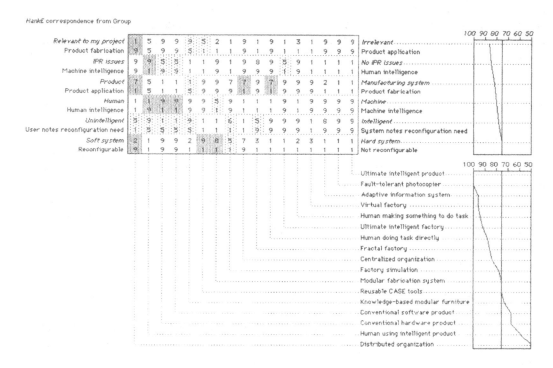

Figure 5. Correspondence and contrast.

Figure 5 shows the WebGrid-II analysis for correspondence and contrast. The newcomer's construct "Relevant to my project—Irrelevant" has been matched against the reference construct "Product fabrication—Product application" which corresponds to the newcomer's interests being in manufacturing systems rather than intelligent products. His construct "IPR issues—No IPR issues" has been matched against "Machine intelligence—Human intelligence" which corresponds to intellectual property rights being associated with the intelligent system developments. His constructs "Product—Manufacturing system" and "Human—Machine" correspond to equivalent ones in the reference grid. His construct "Unintelligent—Intelligent" corresponds to "User notes configuration need—System notes configuration need" and this is essentially a subsumption relationship between a general construct and a specific one that implies it. His construct "Soft system—Hard system" corresponds to "Reconfigurable—Not reconfigurable" which is the way the soft—hard distinction is used in the community. The graph on the right of Figures 5 show these similarities and so helps the user to see the cut-off point where he needs to review his understanding.

A similar comparison analysis provided by WebGrid-II shows the analysis for consensus and conflict.

5 Incorporating WebGrid-II in a Community Web System

WebGrid-II is designed to be used as a service that can be integrated with other web services designed to support Internet communities without the system integrator needing privileged access to, or local support at, our web site. Technical details and examples of how to do this are available (Gaines and Shaw, 1998), and independent user experience of integrating WebGrid-II with other web-based systems has been described (Tennison, 1997; Tennison and Shadbolt, 1998).

6 Conclusions

Communities develop conventions in the use of language that make it difficult for those outside the community to understand the socially situated discourse within it. This article has described and exemplified tools that allow new members of a community to check their usage of terms against those common in the community.

The use of repertory grid methodologies at an early stage sensitizes new members to the issues of constructs and terminology variations within the community, and helps to avoid the confused debates that arise through misunderstanding. It also introduces members of the community to a set of techniques and tools that can be used for a variety of community projects.

Repertory grid analysis can be used to derive social networks based on the capability of one individual to understand the constructs of another (Shaw, 1980), and in RepGrid-Net we used this to facilitate members of a community making contact with like-minded members (Shaw and Gaines, 1991).

In general, the concept of tools that support communities in understanding their discourse and knowledge processes is an important one. Grid-based approaches focus on the modeling of conceptual systems based on actual practice in the use of constructs and terminology. Concept mapping techniques allow users to portray their conceptual structures directly (Gaines and Shaw, 1995b; Gaines and Shaw, 1995a; Kremer and Gaines, 1996; Flores-Mendez, 1997) and can provide a complementary methodology to that described in this article. The derivation of conceptual structures from documents provides yet another approach (Callon, Law and Rip, 1986; Litowski, 1997; Hull and Gomez, 1998), and these various approaches can be combined and integrated to support the reflective processes in communities that can systematically accelerate their effectiveness.

Notes and Acknowledgements

WebGrid-II can be accessed at http://tiger.cpsc.ucalgary.ca/. Financial assistance for this work has been made available by the Natural Sciences and Engineering Research Council of Canada.

References

Atran, S. (1990). **Cognitive foundations of natural history : towards an anthropology of science**. Cambridge, UK, Cambridge University Press.

Bloor, David (1983). **Wittgenstein : a social theory of knowledge**. New York, Columbia University Press.

Bourdieu, P., Passeron, J.-C. and Martin, M. de Saint (1994). **Academic discourse : linguistic misunderstanding and professorial power**. Cambridge, UK, Polity Press.

Bradshaw, J.M., Ford, K.M., Adams-Webber, J.R. and Boose, J.H. (1993). Beyond the repertory grid: new approaches to constructivist knowledge acquisition tool development. **International Journal of Intelligent Systems 8**(2) 287-33.

Brodkey, L. (1987). **Academic writing as social practice**. Philadelphia, Temple University Press.

Callon, M., Law, J. and Rip, A., Ed. (1986). **Mapping the Dynamics of Science and Technology**. Basingstoke, UK, MacMillan.

Flores-Mendez, R.A. (1997). Java concept maps for the learning web. **Proceedings of ED-MEDIA'97 : World Conference on Educational Multimedia and Hypermedia**. Charlottesville, VA, Association for the Advancement of Computing in Education.

Gaines, B.R. and Norrie, D.H. (1997). Coordinating societies of research agents—IMS experience. **Integrated Computer Aided Engineering 4**(3) 179-190.

Gaines, B.R. and Shaw, M.L.G. (1980). New directions in the analysis and interactive elicitation of personal construct systems. **International Journal Man-Machine Studies 13** 81-116.

Gaines, B.R. and Shaw, M.L.G. (1989). Comparing the conceptual systems of experts. **Proceedings of the Eleventh International Joint Conference on Artificial Intelligence**. pp.633-638. San Mateo, California, Morgan Kaufmann.

Gaines, B.R. and Shaw, M.L.G. (1993a). Basing knowledge acquisition tools in personal construct psychology. **Knowledge Engineering Review 8**(1) 49-85.

Gaines, B.R. and Shaw, M.L.G. (1993b). Eliciting knowledge and transferring it effectively to a knowledge-based systems. **IEEE Transactions on Knowledge and Data Engineering 5**(1) 4-14.

Gaines, B.R. and Shaw, M.L.G. (1995a). Collaboration through concept maps. Schnase, J.L. and Cunnius, E.L., Ed. **Proceedings of CSCL95: Computer Support for Collaborative Learning**. pp.135-138. Mahwah, New Jersey, Lawrence Erlbaum.

Gaines, B.R. and Shaw, M.L.G. (1995b). WebMap: concept mapping on the web. **World Wide Web Journal 1**(1) 171-183.

Gaines, B.R. and Shaw, M.L.G. (1997). Knowledge acquisition, modeling and inference through the World Wide Web. **International Journal of Human-Computer Studies 46**(6) 729-759.

Gaines, B.R. and Shaw, M.L.G. (1998). Developing for web integration in Sisyphus-IV: WebGrid-II experience. Gaines, B.R. and Musen, M.A., Ed. **Proceedings of Eleventh Knowledge Acquisition Workshop**. pp.http://ksi.cpsc.ucalgary.ca/KAW/KAW98/gaines/.

Gross, Alan G. (1990). **The rhetoric of science**. Cambridge, Mass., Harvard University Press.

Hull, R. and Gomez, F. (1998). Automatic acquisition of historical knowledge from encyclopedic texts. Gaines, B.R. and Musen, M.A., Ed. **Proceedings of Eleventh Knowledge Acquisition Workshop**. pp.http://ksi.cpsc.ucalgary.ca/KAW/KAW98/hull/.

Kelly, G.A. (1955). **The Psychology of Personal Constructs**. New York, Norton.

Kremer, R.A. and Gaines, B.R. (1996). Embedded interactive concept maps in web documents. Maurer, H., Ed. **Proceedings of WebNet96**. pp.273-280. Charlottesville, VA, Association for the Advancement of Computing in Education.

Litowski, K.C. (1997). Category development based on semantic principles. **Social Sciences Computer Review 15**(4) 394-409.

Phillips, Derek L. (1977). **Wittgenstein and scientific knowledge : a sociological perspective**. Totowa, N.J., Rowman and Littlefield.

Roberts, R.H. and Good, J.M.M., Ed. (1993). **The Recovery of Rhetoric: Persuasive Discourse and Disciplinarity in the Human Sciences**. Charlottesville, University of Virginia.

Selzer, Jack (1993). **Understanding scientific prose**. Madison, Wis., University of Wisconsin Press.

Shaw, M.L.G. (1979). Conversational heuristics for eliciting shared understanding. **International Journal of Man-Machine Studies 11** 621-634.

Shaw, M.L.G. (1980). **On Becoming A Personal Scientist: Interactive Computer Elicitation of Personal Models Of The World**. London, Academic Press.

Shaw, M.L.G. and Gaines, B.R. (1983). A computer aid to knowledge engineering. **Proceedings of British Computer Society Conference on Expert Systems**. pp.263-271. Cambridge, British Computer Society.

Shaw, M.L.G. and Gaines, B.R. (1989). A methodology for recognizing conflict, correspondence, consensus and contrast in a knowledge acquisition system. **Knowledge Acquisition 1**(4) 341-363.

Shaw, M.L.G. and Gaines, B.R. (1991). Supporting personal networking through computer networking. **Proceedings of CHI'91: Human Factors in Computing Systems**. pp.437-438. New York, ACM Publications.

Shotter, John (1993). **Conversational realities : constructing life though language**. London, SAGE Publications.

Tennison, J. (1997). Linking APECKS to WebGrid-II. Department of Psychology, University of Nottingham. http://www.psychology.nottingham.ac.uk/staff/Jenifer.Tennison/APECKS/WebGrid.html.

Tennison, J. and Shadbolt, N.R. (1998). APECKS: a Tool to Support Living Ontologies. Gaines, B.R. and Musen, M.A., Ed. **Proceedings of Eleventh Knowledge Acquisition Workshop**. pp.http://ksi.cpsc.ucalgary.ca/KAW/KAW98/tennison/.

Wittgenstein, Ludwig (1958). **Philosophical investigations**. Oxford, Blackwell.

User Lenses – Achieving 100% Precision on Frequently Asked Questions

Christopher C. Vogt[1], Garrison W. Cottrell[1], Richard K. Belew[1], and Brian T. Bartell[2]*

[1] Department of Computer Science and Engineering, University of California, San Diego, CA, USA
[2] Conceptual Dimensions, Inc., San Diego, CA, USA

Abstract. The concept of a "user lens" is introduced. The lens is a sequence of linear transformations used to reweight the vectors which represent documents or queries in information retrieval systems. It is trained automatically via relevance data provided by the user. Experiments verify the lens can improve performance on training data while not degrading test data performance, and that larger lenses result in nearly perfect performance on the training set. The lens provides a mechanism for automatically capturing long-term, user-specific information about an improved representation scheme for document vectors.

1 Introduction

Information Retrieval (IR) is the task of finding documents which are relevant to a user's query. It is typified in the World Wide Web context by search engines and filtering agents. Search engines are approaches for handling what is known as the "adhoc" task – a user issues a new query against a static collection of documents. Filtering agents, on the other hand, embody the "routing" task – the user has a standing query against which new documents (e.g., newswire articles) are compared.

The division of the IR task into adhoc and routing subtasks is one which researchers naturally make to help them analyze their approaches. Realistically, however, no IR system solves either of these tasks alone, since neither document nor query collections are really static. Viewing each task separately has lead to some standard approaches to one task which are not compatible with the other, making combination more difficult. For example, when solving the adhoc task, traditional IR systems use methods of relevance feedback like term reweighting and term expansion in a short-term fashion. Once the user has finished with a query, the system forgets about the feedback he or she has provided. Systems solving the routing task generally do not fall prey to this problem, since they create and maintain fine-tuned versions of each of the user's queries. On the other hand, each such query is viewed in isolation from the others, with the system making no attempt to create an overall picture of the user's "view of the world." Construction of such a view could make it easier for the system to satisfy future queries (i.e., solve the adhoc task).

Another seemingly unrelated, yet perennial problem in the IR community is that of choosing term weighting schemes. A weighting scheme is just a method for determining how much each term (i.e., word or phrase) in the document will contribute to the representation of the document. These representations are typically in a vector form, with one component of the vector representing each term, and the value of that component (i.e., its weight) indicating how much

---

* This research was supported by NSF grant IRI 92-21276.

the document is about that term. These weights are almost always a function of how often the term occurs in the document (its frequency). Countless researchers have tried to find the best scheme for a particular problem or domain, or even just the best overall scheme (Salton and Buckley, 1988). Searching for the best overall scheme is clearly not the best approach, since the scheme will necessarily be suboptimal in some situations. Likewise, the manual search for the best weighting scheme for a particular domain seems grossly inefficient and unlikely to produce the optimal scheme. A more reasonable approach would be to determine the weighting scheme automatically.

The research presented here addresses both of these problems, and introduces a new way of modeling the user. We introduce the idea of a "user lens." The lens is merely a set of IR system parameters which are automatically adjusted according to the user's relevance feedback. The lens is used to modify the default vector-space weighting scheme, creating a new scheme for representing documents and/or queries. Furthermore, because a modified vector-space approach is used, the system can be used for both routing and adhoc tasks. The lens indirectly preserves all of the user's feedback while simultaneously representing his or her view of the world. This lets the system leverage off of what it has learned from either task when performing the other. The lens presents a simple yet powerful way of modeling the user's behavior, and thus his or her preferences.

2   User Lenses

A "user lens" is simply a sequence of matrices by which the document or query vectors are multiplied to obtain a new representation. The document representations are then compared to the queries using the standard inner-product or cosine measures. The entries in the lens matrices are adjusted automatically using the information gained via relevance feedback. We preface the term lens with "user" to emphasize that each user (or possibly group of users) could have their own lens which gets used whenever they use the system, which they train with their own feedback, and which represents in a crude way their wants, needs, and usage idiosyncrasies. Thus, the lens can be viewed as a rough model of the cognitive processes of the user when he or she is creating the query or interpreting a document.

Figure 1 summarizes our concept of a user lens. We use Latent Semantic Indexing (Deerwester et al., 1990) as our representation. LSI takes the very large document and query vectors and maps them into a smaller dimensional space. We use this technique because if a square matrix were used to modify the original document/query vectors, it would have millions or billions of entries to adjust. Reduced LSI vectors make the lens more manageable, with tens of thousands of entries. The figure is meant to show the entire process through which a ranking score is derived from the document and query vectors. First, each is reduced to a much lower dimensional vector using the LSI matrix S. Then each is optionally multiplied by one of the matrices L_d or L_q. The final score R for the document with reference to the query is calculated using these transformed vectors. Mathematically, this is:

$$R(d, q) = (L_d S d)^T (L_q S q)$$

assuming both lenses are used and the inner-product is the comparison operator. Since there are no restrictions on the lens matrices, any linear transformation can be used to reweight the input vectors.

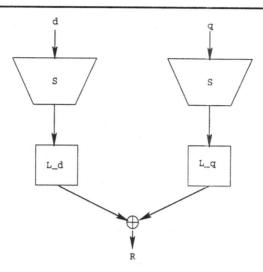

Figure 1. The "user lens" – document and query are first reduced using LSI matrix S, then possibly multiplied by a matrix before being combined into a ranking score R.

Our technique for adjusting the entries in the lens matrices is based on work done by Bartell et al. (1995), (1994). Bartell defines a criterion (hereafter called J) based on Guttman's Point Alienation statistic as follows:

Defn: the ranking function implemented by an IR system is

$$R_\Theta : \Theta \times D \times Q \to \Re$$
where
$\Theta =$ the set of system parameters
$D=$ the set of document vectors
$Q=$ the set of query vectors

Defn: Bartell's J criterion is:

$$J(R_\Theta) = \frac{1}{|Q|} \sum_{q \in Q} \frac{\sum_{d \succ_q d'} (R(\Theta, d, q) - R(\Theta, d', q))}{\sum_{d \succ_q d'} |R(\Theta, d, q) - R(\Theta, d', q)|}$$

where $d \succ_q d'$ indicates the user prefers document d to document d' on query q.

Note that J has a maximum value of 1 when the numerator and denominator are the same (i.e., the IR system ranks documents exactly as the user would), and a minimum value of -1 when the opposite is true. Also note that in order to calculate J, we need to have feedback from a user – for each query, the user needs to label *every* document as either relevant or not relevant to the query. This time consuming and tedious process necessarily limits the amount of training data available.

In our formulation, the entries in the lens matrices L_q, L_d, and S are the system parameters Θ. We then use a multivariate optimization technique like gradient descent or conjugate gradient to determine those values of the matrices which minimize J, by taking the partial derivative of J with respect to the system parameters.

3   Experiments

We have performed two related series of experiments to verify the validity of the lens idea on the adhoc task. The first series verifies the lens as capable of improving system performance, the second series attempts to pinpoint which configuration of lenses produces the most improvement. Because we are examining the adhoc task, two types of improvement are possible: on the training data (this is equivalent to getting better on frequently asked questions) or on the test data (getting better on new queries).

The two most accepted measures of IR system performance are precision and recall. **Precision** is the percentage of retrieved documents which are relevant: $\frac{|R_{EL} \cap R_{ET}|}{|R_{ET}|}$ (where R_{EL} is the set of all relevant documents and R_{ET} is the list of retrieved documents). Precision is a measure of the quality of retrieval. **Recall** is the percentage of relevant documents which have been retrieved: $\frac{|R_{EL} \cap R_{ET}|}{|R_{EL}|}$. Recall measures the coverage of retrieval. Maximizing one of these two measures typically minimizes the other. This tradeoff can be seen in what is a common view of IR system performance: the precision versus recall graph. Precision is calculated at different levels of recall, and these scores are then graphed. Note that high precision corresponds to low recall and vice-versa. The ideal IR system would have a horizontal line across the graph at precision level 1.00, which would correspond to retrieving all and only the relevant documents.

3.1   System Verification

In these experiments, we use both the CISI and MED corpora (distributed with the SMART system (Salton, 1971)). Respectively, these are corpora of Information Science and Medical abstracts, each containing about 1000 documents. Only the query lens L_q is trained, with a cosine comparison operator. The CISI corpus is indexed using the SMART *atc* weighting scheme, and MED is indexed using *ntc*. In both cases, document and query vectors are reduced to 100 dimensions using LSI. The number of training queries is 56 for CISI and 20 for MED, with 10 and 5 test queries respectively. Relevance feedback on all of these 66 and 25 queries are distributed along with the corpora. In both cases, eight different random partitions of the queries in training and testing sets are made, and the average precision/recall figures over these eight partitions are reported below. L_q is initialized to the identity matrix before being trained. Gradient descent with a learning rate of 0.1 is used to minimize J by adjusting the entries of L_q.

For the CISI data, a number of different lenses are trained, each corresponding to a different number of iterations of the gradient descent algorithm. Precision/recall curves corresponding to 200, 1000, and 2000 iterations are shown in Figure 2, along with a baseline of no lens. It is clear from these graphs that a lens can indeed improve performance on the training data and yet not affect performance on the test data. However, as the 1000 and 2000 iteration results show, the large improvement gained by longer training comes at a cost of degradation on the test data. This suggests that a hold-out set be used to determine when to stop training. More importantly, though, this may mean that the lens does not have quite enough power to produce the best possible weighting scheme. This latter idea is explored in the second set of experiments, where we actually train the entries of the LSI matrix S. Because S is so much larger than the L matrices, we hypothesize that training it will allow much better performance on the training data and possibly even some improvement on the test data.

To verify that the results on CISI are not specific to that corpus, we also train a query lens L_q for 2000–5000 iterations of gradient descent on the MED corpus. The results in Figure 3 show the same pattern of improvement on the training data and no effect on the test data performance.

3.2   Finding the Best Configuration

As described above, many options are available when using a lens. In this set of experiments, we explore several configurations in an attempt to determine which results in the best performance on the CISI corpus. The three configurations we use are: training the document lens L_d only, training the document and query lenses simultaneously so that $L_q = L_d$, and as mentioned above, training the LSI matrix S alone. Training the query lens L_q results in performance virtually identical to that of L_d, so it is not shown on the graphs below. Also, in the first two configurations, gradient descent with 200 iterations is used, whereas the faster converging conjugate gradient is used to train S because it is so large.

Figure 4 shows the results of these experiments. As expected, performance on the test data does not change after training, but the performance on the training data improves. Even more importantly, we see that running both the document and the query through a lens results in even better performance. This behavior is not only expected, but desirable, since if a document is used as a query, one would expect the highest possible ranking score when it is compared to itself. Finally, if we are willing to spend the extra time training a much larger set of parameters (i.e., the LSI matrix), then we can get *nearly perfect precision at all levels of recall* on the training data while marginally improving the test data performance (although, this latter improvement is probably not statistically significant). This supports the hypothesis suggested by the first set of experiments that the query lens alone was just not large enough to maximize performance. However, another possibility is that good solutions are not even capable of being represented by transforming the reduced space constructed by LSI. This is an issue we will have to explore in future experiments.

4   Discussion and Conclusions

Use of relevance feedback information as a means of modifying a single query to improve a system's retrieval is becoming a common feature of many IR systems. The second set of experiments imply that modifying the *document* representation, in addition to the query representation, can generate significant improvements. In fact, with the right model (e.g., training the entire LSI matrix), modifying both document and query representations can result in nearly perfect performance on the training data without degrading performance on the test data, producing 100% precision on frequently asked questions.

The two experiments raise a number of interesting and important points. First, we reconfirm Bartell's results: Optimization according to the J criterion results in improved performance as measured by precision. In related work, we have found that optimizing J also worked well in some larger scale experiments (Vogt et al., 1997). Together with the results here, it seems to

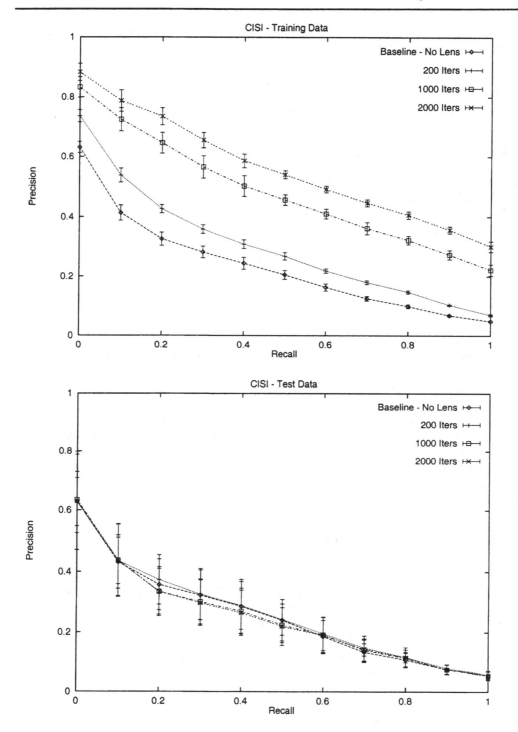

Figure 2. Results of system verification on the CISI training and test data – Comparison of different number of iterations of gradient descent averaged over 8 Runs (error bars are one standard deviation).

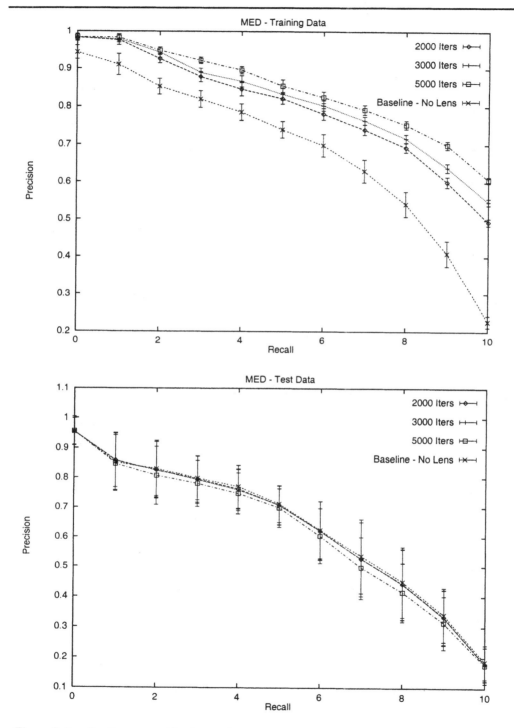

Figure 3. Results of system verification on the MED training and test data, averages over 8 runs (error bars are one standard deviation).

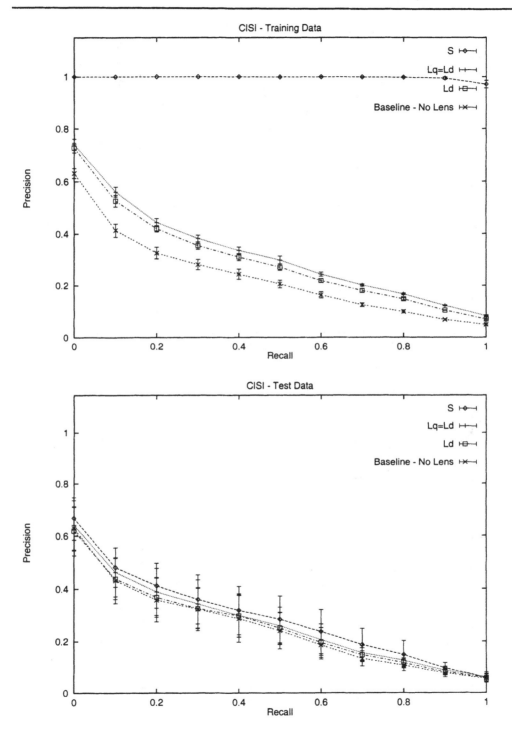

Figure 4. Results of configuration experiment, averages over 8 runs (error bars are one standard deviation).

be a robust approach to determining IR system model parameters. This makes sense, since users typically care most about, and can provide reliable relevance feedback concerning, the *rank order* of retrieved documents rather than their absolute ranking scores. The J criterion is sensitive to just this nonmetric information. Furthermore, we note that optimizing J can be adopted by any adaptive approach to IR, not just user lenses.

Our use of J to adjust the entries in a lens matrix, incorporating a user's preferences, provides a method for improving any existing vector-space weighting scheme. Any document or query, whether part of the original corpus or training set or new and unanticipated, can be "warped" by the lens into a representation more consistent with those they have successfully used in the past. User lenses are also compatible with more traditional forms of feedback, since they can be applied directly to the reweighted or term-expanded form of a query. In terms of the two canonical IR tasks, this suggests improved performance on both the adhoc and routing tasks.

5   Future Work

The work reported here is in its earliest stages and a great deal remains to be done, ranging from straight-forward extensions of experiments done here to much larger designs. First, additional testing must be done to confirm our interpretation of the enormous advantage of training the full S matrix. Second, all of our experiments to date have used more analytically tractable *linear* transformations, but much of this work has grown out of an interest in nonlinear, neural network-style learning methods. We continue to believe that additional benefits may be gained by such nonlinear transformations, and intend to explore these extensions as well. Important questions also remain with regards to the capacity of the lens. That is, how many documents and queries can we reasonably expect the lens to be able to accurately capture?

We are currently in the process of reproducing these results on the the TREC data set (Harman, 1997), and expect that our techniques will scale up to this much larger corpus. We are also formulating a series of experiments that verify that a lens can improve (or at least not degrade) the performance of a routing system.

Ultimately, we envision multiple varieties of lenses, some corresponding to individual users and some to *groups* of users with shared, consensual interpretations of what words and documents mean. Important issues remain concerning how lenses can be trained independently, how users' collective relevance feedback can be aggregated in the appropriate lens, and how compound lenses might be formed automatically, to shape the world of documents each user sees.

References

Bartell, B. T., Cottrell, G. W., and Belew, R. K. (1995). Representing documents using an explicit model of their similarities. *Journal of the American Society for Information Science* 46(4).

Bartell, B. T. (1994). *Optimizing Ranking Functions: A Connectionist Approach to Adaptive Information Retrieval.* thesis, Department of Computer Science and Engineering, The University of California, San Diego, CSE 0114, La Jolla, CA 92093.

Deerwester, S., Dumais, S. T., Furnas, G. W., Landauer, T. K., and Harshman, R. (1990). Indexing by latent semantic analysis. *Journal of the American Society for Information Science* 41(6):391–407.

Harman, D. K., ed. (1997). *The Fifth Text REtrieval Conference (TREC5).* Gaithersberg, MD: National Institute of Standards and Technology. NIST Special Publication 500-238.

Salton, G., and Buckley, C. (1988). Term weighting approaches in automatic text retrieval. *Information Processing and Management* 24:513–23.

Salton, G., ed. (1971). *The SMART Retrieval System – Experiments in Automatic Document Retrieval.* Englewood Cliffs, N.J.: Prentice-Hall Inc.

Vogt, C., Cottrell, G., Belew, R., and Bartell, B. (1997). Using relevance to train a linear mixture of experts. In Harman, D. K., ed., *The Fifth Text REtrieval Conference (TREC5)*, 503–515. Gaithersberg, MD: National Institute of Standards and Technology. NIST Special Publication 500-238.

BUILDING USER MODELS UNOBTRUSIVELY

A Hybrid User Model for News Story Classification

Daniel Billsus and Michael J. Pazzani[*]

Dept. of Information and Computer Science, University of California, Irvine, CA, USA

Abstract. *We present an intelligent agent designed to compile a daily news program for individual users. Based on feedback from the user, the system automatically adapts to the user's preferences and interests. In this paper we focus on the system's user modeling component. First, we motivate the use of a multi-strategy machine learning approach that allows for the induction of user models that consist of separate models for long-term and short-term interests. Second, we investigate the utility of explicitly modeling information that the system has already presented to the user. This allows us to address an important issue that has thus far received virtually no attention in the Information Retrieval community: the fact that a user's information need changes as a direct result of interaction with information. We evaluate the proposed algorithms on user data collected with a prototype of our system, and assess the individual performance contributions of both model components.*

1 Introduction

Research on intelligent information agents has recently attracted much attention. As the amount of information available on-line grows with astonishing speed, people feel overwhelmed navigating through today's information and media landscape. Information overload is no longer just a popular buzzword, but a daily reality for most of us. This leads to a clear demand for automated methods, commonly referred to as intelligent information agents, that locate and retrieve information with respect to users' individual preferences (Lang, 1995; Pazzani and Billsus, 1997; Balabanovic, 1998).

As intelligent information agents aim to automatically adapt to individual users, the development of appropriate user modeling techniques is of central importance. Algorithms for intelligent information agents typically draw on work from the Information Retrieval (IR) and machine learning communities. Both communities have previously explored the potential of established algorithms for user modeling purposes (Belkin et al. 1997; Webb 1998). However, work in this field is still in its infancy and we see "User Modeling for Intelligent Information Access" as an important area for future research.

We describe an intelligent information agent designed to compile a daily news program for individual users. Building such an agent is a challenging task, because traditional Information Retrieval approaches are not directly applicable to this problem setting. Most IR systems assume the user has a specific, well-defined information need. In our setting, however, this is not the case. If at all, the user's query could be phrased as: "What is new in the world that I do not yet know about, but should know?". Computing

---

[*] We thank Daimler-Benz and Sun Microsystems, Inc. for their generous support.

satisfactory results for such a query is non-trivial. The difficulty stems from the range of topics that could interest the user, and the user's changing interest in these topics. We must also take into account that it is the novelty of a story that makes it interesting. Even though a certain topic might match a user's interests perfectly, the user will not be interested in the story if it has been heard before. Therefore, we need to build a system that acquires a model of a user's multiple interests, is flexible enough to account for rapid interest changes, and keeps track of information the user knows.

We focus on two issues related to the automated induction of user profiles for news story classification. First, we motivate the induction of a hybrid user model that consists of separate models for a user's long-term and short-term interests. Second, we show how the user model keeps track of information that has already been presented to the user. This allows us to address an important issue that has thus far received virtually no attention in the Information Retrieval community: the fact that a user's information need changes as a direct result of interaction with information (Belkin, 1997). We evaluate the proposed algorithms on user data collected with a prototype of our system, and assess the individual performance contributions of our proposed approaches separately.

2 A Personal News Agent that Talks and Learns

In this section we present the design and architecture of an agent that is intended to become part of an intelligent, IP-enabled radio, which uses synthesized speech to read news stories to a user. While the system's speech capabilities are not the focus of this paper, we briefly discuss the system's overall functionality and intended purpose in order to motivate various design decisions. Part of our research is based on the observation that most of the work on personalized information access has focused on agents accessible through the World Wide Web. Research in this field has not yet led to the development of interfaces for software agents that do not require access to a computer workstation. However, there is a clear demand for such information systems, as demanding schedules prohibit people from continuous computer access.

The following example motivates the need for personalized information delivery outside of the World Wide Web. Users A and B spend a large portion of their day driving. They can listen to the radio in their cars, but do not have access to any medium that focuses on information specific to their interests. User A is primarily interested in business news in order to follow the current stock market, but he must listen to much unrelated information. To locate information, he must switch news channels and pay attention to the time at which broadcasts start. Similarly, user B must switch news channels to locate information on his interest in local sports.

We have implemented a Java Applet that uses Microsoft's *Agent* library to display an animated character, named *News Dude,* that reads news stories to the user. The Applet requires Microsoft's Internet Explorer 4.0 or newer and is publicly accessible at *http://www.ics.uci.edu/~dbillsus/NewsDude* (see Figure 1). Although our ultimate goal is to work towards a speech-driven agent that does not require graphical user interfaces, we use the web as a medium that allows us to make the system available to a large user base for data collection and testing purposes. Furthermore, we believe that there is a variety of useful applications for speech-driven agent technology for the web. For example, a talking news agent that reacts to voice commands could prove useful for the visually impaired.

Currently, the agent provides access to stories from six different news channels: Top Stories, Politics, World, Business, Technology and Sports. When the user selects a news channel, the Applet connects to a news site on the Internet (*Yahoo!News*) and starts to download stories. Since the Applet is multi-threaded, download of stories continues in the background while the synthesizer is reading, which typically allows filling a queue of stories to be read without any waiting time. The user can interrupt the synthesizer at any point and provide feedback for the story being read. One of the design goals for our system was to provide a variety of feedback options that go beyond the commonly used *interesting/uninteresting* rating options. If we consider an intelligent information agent to be a personal assistant that gradually learns about our interests and retrieves interesting information, it would only be natural to have more informative ways to communicate our preferences. For example, we might want to tell the agent that we already know about a certain topic, or request information related to a certain story. In summary, the system supports the following feedback options: *interesting, not interesting, I already know this,* and *tell me more about this.* After an initial training phase, the user can ask the agent to compile a personal news program. The goal of this process is to compute a sequence of news stories ordered with respect to the user's interests.

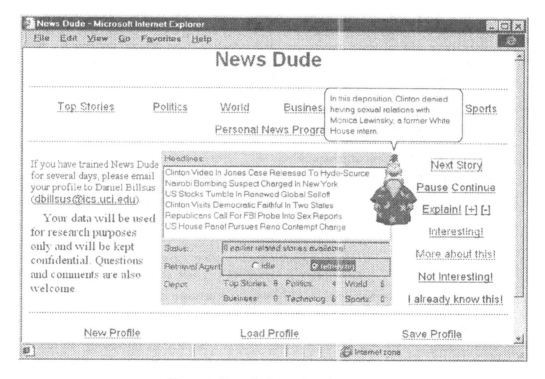

Figure 1. News Dude user interface.

3 Learning a User Model

The specific design of our agent's user model is motivated by a number of observations and requirements. First, the model must be capable of representing a user's multiple interests in different topics. Second, the model must be flexible enough to adapt to a user's changing interests reasonably quickly, even after a long preceding training period. Third, the model should take into account that a user's information needs change as a direct result of interaction with information (Belkin, 1997). Surprisingly, this aspect has received virtually no attention in the IR community. For our application, we take into account the stories the user has recently heard, to avoid presenting the same information twice.

The above requirements led to the development of a multi-strategy learning approach that learns two separate user-models: one represents the user's short-term interests, the other represents the user's long-term interests. Distinguishing between short-term and long-term models has several desirable qualities in domains with temporal characteristics (Chiu and Webb, 1998). Learning a short-term model from only the most recent observations may lead to user models that can adjust more rapidly to the user's changing interests. Here, we restrict the short-term model to the n most recently rated stories (we set n to 100 in the experiments reported in Section 4). The need for two separate models can be further substantiated by the specific task at hand, i.e. classifying news stories. Users typically want to track different "threads" of ongoing recent events - a task that requires short-term information about recent events. For example, if a user has indicated interest in a story about a current Space Shuttle mission, the system should be able to identify follow-up stories and present them to the user during the following days. In addition, users have general news preferences, and modeling these general preferences may prove useful for deciding if a new story, which is not related to a recent rated event, would interest the user. With respect to the Space Shuttle example, we can identify some of the characteristic terminology used in the story and interpret it as evidence for the user's general interest in technology and science related stories. In the following sections we describe these two parts of the user model individually, motivate why they conform to the above requirements, and describe how they can work together to form a comprehensive user model appropriate for our purposes.

For the following description of the user model and its automated induction, we assume that a user provides the system with a set of rated news stories, using the feedback options described in Section 2. Each user rating is then internally converted to a score ranging from 0 to 1, according to the following rules. Let pl be the proportion of a story that the user has heard.

$$\textit{If story was rated as uninteresting, score} = 0.3 * pl$$
$$\textit{If story was rated as interesting, score} = 0.7 + 0.3 * pl$$
$$\textit{If user asked for more information, score} = 1.0$$

This conversion scheme allows for differentiation between different levels of ratings without requiring any extra work by the user. Note that the constants *0.3* and *0.7* were chosen arbitrarily with the only constraint being that the resulting scores for stories rated as uninteresting always receive lower scores than stories rated as interesting. In future work we will determine improved values for these constants experimentally, using a tuning set of user data.

3.1 Modeling Short-Term Interests with the Nearest Neighbor Algorithm

The purpose of the short-term model is two-fold. First, it should contain information about recently rated events, so that stories which belong to the same threads of events can be identified. Second, it should allow for identification of stories that the user already knows. A natural choice to achieve the desired functionality is the nearest neighbor algorithm (NN). The NN algorithm simply stores all its training examples, in our case rated news stories, in memory. In order to classify a new, unlabeled instance, the algorithm compares it to all stored instances given some defined similarity measure, and determines the "nearest neighbor" or the k nearest neighbors. The class label assigned to the new instance can then be derived from the class labels of the nearest neighbors. The utility of the NN algorithm has previously been explored in other text classification applications (Cohen and Hirsh, 1998; Yang, 1998; Allan et al. 1998).

To apply the algorithm to natural language text, we must define a similarity measure that quantifies the similarity between two text documents. This is a well-studied problem in Information Retrieval, and we rely on a commonly used document representation and an associated similarity measure. We convert news stories to TF-IDF vectors (term-frequency / inverse-document-frequency), and use the cosine similarity measure to quantify the similarity of two vectors (Salton, 1989).

Each rated story is converted to its TF-IDF representation and then stored in the user model. A score prediction for a new story is then computed as follows. All stories that are closer than a threshold t_min to the story to be classified become voting stories. The predicted score is then computed as the weighted average over all the voting stories' scores, where the weight is the similarity between a voting story and the new story. If one of the voters is closer than threshold t_max to the new story, the story is labeled as *known*, and its computed score is multiplied by a factor $k << 1.0$, because the system assumes that the user has already heard about the event reported in the story. If a story does not have any voters, the story cannot be classified by the short-term model at all, and is passed on to the long-term model (see Section 3.2).

The nearest neighbor-based short-term model satisfies our requirements that a user model be able to represent a user's multiple interests, and it can quickly adapt to a user's novel interests. The main advantage of the nearest-neighbor approach is that only a single story of a new topic is needed to allow the algorithm to identify future follow-up stories from the same story thread. The "tracking" abilities of the nearest neighbor algorithm have also recently been explored by other researchers in a similar project (Allan et al., 1998). In contrast, most other learning algorithms would require a large number of training examples to identify a strong pattern.

3.2 Modeling Long-Term Interests with a Naïve Bayesian Classifier

The purpose of the long-term user model is to model a user's general preferences for news stories and compute predictions for stories that could not be classified by the short-term model. To achieve this we selected a probabilistic learning algorithm, the naïve Bayesian classifier (Duda and Hart, 73). Naïve Bayes has been shown to perform competitively with more complex algorithms and has become an increasingly popular algorithm in text classification applications (McCallum and Nigam, 1998; Pazzani and Billsus, 1997).

We represent news stories as Boolean feature vectors, where each feature indicates the presence or absence of a word. Not all the words that appear in news stories are used as features. Since it is our explicit goal to model a user's general preferences, we provide the algorithm with background knowledge by hand-selecting a set of domain specific features, i. e. words that are likely to be indicators for commonly recurring themes in daily news stories. Approximately 200 words were selected, ranging from countries to crime, disaster, politics, technology, business and sport related terms. Making the "naïve" assumption that features, here words, are independent given the class label (interesting vs. not interesting), the probability of a story belonging to class j given its feature values, $p(class_j| f_1, f_2, ... f_n)$ is proportional to:

$$p(class_j)\prod_i^n p(f_i \mid class_j)$$

where $p(class_j)$ and $p(f_i \mid class_j)$ can be easily estimated from training data. Specifically, we use the multi-variate Bernoulli event model formulation of naïve Bayes (McCallum and Nigam, 1998), and compute Bayes-optimal estimates of $p(class_j)$ and $p(f_i \mid class_j)$ by straightforward counting of word and class occurrences in the training data. We use Laplace smoothing to prevent zero probabilities for infrequently occurring words. A news story to be classified can thus be labeled with its probability of belonging to the interesting class.

Most applications of the multi-variate Bernoulli formulation of naïve Bayes consider both the presence and absence of words in text documents as evidence in the probability computation. We restrict the evidence used to the presence of words, similar to a naïve Bayes model proposed by Maron (1961). This results in a more conservative classifier that requires examples classified as class c to be similar to other examples in class c.

Finally, we would like to prevent the long-term model from classifying stories that do not contain a sufficient number of features that are indicators for class membership. More formally, we require the story to contain at least n features for which $p(f \mid interesting) > p(f \mid \neg interesting)$ in order to allow a classification as interesting, and likewise, at least n features   for.   which $p(f \mid interesting) < p(f \mid not\ interesting)$ in order to allow a classification as not interesting. In our current implementation we set n to 3, which means a story must contain at least 3 terms that are all indicators for the same class.

3.3 User-Modeling with a Multi-Strategy Learning Approach

Using a hybrid user model consisting of both a short-term and long-term model of the user's interests, a previously unseen news story, u, is classified as follows:

If $\exists d: d \in \{short\text{-}term\text{-}stories\} \wedge cosine\text{-}similarity(d, u) > t\_min$
{
    score = nearest-neighbor-prediction(u, {short-term-stories})
    If $\exists n: n \in \{short\text{-}term\text{-}stories\} \wedge cosine\text{-}similarity(d, n) > t\_max$
        score = score * k, where k << 1.0
}
Else
    If $\exists \{f_1, f_2, ..., f_n\}: \forall f \in \{f_1, f_2, ..., f_n\}\ p(f \mid c) > p(f \mid \neg c)$
        score = naïve-Bayes-prediction(u, {all stories})
    Else
        score = default

In summary, the approach tries to use the short-term model first, because it is based on the most recent observations only, allows the user to track news threads that have previously been rated, and can label stories as already known. If a story cannot be classified with the short-term model, the long-term model is used. If the long-term model decides that the story does not contain sufficient evidence to be classified, a default score is assigned. In the current implementation we set the default score to *0.3*, so that stories that cannot be reliably classified do not appear too high in the recommendation queue, but still receive a higher score than stories that are classified as not interesting.

4 Evaluation

In order to evaluate the recommendation performance of our agent and to assess the performance contribution of its hybrid user model, we used the web-based agent prototype to collect user data. Ten users trained the system on a daily basis over a period ranging from 4 to 8 days, resulting in about 3,000 total rated news stories, i.e. on average 300 stories per user. While this amount of data might not lead to overall performance estimates that generalize to other users or different collection dates, it allows us to analyze the relative performance contributions of the short-term and long-term user models, as well as the benefit of explicitly modeling known stories.

Evaluating the agent's performance is difficult for several reasons. First, standard evaluation methodologies commonly used in the machine learning literature, for example n-fold cross-validation, are not applicable to this scenario. This is mainly due to the chronological order of the training examples, which cannot be presented to the learning algorithm in random order, without skewing results. Second, if we measure the agent's performance on a daily basis, we not only measure the effects of the agent's updated user model, but also of the changing distribution of news stories. Finally, we are trying to approximate a model of user interests that can be assumed to be neither static nor consistent. A user going through the same list of stories at a later time might assign different labels.

We chose to evaluate the agent's performance as follows. We divided each user's data into separate training sessions, corresponding to the user's use of the system, i.e. typically one training session per day. We started to train the algorithm with all rated examples from the first training session, and compared its predictions for class labels of stories from the second training session to the user's ratings. We then incremented the training set session by session and measured the agent's performance on the following session. Finally, we averaged the results over all users. This methodology models the way the system is used realistically, because all training data available up to a certain day was used to classify stories.

In addition to the system's classification accuracy, i.e. the proportion of correctly classified news stories, we used common Information Retrieval performance measures, *precision, recall* and F_1 to evaluate the system. In our domain, precision is the percentage of stories classified as interesting that are interesting, and recall is the percentage of interesting stories that were classified as interesting. It is important to evaluate precision and recall in conjunction, because it is easy to optimize either one separately. For a classifier to be useful for our purposes we demand that it be precise as well as have high recall. In order to quantify this with a single measure, Lewis and Gale (1994) proposed the *F-measure*, a weighted combination of precision and recall that produces scores ranging from 0 to 1. Here we assign equal importance to precision and recall, resulting in the following definition for F_1:

$$F_1 = \frac{2 \cdot precision \cdot recall}{precision + recall}$$

Figure 2 summarizes the system's performance averaged over all users, showing a rapid increase of classification performance during the first three training sessions. Results for more training sessions are only available for a subset of the users and therefore cannot be presented in one plot. However, results for users that collected data of up to 8 training sessions revealed that performance increases rapidly during the first few training sessions and then starts to fluctuate as a result of changing distributions of daily news stories. Figure 2 also shows the relative performance of the two user model components. As expected, the hybrid approach combining a short-term and long-term user model performs better than each individual approach with respect to both classification accuracy and the F_1 measure. Further inspection of the achieved performance revealed that the short-term model tends to have high precision, but low recall. In contrast, the long-term model has higher recall than the short-term model, but lower precision. Combining both models allows taking advantage of both models' strengths, resulting in substantially higher F_1 values as well as overall classification accuracy.

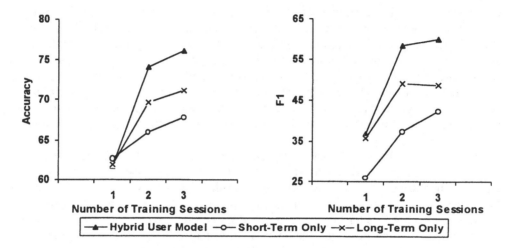

Figure 2. Overall system performance.

In an additional experiment we quantified the utility of explicitly representing stories previously presented to the user. Figure 3 compares the performance of two approaches, here labeled as knowledge-dependent and knowledge-independent classification. The knowledge-dependent approach is the full multi-strategy user modeling algorithm as described in Section 3.3. This approach can classify stories as uninteresting if they are assumed to be known by the user. In contrast, the knowledge-independent approach does not take into account that the user might already know about certain events. Algorithmically, this simply amounts to setting t_max to a value > 1 (see Section 3.1), so that predicted scores are never reduced due to the presence of similar stories in the short-term model. Figure 3 shows that knowledge-dependent classification leads to an overall increase of classification accuracy. Knowledge-dependent classification reduces the relevance scores for stories that are assumed to be known, and therefore leads to a substantial increase in precision, but to a decrease in recall (since fewer stories are classified as interesting). Since the overall increase in precision is larger than the decrease in recall, we observed both higher classification accuracy as well as increased retrieval performance as measured by the F_1 statistic.

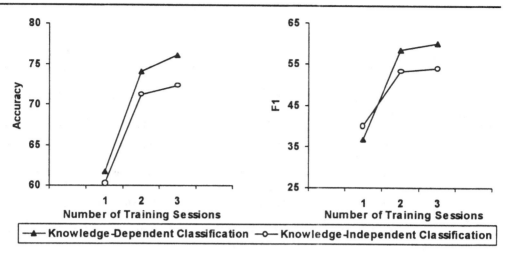

Figure 3. Effect of knowledge-dependent classification

5   Related Work

Chiu and Webb (1998) have previously studied the utility of the induction of a dual user model in the context of student modeling. While the studied domain, data representation and learning algorithms differ significantly from the text classification approach presented here, the underlying motivation for the use of a dual model is similar. In general, user modeling is a task with inherent temporal characteristics. We can assume recently collected user data to reflect the current knowledge, preferences or abilities of a user more accurately than data from previous time periods. However, restricting models to recent data can lead to overly specific models, i.e. models that classify instances that are similar to recently collected data with high precision, but perform poorly on instances that deviate from data used to induce the model. To overcome this problem, Chiu and Webb use a dual model that classifies instances by first consulting a model trained on recent data, and delegating classification to a model trained over a longer time period if the recent model is unable to make an accurate prediction.

6   Summary and Conclusions

We have presented the functionality, design and underlying algorithms of a news agent that learns about a user's interests in daily news stories. The agent uses a multi-strategy machine learning approach to induce user models that model a user's short-term and long-term interests separately. The two models were experimentally shown to complement each other. Furthermore, we have investigated the utility of explicitly representing stories a user has heard before. This allows us to take into account that a user's information need changes as a direct result of interaction with information. Similar news stories can be prevented from being presented multiple times, which was experimentally shown to lead to increased predictive performance.

References

Allan, J., Carbonell, J., Doddington, G., Yamron, J. and Yang Y. (1998). Topic detection and tracking pilot study final report. *Proceedings of the DARPA Broadcast News Transcription and Understanding Workshop,* Lansdowne, Virginia.

Balabanovic, M. (1998). *Learning to Surf: Multiagent Systems for Adaptive Web Page Recommendation.* Ph.D. Thesis, Stanford University.

Belkin, N. (1997). User modeling in Information Retrieval. Tutorial Overheads, available at http://www.scils.rutgers.edu/~belkin/um97oh/, *Sixth International Conference on User Modeling,* Chia Laguna, Sardinia.

Belkin, N., Kay, J., Tasso, C. (eds) (1997). Special Issue on User Modeling and Information Filtering. *User Modeling and User Adapted Interaction, 7*(3).

Chiu, B. and Webb, G. (1998). Using decision trees for agent modeling: improving prediction performance. *User Modeling and User-Adapted Interaction* 8:131-152.

Cohen, W. and Hirsh, H. (1998). Joins that generalize: text classification using WHIRL. In *Proceedings of the Fourth International Conference on Knowledge Discovery & Data Mining,* New York, New York, 169-173.

Duda, R., and Hart, P. (1973). *Pattern Classification and Scene Analysis.* John Wiley & Sons, New York.

Lang, K. (1995). NewsWeeder: learning to filter news. *Proceedings of the Twelfth International Conference on Machine Learning.* Lake Tahoe, CA, 331–339.

Lewis, D. and Gale, W. A. (1994). A sequential algorithm for training text classifiers. *Proceedings of the Seventeenth Annual International ACM-SIGIR Conference on.Research and Development in Information Retrieval.* London, Springer Verlag, 3-12.

Maron, M. (1961). Automatic indexing: an experimental inquiry. *Journal of the Association for Computing Machinery,* 8:404-417.

McCallum, A. and Nigam, K. (1998). A comparison of event models for naïve Bayes text classification. *American Association for Artificial Intelligence (AAAI) Workshop on Learning for Text Categorization.* Available as Technical Report WS-98-05, AAAI Press.

Pazzani M., and Billsus, D. (1997). Learning and revising user profiles: the identification of interesting web sites. *Machine Learning 27,* 313-331.

Salton, G. (1989). *Automatic Text Processing.* Addison-Wesley.

Webb, G. (ed) (1998). Special Issue on Machine Learning for User Modeling. *User Modeling and User-Adapted Interaction,* 8(1-2).

Yang, Y. (1999). An evaluation of statistical approaches to text categorization. Manuscript submitted for publication.

The Development of Behavior-Based User Models for a Computer System

By Robert Bushey[1], Jennifer Mitchell Mauney[2], and Thomas Deelman[1]

[1] SBC Technology Resources, Inc., Austin, TX, USA
[2] Mauney Consulting, Austin, TX, USA

Abstract. This paper examines the development of user models for the graphical user interface of a telecommunication computer system used during service and sales negotiations. User models enhance the requirements gathering phase of system design by capturing the diversity of the user population and capitalizing on the variety of distinguishable and categorizable strategies that affect performance. The CDM method (Categorizing, Describing, and Modeling method) was developed as a technique to generate user models. In the CDM method, the user population is first categorized into a reasonable number of groups. The behaviors for each group are described and then qualitatively and quantitatively modeled. These models are subsequently used during the system design and operational processes to optimize performance of the entire user population.

1 Introduction

In gathering requirements for the design phase of system development, it is common practice to interview and observe the behaviors of a random sample of users from the intended user population. System design requirements typically characterize the user as one entity with a single set of behaviors, namely expert, novice, or a composite of all the users. For example, if the system development team is emphasizing the high-end performance, the behaviors and characteristics that emerge are items related to the expert user. Therefore, the designers tune their comments and suggestions towards the expert users. However, in some design projects, ease of learning, training, or novice aspects are emphasized to a greater extent. In this case, interviewers focus on the comments and suggestions by novices. If there is no overwhelming performance issue or training issue that directs the team, then anecdotal behavioral information is obtained on a variety of users. Typically, these approaches limit the overall performance when the system is implemented because not all of the users' behaviors are accounted for during the design phase.

The development of a system that accommodates the diversity of the user population and improves the users' performance is optimal. One method to improve the users' performance is to categorize the system users into groups, describe and model each group's behaviors, and then incorporate this information in the design and operational processes. Currently, there is no technique that will do all three phases of the above, rather tools and techniques exist that accomplish only small portions of the desired process.

Due to this lack of an encompassing technique that incorporates categorizing, describing, and modeling users and then applying this information to the system design and process operation, the CDM (Categorize, Describe, and Model) method was developed. The purpose of the CDM method is to build a set of precise and accurate models that represent the interaction of diverse user behaviors with the system. The results of these models are then applied during the system design and operational processes to optimize performance for all users.

Since the CDM method focuses on modeling different users' behaviors, it is best implemented on systems where users' behaviors are measurably different. One illustration of users' behaviors being measurably different is shown in Figure 1.

Figure 1 presents a wide range in variability on a metric used to measure users' performance. Note that there is more than a "500%" difference from the lowest to the highest value. In the current and previous projects, a broad range of user performance has been a key indicator that user behaviors are indeed different.

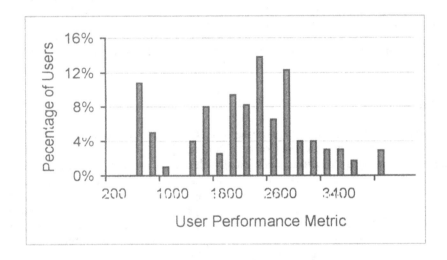

Figure 1. Histogram of user's performance.

When it has been determined that users' behaviors differ, the first step in the CDM method is to categorize the users. Both cognitive and performance measures are calculated for each user and the users are categorized into groups with similar results.

Next, a subset of users from each group are selected and their behaviors observed and documented. Behaviors are examined and should demonstrate similarities within a group and differences between groups of users. The emphasis of these descriptions focuses on behaviors that affect performance and are incorporated into the user models (Eberts, 1994; John and Kieras, 1996; and Kieras, 1996).

When the users' behaviors are well understood within a given user group, a user model is constructed. There are two types or levels of models: qualitative and quantitative. The qualitative models include statements of a user's behavior from the specific user group in certain situations or performing certain functions. The quantitative models also represent the behavior of a specific user group, but are more formal by incorporating the capability to make numerical performance predictions (Harrell and Tumay, 1995; Pegden, 1990).

2   Categorization of Users

As previously mentioned, users are categorized based upon similar behavioral characteristics that are important to system interface design and use. Users are categorized using mental workload measures, user characteristic measures, and performance measures.

Since it is expected that differences in mental workload relate to types of strategies (Shingledecker, 1980; Welford, 1978; Wei, 1997), measuring mental workload is an indirect way to measure types of strategies. Furthermore, measuring mental workload can be quick, easy to perform, and inexpensive (Eggemeier, 1988). Conversely, determining each user's strategy that is evidenced by their behaviors for each task would take a considerable amount of time, requires a lot of effort, and be very expensive.

The NASA Task Load Index (NASA-TLX) (Hart and Staveland, 1988) was chosen as a mental workload measure to facilitate the categorization of users. However, it was modified for this system. The original NASA-TLX contains six measures: mental demand, physical demand, temporal demand, performance, effort, and frustration. Physical demand was removed due to its absence in the users' duties. Effort was confused with mental demand in pre-study testing; therefore effort was removed from the TLX. Furthermore, the performance measure was removed. Users may have viewed the performance measure as a scale relating to their performance reviews. Lastly, the label "temporal demand" was changed to "time pressure". The modified TLX contained the three measures of mental demand, time pressure, and frustration.

Another method for facilitating the categorizing of users is to assess user characteristics. User characteristics refer to qualities or traits that are measurable and differ between users. Since the CDM method is based on modeling different behaviors and because user characteristics should, to some degree, reflect user behaviors, it was hypothesized that user characteristics may facilitate the categorization of users.

An example of a user characteristic is the users' ability and preferred method to navigate through the system. For the system examined, the ability to navigate is a user characteristic that was measurable, differed between users, could be modeled, and reflected users' behaviors of interacting with the system. This characteristic was also important to system design. For example, users who rated themselves as having difficulty navigating to specific areas in the system were expected to benefit from a menu-based interface. Menu-based interfaces require less mental demand (memorizing) than other types of interfaces. Users who rated themselves as having no difficulty navigating through the system and wanted to quickly navigate were expected to benefit from an interface where menus could be skipped and shortcut keys could be used.

Using preliminary surveys on a small subset of users, the general characteristics regarding navigation through the system and recall of packages/services and prices were found to be important differentiators in the system design and thus, for establishing user groups. In addition, the user characteristic of cross-selling was also found to be an important differentiator for establishing user groups. Cross-selling is the act of selling additional products or services to a customer. In the system examined, it was found that some users almost always tried to cross-sell, others never cross-sold, and still others only cross-sold in certain situations.

In applying the CDM method to this system, the users were given a survey containing the modified NASA-TLX and the user characteristic questions. The users rated the three measures (mental demand, time pressure, and frustration) of the modified NASA-TLX on a twenty-point scale. The users then performed paired comparisons between these three measures. The paired comparisons were used to weight the measures and facilitate the development of a score representing the mental workload experienced.

The users also rated themselves on the user characteristic questions regarding navigation, recall, and cross-selling. The questions were rated on a nine-point scale. An example of a user characteristic question can be seen in Table 1.

Table 1. Example of a user characteristic recall question.

How easy was it to recall the various products and services while you were on the phone with a customer?

Very Easy									Almost Impossible

Since system users from more than one center were examined, the centers were examined for consistency of user responses. Table 2 presents the modified NASA-TLX data and the normalized, collapsed user characteristic data for 262 users. Bushey, Mauney, and Deelman (1998) present this data in more detail along with a more detailed account of the categorizing section of the CDM method.

The mental workload scores display a high degree of consistency between the different centers. In addition, the normalized recall, purchase, and navigation data show consistency between centers.

The normalized data from both the modified NASA-TLX and the user characteristic questions were weighted and incorporated into an equation called the cognitive metric. The values were weighted based on their importance to system operation. The cognitive metric, along with the performance measures, facilitated the categorization of users.

Table 2. Modified NASA-TLX scores and user characteristic scores for each center.

Centers	Mental Workload Score*	Normalized Navigation Questions **	Normalized Recall Questions **	Normalized Cross-Selling Questions **
Center A	64	0.7	0.7	1.6
Center B	61	0.8	0.9	1.3
Center C	65	0.7	1.0	1.3
Center D	68	0.7	0.8	1.5
Center E	66	0.7	0.8	1.6
Center F	55	0.8	0.8	1.4
Center G	63	0.6	0.8	1.6
Average	62.7	0.7	0.8	1.5

* Denotes a range of 1-100, 1-low, 100-high.
** Normalized to individual average and denotes a 9 point Likert scale, 1-very easy, 9-impossible.

There may be multiple performance measures for a telecommunication system. These measures may include, net sales, gross sales, cross-selling sales, sales per call type, retention of sales, customer satisfaction, number of calls per time period, etc. The performance measures used for the CDM method were the primary performance measures used by the systems operation management. Currently, the users are monetarily compensated based on their performance based on these specific measures. It was hypothesized that these performance measures would also facilitate the categorization of users since the users' behaviors should be reflected in these measures.

Performance measures were acquired on the same subset of users who performed the mental workload and user characteristic survey. The performance metric is an equation that incorporates the performance measures for the specific system. Each normalized performance measure in the equation is weighted based on its importance to system operation.

In order to categorize the users into specific groups, data from the cognitive metric and performance metric were plotted. Next, Ward's minimum variance method (Milligan, 1980) was used to cluster similar data points based on both the cognitive metric and performance metric. The users were initially categorized into four groups. Observational data was then collected in order to validate and refine the original groupings.

3   Description of Users

In the describing section of the CDM method, a subset of individuals in each categorized group was observed for behaviors used to perform their tasks. In this stage of the CDM methodology, an observer unobtrusively recorded a variety of activities including the manner in which users navigated through the current interface and details of the sales negotiation performed between the user and actual customers.

Two behaviors that made a predominant impact on users' job performance were the number of cross-selling attempts made to the customer and the length of the call. For example, users who did not make any cross-selling attempts and quickly performed the service requested by the customer, rapidly completed a large number of customer sales. This behavior typically resulted in a large number of low revenue calls. Other users talked longer to the customer to determine the most likely types of products or services that they could successfully cross-sell to the customer. This behavior typically resulted in a smaller number of high revenue calls.

It was also determined that cross-selling behavior was dependent on the task of the customer. For example, customers may have the task of "I need to get a product/service". Therefore, some tasks allow for more successful cross-selling attempts by a user.

Since users from more than one call center were examined, the call centers were examined for consistency on a variety of measures. One measure was the consistency of customer tasks. Overall, customer tasks could be divided into three basic types. Table 3 presents the data for the customer tasks by center.

Table 3. Percent of customer task types for each center.

Centers	Type A Customer Tasks	Type B Customer Tasks	Type C Customer Tasks
Center A	75%	17%	8%
Center D	74%	15%	11%
Center E	79%	19%	2%
Center F	73%	19%	8%
Center H	78%	15%	7%
Center I*	74%	9%	17%
Center J*	76%	12%	13%

* After hours centers.

Centers A through H are relatively consistent for customers' tasks. Although Center E has a lower percentage of Type C customer tasks, these C tasks were not used in any of the analyses. Centers I and J are after hours centers, meaning they received calls between the hours of 5:00pm and 8:00am. These centers tended to have a relatively smaller number of Type B customer tasks and a relatively larger number of Type C customer tasks. For this reason, and because there were some job differences at these two centers, the users from Centers F and G were not included in the rest of the analyses or results. Over 1000 customer tasks (calls) were used to calculate the percentages in the table above.

Based on the number of cross-selling attempts per call and average length of call, the users were grouped by similar behaviors. The results of this grouping technique are shown with a subset of users in Figure 2.

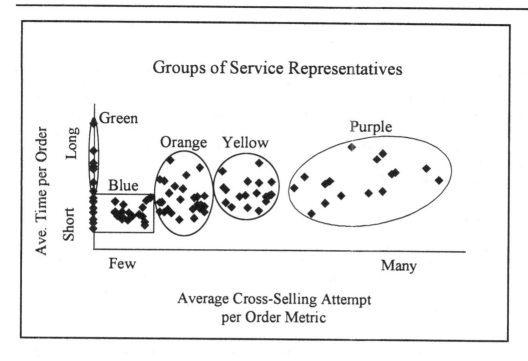

Figure 2. Groupings based on observational data.

Based on the observed, objective data, five groupings of users emerged. In the figure above, members of the Blue group are quick call takers who rarely or never make cross-selling attempts. In contrast, members of the Green group average spending over twice as much time on a call and never make sales attempts. Members of the Purple group also average spending more time on a call, but make several sales attempts.

As discussed previously, users were originally categorized into four groups. This divergence in the number of user groups is due to the detail in the data collection procedures. The users were originally categorized into four groups based on a short, subjective survey. The observed, behavioral data not only were collected using objective methods, but also contained much more detail. Due to the greater level of detail in the objective measures, the users were more distinctly categorized, resulting in five user groups.

The categorization of users based on survey and performance data was intended to be at a validity level such that the labor and cost intensive task of grouping users based on observable behaviors was not needed. For this system development, categorizing users based on the cognitive and performance data compared to categorizing users based on observable behaviors was not optimal. However, the quality of information gained from the cognitive and performance metrics greatly facilitated the system development and notably contributed to the describing and modeling sections of the CDM method. In addition, this information also contributed to the design of the user interface. For these reasons, the initial categorizing step of the CDM process was highly beneficial and necessary.

The groupings that emerged through the survey and performance data collections and from the observed behaviors provide a rich combination of information that is currently being applied to interface design. The observational data is particularly useful when the types and order of interface screens that users visit are linked with the user's group membership. The current set of user behaviors and characteristics enable detailed descriptions of each group to be made. These descriptions take the form of qualitative and quantitative models. These models represent the diversity of the user population and show the particular needs required of each group that can be incorporated into interface design.

4   Modeling the Users

The qualitative models include statements of how users within a specific user group behave in certain situations or perform certain functions. These models allow the design team to represent each of the various user groups in the design process. As the various design decisions are addressed, these models are extremely valuable by ensuring that the various user group needs are not lost in the development process.

Since there are five groups of users, five qualitative models were developed. A section of the Blue Qualitative Model included the following. The Blue group tends to be efficient call takers who most likely do only what the customer requests. They will want a system that allows them to process calls very quickly. They tend not to cross-sell. To facilitate members of the Blue group to make cross-selling attempts, incorporating sales incentives would be appropriate. In addition, some members may need to be trained on successful cross-selling techniques.

Another a section from a qualitative model included the following. The Yellow group consists of average call takers who try to engage customers with a specific task into buying at least one additional product or service. They will optimally perform using a system that allows them to easily make cross-selling attempts without having to decrease the time they spend conversing with the customer since it is the conversation with the customer that facilitates the successful cross-selling attempt.

Quantitative models represent the behaviors of the user groups in more detail than those of the qualitative models. Specifically, the quantitative models incorporate the capability to make numerical performance predictions. Items such as arrival patterns, resources allocations, and task duration times are also included and combined with the flow of incoming work. These quantitative models are developed only to the degree of detail necessary to adequately represent the user groups for the design team during the system development process.

These quantitative models show how certain groups of service representatives could perform more in accordance with business goals. The quantitative models could also be used to make predictions about changes to the system and in operational processes. For example, if operational management wanted to stress customer accessibility, these models could be used to predict how long customers would have to wait in the queue if no more than one cross-selling attempt were made per customer. It would also predict the decrease in sales if no more than one cross-selling attempt were made per customer.

5 Conclusion

Given that the users of this system differed, the CDM method facilitated the categorization of similar groups of users. It also facilitated the interface designers' understanding of the requirements of different types of users through applying qualitative and quantitative models. For example, qualitative models of the most distinctive user groups that positively contribute to operational efficiency were applied during the design stage of interface design. Specifically, each design implementation was evaluated to ensure that the needs of these user groups were accommodated. This way, the system is designed to accommodate the behavioral diversity of the user groups that most strongly contribute to meeting business goals. This method essentially allows the system to be customized to facilitate desired behavior and optimize preexisting behavior that has proven to be successful in the competitive sales and service environment.

The CDM method has only been applied to the sales negotiation telecommunication computer system described in this paper. Future work will focus on a variety of areas including the application of the CDM method to other systems including the documentation of the successes and failures of those applications, the development of a heuristic categorization technique that captures the type of data collected in the describing section of the CDM method, and the optimization of the user interface design and the system operation.

A patent has been filed regarding the work contained in this paper.

6 References

Bushey, R., Mauney, J. M., and Deelman, T. (1998). The application of a behavioral categorization technique in the development of user models. *The Proceedings of the Human Factors and Ergonomics Society 42nd Annual Meeting*, 434-438.

Eberts, Ray E. (1994). *User interface design.* Englewood Cliffs, NJ: Prentice Hall.

Eggemeier, F. T. (1988). Properties of workload assessment techniques. In P. A. Hancock and N. Meshkati (Eds.), *Human mental workload.* (pp. 139-183) Amsterdam: North-Holland

Harrell, C. R. and Tumay, K. (1995). *Simulation Made Easy.* Industrial Engineering and Management Press.

Hart, S. G., and Staveland, L. E. (1988). Development of the NASA-TLX (task load index): Results of empirical and theoretical research. In P. A. Hancock and N. Meshkati (Eds.), *Human mental workload.* (pp. 139-183) Amsterdam: North-Holland.

John, Bonnie E. and Kieras, David E. (1996). Using GOMS for user interface design and evaluation: Which technique? *ACM Transactions on Computer-Human Interaction, 3* (4), 287-319.

Kieras, David E. (1996). Task analysis and the design of functionality. In T. Allen (Ed,), *Handbook of computer science and engineering.* Boca Raton, FL: CRC Press.

Milligan, G. W. (1980). An examination of the effects of six types of error perturbation on fifteen clustering algorithms. *Psychometrika, 45,* 325–342.

Pegden, C. D., Shannon, R. E., and Sadowski, R. P. (1990*). Introduction to Simulation Using SIMAN.* McGraw – Hill, Inc.

Shingledecker, C. A. (1980). Operator strategy: A neglected variable in workload assessment. *The American Psychological Association, Division 21 Symposium on "Mental Workload Measurement: The Theory Application Interface".* Montreal, Quebec, Canada: American Psychological Association.

Wei, Z. G. (1997). *Mental load and performance at different automation levels.* Delft, Netherlands: WEI, Z. G.

Welford, A. T. (1978). Mental work-load as a function of demand, capacity, strategy, and skill. *Ergonomics, 21* (3), 151-167.

Patterns of Search: Analyzing and Modeling Web Query Refinement

Tessa Lau[1] and Eric Horvitz[2]

[1] Department of Computer Science & Engineering, University of Washington, Seattle, WA, USA
[2] Decision Theory & Adaptive Systems, Microsoft Research, Redmond, WA, USA

Abstract. We discuss the construction of probabilistic models centering on temporal patterns of query refinement. Our analyses are derived from a large corpus of Web search queries extracted from server logs recorded by a popular Internet search service. We frame the modeling task in terms of pursuing an understanding of probabilistic relationships among temporal patterns of activity, informational goals, and classes of query refinement. We construct Bayesian networks that predict search behavior, with a focus on the progression of queries over time. We review a methodology for abstracting and tagging user queries. After presenting key statistics on query length, query frequency, and informational goals, we describe user models that capture the dynamics of query refinement.

1 Introduction

The evolution of the World Wide Web has provided rich opportunities for gathering and analyzing anonymous log data generated by user interactions with network-based services. Web-based search engines such as Excite, AltaVista, and Lycos provide search services by crawling and indexing large portions of the Web. In a typical session, a user enters a string of words into the search engine's input field and receives an HTML page containing a list of web documents matching the user's query. This list may include hundreds of documents. Web search engines rank this list and present the results in small groups. The user may follow one or more of the returned links, request additional results, or refine and resubmit a query.

We review our work in developing models of users' search behaviors from log data. Our motivation is to enhance information retrieval by developing models with the ability to diagnose a user's informational goals. In this paper, we describe probabilistic models that are used to infer a probability distribution over user's goals from the time-stamped data available in server logs. More specifically, we elucidate probabilistic relationships between user goals and temporal patterns of query refinement activity. In contrast with the work of Maglio and Barrett (1997), who study several users' complete web searches, we consider only interactions with the search service itself. In distinction to the work of Silverstein et al. (1998), which reported statistics over a large corpus of unprocessed log data, we mine a corpus that has been hand-tagged to provide information about the refinements and goals associated with queries.

We shall first describe the initial data set and our methodology for transforming the data into a representation of user behavior with richer semantics. We review a set of definitions that abstract queries into classes of query refinement and informational goals. We then present key statistics of our corpus. Finally, we describe the construction of Bayesian network models that capture dependencies among variables of interest.

2   Server Log Corpus

We analyzed a data set derived from the server logs generated by the Excite Internet search engine. The server log data was made available for research purposes by Excite. The server logs capture an unspecified portion of all queries to the Excite search engine over a twenty-four hour time period on Tuesday, September 16, 1997.

Each entry in the initial log file records a single query, the time the query was input, and a globally unique identifier (GUID), which uniquely identifies each client using the search service. The total size of the data set is 48 megabytes, representing approximately one million queries. We extracted a 200-kilobyte portion of the corpus, representing 4,690 queries. The unprocessed logs contain data of the following form:

```
8A563CBE26CA77A9    970916144332    rhubarb
8A563CBE26CA77A9    970916144534    rhubarb pie
8A563CBE26CA77A9    970916144836    rhubarb pie
B04ABFA483164552    970916080514    trac right
5F5338040B2A4285    970916225207    peace, adrian paul fan club
```

The first column contains the GUID. The second column shows the time at which the query was made in YYMMDDHHMMSS format (year, month, day, hour, minutes, seconds). The remainder of the line contains the user's query.

3   Enriching the Semantics of Server Data

This server data is limited in that it shows only users' interactions with the Excite search engine. No information is provided about the user's selection of links offered by the search engine or about navigation to content beyond the search engine. We are also limited in our ability to assess the ultimate success or failure of users to find what they were seeking. Nevertheless, informational goals and query actions can be inferred via deliberate inspection of queries. We have tagged the server logs by hand to extend the data set with a human interpretation of search actions and informational goals of users.

3.1   Assigning Query Refinement Classes

In an initial phase of hand tagging, we partitioned queries into classes representing different search actions. We focused in particular on the inferred refinement strategy of query sequences. We abstracted search actions into a set of mutually exclusive refinement classes, where the refinement class of a query represents a user's intent relative to his prior query. Refinement classes include:

- New: A query for a topic not previously searched for by this user within the scope of the dataset (twenty-four hours).
- Generalization: A query on the same topic as the previous query, but seeking more general information than the previous query.
- Specialization: A query on the same topic as the previous query, but seeking more specific information than the previous query.

- Reformulation: A query on the same topic that can be viewed as neither a generalization nor a specialization, but a reformulation of the prior query.
- Interruption: A query on a topic searched on earlier by a user that has been interrupted by a search on another topic.
- Request for Additional Results: A request for another set of results on the same query from the search service. Duplicate queries appear in the data when a person requests another set of results for the query, as detailed by Spencer (1998).
- Blank queries: Log entries containing no query. These entries arise when a user clicks on the search button with no query specified or when a query by example is performed, as explained by Spencer (1998). We removed blank queries from consideration.

Our original set of refinement classes did not include interruptions. However, we found a small proportion of query sequences in which users had two distinct goals (such as lawnmowers and pornography), and interleaved queries on both of these topics over the span of our study. We introduced the *Interruption* refinement class to capture this type of behavior.

While annotating queries, we noted several opportunities for automating the assignment of refinement class. For example, a request for additional results appears in the logs as a duplicate of the previous query. Generalizations and specializations can often be identified by query contractions or extensions, or by the addition of new terms with the use of Boolean connectives such as *and* and *or*. Although complete automation of the tagging of refinement classes is likely infeasible, there are opportunities for recognizing a subset of refinements in an unsupervised manner.

3.2   Assigning Informational Goals

A second phase of annotation of the data set focused on the classification of each query in terms of our best guess about the user's goal. We created a broad ontology of fifteen informational goals. To support our inferences about a user's goals, we reviewed the hits returned by Excite on the queries and carefully examined the other queries made by the same user. We implemented an editorial tool for assigning informational goals that allowed the editor to have immediate access to web pages recommended by a later version of the Excite service for each query in the data set.

Our ontology of the informational goals of users included *Current Events, Weather, People, Health Information, Products and Services, Recreation and Sports, Entertainment, Business, Adult Content, Science and Technical, Places, Education, Career Opportunities,* and *Non-Scientific Reference*.

We were unable to classify some queries into any of the above categories and labeled these queries as *Unclassifiable*. Unclassifiable queries included foreign-language queries ("consorzio lecole" or ljuba vrtovec pribec), malformed queries for nonexistent web sites (www.hahoo .com), and short or cryptic queries with little information content such as http or hello.

Many queries were difficult to classify because of the small amount of context available or the editor's unfamiliarity with the query topics. In some cases, review of a sequence of queries revealed the nature of a query. For example, a query of dr-511 was only classifiable after noting the query pioneer 24x cd in the same session. In this context, the editor could infer that dr-511 is likely to be the model number of a CDROM drive, and that the searcher was most likely looking for a product.

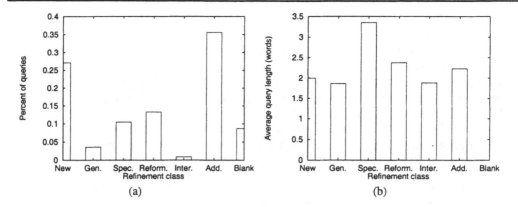

Figure 1. (a) Distribution of user query behavior in 4690 queries analyzed. Fraction of queries is indicated on left axis. (b) Graph of average query length for each refinement class. Query length for additional results refers to active query when more results are requested.

Other queries, such as harvest moon, have several meanings. Harvest Moon is the name of a video game, the name of a furniture company, another name for the September moon, an album by musical artist Neil Young, the name of a natural foods company, and a poem by Ted Hughes. In this case, we classified harvest moon as a non-scientific reference. Because of the difficulty we encountered in assigning informational goals to queries, the prospect of fully automating this coding process is unlikely.

4 Key Statistics

We shall first present several fundamental statistics we derived from the data set. Then we shall explore temporal trends. Finally, we will construct and exercise Bayesian network user models.

Users made on average 4.28 queries over the course of a day, with a standard deviation (sd) of 5.39. The average length of queries was 2.30 words (sd: 1.42). Users averaged 1.31 distinct informational goals per day (sd: 0.78), and performed 3.27 queries per goal (sd: 3.91).

4.1 Distribution and Query Length for Refinement Classes

The graph in Figure 1a displays the probability distribution over queries for the different query refinement classes. We found that most actions were either new queries or requests for additional information. Relatively few users refined their searches by specialization, generalization, or reformulation. A very small number of people interleaved searches on different topics (the *Interrupted* class of queries).

Figure 1b shows the breakdown of query length conditioned on different classes of query refinement. Specialization queries tended to contain more words than any other type of query; this was evidenced by the fact that people tended to add more words to queries in order to narrow the scope of their search. Reformulated queries tended to be longer than the initial queries they heralded from. These results highlight the opportunity for harnessing query length as an indicator of the refinement class of a query.

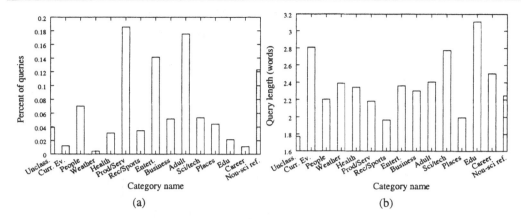

Figure 2. (a) Distribution of informational goals in tagged data set. (b) Relationship between query length and information goal of query.

4.2 Distribution and Query Length for Informational Goals

We analyzed the distribution of informational goals in the tagged corpus (Figure 2a). We found that the largest category was *Products and Services*, describing 19% of all queries. The second largest category was *Adult Content* covering 18% of the queries. The smallest category was *Weather*, which occupied less than one percent of all queries.

We explored the influence of informational category on query length (Figure 2b). Compared to the overall average query length of 2.30 words, the longest queries were in the *Education* category, with a mean of over 3 words per query, followed by *Current Events* and *Scientific/Technical*. The shortest queries were in the *Unclassified* category. This is not surprising since shorter queries contain less information and are thus harder to classify into informational goals.

5 Temporal Dynamics of Query Behavior

The analyses we have described so far capture snapshots of a potentially complex process of formulation and iterative refinement of queries. We shall now review our work on generalizing the analyses of the tagged log data to probe temporal patterns of query behavior.

5.1 Inter-query Interval and Refinement Actions

We pursued an understanding of relationships between the time taken to browse or process the results of a search and the nature of refinement actions. As one approach to this problem, we examined pairs of adjacent queries from individual users, and assigned the pairs to buckets representing different inter-query time intervals according to a predefined discretization of intervals, ranging from the shortest interval of *0-10 seconds* to the largest of *Greater than 20 minutes*. For each inter-query interval, we computed the conditional probability that the next query would be in each refinement class. The results of this analysis are displayed in the graph in Figure 3. For each time bucket, the probabilities of all of the different refinement classes sum to 1.

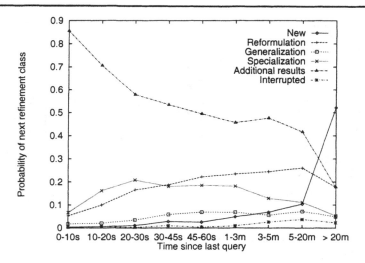

Figure 3. Relationships between the inter-query interval and next refinement class.

We discovered distinct relationships between the time interval separating adjacent query actions and the refinement class of the successive query. For example, the probability that a new query will be issued increases as the inter-query interval increases, growing to over a 0.5 probability when the inter-query interval is greater than 20 minutes. The probability of requesting additional results on a previous query is greater than 0.8 for the 0-10 second interval, but decreases to approximately 0.5 for the 1-3 minute interval, where it remains relatively stable until the interval becomes greater than 20 minutes. The probability that a user will specialize a previous query rises to a maximum in the 20-30 second interval, and holds steady at a probability of nearly 0.2 until it begins to diminish when the inter-query interval grows to 1-3 minutes. The probability of a generalization is always a small fraction of the probability of a specialization; this probability grows with the interval size, peaking in the 5-20 minute interval before diminishing. The probability of seeing a reformulation grows with the interval duration, peaking at 5-20 minutes before beginning to diminish.

The dynamics of the probabilities of alternative actions likely represent common behavioral patterns. For example, we believe the larger amount of time without interaction with the Excite service tends to indicate that the precursory query pointed the user towards a region of the Internet that provided either the desired information or a path to relevant information.

6   Constructing Probabilistic User Models

Our interest in characterizing—and predicting—a user's web search behavior under uncertainty led us to pursue the construction of general probabilistic dependency models that could take into consideration multiple observations including the timing of subsequent interactions, the pattern of query refinements, the length of a user's query, and prior probabilities of informational goals.

We have constructed Bayesian network models and parameterized the models with data drawn from the tagged Excite logs. A Bayesian network is a directed acyclic graph (DAG) representation of the joint probability distribution for a set of random variables Horvitz et al.; Pearl (1988; 1991). Nodes in Bayesian networks represent random variables and arcs represent probabilistic dependencies among pairs of variables. Several user modeling applications have benefited from Bayesian networks: Charniak and Goldman (1993) have used Bayesian networks for plan understanding; Horvitz and Barry (1995) and Jameson (1995) apply them to time-critical decision support and utility directed display of information; Conati et al. (1997), Horvitz et al. (1998) and Jameson (1995) diagnose a user's goals and needs; and Albrecht et al. (1997) model actions in a game setting using Bayesian networks.

6.1   Considering Inter-query Interval and Adjacent Actions

We constructed a Bayesian-network model for modeling a user's search behavior that considers the probabilistic relationships between inter-query intervals and the refinement classes of adjacent queries. As displayed by the Bayesian network in Figure 4, we consider relationships among the variables *User Search Action*, representing the first of two adjacent search actions, *Time Interval*, representing the inter-query interval, and *Next Search Action*, representing the next action taken with the search service. Arcs represent the assumption that the current search action and inter-query time interval may both influence the probability distribution over the next search action. As evidenced by the arc from *User Search Action* to *Time Interval*, we also allow for the possibility that the current search action also directly influences the delay before the next interaction with the service. The states for each variable in the model are displayed adjacent to the nodes.

After constructing the overall dependency model, we generated from the initial data set conditional probability tables with probabilities of the states of each variable, conditioned on combinations of the states of nodes that are its immediate parents in the directed graph. The completed Bayesian network can be harnessed to infer probability distributions over the states of all variables given the explicit setting of the value of the states of one or more variables. The probabilities computed for each state are displayed as the length of bars adjacent to the nodes representing network variables.

Figure 4a displays the inferred probability distributions for the inter-query time interval and for the next search action in the situation where we input only the information that a new query was performed. The explicit setting of the variable *User Search Action* to the state *New Query* is indicated by that state having probability 1.0 and the other states having probability zero. Following a new query, the maximum likelihood delay before the next action taken with the search service is 1-3 minutes (p=0.22), and the action with highest likelihood is a request for additional results (p=0.46).

Figure 4b highlights the ability to make inferences about the probability of the next action in response to the current query and the delay before the next action occurs. Suppose we know that no action has occurred in the 20 minutes since a new query was input. Probabilities are inferred over the next action. In this case, the maximum likelihood action is a new query (p=0.54), followed by a request for an additional page of results (p=0.25).

6.2   Extending the User Model to Consider Informational Goals

We extended the Bayesian-network introduced in section 6.1 by introducing additional context in the form of the inferred informational goals of users. We were interested in predictive power

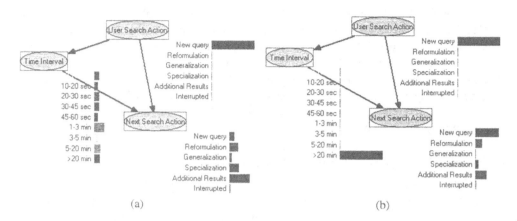

(a)   (b)

Figure 4. A Bayesian-network model representing dependencies among a user's prior action, next action, and inter-query interval. The states of each variable are listed next to the variables, and probabilities of each state are captured by the length of the adjacent bars. (a) The probability distributions for *Next Search Action* and *Time Interval* show the implications of setting the variable *User Search Action* to *New query*. (b) Display of the inferred probabilities for the next search action in the case where the user composes a new query and then does not perform another search action within 20 minutes.

associated with including the context of a user's goals in the model, and in the feasibility of inferring information goals from search action and inter-query interval information. As portrayed in Figure 5, we conditioned all of the variables in the model introduced in Section 6.1 on the variable *Search Goal*, and derived conditional probabilities for the model from the tagged data set.

Figure 5a considers the specific case where a specialization of an earlier query has occurred followed by delay of 10-20 seconds before the user takes another action with the search service. We set the initial query and time interval to these states and infer probability distributions over the states of the other variables. The inferred probability distribution over the next search action shows us that exploring additional results is the most likely action (p=0.53), with additional specialization of the query occurring at about half that likelihood (p=0.26), trailed by generalization (p=0.12) and reformulation of the query (p=0.09). The inference over goals shows that a specialization followed by another action at 10-20 seconds implies that a user is most likely searching for entertainment-related information, and then, with diminishing likelihood, for adult-related content, education, business, and places.

Figure 5b shows the probability distributions resulting from a single generalization action. Given this action, the most likely informational goal is a search for products and services, the next search action will occur within 10-20 seconds, and it will most likely be a specialization. This result evinces the common pattern of a generalization followed quickly by a specialization, perhaps because the generalization resulted in too many matching results.

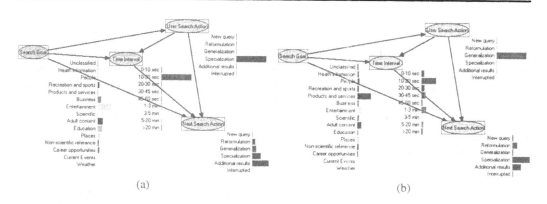

Figure 5. Bayesian network conditioning adjacent search actions and inter-query interval on the informational goals of users. (a) Probabilistic implications of a specialization followed by another action within 10-20 seconds. (b) Probabilistic implications of performing a generalization.

6.3 Opportunities for Leveraging Models of Search Dynamics

We are impressed by the power of the Bayesian network models to identify the most likely informational goals of users and the timing and nature of the next search actions given extremely limited observations of activity. Experimentation with the models reveals that informative distributions about the informational goals of users can be generated by simply considering the timing between queries. Knowledge about the status of a user's current query and the timing of the next search action often can be used to generate relatively peaked distributions over the type of refinement that will occur next.

The ability of the probabilistic models to predict user activity from such simple observations as timing highlights opportunities for enhancing the user search experience. Future search services may leverage such models to assist a user in forming queries. For example, a search service could calculate the probabilities of next search actions based on the length of the delay noted since the last search. If the user has not performed an action within two minutes, the search service might conclude that the user is likely to desire a reformulation of his query and suggest an alternate query using synonyms of the original query—or invoke a larger help system targeted at reformulation of the query.

We believe it is feasible to detect adjacent refinements in an automated manner and to use such information in conjuction with the interquery interval to diagnose a user's informational goals with probabilistic user models. As we mentioned in Section 3.1, it is often possible to identify the refinement class of a query by examining how it differs from the previous query. An ability to identify likely user goals through detecting one or more query refinements could be exploited in a variety of ways to enhance search from the user's or provider's perspectives. Consider the likely informational goal of *Entertainment* inferred in the case displayed in Figure 5. Armed with this goal, a search service might highlight links to entertainment-related web pages. Such inferences can also be harnessed by search services to perform targeted advertising.

7 Conclusion

We have reviewed analyses of a large data set of log information capturing the interaction of users with an Internet search service. We described ontologies that we created to classify query actions and informational goals, and reviewed key statistics characterizing user web search activity. We then explored patterns of query refinement over time and reviewed several trends. We constructed Bayesian networks and demonstrated the power of these probabilistic user models for capturing relationships about the dynamics of users' search activities. We presented several illustrative examples of the use of the Bayesian networks to infer the probability of a user's next action, the time delay before taking the action, and the user's informational goal, based on a consideration of partial evidence about the status of a search. Our ongoing work is focusing on further generalizing the model to consider more complex temporal patterns of activity and exploring the variety of ways that such inferences might be leveraged to enhance the search experience for users in pursuit of specific information from large unstructured corpora.

References

Albrecht, D., Zukerman, I., Nicholson, A., and Bud, A. (1997). Towards a Bayesian model for keyhole plan recognition in large domains. In Jameson, A., Paris, C., and Tasso, C., eds., *Proceedings of the Sixth International Conference on User Modeling*. New York: Springer-Verlag. 365–376.

Charniak, E., and Goldman, R. (1993). A Bayesian model of plan recognition. *Artificial Intelligence* 64(1):53–79.

Conati, C., Gertner, A., VanLehn, K., and Druzdzel, M. (1997). Online student modeling for coached problem solving using Bayesian networks. In Jameson, A., Paris, C., , and Tasso, C., eds., *Proceedings of the Sixth International Conference on User Modeling*. New York: Springer-Verlag. 231–242.

Horvitz, E., and Barry, M. (1995). Display of information for time-critical decision making. In Besnard, P., and Hanks, S., eds., *Proceedings of the Eleventh Conference on Uncertainty in Artificial Intelligence*, 296–305. San Francisco: Morgan Kaufmann.

Horvitz, E., Breese, J., and Henrion, M. (1988). Decision theory in expert systems and artificial intelligence. *International Journal of Approximate Reasoning, Special Issue on Uncertainty in Artificial Intelligence* 2:247–302.

Horvitz, E., Breese, J., Heckerman, D., Hovel, D., and Rommelse, D. (1998). The Lumiere Project: Bayesian User Modeling for Inferring the Goals and Needs of Software Users. In *Fourteenth Conference on Uncertainty in Artificial Intelligence*, 256–265. Morgan Kaufmann Publishers.

Jameson, A. (1995). Numerical uncertainty management in user and student modeling: An overview of systems and issues. *User Modeling and User-Adapted Interaction* 5:193–251.

Maglio, P. P., and Barrett, R. (1997). How to Build Modeling Agents to Support Web Searchers. In Jameson, A., Paris, C., and Tasso, C., eds., *User Modeling: Proceedings of the Sixth International Conference, UM97*, 5–16. Vienna, New York: Springer Wien New York.

Pearl, J. (1991). *Probabilistic Reasoning in Intelligent Systems: Networks of Plausible Inference*. San Francisco: Morgan Kaufmann Publishers.

Silverstein, C., Henzinger, M., Marais, H., and Moricz, M. (1998). Analysis of a Very Large AltaVista Query Log. Technical Report 1998-014, Digital Systems Research Center, Palo Alto, CA.

Spencer, G. (1998). Personal communication. Email correspondence between Eric Horvitz and Excite CTO, 8/30/98 and 9/9/98.

Building User and Expert Models by Long-Term Observation of Application Usage

Frank Linton, Deborah Joy, Hans-Peter Schaefer

The MITRE Corporation, Bedford MA, USA

Abstract. We describe a new kind of user model and a new kind of expert model and show how these models can be used to individualize the selection of instructional topics. The new user model is based on observing the individual's behavior in a natural environment over a long period of time, while the new expert model is based on pooling the knowledge of numerous individuals. Individualized instructional topics are selected by comparing an individual's knowledge to the pooled knowledge of her peers.

1 Keywords

OWL, recommender system, logging, organization-wide learning, learning recommendations.

2 Introduction

The goal of this research is to provide individualized instruction based on a new kind of user model and a new kind of expert model. This new user model is based on observing the individual's behavior in a natural environment over a long period of time, while the new expert model is based on pooling the knowledge of numerous individuals. Individualized instructional topics are selected by comparing an individual's knowledge to the pooled knowledge of her peers, which is expected to evolve over time.

This approach is quite distinct from that of other systems, such as Microsoft's Tip Wizard, which recommend new commands to users based on their logical equivalence to the less-efficient way a user may be performing a task, and it is much simpler than the more ambitious Office Assistant which uses Bayesian analysis to understand users' actions and questions and provide intelligent assistance (Horvitz, et.al., 1998). It is also distinct from that of Intelligent Tutoring Systems, which recommend learning actions and activities based on a user's capability to perform specific actions in a defined set of exercises.

Learning often takes place outside formal training or educational classes. Some of this informal learning is accomplished by the exchange of information among people with similar interests. More than ever before, information technology (IT) is the medium of work, and much informal learning in recent years has focused on IT skills.

The purpose of the research reported here is to study informal knowledge acquisition processes and, ultimately, to provide mechanisms that support them. The domain of interest is the use of information technology in the workplace, and the support mechanisms will be based on information technology as well.

As a domain of interest, information technology skills have the advantage of being observable. It is possible to observe text editing skills such as use of the outline tools. In contrast, other workplace skills such as writing skills, e.g., generating an outline, are primarily mental activities, and can only be inferred.

While some familiar workplace technologies, such as e-mail and intranets, support the processes of informal learning, other less familiar technologies such as recommender systems (Resnick and Varian, 1997), which enable the pooling and sharing of information, may be applied to support informal learning as well.

In the first section of this paper we describe the process of logging users' commands; we build models of the users of information technology as they go about their everyday tasks in the workplace. Next, we present an analysis of that data, characterize the users, provide views of the pooled data, and show how contrasting individual user models with the pooled expertise points to learning opportunities. Finally, we examine some of the other uses of this sort of user and expert modeling.

3 The Logging Process

A software application is a computer-based tool; thus details of how the application is used by individuals can be logged. The recent shift from standalone to networked PC computing has resulted in the capability of logging the actions of a large population of individuals performing a variety of tasks with a particular software application for a prolonged period of time. These logged observations can be analyzed and used for designing or refining training programs and for automated coaching. The data can be analyzed and synthesized to build models of current use, and models of expertise. Users can be individually coached by a module that compares individual performance to a synthesized expert's. Finally, the data can be analyzed to observe and promote the evolution of expertise over time.

From a practical standpoint, it is crucial that the logging process be reliable, unobtrusive, and frugal with resources, as observation takes place for extended periods of time (Kay and Thomas, 1995). The research reported here is based on logs of Microsoft Word users. The logger was written in the Word Basic macro language. In general, it is difficult to implement a logger without access to the application's source code, but Cheikes, et.al. (1998) make available a tool for instrumenting UNIX applications without modifying the application.

In our system, each time a user issues a Word command such as Cut or Paste, the command is written to the log, together with a time stamp, and then executed. The logger, called OWL for Organization-Wide Learning, comes up when the user opens Word; it creates a separate log for each file the user edits, and when the user quits Word, it sends the logs to a server where they are periodically loaded into a database for analysis. A toolbar button, Figure 1, labeled 'OWL is ON' (or OFF) informs users of OWL's state and gives them control.

Figure 1. The OWL toolbar button.

Figure 2 displays a sample OWL log. The first five lines record general information: the logger version, the date and time stamp, and the author, followed by the platform, processor, and version of Word. At this point detailed logging begins. Each time the user enters a Word command, the logger adds a line to the log file. Each line contains a time stamp, the command name, and possibly one or more arguments. For example, the line beginning 17:11:34 records these facts: at 5:11:34 p.m. the author used the FileOpen command to open the file entitled "Notes for UM'99." The author then performed some minor editing (copy, paste, etc.), then printed the file. The log does not record text a user enters; this omits some potentially useful information but preserves users' privacy and makes logging more acceptable.

Logging captures a detailed record of users' activities but the record may be sketchy for several reasons. First, an individual may also edit text on other systems without loggers, so some of their activity may not be captured. Second, a macro-based logger besides omitting text, does not capture certain other keyboard actions such as Tab and Return, nor does it capture certain mouse actions such as scrolling, nor does it distinguish *how* commands are entered (by menu, icon, or keyboard command). Finally, permitting user control over logging means that logging can be turned on and off at will, though the default is that OWL is on. To summarize then, the logged data is neither a census of the user's actions, nor a random sample, but rather an arbitrary selection of them.

```
Initiated OWL 4.4 Logging at 11/5/98 17:11:34
System Identfier/Author m300
Platform = Macintosh 8.1
Processor: 68040
Microsoft Word Version 6.0.1
17:11:34 FileOpen Frobnut:Conferences 99:UM'99:Notes for UM'99
17:11:36 Doc size: 4,790
17:12:05 EditCopy
17:12:15 EditPaste
17:12:40 EditClear
17:12:49 EditCut
17:12:55 FormatBold
17:13:12 FilePrint
17:13:34 FileDocClose
17:13:34 Doc size: 4,834
17:13:34 Filename: Notes for UM'99
17:13:34 Path: Frobnut:Conferences 99:UM'99:
```

Figure 2. Sample OWL log.

4 Analysis

This section presents an analysis of log data. Much of the data is publicly accessible (Linton, 1999). First we present summary statistics of the users and their log data. Next we describe the relative frequencies of the different types of commands. We then present a table showing relative frequencies of each individual command, and give an equation characterizing their sequential relationship. Fourth, we show how the total volume of data logged for an individual influences their apparent level of expertise. We then show that the structure of individual user data is similar to the structure of the pooled data. Finally we show how we find learning opportunities by comparing individual user models to the expert model created by pooling the knowledge of the group.

The analysis presented here is exploratory in nature. The method we have used is Naturalistic Inquiry, which, to parapingse Patton (1990, p. 40, 41) involves studying real-world situations as they unfold naturally in a non-manipulative, unobtrusive, and non-controlling manner, with openness to whatever emerges and a lack of predetermined constraints on outcomes. The point is to understand naturally occurring phenomena in their naturally occurring states. This data has been acquired from a set of users who were not randomly selected from the population, and the logged data is not a random sample of the users' actions. Therefore, all statistics presented are descriptive (of this data for this group), not predictive. Any generalizations inferred from this data must be treated cautiously until tested further.

4.1 The Subjects (Users)

The project obtained substantive logs from 16 users. The majority of them were members of one department of The MITRE Corporation's Advanced Information Systems Center. MITRE is a federally funded not-for-profit corporation performing research in the public interest. The users consisted of one group leader, ten Artificial Intelligence Engineers at four levels of responsibility, three technical staff, and two support staff. There were eight males and eight females. The users had been employed at MITRE from one to twenty-nine years with a median of eight years. The users worked on four different Apple Macintosh platforms, three versions of the Macintosh Operating System, and three versions of Word 6.0 for the Macintosh. The data presented here was obtained during 1997, the period of logging ranged from 3 to 11 months per person. The project acquired a total of 96 user-months of data.

During the time they were logged, the users -- as a group -- applied 152 of the 642 available Word commands a total of 39,321 times. The average person used 56 ($SD = 25$) different commands in the period they were logged (the average logging period was 6 months per person); applying 25 different commands 409 ($SD = 545$) times in an average month.

4.2 Pooled Knowledge: Overall

We now switch focus from the subjects to the commands they used, beginning with an overall, descriptive view. One of the most salient characteristics of the recorded data is the relative inequality in the use of each type of command. For example, as shown in Figure 3, the File commands, i.e., the commands under 'File' in Word's main menu, make up nearly 48% of all commands used, while the Help commands account for only 0.09 % of the commands logged.

Table 1 lists the 20 most frequently occurring Word commands sequenced by their frequency of occurrence, together with the percentage occurrence of each, and the cumulative percent of usage for all commands up to that point in the sequence. Command names are preceded by their main menu type, e.g., FileOpen is the Open command on the File menu. The first two commands account for 25% of all use, the first 10 commands account for 80%, the first 20 commands account for 90%, etc.

The inequalities in command counts (for example, the log shows more FileOpen commands than FileClose commands) may be accounted for by recalling that there are multiple ways of accomplishing the same effect, that is, a file may be closed by FileClose, by FileQuit, by FileSaveAs, or by crashing the system; this last method is not logged.

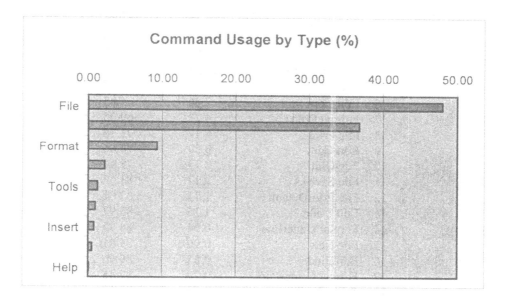

Figure 3. Command usage by type.

The chart in Figure 4 presents command usage data for the 100 most-frequently-used Word commands. The horizontal axis represents commands 1 through 100 (the names of the first 20 of these commands were itemized in Table 1). Each command's usage is indicated by the Percent line relating to the logarithmic scale on the left margin of the chart. Note that command usage (expressed in percent) varies by more than three orders of magnitude. The trendline plotted, which most-closely fits the observed data ($R^2 = 0.96$), is a power curve. An exponential curve also provides a close fit ($R^2 = 0.90$) but it badly mis-estimates the first 12 values (in contrast, the power curve mis-estimates only the first four values). The power curve equation describing Word command frequency of use is

$$y = 137x^{-1.88}$$

This equation is in contrast to the exponential distribution reported by Thomas (1996) for Sam editing commands, and the Zipf distribution reported by others (Thomas, 1996) for the UNIX domain.

The line formed by the light-colored triangles in the chart in Figure 4 plots the cumulative percent of data against the axis on the right margin of the chart. As mentioned, relatively few commands account for the bulk of the commands used.

Table 1. Command sequences and percentages.

Sequence	Command	Percent	Cumulative Percent
1	File Open	13.68	13.68
2	Edit Paste	12.50	26.18
3	File Save	11.03	37.22
4	File DocClose	10.25	47.47
5	Edit Clear	9.50	56.97
6	Edit Copy	7.86	64.83
7	Format Bold	4.22	69.05
8	File Print	4.12	73.16
9	Edit Cut	3.50	76.66
10	File Quit	2.73	79.40
11	File SaveAs	2.17	81.57
12	File PrintDefault	1.23	82.81
13	Edit Undo	1.16	83.97
14	Format Underline	0.94	84.90
15	File New	0.90	85.81
16	Edit Find	0.85	86.66
17	Format CenterPara	0.79	87.45
18	Tools Spelling	0.75	88.19
19	File PrintPreview	0.74	88.94
20	View Header	0.68	89.62

These figures and tables above are based on *all* the collected data. Since there are many short data samples and only a few long ones (Figure 5), and since the frequency of occurrence of commands is a function of the total length of an individual's data sample, it might be expected that frequently-occurring commands are somewhat over-represented, and rarely-occurring commands are somewhat under-represented. However fitting trendlines to selected subsets of data, such as the first 1000 data points of all the logs longer than 1K, and the first 4000 data points of all the logs longer than 4K revealed no systematic changes in the curve.

4.3 Pooled Knowledge: Details

One might hypothesize that it would be adequate to observe an individual for a relatively short period of time to determine their level of expertise, or hypothesize that a graph of an individual's use of distinct commands would rise over time to the user's level of knowledge and then plateau. However, contrary to what one might expect, the number of distinct commands observed is highly correlated ($R^2 = 0.83$) with the total length of an individual's data sample. In other words, the longer an individual is observed the more knowledgeable she appears to be! The explanation for this phenomenon can be found in the command trendline in Figure 4. The less frequently a command is used in general, the longer an individual must be logged before the command will appear in their record. The chart in Figure 5 plots distinct commands vs the total logged data for each individual in our study.

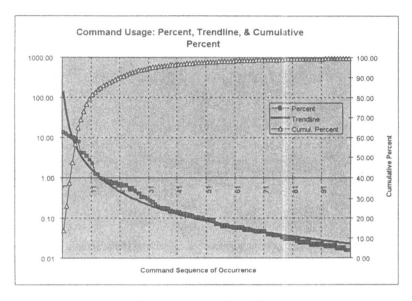

Figure 4. Command trendline.

The apparent differences in knowledge among the individuals that we observed can mostly - but not entirely - be accounted for by differences in the volume of logged data. In the following section we will examine the genuine individual differences and the learning opportunities they present.

The graph in Figure 4 shows the command frequency-of-occurrence trendline, based on all the collected data, as a power curve. We might question whether a power curve also provides the best fit to the data of individual users. Curves were fit to the data from several individual users; indeed, power curves do describe individual as well as group data.

It is tempting to hypothesize a relationship between users' job tasks and their editing tasks, such that certain sets of users would exhibit a preference for certain sets of commands, but in the observed group of users (perhaps too small and too diverse), no such relationship was found. If such a relationship were to be found, the users should then be partitioned or clustered into subgroups which share similar tasks and similar usage patterns, so that recommendations to each user are based on the pooled knowledge of their peers.

Also, one might hypothesize that more-expert users would use a different subset of commands from novices, but they did not; instead they added more commands to their repertoire.

If the hypothesis had been true, individual learning recommendations would have a different character, focusing on mastering a subset of commands at each level.

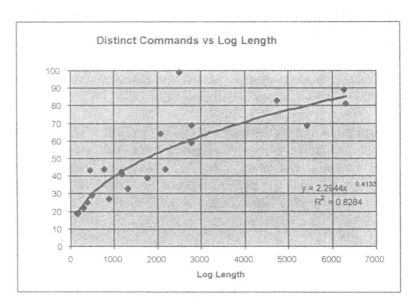

Figure 5. Distinct commands occur as a function of log length.

4.4 Individual Models Point to Learning Opportunities

Our user model is a simple one. It is the list of distinct commands each person has logged, together with their respective frequencies of use. Our expert models are equally simple; they are the commands and frequencies each person would use if her behavior were consistent with that of her peers. By comparing an individual's actual and expert models we can determine whether a particular command is not used, underused, overused, or at the boundary of use.

The pooled data exhibits strong regularities, while individual user models vary not only in the number of distinct commands used, but also in the relative proportions of the commands used. For example, the second most frequently used Edit command, the Delete Forward key, was used by only ten of the sixteen users: four users did not use the command at all and two others used it only once or twice, probably accidentally.

Let us assume for the moment that we have an adequate sample of a user's behavior. In that case, when an individual is seen not to use a command that her peers have found useful, we can assume she might use the command if she were to learn about it. Similarly, underuse of a command may indicate a willingness to learn other ways to apply the command.

Overuse may indicate reliance on a weak general-purpose command, such as Delete, when a more powerful specific command, such as DeleteWord, might be more appropriate.

A given volume of logged data will provide more reliable estimates of the user's knowledge of the more frequently used commands than of the less frequently used ones. For the less frequently used commands we must do a different sort of analysis. First, the high correlation between volume of logged data and number of distinct commands used (Figure 5) means we must be careful not to equate non-observation of a command with a lack of knowledge of that command by the user. It may be that we have not yet acquired enough data to observe it.

For analyzing the usage of the less frequently occurring commands and making learning recommendations regarding them, we turn to the notion of *confidence interval* (Triola, 1983). The confidence interval is determined by the relative frequency of use of a command and the total volume of logged data. The confidence interval describes the range around the observed value within which the actual value may lie. Thus if a user is observed to use a command zero times, and the confidence interval around the zero value includes the expected value, we cannot conclude that the user does not know the command. For infrequently used commands, the confidence interval is broad. Consequently, estimates of the limits of a user's knowledge must be tempered by the broad confidence interval required by the infrequent use of the commands and the small volume of logged data.

We are interested in determining the boundaries of a user's knowledge because, of all the commands an individual is not using, the commands just beyond the edge of a user's knowledge (in terms of frequency of use) are the most likely to be useful; they represent another learning opportunity.

We assume that the features of an application that are most useful to an individual will evolve over time, not only as her own knowledge and that of her peers grows, but also as their tasks and organizational circumstances change.

These learning opportunities (nonuse, underuse, overuse, and edge of use) can be prioritized and presented to the user in terms of learning recommendations. Learning recommendations determined by pooling the knowledge of a set of peers and by individualizing the instruction (by showing a user what her peers have found useful that she is not yet doing), may result in recommendations that the individual finds particularly helpful in deciding what to learn next, thus reducing learners' efforts while simultaneously increasing their benefits.

Earlier we noted that the high correlation between volume of observed data and number of distinct commands used (Figure 5) means we must be careful not to equate non-observation of a command with a lack of knowledge of that command on the user's part, since we may not have acquired enough data to observe it. Our first observation of a command is not necessarily the individual's first use of the command. We observe *learning* when we observe first use after confidently concluding nonuse.

5   Further Applications of the User and Expert Models

In this section we list some further research questions that can be addressed by this sort of user modeling, describe some practical applications of the models, describe some other activities which could be analyzed fruitfully in this same manner, and summarize the paper.

The user modeling described here can be applied to a number of questions regarding skill development in individuals. How do individuals acquire application software skills? What is their rate of learning? What factors influence learning rate? What factors influence plateauing? What factors distinguish expert users from others?

Researchers in the training arena have their own set of questions. How to encourage low-skilled and average users to become more expert, and experts to continue developing, evolving, and contributing their expertise? What sort of training interventions are the most effective, at the individual, group, and organizational levels? How to build systems that 'automatically' recognize, capture, and instruct new knowledge.

Besides using individual and expert models for individualized coaching and feedback, as described above, the data can be analyzed to improve the content of conventional training (what are users doing that we should be training but aren't), and to improve the methods of conventional training (what have we 'trained' users to do that they aren't actually doing). Data may also be analyzed to improve the application itself, and the data may be combined with network traffic data to analyze the effect of operator actions on network loads.

The model building process described here may be applied to modeling other kinds of user actions besides invoking application commands. For example, an organization's intranet contains a large numbers of information sources. The intranet server logs record who viewed which sources; these can be analyzed to recommend sources to peer groups of users. Lastly, certain programming languages have large numbers of commands or objects; again, an analysis of how they are used, and by whom, could result in an ongoing series of recommendations of certain objects to certain programmers.

To summarize, not only has IT become the medium in which much work is performed, IT skills have become a significant portion of workers' knowledge. In contrast to other tasks, IT tasks are observable, and can be logged and analyzed for several purposes. Here we have focused on analyzing IT usage for the purpose of constructing individual user models based on long term observation of users in their natural environment and on building expert models based on pooling the knowledge of individual users. Finally, we have shown how we might create individualized instruction based on comparing the knowledge of each individual to the pooled knowledge of her peers.

References

Cheikes, B., Geier, M., Hyland, R., Linton, F., Rodi, L., and Schaefer, H. (1998). Embedded Training for Complex Information Systems. In *Proceedings of ITS 98*. Springer-Verlag.

Horvitz, E., Breese, J., Heckerman, D., Hovel, D., and Rommelse, K. (1998). The Lumiere Project: Bayesian User Modeling for Inferring the Goals and Needs of Software Users. In *Proceedings of the Fourteenth Conference on Uncertainty in Artificial Intelligence, Madison, WI, July 1998*. pages 256-265. Morgan Kaufmann: San Francisco.

Kay, J., and Thomas, R. (1995). Studying long-term system use; computers, end-user training and learning. Communications of the ACM Volume 38 number 7.

Linton, F. (1999). Dataset: Usage of Microsoft Word Commands. A repository of 70,000 rows of data at the Machine Learning for User Modeling web site: http://zeus.gmd.de/ml4um/

Patton, M. (1990). Qualitative evaluation and research methods. 2nd. Ed. London: Sage.

Resnick, P., and Varian, H. (1997). Introduction to Special Section on Recommender Systems. Communications of the ACM Volume 40 number 3.

Thomas, R. (1996). Long term exploration and use of a text editor. Unpublished doctoral dissertation. University of Western Australia.

Triola, M. (1983). Elementary Statistics. 2nd. Ed. Menlo Park CA: Benjamin/Cummings.

Capability, Potential and Collaborative Assistance

Rosemary Luckin and Benedict du Boulay

School of Cognitive & Computing Sciences, University of Sussex, Brighton, BN1 9QH, UK

Abstract. This paper is concerned with the issue of adjusting the complexity, content and assistance in interactive learning environments (ILEs). In particular, it describes the structure and evaluation of the learner model implemented within VIS (the Vygotskian Instructional System). This software explores the way that Vygotsky's Zone of Proximal Development can be used in the design of learner models. This theoretical foundation requires the system to adopt the role of a more able assistant for a learner. It must provide appropriately challenging activities and the right quantity and quality of assistance. The learner model must track both the learner's capability and her potential in order to maintain the appropriate degree of collaborative assistance. Within VIS the learner model is a Bayesian Belief Model overlay of the domain knowledge structure. An evaluation of the system illustrates that the approach adopted by VIS promotes the construction of productive interactions with the majority of learners, across a range of abilities. The learner model within VIS is in effect an operational definition of the ZPD of each learner who interacts with the system

1 Introduction and outline of what is to come

The Zone of Proximal Development (ZPD) (Vygotsky, 1978) is created when two or more people form a collaborative learning partnership in which the more able members enable the less able members to achieve their goal. In order for a collaborator to be successful in the role of a more able learning partner she must construct a shared situation definition (Wertsch, 1984) where all members have some common knowledge about the current problem. This intersubjectivity can only be achieved if the teacher/collaborator has a dynamic representation of the learner's current knowledge and understanding. The ZPD also has a spatial analogy which quantifies a learner's potential (Vygotsky, 1986). It is the fertile area between what she can achieve independently and what she can achieve with assistance from another. In essence the ZPD requires collaboration or assistance for a learner from another more able partner. The activities which form a part of the child's effective education must be (just) beyond the range of her independent ability. The learning partner must provide appropriately challenging activities and the right quantity and quality of assistance. In VIS the learning partner role is adopted by the system, and so the learner model must track both the learner's capability and her potential in order to maintain the appropriate degree of collaborative assistance. This paper discusses the design of the learner model implemented in VIS. An evaluation of VIS enabled us to explore the types of computer experiences which appeared to lead to productive interactivity for children learning about food web concepts. Through examination of the way that the learner model in VIS helped to ensure this type of productive interactivity for each child, the following question could be addressed: What instructional leverage is gained through using the ZPD in the design framework?

The strong focus on adapting to the user by adjusting the amount of help that is initially offered is similar to the adaptive mechanisms in the SHERLOCK tutors (see e.g., Katz,

Lesgold, Eggan, & Gordin, 1993; Lesgold, Lajoie, Bunzo, & Eggan, 1992). A difference is that there is also adjustment both to the nature of the activities undertaken by users and to the language in which these activities are expressed. The emphasis which VIS places upon extending the learner beyond what she can achieve alone and then providing sufficient assistance to ensure that she does not fail also sets it apart from other system's such as that of Beck, Stern and Woolf (1997), which generate problems of controlled difficulty and aim to tailor the hints and help the system offers to the individual's particular needs. VIS extends the work done with other systems which have used the ZPD concept in the learner modelling (e.g. Gegg-Harrison, 1992).

2   VIS and the Ecolab

The Vygotskian Instructional System (VIS) is part of the Ecolab Interactive Learning Environment (ILE) which aims to help children aged 10 -11 years learn about food chains and webs. The Ecolab provides a flexible environment which can be viewed from different perspectives and run in different modes and in increasingly complex phases. In addition to providing the child with the facilities to build, activate and observe a simulated ecological community, the Ecolab also provides the child with small activities of different types. The activities are designed to structure the child's interactions with the system. They provide a goal towards which the child's actions can be directed and vary in the complexity of the relationships which the child is required to investigate. The Ecolab can assist the child in several ways. First, it can offer 5 levels of graded help specific to the particular situation; second, the difficulty level of the activity itself can also be adjusted (activity differentiation). Finally, the definition of the domain itself allows topics to be addressed by the learner at varying levels of generality.

3   The learner model in VIS

In order to provide the collaborative support just described the learner model in VIS is based upon a set of beliefs about the child's ZPD. It is an overlay of the curriculum knowledge representation and consists of two hierarchies of linked nodes. One defines the phases of environment complexity and the other defines the levels of terminology abstractness. This structure is based upon an adaptation of Goldstein's Genetic Graph (Goldstein, 1982). The resultant links between the different organisms can be divided into two main categories:

Vertical dimension links: These connect concepts within the taxonomy in terms of their level of abstraction. For example, specific instances of concepts such as *rabbit* are linked to the more general concept *herbivore* which in turn is linked to *primary consumer*. Although this taxonomy may not be entirely based upon the abstraction relationship, as the level increases the concepts are those which are less familiar to the child and more inclusive of the subordinate concepts. This dimension is represented in the Ecolab by the different levels of abstraction applied to the language used to describe the organisms in the simulated community.

Horizontal dimension links: These links define the concepts' degree of complexity within the world and the relationship which each concept bears to another (see Figure 1).

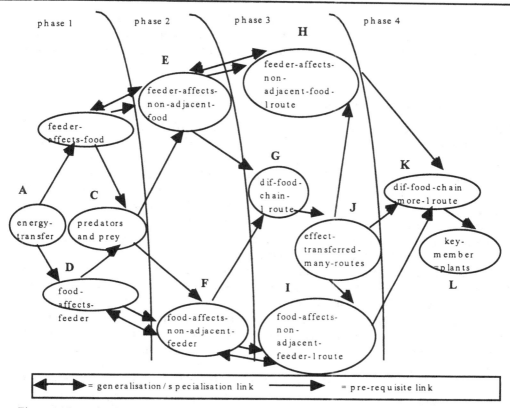

Figure 1 Network of food-web rules representing the horizontal dimension of the domain knowledge

These relationships themselves form a hierarchical structure put together in terms of the complexity of the particular relationship. For example, the *eat* relationship existing between rabbit and grass is simpler and needs to be understood before the relationship which exists between grass and fox which are non-adjacent members of the same food chain. Each relationship which is possible between organisms in the Ecolab is defined by a rule represented by a node in Figure 1. Each of these rules is associated with one of the commands the child uses to activate organisms in her environment. For example, one of the rules states that a change in the state of a *food organism affects the state of a feeder organism*. The command associated with this rule is the *eat* command. A set of activity templates is associated with each rule node, these present her with activities which focus on the associated rule. The complexity of the relationship described by the rule defines the phase (from 1 - 4) to which the node is allocated within this hierarchy. Phase 1 is the simplest and phase 4 the most complex.

In the domain knowledge representation each node represents an element of the curriculum, something which the child needs to understand: a relationship or a level of terminology abstraction. In the overlay learner model there are 2 values, or *tags*, associated with each node. The first value: the *ability belief* tag is the system's 'belief' about the child's independent ability. The second value: the *collaborative support tag* is a quantitative representation of the amount of collaborative support which the system needs to provide for the child in order to ensure her success at that node. These tags allow the modelling of the system's beliefs about which areas of the curriculum are outside the child's independent ability and the extent of the collaborative support required to bring each of these areas within her collaborative capability.

3.1 Forming Beliefs about the learner's capability

The learner model must enable VIS to quantify which areas of the curriculum are beyond what the learner can use on her own, but within the bounds of what she can use successfully when the system provides appropriate support. Within VIS this entails decisions about: which nodes in the system's model of the learner are within, or close to being within, her independent ability and therefore have a high *ability tag value* close to 1; which nodes are outside her independent ability and have a lower *ability tag value*; how much support needs to be provided in order to ensure that the learner is successful when interacting at a node with an *ability tag value* lower than 1. The overall instructional strategy is to aim for success at each node, rather than failure followed by remediation.

The amount of collaborative support a child actually used with a particular curriculum element (represented by a node in the learner model) is recorded. This may well be different to what the system predicted. This record is the node's *collaborative support tag*. Once an activity has been completed the amount of collaborative support that the system actually provided for that activity is used to assess the probability that this activity was within the child's independent ability. There are 18 possible combinations of help and differentiation (collaborative support). Each carries with it a certainty value which represents the extent to which a particular activity was within the child's independent ability when this amount of support was used. The higher the value, the greater the system's belief that this activity is within the child's <u>independent</u> ability. In VIS the probability values have been equally spaced across the range 0 - 1 and are an initial 'best guess' at appropriate values (see Table 1).

Help Level	0	0	0	1	1	1	2	2	2	3	3	3	4	4	4	5	5	5
Differentiation	0	1	2	0	1	2	0	1	2	0	1	2	0	1	2	0	1	2
Certainty	1	.83	.67	.90	.73	.56	.80	.63	.46	.70	.53	.36	.60	.43	.26	.50	.33	.16

Table 1: certainty values attributable to the possible combinations of help and differentiation

3.2 Drawing inferences about a learner's potential.

The pre-requisite relationships within the domain knowledge allow a partial ordering of the curriculum elements. In the horizontal (complexity) dimension node *n* needs to be tackled before node *n+1* where *n* is connected to *n+1* by a pre-requisite link. In the vertical (terminology abstractness) dimension the hierarchy is quite specific, level 1 first then 2 and so on. This partial ordering allows the use of conditional probabilities in a Bayesian Belief Network (BBN). Each *ability belief tag* in the learner model is a representation of the system's belief about the extent to which that element of the curriculum is within her independent ability. This information is used to quantify the child's ZPD. Evidence from interactions at a particular rule node will alter the system's belief about that node and its membership to the set of nodes which constitute the child's independent ability. In addition, if the node in question is linked to another node via a pre-requisite link it is part of an influential relationship and the system's belief about this linked node will also be affected (Reye, 1995). The learner model must be constantly updated to take into account the changing situation as the child continues to interact with the system. The conditional probability element within VIS allows the maintenance of this dynamic representation of the extent of the child's ability. Once an *ability belief tag* value has been calculated, Bayes Theorem is used as the basis for propagating a new value for each of the other *ability belief tags* in the learner model (Jensen, 1996).

In addition to the existence of influential relationships within both the horizontal and vertical dimensions, and the potential for inference passing that these relationships afford, there is also the possibility of being able to pass inferences in both directions of the network. This possibility requires that there is a specification of the reverse relationships which exist between nodes. An allowance for the possibility of forgetting as well as acknowledgement of the value assigned to the forward transition counterpart is included in these reverse relationships.

4 Using the ZPD learner model to individualise instruction

Before the child starts an activity the system will have allocated a value to the *ability belief tag* for the current rule node in the learner model. This value represents the system's belief about the extent to which this rule is within the child's ability. As the child interacts with the system and completes the activities based around this rule, the belief held by the system will vary in accordance with the amount of collaborative support the child actually uses (see Table 1). In the current implementation of VIS a very conservative view of prior knowledge is taken and so all values start at zero. All children start at the first node *energy transfer*. As soon as the child starts interacting at this rule node, records of help and differentiation level are recorded and these are used to update the *ability belief tag* from zero.

4.1 Deciding what activity to offer next

When deciding which node to offer the child next there are various possibilities: stay at the same rule node at the same level of terminology abstraction (the same activity can be re-done or a different type of activity on the same topic is tackled), or move to a new node. The new node may be a more or less complex rule node (a move forward, to the right in Figure 1, across the horizontal dimension OR backward across the horizontal dimension) and/or a rule node using a different level of terminology abstraction (a move up or down the vertical dimension)

In the current implementation of VIS decisions are made on the following basis: upon completion of each activity the *ability belief tag* values in the BBN are updated to take account of the collaborative support most recently provided (see Table 1). If the activity is other than the introductory activity the *ability belief tag* value associated with a particular node in the learner model is compared to a threshold value (currently set at .3). If the *ability belief tag* value is equal to or greater than the threshold then a new node in the curriculum will be selected. The next node is selected as the node with an associated *ability belief tag* value which comes closest to, but below, the value associated with the just completed node. This algorithm was selected in the current implementation in order to select a node which is not too far from the learner's current capability. If the threshold value has not been reached then the child is offered another activity at the same node in the curriculum. Once all activities at a node have been completed, the network is updated and searched for a node with an *ability belief tag* value which is closest to, but higher than the current node. The choice of a value of .3 for the threshold was motivated by the desire to set a value which reflected that the system is aiming to extend the child onto activities which are outside her independent ability whilst at the same time avoiding over-extension beyond what she can achieve even with support. The choice of this threshold and the implementation of this decision algorithm are issues which are on this first implementation a 'best guess'. They are areas which require further attention.

4.2 Using the model to decide how much collaborative support to offer

Recall that the educational strategy is that the learner should successfully complete any node tackled if at all possible even if that means that the system, as the more able partner, provides a huge amount of assistance. When the next node within the curriculum has been selected a decision about how much collaborative support to provide is made using the *ability belief tag* value associated with the newly selected node and the *collaborative support tag* values which contain information about how much support the child has used previously.

The level of help is the more flexible component of collaborative support. The historical record of past help given to a learner is used to calculate the amount of help considered most appropriate for a particular learner: that learner's preferred help level (pfH). The help value for each previously visited node is weighted so that the most recently tackled activities contribute most to future decisions. The value of the next level of help to be offered to the child is set at the level of pfH (preferred help level), modified by the *ability belief tag* value associated with the next node and the difficulty of the transition from current to next node. The difficulty of the transition $p(n+1|n)$ to the next node $(n+1)$ is specified in the probability table reflecting the relationship between it and the just completed node n. The lower the value assigned to the relationship, the harder the transition from n to n+1 is perceived to be. A fragment of this table for movement across the horizontal dimension of Figure 1 is shown in Table 2.

Relationship	$p(A)$	$p(B|A)$	$p(D|A)$	$P(C|B,D)$	$p(E|B,C)$	$p(F|C,D)$
Associated Value	.8	.6	.8	.5	.5	.6
Relationship	$p(G|E,F)$	$p(H|E,J)$	$p(I|J,F)$	$p(J|G)$	$p(K|H,I,J)$	$P(L|K)$
Associated Value	.8	.5	.8	.5	.7	.6

Table 2 : Conditional probabilities in the horizontal dimension

Differentiation is measured in terms of the level of differentiation employed at the start of a particular activity. When deciding which of the three levels of Differentiation to use next there are three possibilities: increase, decrease or stay the same. The aim is to ensure strenuous mental activity on the part of the child. This results in adherence to the motto "if possible reduce the amount of Differentiation used". In other words, the next level of Differentiation to be used is modified by the amount of Differentiation just implemented and the help this required.

5   Evaluation

In addition to VIS there are two other system variations in the Ecolab: WIS and NIS. WIS is a system inspired by the contingent instructional approach (Wood & Middleton, 1975) and NIS is a system which allows the user a greater amount of autonomy in her selection of the collaborative support which the system will provide. The contingent teaching strategy requires a more able partner to take more control when the learner makes an error and then relinquish some of that control if the child is subsequently successful. WIS offers the child suggestions about the type of relationship she should investigate and the type of activity she should tackle. It also sets the initial level of help which will be offered to the child the first time she asks. The learner model in WIS is simply a record of which activities have been completed, the identity of the most recent level of help used and whether or not this help lead the child towards success. By contrast, NIS maintains no learner model and allows the child herself to select the complexity and nature of the task, and the level of system support. With the exception of the quality and quantity of collaborative support given by the system and the implications this has for the interface, all three variations, VIS, WIS and NIS are identical.

The purpose of WIS and NIS is to allow a comparative evaluation of VIS. Observations of the way that learners interacted with the three systems were made as well as pre-post comparisons. This allowed an analysis of how the learner modelling in VIS affected learners of differing ability, and it also allowed a comparative analysis of the effects of switching out some (WIS) or all (NIS) of the adaptivity derived from detailed modelling. For full details of this evaluation see Luckin (1998) and Luckin and du Boulay (forthcoming). The children were all aged between 10 and 11 years of age. For the learner model within a system to claim efficacy it must be able to assist children of varying abilities. Prior to conducting this study the children had completed practice National and cognitive ability tests as part of the school's routine assessment procedure. These scores were used as the basis for allocating each child to one of three ability ranges: high, average and low.

There was a significant interaction $(F(2,17) = 3.79$ p $<.05)$ between learning gain and system variation. Overall the mean learning gain amongst VIS users was greatest at 16.67% as opposed to 10.92% for WIS and 7.29% for NIS. A post hoc analysis indicated that the significant difference (p < .05) was between VIS and both WIS and NIS. There was a significant interaction $(F(2,17) = 5.63$ p $<.01)$ between learning gain, system variation and ability. This evidence highlights the impact upon of the child's ability at the outset. A good learner model needs to be able to adjust to all abilities and offer appropriate support.

6   So Why was VIS more effective?

In order to examine the learner modelling in VIS as an implementation of its ZPD inspired design framework and to evaluate how well it adapted the system's collaborative assistance to children of differing abilities, the available assistance and the children's use of it was analysed. The range of assistance which can be made available to the child when using the Ecolab software consists of the following basic elements of assistance:

1. Extension: **Across** to a more complex node OR **Up** to a more abstract level of description in the food web curriculum
2. Collaborative Support: Alterations to the complexity of the Ecolab environment: World differentiation i.e. moving between phases OR Alterations to the difficulty of the activities: activity differentiation OR Help of 5 different levels

During the evaluation each time a child used one of these forms of assistance it was recorded. VIS and WIS learners accessed a greater number of the different types of assistance than their NIS counterparts. All of the children using VIS and 79.2% of the children using WIS accessed 4 or more of the different types of assistance available. However, 87% of the NIS children tried less than 4 different types of assistance and none of this group tried more than 4. There were members of the WIS and VIS groups who made use of all the different types of assistance available A greater percentage of VIS children used each of the different types of assistance than either WIS or NIS. A one way ANOVA examined the effects of system variation on the number of types of assistance used. This effect was significant (F(2,25) = 16.38, p <.01). A post hoc Bonferroni test indicated that the significant difference was between the number of assistance types used by NIS children and that used by WIS and VIS children (p < .05).

These results support the suggestion that VIS users took the greatest advantage of the system's collaborative support. The overall efficacy of VIS in terms of learning gains provides some support for the appropriateness of the system adjustments that VIS users experienced. However, for there to be more conclusive support for the hypothesis that VIS gains extra instructional leverage through operationally defining a child's ZPD, this assistance needs to be shown to have been effective in terms of learning gain. Figure 2 (left) differentiates the types of assistance used by learners who made an above average learning gain from the assistance used by learners making a below average learning gain. Figure 2 (right) differentiates the types of assistance used by learners according to system variation. These charts suggest that learners benefited from being challenged and extended *provided that* the activities were both differentiated appropriately and sufficient help was provided. VIS clearly extends all learners, indeed it is the only system variation to explicitly challenge learners in this way.

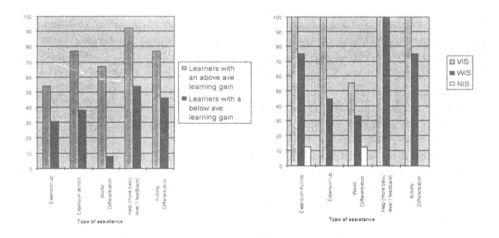

Figure 2: Assistance used by learning (left) and by system variation (right).

As has already been indicated, there was a significant interaction between the system variation a child used and her post-test learning gain. VIS was the most consistent variation across the ability groups. There is, however, some evidence that the needs of the lower ability children require further attention. Perhaps VIS extended the lower ability children too much, due perhaps to incorrect setting of probability values in the BBN. To this extent VIS has not completely met its design specification in terms of the operationalisation of a learner model that reflects the child's potential effectively. Certainly VIS adjusts to its users to a greater extent and some of its users learn significantly more than WIS and NIS users, however, these adjustments may or may not be optimal for each child's ZPD. The conditional probabilities used in the BBN were based upon information about which areas of the curriculum were known to cause children problems. These values could now be refined using the information about children's actual performance at the different nodes to inform this adjustment.

7 Conclusion

This paper has described a BBN-based learner model that operationalises Vygotsky's Zone of Proximal Development. This model has been implemented and evaluated both across a range abilities as well as against systems that switch out part of its functionality in an experiment similar to that carried out by Mark and Greer (1995). This has shown that the extra adaptivity enabled by the detailed model does lead to changes in learner behaviour and to learning gains.

Future work will involve refinement of the current model to take account of the inadequacies of its mechanisms and will increase its knowledge about how children learn about food webs. With regard to this latter point, and in accordance with the discussion of a dynamic ZPD above, the ability to alter the probability values attributed to each link in the learner model in the light of information gained as more children use the system will need consideration. Refinement of the learner model must also include attention to two particular aspects of the *individual differences* which were of particular note in the current evaluation: ability and learning style.

8 References

Beck, J., Stern, M., & Woolf, B. P. (1997). Using the student model to control problem difficulty. In A. Jameson, C. Paris, & C. Tasso (Eds.), User Modeling: Proceedings of *Sixth International Conferenceon User Modeling*, UM97. New York: Springer Wien. 278-288.

Goldstein, P. (1982). The genetic graph: a representation for the evolution of procedural knowledge. In D. Sleeman & J. S. Brown. (Eds.), *Intelligent Tutoring Systems*. New York: Academic Press.

Gegg-Harrison, T. S. (1992). Adapting instruction to the students capabilities. *Journal of Artificial Intelligence in Education*, 3(2), 169-181.

Katz, S., Lesgold, A., Eggan, G., & Gordin, M. (1993). Modelling the student in SHERLOCK II. *Journal of Artificial Intelligence in Education*, 3(4), 495-418.

Lesgold, A., Lajoie, S., Bunzo, M., & Eggan, G. (1992). SHERLOCK: A coached practice environment for an electronics troublshooting job. In J.H. Larkin & W. Chabay (Ed.), *Computer-Assisted Instructions and Intelligent Tutoring Systems*, pp 289-317 Hillsdale, NJ: Lawrence Erlbaum Associates.

Luckin, R. (1998). *'ECOLAB': Explorations in the Zone of Proximal Development* (CSRP Technical Report 386): School of Cognitive and Computing Sciences, University of Sussex.

Luckin, R. & du Boulay, J.B.H. (forthcoming). Designing a Zone of Proximal Adjustment.to appear in *International Journal of Artificial Intelligence and Education*. Volume 10, 1999

Mark, M. A., & Greer, J. E. (1995). The VCR tutor: effective instructions for device operation. *Journal of the Learning Sciences*, 4(2), 209-246.

Jensen, F. V. (1996). Bayesian networks basics. *Society for the Study of Artificial Intelligence and Simulation of Behaviour Quarterly Newsletter*, 94, 9-23.

Reye, J. (1995). A belief net backbone for student modelling. In Frasson, C.; Gauthier, G & Lesgold, A. (Eds.), *3rd International Conference on Intelligent Tutoring Systems*. Lecture notes in Computer Science 1086 Berlin: Springer. 596-604.

Vygotsky, L. S. (1978). *Mind in society: the development of higher psychological processes* (M. Cole, V. John-Steiner, S. Scribner, E. Souberman, Trans.). Cambridge, MA: Harvard University Press.

Vygotsky, L. S. (1986). *Thought and language.* Cambridge, MA: M.I.T. Press

Wertsch, J. V. (1984). The zone of proximal development: Some conceptual issues. In B. Rogoff & J. V. Wertsch (Ed.), *Children's Learning in the "Zone of Proximal Development"* (Vol. 23, pp. 7-18). San Francisco: Jossey-Bass.

Wood, D. J., & Middleton, D. (1975). A study of assisted problem solving. *British Journal of Psychology,* 66, 181-191.

Strategic Support of Algebraic Expression Writing

Mary A. Mark and Kenneth R. Koedinger

School of Computer Science, Carnegie Mellon University, Pittsburgh, PA, USA

Abstract. The examination of user data as a basis for developing production models of user behavior has been a major focus in the PAT Algebra I Tutor's development. In recent work, we have investigated relationships between related tasks and the solution strategies displayed by students. To solve a PAT Algebra I problem, students must complete several related arithmetic and algebraic tasks. The sequences in which these tasks are completed suggest problem-solving strategies of students. We have observed a characteristic pattern of students' success rates on related tasks. We have also observed that students' success on specific skills (e.g. constructing a symbolic representation) may differ depending on whether students previously carried out related tasks in the same problem (e.g. solving an analogous arithmetic question). This information has important implications for our user model and our modeling approach.

1 Introduction

Users with different experience and expertise may interact quite differently with the same application. As users move up the not-so-gentle slope from novice to expert, the strategies they use often change (Siegler and Jenkins, 1989). Ideally, user modeling applications should be able to track the use of multiple strategies by users, and suggest desirable strategies for individual users.

One ubiquitous pattern of change in the process of skill acquisition is the transition from more concrete instance-based modes of interaction (e.g. direct manipulation in spreadsheets or word processors) to the use of more abstract symbols and functions (e.g. use of formulas and style specifications). In mathematics, the concrete-instance to abstract-symbol transition corresponds broadly to the advance from arithmetic to algebraic competence. We are investigating this pattern of development with an intelligent tutoring system for grade 9 algebra, the PAT Algebra I Tutor.

In traditional views of problem-solving in this domain, students must first develop equation solving competence and then use equations to solve story problems. Even research into multiple solution strategies has focused on symbolic manipulations (Mayer, 1982). However, cognitive research by Koedinger and Nathan (1999) shows that initially students can comprehend and solve quantitative constraints better when constraints are presented in concrete verbal and numerical form rather than abstract symbolic form. Students use concrete instance-based strategies to solve quantitative constraints, in addition to the formal translate-to-algebra strategy. Instruction which connects concrete strategies to abstract ones is more effective (Koedinger and Anderson, 1998).

In this paper we present a detailed analysis of on-line data collected by PAT's user model. We focus on a set of skills related to the concrete-instance to abstract-symbol transition in mathematics, involving solution of concrete cases and writing of abstract expressions. The data collected enables us to identify different strategies chosen by students, the proportion of students choosing them, and student success rates at the tasks involved. One concern is to compare the relative difficulty of these skills. We also want to know if solving one task in a problem enables students to more successfully complete related tasks in the same problem. Is writing an expression after successful completion of a related skill really the same task as writing an expression without previously completing a related skill? How should this be modeled? Also, at a strategic level, do students prefer certain solution paths? If working on concrete cases can help students to write expressions, are students making strategic choices that reflect this? To what extent can our existing tutors track and support more effective strategy use by students? What implications does this have for our approach to student modeling?

2 The PAT Algebra I Tutor

The PAT Algebra I tutor focuses on the mathematical analysis of real world situations and the use of multiple representations for problem-solving. Checking charges on a phone bill and comparing the costs of different car rentals are examples of such real-world situations. To solve a PAT problem, students read a textual description of a situation with some questions. Students use multiple representations of the situation including words, numbers, symbols, tables, and graphs, to reason about the situation and answer questions. (Koedinger et al., 1997). At the tutor's core is a production rule model of student behavior which enables the tutor to diagnose correct and incorrect actions, provide help and feedback, and control the student's progress through the curriculum. Previous papers discuss the overall educational impact of PAT (Koedinger et al., 1997; Koedinger and Sueker, 1996) and learning of expression writing skills (Mark et al., 1998).

Figure 1 shows a partial solution for a single linear equation problem from Lesson 1 of the PAT Algebra I curriculum for the 1996-1997 school year. In Lesson 1 the student must construct a table by finding solutions to questions and by writing an expression. More complex problems and additional tools are introduced in later lessons. The Problem Description (upper left of Figure 1) describes the cost of skating at Sky Rink, based on a flat fee for renting skates and a per-hour fee for time at the rink. Students investigate the situation using a spreadsheet tool (the "Worksheet" window) and a specialized tool for identifying algebraic expressions from concrete cases (the "Pattern Finder" window). Students construct the Worksheet (lower left) by labeling the columns with quantities from the situation, entering units, writing an algebraic expression, identifying givens, and answering the numbered result unknown questions. Once the relevant quantities have been identified a student can complete the rest of the table in any order desired. The Pattern Finder (center right) can be used at any time to work out the form of the algebraic expression. On average, students spend about twelve minutes solving a tutor problem like this.

The tutor monitors and responds to students through the use of a production rule based user model. As detailed in previous papers (Koedinger et al., 1997; Mark et al., 1998), *model tracing* monitors student behavior within a problem, diagnosing student success and failure on individual skills, and generating help and feedback, through the matching and firing of production rules. The "Messages" Window (lower right of Figure 2) displays these messages to the student. *Knowledge tracing* monitors learning across problems. Information about the success and failure of a student's attempts at a skill is incorporated through mathematical modeling into a current assessment of the likelihood that the student has learned the skill. Assessments of what the student knows are used to individualize the tutor's curriculum, assigning remedial problems in areas where the student is weak. The tutor's current assessment of the student's learning is shown in the skillometer window (upper right: entitled with the student's name, e.g. "Mary Mark".)

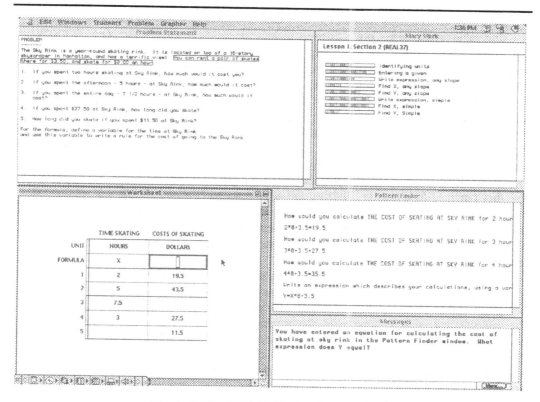

Figure 1. The PAT Algebra I Tutor, Lesson 1.

3 Expression Writing and Related Skills

One of the primary skills that the student is expected to learn is the writing of an algebraic expression to describe a problem situation. The ability to capture complex mathematical relationships in a concise algebraic form is seen as a meaningful indicator of students' understanding of a situation and the mathematical relationships involved. The ability to translate a quantitative problem situation into algebraic symbols and to use that symbolic form is important for effective use of real-world tools like symbolic calculators (Koedinger and Anderson, 1998).

Writing an expression requires the composition of an algebraic representation involving a variable, numbers, and operators. To experts, writing an algebraic expression like "8.0*x+3.50" to describe the Sky Rink problem seems like a fairly obvious process: you read the problem statement, identify the changing quantity and rate of change in the problem, check for an initial value, and put the appropriate numbers into the appropriate places in the formula. Novices find it considerably more difficult, and are affected by features of the problem situation such as the use of integer vs. non-integer numbers, and the presence and sign of y-intercepts (Mark et al., 1998).

Novices display more success with the type of concrete case called a *Result Unknown* (Koedinger and Anderson, 1998). Question 2 in the "Problem Statement" window involves a result unknown: "If you spent two hours skating at Sky Rink, how much would it cost you?"

The student is given a numeric value for the number of hours skated and asked to find the resulting value for the cost. Correct answers include the final calculated value, (e.g. "19.50") and any arithmetic expressions evaluating to this answer (e.g. "3.5+16" or "8+8+3.5"). Students may solve result unknowns by translating the problem into symbolic form and then substituting a value for the variable. They may also engage in a process of arithmetic problem-solving in which the problem is broken down into arithmetically tractable sub-tasks which are completed to obtain a result without ever combining the sub-tasks in ways that symbolically relate them. For example, a student calculating the cost of skating at Sky Rink for 2 hours might multiply 2 times 8 first, and then take this intermediate result and add 3.5 to get 19.5. These two operations are usually performed as separate arithmetic steps with equal signs in a calculator, or as separate summations in column arithmetic on paper. When asked how they obtained their answer, students will often respond "I added 16 and 3.5" and have trouble remembering how they got 16. This strategy avoids the application of skills for *composing* the two operators into a single symbolic sentence. Work by Heffernan and Koedinger (1997) suggests that composing an arithmetic symbolization may be almost as hard for students as writing an expression with a variable.

The "Pattern Finder" isolates this composition skill by asking students to write a concrete symbolization, a *Pattern Instance*. In the first concrete case in the "Pattern Finder" window, students are asked "How would you calculate the cost of skating at Sky Rink for 2 hours?" The student must indicate how he or she would get an answer, by entering a symbolic mathematical expression as a solution for the cost (e.g. "2*8+3.5"). The numeric result (e.g. "19.5") or a random mathematical expression which yields it (e.g. "10+9.5") will not be accepted. When a correct answer is given by the student (e.g. "2*8+3.5"), the Pattern Finder displays the calculation and its result as an equation (e.g. "2*8+3.5=19.5").

The Pattern Finder is structured so that students work through a progression of pattern instances, using a fixed sequence of values for x of 2, 3, and 4. After the student has solved three or more such concrete cases, he is requested to "Write an expression which describes your calculations, using a variable." In this final *Generalization* step the student is expected to examine the preceding arithmetic symbolizations for underlying patterns, and make the generalization to using a variable in place of the changing numeric value.

Consider which of these the steps in the Pattern Finder window is likely to be the most difficult for students. Is it writing an expression when x=2, x=3, x=4, or explicitly using the variable x? Most people, when asked this question, predict that the final step of generalizing from the arithmetic expressions to the algebraic expression is the most difficult. Indeed, this was our original intuition when designing the Pattern Finder. We hoped that doing multiple instances (2, 3, 4) would help students make this difficult generalization step. Data collected by PAT's user model is particularly interesting with respect to this question!

4   Student Success Rates on Related Skills

Data was collected by the PAT tutoring system during the 1996-1997 school year at Langley, a typical urban high school. Classes at Langley used the PAT tutor as part of their regular grade nine algebra I program, spending two out of five 40-minute classes per week on the tutor. As students worked, the PAT tutor saved protocol files recording student actions, their success or failure, and the production rules fired. The production model of the 1996-1997 tutor did not identify skills by order of completion, so we generated the necessary sequence-based production information from the protocol data during analysis. The data presented comes from 75 students, who completed a total of 1026 problems in the first lesson of the grade nine tutor curriculum (an average of 13.68 per student). Lesson 1 contained a demonstration problem (ignored in this analysis), 8 required problems, and a pool of 16 remedial problems. Students worked independently through the lesson. The basic curriculum was individualized for each student as the tutor assigned differing orders and numbers of problems. Not all students completed the lesson.

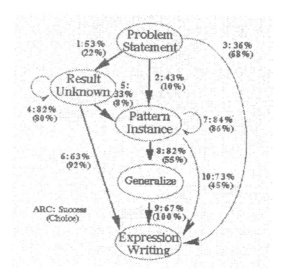

Figure 2. Student solution paths.

Figure 2 shows a partial graph of the sequences in which a student can complete the related skills when working through a problem. A node in the graph represents a state in which certain tasks have been successfully completed. A student may begin the problem by writing the expression, or do one or more result unknowns first, or use the Pattern Finder. In the Pattern Finder, a student must complete at least three pattern instances before the generalizing step. It is also possible to change course mid-way and skip from the Pattern Finder to writing the expression in the Worksheet, for example. Unrelated skills such as identifying quantities and units and entering givens were ignored. Since our main concern was to examine the effect of concrete cases on writing of expressions, we also ignored activities which occurred after writing Worksheet expressions.

For any transition in the graph, we can calculate the percentage of students in a state who follow a particular solution path out of that state by successfully completing a related action. We can also calculate the percentage of students who make this transition successfully on their first attempt at the transition skill. For the purposes of this analysis, to ensure that the success rates are comparable, succeeding at one of the related skills causes the other related skills to be treated as if they have not been previously attempted. Thus, success rates at any transition reflect the most immediate state of the student's knowledge and abilities. In this way, we avoid the problem of contamination due to a change in strategy: unsuccessfully attempting a skill early on will not affect the success rate calculated for that skill after completing a sequence of other related tasks. Table 1 contains a summary of these skill transitions, the cognitive task components which we believe are involved, and the strategy choice and success rates observed.

Table 1. Success rates and strategy choices.

Sequence of Skills Completed	Cognitive Task Components	Success Rate	Strategy Choice
1. Problem -> Result Unknown	Concrete case: Symbolization or Arithmetic problem solving	53%	22%
2. Problem -> 1st Pattern Instance	Concrete case: Symbolization	43%	10%
3. Problem -> Expression	Symbolization and Generalization	36%	68%
4. Result unknown -> Result unknown	Concrete case: Symbolization or Arithmetic problem solving	82%	80%
5. Result unknown -> Pattern	Concrete case: Symbolization	33%	8%
6. Result unknown -> Expression	Symbolization and Generalization	63%	92%
7. Pattern -> Pattern	Concrete case: Symbolization	84%	86%
8. Pattern -> Generalization	Generalization	82%	55%
9. Generalization -> Expression	Transfer	67%	100%
10. Pattern -> Expression	Generalization	73%	45%

The students' first actions give us a comparison of the relative difficulty of writing an expression, a pattern instance, and a result unknown. Students succeeded 36% of the time on their first attempt to write an expression, 43% on their first attempt at a pattern instance, and 53% on their first attempt at a result unknown. This supports our hypothesis that abstract symbolizations involving variables (expression writing) are harder for students than the solution of concrete cases (result unknown, pattern instance). This replicates the pre-and-post-test results for symbolization and result unknown skills of Koedinger and Anderson (1998), at the level of specific traceable skills. Students also found it harder to write their first pattern instance (a concrete case requiring symbolization) than to solve their first result unknown (a concrete case not requiring symbolization). This agrees with the composition effect reported by Heffernan and Koedinger (1997), in which solving the whole was more difficult than finding the sum of its parts, independent of variable use. However, PAT students found it easier to write a pattern instance than an expression when using the tutor. Somewhat in contrast, Heffernan and Koedinger reported only a small not significant effect of variable (abstract symbolization) vs. no variable (pattern instance) problems.

If we follow students through a sequence of tasks in the Pattern Finder (center right of Figure 1), we can see that students improve substantially from their first pattern instance (43%), to subsequent pattern instances (84%). Breaking this out into the first, second, third, etc. pattern instances showed a substantial increase after the first pattern was solved, and a much smaller increase for each successive instance. This supports the hypothesis that completing the arithmetic symbolization in the first concrete case is a important step enabling students to more effectively solve further pattern instances. However, the transition from the concrete cases to the abstract symbolization (82% success) is only marginally harder than doing another concrete case (84%). In contrast to our expectation, students did not have great difficulty making this generalization step (82%); rather, it was writing the first pattern instance (43%) that was most difficult for them.

Comparing the first result unknown in a sequence with later result unknowns we see that students have the most difficulty solving their first result unknown (53%), and improve considerably on later result unknowns (82%). Again, the first concrete case was the most crucial, with small increments in success rate for each later concrete case. However, after writing a result unknown, it is still substantially harder to write an expression (63%) than to do another result unknown (82%). This supports the idea that students who solve result unknowns may be doing so either by engaging in a concrete case symbolization, or through a process of arithmetic problem solving which does not involve symbolization, while students who write pattern instances are required to compose symbolic representations.

Students are more successful when writing an expression after completing some result unknowns (63%) than when writing an expression without completing any concrete cases (36%). Students using the Pattern Finder were more successful at writing expressions in the Worksheet after completing only pattern instances (73%) or both pattern instances and the generalization step (67%). While these two success rates are similar, the types of errors displayed on the transitions are different. Students who completed the generalization in the Pattern Finder had more difficulty transferring the expression back to the Worksheet than we expected. However, they did tend to make errors consistent with a transfer attempt (e.g. "Y=X*8+3.5" for "X*8+3.5"). The errors of students who went from a pattern instance to writing a Worksheet expression suggest serious difficulties in symbolization. Such students are 20% more likely to enter unrelated or unparseable solutions, and 22% more likely to request help. Protocols suggest that we may have two populations of students on this arc: one which is somewhat skillful, and one which has great difficulties.

5   Solution Paths and Strategic Choices

An examination of solution paths shows that 68% of the time, students successfully wrote the expression before completing any concrete instances in the Pattern Finder or the Worksheet. This preference may partly reflect the layout of the Worksheet: the expression appeared at the top as in a spreadsheet. Twenty-two percent of the time, students successfully calculated a result unknown first. Only 10% of the time did students begin by completing the first pattern instance in the Pattern Finder. Eighty percent of the time, students who successfully calculated one result unknown did additional result unknowns before writing the expression. After one or more result unknowns, 92% of students wrote the expression, while 8% did further concrete cases with the Pattern Finder. Eighty-six percent of the time, students who completed one pattern instance did additional concrete cases with the Pattern Finder before generalizing in the Pattern Finder or writing an expression in the Worksheet. Fifty-five percent of students who completed at least one pattern instance went on to generalize an expression in the Pattern Finder, while 45% went from the concrete instances to writing the expression in the Worksheet. Although there is evidence to suggest that students can benefit by doing concrete instances before writing expressions, students do not generally use the Pattern Finder for this. More often they solve result unknowns, but in general they follow the layout of the table and immediately try to write an expression.

A student may not depend on a single strategy while using the tutor. "Student A" is a particularly good case study for demonstrating that a student may acquire strategic knowledge about what solution paths to follow, as well as learning individual skills. "Student A" illustrates several solution strategies which students may use when working on tutor problems. Her early solution paths are somewhat erratic, but she starts to use the Pattern Finder consistently as a support tool, and then, as she becomes more proficient, leaves it behind.

In Lesson 1 the teacher introduced the tutor by working through a demonstration problem in a recommended sequence, identifying quantities and units in the Worksheet, and then completing the Pattern Finder. The Pattern Finder was recommended as a tool which students could use to find expressions if they were having difficulty. "Student A" follows the teacher through the MX demonstration problem without difficulty. She then solves her first randomly assigned problem, following the suggested sequence of steps, and starts a third problem before the class adjourns.

Despite this promising beginning, she has considerable difficulty in subsequent classes. Her initial answers are often correct or nearly correct but she frequently enters them in inappropriate cells, putting an expression in place of a variable or switching a given and a result. She is easily distracted by additional information in the problem (other givens or distractors). Once she gets off-track, she tends to flounder, and to generate increasingly unlikely solutions.

In her fourth problem, "Student A" enters a sequence of pattern instances and then, without entering an abstraction, goes directly to entering an expression in the Worksheet. She gets it wrong because she puts the expression in the wrong column. Several similar error sequences seem to convince her that it is better to work through a complete Pattern Finder sequence before entering the expression in the Worksheet.

In problems 8-12, "Student A" consistently goes to the Pattern Finder before attempting the expression or any of the concrete cases in the table. She succeeds about 50% of the time in her first attempt at a pattern instance, but once she has completed one (e.g. "8.0*2+3.5"), she almost invariably writes the rest without difficulty (90% success), and generalizes correctly (100% success). She is increasingly successful at transferring the expression back to the Worksheet.

In problems 11 and 12, "Student A" is able to write the first pattern instance without errors, even though she sees a problem of the form MX-B for the first time in Problem 12. These successes appear to give her confidence, and in problems 13 and 14, she labels the Worksheet columns, enters units, indicates the variable (X) and correctly enters the MX expression, without using the Pattern Finder. Her next problem is an MX+B form. Unfortunately she overgeneralizes from the previous two problems, and her initial MX solution is incorrect.

In many ways, "Student A" displays an ideal pattern of strategy choice. When in difficulties, she turns to the Pattern Finder as a useful tool, and uses it until she considers herself to be mastering the relevant skills, at which point she discards it. In the same way, an expert tutor might suggest that a student use tools for support on an as-needed basis.

Other students find the result unknowns in the table useful as concrete cases. "Student B" shows a consistent pattern of strategy choice (19/24 problems) in which he solves result unknowns in the Worksheet before entering an expression. In other cases (4/24), he asks for help for a result unknown and then attempts the expression directly, without completing a result unknown. His success rates show a characteristic pattern: he is successful on 30% of his first result unknowns, but his success rate on subsequent result unknowns improves to 70%. His success rate for entering a subsequent expression, however, is only 60%, indicating that symbolization with a variable still gives him difficulty. When he attempts an expression without first completing concrete cases, his success rate is only 50%.

Students who tend to go straight for the expression without doing concrete cases vary considerably in skill. Students "C" and "D" consistently complete the expression before doing other work, and succeed on 64% and 80% of their first attempts at expression writing, respectively. In contrast, Students "E" and "F" succeed about 24% and 30% of the time. These low-achieving students could potentially benefit from working out concrete cases first, but tend not to do so.

6 Conclusions

Deriving expressions through induction. We hypothesized that the cognitive tasks of symbolic composition and generalization of variables would affect students' success at expression writing and other related skills. Our results show that students find it easier to solve concrete cases that do not require symbolization than concrete cases that do; and that either type of concrete case is easier than writing an expression with a variable. Our results support the idea that students learn to construct expressions through induction from concrete cases. Requiring students to show their work symbolically can help them to make this transition. We found further support for the surprising result that students find composition much more difficult than generalization.

Several changes were made to the 1998-1999 PAT tutor and curriculum as a result of these observations. We reduced the number of concrete cases in each problem, since results suggest that solving the first concrete case in either the Pattern Finder or the Worksheet has the most impact, and subsequent cases yield little further improvement. We also moved the expression writing row to the bottom of the Worksheet after the result unknowns. This may prompt students to solve result unknowns before writing the expression. More substantial changes can also suggested:

Refining production models to reflect cognition. Our comparison of solution paths and success rates leads us to the conclusion that expression writing is not always the same skill. Depending on the sequence in which tasks are completed, tasks like expression writing may involve various cognitive components. PAT's productions should be redesigned to model both surface goals that students are trying to satisfy (expression writing, solving result unknowns, and writing pattern instances), and deeper underlying cognitive skills (symbolization, generalization, and transfer). However, a behavior like solving result unknowns, which is ambiguously related to underlying skills, may considerably complicate the tracing and attribution of production skills. Luckily, other researchers are already dealing with some of the issues this may involve, such as uncertain knowledge (Katz et al, 1994), and relating subskills and factors (VanLehn et al, 1998).

Identifying strategic behavior. As case studies for "Student A" and "Student B" suggest, students may strategically select solution paths when working on a problem. Students can learn strategic knowledge about approaching an overall problem, just as they learn individual skills. Many students, however, remain unaware of the possible benefits of strategic choices. Currently, the tutor allows students to follow a variety of strategies, but does not attempt to track their use of such strategies. Diagnosis of strategic choices along solution paths within problems could be achieved by writing production rules which are more sensitive to information about the student's current working context and solution state. We can diagnose strategic behavior within problems in the same way that we diagnose a student's current actions, in our existing modeling paradigm.

Reflective modeling of strategic behavior. A student makes strategic choices about how to solve a problem in part on the basis of self-assessments of his or her skills, as shown by "Student A" and "Student B". In our current modeling approach, information about the problem structure, the current solution state, and the student's behavior, is available to model tracing for diagnosis. Information that captures student behavior across problems is not accessible to model tracing. The tutor's assessments of what the student knows are available only to the knowledge tracing component which individualizes the curriculum. To determine not only what strategy choice a student is making, but what strategy choices a student should make, and when to recommend such actions, further information about the student is needed. Assessments of student knowledge are an important source of information, available in the tutor, which could be accessed by the production model. A reflective model that used assessments of a student's learning of skills could provide students with individualized strategic advice about desirable solution processes. "Student A", who experiences success with pattern instances, but not with result unknowns, could be given different help from "Student B", who is successful at writing result unknowns. Such a tutor could also distinguish between "Student D", who displays considerable skill at expression writing, and "Student E", who is unsuccessful at this skill. Developing a more self-reflective user model, which could utilize knowledge tracing information about individual students to teach strategic skills, would be an exciting extension of our current user modeling approach.

References

Heffernan, N. T., and Koedinger, K. R. (1997). The composition effect in symbolizing: The role of symbol production vs. text comprehension, *Proceedings of the Nineteenth Annual Meeting of the Cognitive Science Society*. Mahwah, NJ: Erlbaum.

Katz, S., Lesgold, A., Eggan, G., and Gordin, M. (1994). Modeling the student in Sherlock II. In Greer, J. E., and McCalla, G. I., eds., *Student Modelling: The Key to Individualized Knowledge-Based Instruction*, New York: Springer-Verlag. 99-125.

Koedinger, K. R., and Anderson, J. R. (1998). Illustrating principled design: The early evolution of a cognitive tutor for algebra symbolization. *Interactive Learning Environments, 5*, 161-179.

Koedinger, K. R., Anderson, J. R., Hadley, W. H., and Mark, M. A. (1997). Intelligent tutoring goes to school in the big city. *International Journal of Artificial Intelligence in Education, 8*, 30-43.

Koedinger, K. R. and Nathan, M. J. *The real story behind story problems: Effects of representations on quantitative reasoning*. Manuscript submitted for publication.

Koedinger, K. R. and Sueker, E. L. F. (1996). PAT goes to college. In *Proceedings of the Second International Conference on the Learning Sciences*, Charlottesville, VA: Association for the Advancement of Computing in Education.

Mark, M. A., Koedinger, K. R., and Hadley, W. H. (1998) Elaborating models of algebraic expression writing. In *Intelligent Tutoring Systems: 4th International Conference Proceedings (ITS '98)*. New York: Springer-Verlag.

Mayer, R. E. (1982). Different problem-solving strategies for algebra word and equation problems. *Journal of Experimental Psychology: Learning, Memory and Cognition, 8*, 448-462.

Siegler, R. S. and Jenkins, E. (1989). *How Children Discover New Strategies*. Hillsdale, N. J.: Lawrence Erlbaum Associates.

Van Lehn, K., Niu, Z., Siler, S., and Gertner, A. S. (1998) Student modeling from conventional test data: A Bayesian approach without priors. In *Intelligent Tutoring Systems: 4th International Conference Proceedings (ITS '98)*. New York: Springer-Verlag.

Modelling of Novices' Control Skills With Machine Learning

Rafael Morales and Helen Pain*

School of Artificial Intelligence, University of Edinburgh, United Kingdom

Abstract. We report an empirical study on the application of machine learning to the modelling of novice controllers' skills in balancing a pole (inverted pendulum) on top of a cart. Results are presented on the predictive power of the models, and the extent to which they were tailored to each controller. The behaviour of the participants in the study and the behaviour of an interpreter executing their models are compared with respect to the amount of time they were able to keep the pole and cart under control, the degree of stability achieved, and the conditions of failure. We discuss the results of the study, the limitations of the methodology in relation to learner modelling, and we point out future directions of research.

1 Introduction

Previous research on supporting teaching and learning cognitive tasks has concentrated on high-level skills such as problem-solving in mathematics and physics, programming, and second language learning. Acquisition of real-time control skills of the sort required for playing a musical instrument, driving a vehicle or operating a tool have received much less attention. This paper attempts to make a contribution to the latter, more neglected area, with respect to learner modelling. Descriptions of strategies followed by apprentices of the simple task of balancing a pole attached to a cart are obtained by applying machine learning techniques to traces of the apprentices' behaviour. We consider whether these can be regarded as adequate representations of the evolving control skills of novices.

Machine learning techniques have been applied to pole balancing and other controlling tasks like flying a plane, operating a crane, and production scheduling (see Bratko et al., 1997, for an overview; Michie et al., 1990; Michie and Camacho, 1994; Urbančič and Bratko, 1994). The methodology, termed *behavioural cloning* (Michie et al., 1990), was originally motivated by the difficulties encountered in getting expert controllers to produce detailed explanations of their skills that can be embedded in programs. Learner modelling differs, however, in a number of respects from expert modelling, owing to the fact that the subject is not an expert, but a beginner whose behaviour manifests faulty and inconsistent performances.

The use of machine learning techniques for learner modelling has a long history (e.g. Gilmore and Self, 1988; Langley et al., 1984; Sleeman, 1982; Webb and Kuzmycz, 1996; see also Sison and Shimura, 1988). Machine learning offers the possibility of data-driven learner modelling, focused on the actual behaviour of the learner, without the prerequisite of detailed descriptions

* We thank Tom Conlon, Donald Michie, Kaśka Porayska-Pomsta, Michael Ramscar, Shari Trewin, Angel de Vicente, and three anonymous reviewers for comments on this paper. William Cohen deserves special thanks for allowing free use of RIPPER, and his prompt and kind response to all our questions. Rafael Morales is being supported by CONACYT and the Instituto de Investigaciones Eléctricas, Mexico, under scholarship 64999/111091.

of domain knowledge and its common variations (the latter usually referred to as 'misconceptions', 'bugs', or 'mal-rules'; cf. Sison and Shimura, 1988). The reduction of assumptions about domain knowledge gives grounds for expecting a decrease in the bias of the diagnosis, and hence greater flexibility to accommodate different (human) learning styles and different conceptions of domain knowledge (Jonassen and Grabowski, 1993). However, because machine learning does not necessarily relate to human learning, claims about the psychological status of models constructed with it have varied. Advocates of the approach have either attempted to embed their techniques in broader psychological theories (e.g. Langley et al., 1984), or they have assumed to model solely competence in the task, without claiming to describe plausible cognitive processes of human learners (e.g. Gilmore and Self, 1988; Webb and Kuzmycz, 1996).

Our research differs from related work on behavioural cloning in that it focuses on apprentices, rather than experts. We are interested in making matches between subject and clone behaviour, whereas research on behavioural cloning has focused on maximising the clone's expertise. Our work differs from previous work on using machine learning for learner modelling in the time-constrained and highly dynamic nature of the domain, which demands a different approach to preparing the input data and evaluating the adequacy of the models. We focus on devising methods for diagnosing novice performers of real-time, control-like tasks, constructing representations of their strategies based on traces of their behaviour, and checking that the representations are faithful models of the novices' competence in the task. As to the psychological credibility of the models, we adopt a conservative approach: our intention is not to build accurate psychological models, but rather models that we could offer to learners as abstract representations of the strategies they follow; models that learners can identify themselves with and inspect as part of their learning process. This facet of the present work derives from our ongoing research on *participative learner modelling* (Morales et al., 1998).

To briefly summarize the rest of this paper, Section 2 describes an empirical study used to gather subject data. Section 3 we describes the behaviour of the participants in the task. The procedure of preparing the traces and inducing the models is presented in Section 4. The predictive power of the models is analysed in Section 5, their individualised nature is discussed in Section 6, and a comparison between the behaviour of participants and their respective models is made in Section 7. The general discussion of results and conclusions are given in Section 8.

2   The study

The basic task explored involved balancing a pole (inverted pendulum) attached to the top of a cart (wheeled vehicle) mounted on a straight track of finite length (Figure 1); the pole could fall over the cart only along the vertical plane passing through the track. The whole device could be controlled only by the application (or not) of a force of fixed magnitude, parallel to the track, but with a choice of left or right direction. A simulator based on existing code made available by Finton (1994) was coupled with a graphical user interface and then used instead of a physical device. In the empirical study, every *control run* started with a still pole tilted randomly ±6 degrees on a still cart placed in the centre of the track, and ended whenever a *crash* occurred (i.e. any time the cart fell off the end of the track or the pole reached a horizontal position). User input was restricted to pressing arrow keys: ↑ to start a control run, ← to push the cart to the left, and → to push the cart to the right. User keystrokes were collected for every 100 ms, the action corresponding to the last keystroke sent to the simulator, and the subsequent new state of the device displayed. The simulator was set up to calculate the state of the device in time increments of 20 ms. The combination of timings, of the interface and the simulator, resulted in a simulation five times slower than the real pole and cart device.

Six subjects took part in the study. They received a brief introduction to the task and the interface, and then were instructed to try keeping the pole in a non-horizontal position and the cart on the track. They were told to start a new control run after every crash. After five minutes of playing with the system, the participants were instructed to continue for another five minutes, and prompted to try harder in pursuing the task.

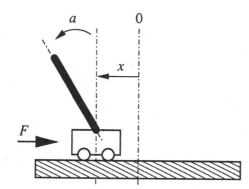

Parameter	Value
Cart mass	1 kg
Pole mass	0.1 kg
Pole length	1 m
Magnitude of force	10 N
Length of track	4.8 m

Figure 1. The pole and cart device. A position of the cart on the right (left) half of the track is taken to be positive (negative). An inclination of the pole to the right (left) of the vertical is considered positive (negative).

3 Behaviour of the participants

A straightforward measure of the performance of the participants is *control run length*, i.e. the amount of time they were able to avoid a crash. Because a participant could achieve a given control run length in several different ways, exhibiting different "control styles," we conceived an additional *index of stability* to give a more detailed account of the control process than the raw end result. The control strategy shown in Figure 2 defines a decreasing order of relevance of the state variables for controlling purposes, from the angular velocity of the pole to the position of the cart. Following it every state of the pole and cart was classified into one of five categories, in increasing order of stability: *falling* (0.0025), *tilted* (0.0474), *leaving* (0.5), *displaced* (0.9526), and *stable* (0.9975); the stability index per category was obtained by evaluating the sigmoid function $s(x) = 1/(1+e^{-3x})$ at $x = -2, -1, 0, 1, 2$. The stability of a control run was then calculated by summing up the stability of all its states, divided by the total of states in it. An overall stability index per participant was calculated as the cumulative effect of the whole set of states of the pole and cart generated by each participant. The last characteristic of the participants' behaviour we considered

falling:	**if** $\dot{a} > 0.5$ **push** right **else if** $\dot{a} < -0.5$ **push** left
tilted:	**else if** $a > 0.07$ **push** right **else if** $a < -0.07$ **push** left
leaving:	**else if** $\dot{x} > 0.4$ **push** right **else if** $\dot{x} < -0.4$ **push** left
displaced:	**else if** $x > 0.5$ **push** right **else if** $x < -0.5$ **push** left
stable:	**else** do nothing

Figure 2. Adaptation of a succesful control strategy from (Michie et al., 1990). Angles (a) are measured in radians (clockwise direction is positive), angular velocities ($\dot{a}$) in radians per second; cart positions (x) in metres, and cart velocities ($\dot{x}$) in metres per second. The adaptation consists in a change of the tresholds for the position of the cart, from zero to ± 0.5.

was the object they finally crashed, either the pole or the cart. Statistics per participant of these three aspects of their behaviour are presented in Table 1.

The behaviour exhibited by the group was far from the expert behaviour reported by Michie et al. (1990), whose expert was able to control the device for five minutes. In our study the longest control run lasted only two minutes, and even that was atypical of the performance of the participants. According to control run length, the participants seem to split into three categories: "short run" performers (participants S_3 and S_6), "medium run" performers (participants S_2 and S_4), and "long run" performers (participants S_1 and S_5). The lack of expertise and the variety in the group of participants can be regarded as a useful test of the robustness of the methodology and the adequacy of the models it produces.

Although it was possible to achieve long runs within a adventurous style (low stability), and to get short runs in a cautious manner, we expected a positive correlation between the index of stability and control run length. The results on overall stability, shown in Table 1, indicate that participants S_3 and S_6 had great difficulties at controlling the angular velocity of the pole; they achieved a very small number of stable and displaced states. S_1, S_2, and S_4 performed better, achieving higher stability scores, but below the outcome of S_5. In general, there was high variability in stability across control runs for all participants, although with a tendency to gain in stability over time. The performance of participant S_6 showed the least variation.

To prevent miscounting as a cart crash a loss of control of the pole from which it is impossible to recover even if there were more space in the track, a pole with an inclination of more than twelve degrees in either direction was regarded as crashed, as in (Bratko, 1995; Michie et al., 1990). As before, the behaviours of participants S_3 and S_6 were quite similar: both had difficulties in controlling the pole. Participants S_2 and S_4 again had similar behaviour, exhibiting less difficulties in controlling the pole than S_3 and S_6. Participant S_1 achieved relatively good control over the pole early in the study, but did not improve very much afterwards. On the other hand, participant S_5 had initial difficulties at controlling the pole, followed by a dramatic improvement.

4   Modelling procedure

All user actions on the simulated pole and cart were recorded in trace files in the general form *device status* → *user action*. The *device status* contained the values of the pole and cart positions and velocities, as displayed on the screen for the last 100 ms. The *user action* was either the

Table 1. Statistics per participant of control run length, stability index, and crashing conditions. Medians and geometric means are included because the distributions are skewed positively. Runs lasting less than 2.5 seconds were not taken into account in calculating the statistics of control run length and stability. There were five such control runs, and three of them are counted in the *Other* category in the section on crashing conditions.

Property	Statistics	S_1	S_2	S_3	S_4	S_5	S_6
Control run length	Median	23.1	16.7	9.4	18.6	19.8	9.4
(in seconds)	Geom. mean	22.6	17.1	9.4	18.5	20.3	9.7
	Mean	32.0	20.7	10.8	21.6	31.9	10.5
	Std dev.	29.1	13.3	5.9	12.9	29.2	5.0
Overall stability index		0.25	0.30	0.10	0.27	0.47	0.03
Crashing conditions	Pole	12	22	48	19	13	56
	Cart	7	8	0	9	5	2
	Other	0	0	1	0	4	0

action corresponding to the user's last keystroke in the last 100 ms, or a "no action" encoding the lack of a user keystroke in the same period. The procedure for extracting the models consisted of three steps: preparation of the traces for diagnosis, induction of a set of production rules, and informed refinement of it into a learner model.

Two problems had to be solved in the preparation stage. Due to possible delays between perception and action, we could not simply assume that the user action stored in a record corresponded to the pole and cart status in that same record: it could correspond to an earlier status of the device, displayed some hundreds of milliseconds before and hence stored in a previous record. A related problem was the treatment of no-actions, introduced by the system every time no keypress ocurred for the last 100 ms; the greater the reaction delay, the more *undesired no-actions* it caused. Observations during the study made clear that some no-actions were the correct interpretation of the participants' intentions, and hence it would be unwise for us simply to remove all no-actions from the traces.

The mean of the lag between the start of a control run and the issue of the participants' first action provides an estimated upper limit to reaction time in the task ($N = 202$, mean $= 706.4$ ms, std $= 318.0$ ms; median $= 647.5$ ms). It is likely for the task to become less dependent on raw reaction time after the first action has been issued[1]. We chose the value of 300 ms for reaction time, based on the mean lag of 343.2 ms between pairs of consecutive actions ($N = 10022$, std $= 442.3$ ms; median $= 180.0$ ms), remarkably close to the estimated reaction time of 350 ms to pressing a key in response to a simple visual stimulus produced on the screen (Cotterill, 1989, cited by Michie et al., 1990). In practice, that meant aligning the device state and user actions with a shift of three, *device status$_k$* $\rightarrow$ *user action$_{k+3}$*, and stripping the traces of all sequences of no-actions with less than three elements (cf. Michie et al., 1990).

---

[1] Decisions and actions, even if elicited in response to the present state of the device, are primed by previous states and actions; accumulated knowledge of the task allows some actions to be planned in advance; and some degree of parallelism of the cognitive processes of states perception, selection of responses, and execution of motor actions evolves.

We divided the sequence of control runs of each participant up in overlapping sections of roughly five minutes long (such that they did not split any control run). A five minute window was displaced over the sequence of control runs in steps of around thirty seconds, resulting in six sections for all participants apart from S_1, who got only four sections. Variations in the number of sections and their span came as a result of not splitting control runs and the variability in the length of control runs achieved by the participants. The groups of records resulting from the alignment, filtering, and sorting out described above were finally presented as input data to RIPPER, a domain-independent rule-learning system (Cohen, 1995).

Specific traits of the domain, such as symmetry, the range of the variables, and their interrelationship, could not be dealt with in the induction process itself. The limited amount of data, and the fact that both the starting and final states in every control run are necessarily asymmetrical, obscured the symmetry of the domain. In order to compensate for these limitations, we introduced symmetrical cases as input to the induction process: for every case *device status* → *user action*, a new case with a symmetrical device status and opposite action was included too. Post-processing of rule sets consisted of substituting a default rule for all the rules issuing no-actions.

5 Predictive power of the models

The procedure described in the previous section produced a number of rule sets per participant— four from S_1, and six from all other participants. For these rule sets to be properly called *individualised* models, they should exhibit two properties: first, they should match the subjects they were extracted from, and second, they should differ from each other[2].

For each five minute window (as described above) a model was induced. The predictive power of this model was tested on the following (roughly) thirty second window of control runs (again avoiding splitting individual runs). The final five minute window in each case was not verified. The results, presented in Table 2, were error rates between 8.4 and 44.2 percent ($N = 28$, mean $= 30.0$, std $= 8.7$). There is a significant difference between lower error rates for participant S_3, and higher error rates for S_2, S_3, S_4, and S_5 (One-way analysis of variance: $dfs = 4, 20, 24$; $F = 7.1407$, $p < 0.001$. Tukey-HSD test with significance level 0.05. Results on participant S_1 are excluded from the tests because of their different number of models).

Table 2. Predictive power of the models per participant.

Property	S_1	S_2	S_3	S_4	S_5	S_6
Mean no. of cases	366.7	154.0	167.0	213.8	235.2	207.2
Min. error (%)	27.0	26.8	21.7	28.5	23.1	8.4
Max. error (%)	36.4	39.9	42.3	44.2	41.7	21.6

Although these results are statistically highly significant when compared to raw random guessing (the binomial test of the combination of the least number of cases, $N = 118$, and the

---

[2] If the models were all very similar, they could still be individualised models, but we would not have evidence supporting that.

worst error rate gives $p < 0.001$), they do not argue for a good match by themselves. It could be argued instead that an undetermined amount of the error rates is due to errors in the alignment of states and actions (Section 4). Despite this caveat, it is worth mentioning that a mean of 72.4% of actions per participant were predicted by their models (min = 49.4, max = 93.5, std = 11.9), and that only a mean of 5.3% of actions per participant were predicted in the wrong direction (min = 0, max = 14.5, std = 4.8).

6 Differentiability of the models

Because participants in the study exhibited clear differences of behaviour in their attempts to control the pole and cart, we expected such differences to be apparent also in their models; i.e. models from the same participant should be similar among themselves and different to those from other participants. We opted for a simple dissimilarity measure between models: the level of disagreement in their predictions. A straightforward measure was defined in terms of the traces of the participants' behaviour as

$$d(M_a, M_b) = \frac{1}{\#C_a + \#C_b} \left(\sum_{c \in C_a} (M_b(c) - C_a(c))^2 + \sum_{c \in C_b} (M_a(c) - C_b(c))^2 \right), \tag{1}$$

where M_a and M_b are models; C_a and C_b are case sets from which M_a and M_b were extracted, respectively; $C_x(c)$ is the action corresponding to case c in C_x; $M_x(c)$ is the action predicted by model M_x for case c; and actions are encoded as -1 for pushing-left, 1 for pushing-right, and 0 for no-action. The problem with this measure is that it depends on the accuracy of the alignment between states and actions, as recorded in the case sets. A second measure allows to compare directly the predictions given by models on the basis of a sample of the set of states generated by the participants during the study. It is defined as

$$d(M_a, M_b) = \frac{1}{1000} \sum_{s \in S} (M_a(s) - M_b(s))^2, \tag{2}$$

where S is a sample of one thousand of such states.

Two cluster analyses were then applied to both dissimilarity matrices, using average group and Ward's method (Everitt, 1993). The number of groups were selected on the basis of visual inspection of the dendrograms produced by the clustering methods and plots generated by multidimensional scaling. The analyses suggested three and four groups using dissimilarity measure (1), and five groups using dissimilarity measure (2). Overall, they identify models corresponding to participants S_3 and S_6; Ward's methods also distinguished (some) models corresponding to S_1 and S_2; but none of the analyses distinguished between models of S_4 and S_5. The analyses agreed among them in 405 of 561 decisions (72%), and agreed with the known grouping in 360 of the decisions (64%)—there were $\binom{34}{2} = 561$ pairs of models that could be classified either in the same or different group. The best match with the known grouping was given by the Ward's method using dissimilarity measure (2): 480 of 561 decisions (86%). A binomial test shows that all results are highly significant in reproducing the correspondence between models and participants (random guess with $N = 561$ and $k = 360$ gives $p \ll 0.0001$).

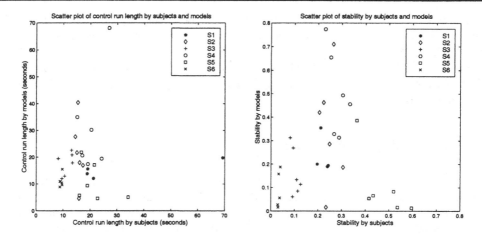

Figure 3. Comparison of control run length and stability achieved by subjects and models. For clarity, control run length for model $M_{4,6}$ is not shown (235.06 seconds).

7 Behaviour of the models

We built an interpreter for the models with a fixed reaction time of 300 ms, and ran every model fifty times, with the starting state of the pole and cart as before. The geometric mean of control run length and overall stability were measured both in the control runs produced by executing each model and in the control runs the model was derived from in the first place (Figure 3). The comparison between subjects' and models' performance gave three general results:

1. Models of participants S_3 and S_6 exhibited behaviour very similar to their respective subjects: short control runs, low stability, and difficulties in controlling the pole. Models of S_6 also showed high predictive power.
2. Models of participant S_4 usually outperformed participant S_4, with long control runs of high stability and good control. This relates to the *clean-up effect* observed by Michie et al. (1990), consisting of the behavioural clone outperforming the expert it was derived from.
3. Models of participant S_5 often performed considerably worse than participant S_5, and on several occasions performed worse than models of S_3 and S_6, despite the fact that S_5 was far better at controlling the pole and cart.

8 Discussion and conclusions

The assumption of a fixed amount of reaction time, both within a participant's control runs and among participants, made the alignment of states and actions in traces of the participants' behaviour easier, and we did not have any good arguments for doing otherwise. However, this neglects differences in sensorimotor abilities among participants, and the possibility of improvement with practice. It is possible that some participants overcame their sensorimotor limitations by taking into account additional information for short term planning, and issued actions more accurately.

Poorer control of the pole and cart produces a good sample of the whole space of possible states of the device, and corresponding control actions, from which accurate models can be induced. Behavioural cloning produces a small cleanup from low quality control and improves considerably medium quality control. In contrast, tight control of the pole and cart produces a biased sample of the whole space of control from which it is more difficult to induce a complete model of the control strategy followed by the subject. This, combined with the clean up attempted by behavioural cloning, resulted in brittle, low quality control strategies. Furthermore, participant S_5 had the most economical control strategy, in terms of the number of actions issued. That property translated into traces containing lots of *no-actions* that were overestimated by the machine learning algorithm[3], which in turn produced extremely economical models that were unable to keep the pole and cart in conditions such as those contained in the sample of the control space from which the models were induced.

Some issues concerning the application of machine learning to learner modelling, as performed in our study, need to be considered. Very little knowledge about the domain was taken into account for the production of the models. More information about the symmetry of the domain, the nature of the actions, and critical regions in the space of control during the process of induction, would produce better results. Also, the resulting models are "flat," embodying a purely reactive conception of the task. However, participants were presented with a goal: keep the pole and cart under control for as much time as possible; at least some of them appeared behaving in a goal-oriented way. In this respect, other machine learning approaches, like inductive logic programming, could be interesting alternatives to the more traditional machine learning techniques employed in our study (cf. Chiu et al., 1997). An approach to learner modelling simply based on extraction of the current model from the last minutes of the learner's behaviour appears to be too limiting, resulting in high variability of the models over time. A proper learner model maintenance module, comprising machine learning techniques as subcomponents, would be needed. Ten minutes of controlling behaviour per participant provides too little data to say anything conclusive about the learning of the participants and the evolution of their models.

In conclusion, we have presented an empirical study in applying machine learning to model novices in the task of controlling a pole on a cart. Our results indicate it succeeded in distinguishing between different subjects, hence producing clearly different models for them. A static test on data collected from the participants showed the models performed well at predicting the actions of the subjects in the short term, especially if the likely presence of noise due to our assumption of fixed reaction time is taken into account. Dynamic tests of the models consisted of executing them and comparing their performance with the original performance of the participants. A close correlation was noticed for three of the participants, while an evident discrepancy was discernible in the remaining cases. We advanced an explanation for the latter failure in terms of reaction time, the clean up of control behaviour and the high degree of stability achieved by some participants, and suggested some ways to overcome the deficiencies of our approach. Our results show machine learning can be a useful tool for diagnosis in learner modelling in domains involving control tasks, although it needs to be enhanced with more domain-specific knowledge, and embedded into a more comprehensive learner model maintenance system.

---

[3] We tried to ameliorate this effect by weighting false positives and false negatives in RIPPER. The effect was clearly appreciated in better performance of models from S_2.

References

Bratko, I., Urbančič, T., and Sammut, C. (1997). Behavioural cloning of control skill. In Michalski, R. S., Bratko, I., and Kubat, M., eds., *Machine Learning and Data Mining: Methods and Applications*. John Wiley & Sons. chapter 14, 335–351.

Bratko, I. (1995). Derivating qualitative control for dynamic systems. In Furukawa, K., Michie, D., and Muggleton, S., eds., *Machine Intelligence*, volume 14. Oxford: Clarendon Press. 367–386.

Chiu, B. C., Webb, G. I., and Kuzmycz, M. (1997). A comparison of first-order and zeroth-order induction for Input-Output Agent Modelling. In Jameson, A., Paris, C., and Tasso, C., eds., *User Modeling: Proceedings of the Sixth International Conference, UM97*, 347–358. Chia Laguna, Sardinia, Italy: Springer Wien New York.

Cohen, W. W. (1995). Fast effective rule induction. In Prieditis, A., and Russell, S., eds., *Machine Learning: Proceedings of the Twelfth International Conference*. Tahoe City, CA: Morgan Kaufmann.

Cotterill, R. (1989). *No Ghost in the Machine*. London: Heinemann.

Everitt, B. (1993). *Cluster Analysis*. London: Edward Arnold, 3 edition.

Finton, D. J. (1994). Controller-less driver for the cart-pole problem. Available on the World Wide Web at http://www.cs.wisc.edu/~finton/poledriver.html.

Gilmore, D., and Self, J. (1988). The application of machine learning to intelligent tutoring systems. In Self, J., ed., *Artificial Intelligence and Human Learning: Intelligent Computer-Aided Instruction*. London: Chapman and Hall Computing. chapter 1, 179–196.

Jonassen, D. H., and Grabowski, B. L. (1993). *Handbook of Individual Differences, Learning, and Instruction*. Lawrence Erlbaum Associates.

Langley, P., Ohlsson, S., and Sage, S. (1984). A machine learning approach to student modeling. Technical Report CMU-RI-TR-84-7, The Robotics Institute, Carnegie-Mellon University, Pittsburgh, Pennsylvania, USA.

Michie, D., and Camacho, R. (1994). Building symbolic representations of intuitive real-time skills from performance data. In Furukawa, K., Michie, D., and Muggleton, S., eds., *Machine Intelligence*, volume 13. Oxford: Clarendon Press. 385–418.

Michie, D., Bain, M., and Hayes-Michie, J. (1990). Cognitive models from subcognitive skills. In McGhee, J., Grimble, M. J., and Mowforth, P., eds., *Knowledge-Based Systems for Industrial Control*. London: Peter Peregrinus. chapter 5, 71–99.

Morales, R., Ramscar, M., and Pain, H. (1998). Cognitive effects of participative learner modelling. In Ayala, G., ed., *Proceedings of the Current Trends and Applications of Artificial Intelligence in Education Workshop*, 49–56. Mexico City, Mexico: ITESM.

Quinlan, R. J. (1993). *C4.5: Programs for Machine Learning*. Morgan Kaufmann.

Sison, R., and Shimura, M. (1988). Student modeling and machine learning. *International Journal of Artificial Intelligence in Education* 9:128–158.

Sleeman, D. H. (1982). Inferring (mal) rules from pupil's protocols. In *ECAI-82 : 1982 European Conference on Artificial Intelligence*, 160–164.

Urbančič, T., and Bratko, I. (1994). Reconstructing human skill with machine learning. In Cohn, A. G., ed., *ECAI 94: 11th European Conference on Artificial Intelligence*, 498–502. Amsterdam, The Netherlands: John Wiley & Sons.

Webb, G. I., and Kuzmycz, M. (1996). Feature based modelling: A methodology for producing coherent, consistent, dynamically changing models of agents' competencies. *User Modeling and User-Adapted Interaction* 5:117–150.

Exploiting Learning Techniques for the Acquisition of User Stereotypes and Communities

Georgios Paliouras[1], Vangelis Karkaletsis[1],
Christos Papatheodorou[2], Constantine D. Spyropoulos[1]

[1]Institute of Informatics and Telecommunications, [2]Division of Applied Technologies,
National Centre for Scientific Research (NCSR) "Demokritos", 15310, Aghia Paraskevi Attikis, Greece.
E-mail:{paliourg, vangelis, costass}@iit.demokritos.gr, papatheodor@lib.demokritos.gr

Abstract. In this paper we examine the acquisition of user stereotypes and communities automatically from users' data. Stereotypes are built using supervised learning (C4.5) on personal data extracted from a set of questionnaires answered by the users of a news filtering system. Particular emphasis is given to the characteristic features of the task of learning stereotypes and, in this context, the new notion of community stereotype is introduced. On the other hand, the communities are built using unsupervised learning (COBWEB) on data containing users' interests on the news categories covered by the news filtering system. Our main concern is whether meaningful communities can be constructed and for this purpose we specify a metric to decide on the representative news categories for each community. The encouraging results presented in this paper, suggest that established machine learning methods can be particularly useful for the acquisition of stereotypes and communities.

1 Introduction

User modeling technology aims to make information systems really user-friendly, by adapting the behaviour of the system to the needs of the individual. The importance of adding this capability to information systems is proven by the variety of areas in which user modeling has already been applied: information retrieval, filtering and extraction, adaptive user interfaces, tutoring systems. In this paper we examine the exploitation of machine learning techniques in user modeling technology for news filtering services. More specifically, we examine the organisation of the users of a news filtering system into groups with common characteristics (*stereotypes*) and groups with common interests (*communities*). The choice of the appropriate learning techniques, the use of stereotypes or communities, as well as the construction of meaningful communities are some of the important issues examined in this paper.

Stereotypes have been widely used in user modeling, but their construction has been almost exclusively manual (Brajnik & Tasso, 1994 and Kay, 1995). Attempts to automate the acquisition of stereotypes have been limited to the adaptive refinement of numeric parameters, rather than the construction of the stereotype (Rich, 1983). The manual construction process usually involves the classification of users by an expert and/or the analysis of data relating to the interests of individual users. Acquiring the stereotypes in this way is a difficult task. Similar difficulties have been encountered in other classification tasks and one solution that has yielded positive results is the automatic acquisition of knowledge, using machine learning. The work presented here focuses on the characteristics of the task of learning stereotypes and introduces the new notion of community stereotype. The method examined (*C4.5*) performs *supervised learning* from personal data extracted from questionnaires answered by the users of a news filtering system. These are data about the company the user is working in (type, department, location, size, market) and his interests on specific news categories.

The lack of sufficient personal data about the users of the news filtering system led us to the use of community modeling. Communities are built from data containing only the users' interests on news categories. These interests are determined by the users themselves. In this paper we examine *unsupervised learning* (*COBWEB*) for the acquisition of user communities. The resulting communities can be used to improve the services provided by the news filtering system. However, this can be done effectively only when the communities are meaningful, that is if they associate users with a limited set of common interests. For this reason we use a metric to decide which news categories are most representative for each community.

The work presented in this paper has been performed in the context of the research project ECRAN project (Language Engineering 2110, Telematics Applications Programme) which focuses on the adaptation of information extraction systems to new domains and users. Section 2 of the paper explains how machine learning techniques can be exploited for the acquisition of user stereotypes and communities and describes the learning algorithms that were applied in this work. Sections 3 and 4 present the setting of the two experiments for stereotype and community acquisition respectively and discuss the experimental results. Finally, section 5 describes ongoing work and introduces our plans for future work.

2   Learning User Stereotypes and Communities

Machine learning methods have been applied to user modeling problems mainly for acquiring models of individual users interacting with an information system (Bloedorn et al., 1997, Chiu, 1997 and Raskutti & Beitz, 1996). In such situations, the use of the system by an individual is monitored and the collected data are used to construct the *user's model*, i.e., his individual requirements. We are concerned with a higher level of generalisation of the users' interests: the construction of user stereotypes and communities. This task requires the application of learning techniques to user models, which are assumed to have been constructed by a separate process, either manual or automatic.

The choice of learning method depends largely on the type of training data that are available. The main distinction in machine learning research is between *supervised* and *unsupervised* learning. *Supervised learning requires the training data to be preclassified*. This means that each training item (*example*) is assigned a unique label, signifying the class in which the item belongs. In our case, this would mean that each user model must be associated with a class label out of a set of possible classes that have been defined beforehand. Given these data, the learning algorithm builds a characteristic description for each class, covering the examples of this class, i.e., the users belonging to the class, and only them, i.e., none of the users of other classes. The important feature of this approach is that the class descriptions are built conditional to the preclassification of the examples in the training set. *In contrast, unsupervised learning methods do not require preclassification of the training examples*. These methods form clusters of examples, which share common characteristics. When the cohesion of a cluster is high, i.e., the examples in it are similar, it defines a new class.

2.1 Learning User Stereotypes

The problem of learning user stereotypes cannot easily be categorised as a supervised or an unsupervised learning task. This is due to the nature of user models, i.e., the training data. Typically, user models contain two types of information for the user: personal characteristics and the user's requirements from the system. In a news-filtering system, the personal characteristics for the user could be age, education and occupation, while the user's requirements are news categories that the user is interested in. The former type of information is *system-independent*, while the latter is *system-dependent*.

The peculiarity of the task of learning user stereotypes stems from the fact that each user model is not labelled by a user class. In Fig.1 the class label is shown in a shaded box, signifying that the label is latent information, not provided in the data. However, this information acts as a link between the system-independent and the system-dependent information. The system-dependent information can be used to build a description of a user community, while the system-independent information to associate a stereotypical behaviour with that community. If the class was known for each user, then the task of learning the stereotypes could be split into two supervised learning subtasks: learning the description of a user class and learning the stereotypical behaviour of a class. Lacking the information about the class label, this two-stage approach requires the combination of an unsupervised with a supervised learning method. For instance, using an unsupervised learning method to form communities and a supervised learning method to learn the stereotypical behaviour of each community. Henceforth, this approach will be referred to as *community stereotype learning*. The symmetric approach, i.e., performing unsupervised learning on the system-independent information, is less interesting, because it contradicts the goal of maximising the similarity of user requirements within each user class.

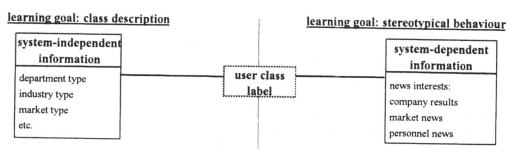

Figure 1. Information available in the training data and the role of the latent user category.

An alternative approach that is adopted here is to ignore the latent class label and use the system-dependent information as the classification data. Thus, *instead of classifying users into communities, the goal is to learn the description of the user classes associated with each of the system-dependent pieces of information*. For instance, in the news-filtering task the goal of the learning method is to construct a user class for each news category. The class description is in terms of the system-independent information, e.g. "people who work in the marketing department of financial companies are interested in company results". Such a class would ideally cover all people who are interested in company results and none of the others. This approach is a valid alternative to community stereotype learning. Its main advantage is that the construction of user classes is driven directly by the system-dependent information. There is no need for the construction of intermediate concepts, such as the user communities. In this manner, more cohesive user classes can be constructed.

The machine learning method used in this study is called *C4.5* (Quinlan, 1993) and performs induction of *decision trees*, i.e., it constructs decision trees from training data. In the case of stereotype learning, each decision tree corresponds to the stereotype for one system-dependent variable, e.g. a news category. Figure 2 shows a decision tree focusing on users' interest in company results.

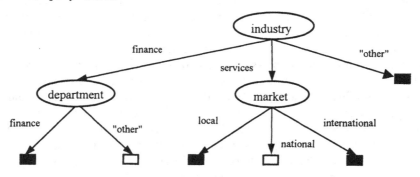

Figure 2. Part of the decision tree representing stereotypes for the company results category (clear boxes indicate interest in the category while filled boxes represent lack of interest)

The decision tree of Fig. 2 could be interpreted into the following simple stereotype rule for the company results category:

IF (industry = finance AND department ≠ finance) OR (industry = services AND market = national) THEN AND ONLY THEN the user is interested in company results.

Similar decision trees can be constructed for other news categories. The resulting set of trees is the set of stereotypes, which can be used to determine the interests of a user, based on his personal characteristics. The construction of multiple decision trees is atypical of work on decision tree induction. However, this approach is necessary here, since the goal is not to discriminate between the various news categories, but between people being interested in each category and those who are not.

2.2 Learning User Communities

User communities can be constructed automatically using an unsupervised learning method. Unsupervised learning tasks have been approached by a variety of methods, ranging from statistical clustering techniques to neural networks and symbolic machine learning. In this work, we have opted for the symbolic learning methods, because we are interested in the comprehensibility of the results. The branch of symbolic machine learning that deals with unsupervised learning is called *conceptual clustering* and a popular representative of this approach is the algorithm COBWEB (Fisher, 1987). Conceptual clustering is a type of learning by observation that is particularly suitable for summarising and explaining data. Summarisation is achieved through the discovery of appropriate clusters, which involves determining useful subsets of an object set. In unsupervised learning, the object set is the set of training examples, i.e., each example is an object. Explanation involves concept characterisation, i.e., determining a useful concept description for each cluster.

COBWEB is an incremental algorithm that uses hill-climbing search to obtain a concept (cluster) hierarchy, partitioning the object space. The term *incremental* means that objects are incorporated into the concept structure as they are observed. An object is a vector of feature-value pairs. In our case, objects are user models and features are the news categories taking the values true and false for each user. Each concept in the hierarchy produced by COBWEB, is a probabilistic structure that summarises the objects classified under that concept.

In order to construct the clusters, COBWEB uses *category utility* (Gluck & Corter, 1985), which is a probabilistic measure of the usefulness of a cluster. COBWEB incorporates objects into the concept hierarchy using four clustering operators: placing the object in an existing cluster, creating a new cluster, combining two clusters into a new one (merging) and dividing a cluster (splitting). Given a new object, the algorithm applies each of the previous operators and selects the hierarchy that maximises category utility.

3 Case Study I: Learning User Stereotypes

3.1 Experimental Setting

In the framework of the ECRAN project, we developed a prototype user modeling module (UMIE, *http://www.iit.demokritos.gr/UMIE*) that filters, according to the user's interests, the facts extracted by the ECRAN information extraction system (Benaki et al., 1997). The interests of an individual user are stored in his user model. In addition, the system uses a set of stereotypes, in order to anticipate the interests of a new user.

At a first stage, the stereotypes were built manually by analysing questionnaires answered by the users. The questionnaires contained information about the company the user is working in and the news categories that the user is interested in. Thirty-one questionnaires were analysed and it was decided that only one feature was informative of the interests of the user: the department in which he/she works. Nine stereotypes were constructed, corresponding to nine different company department types, and each was associated with a list of news categories, covering the interests of all the users in the stereotype. This manual acquisition process was difficult and the generated stereotypes did not prove particularly useful. The first difficulty was the interpretation of the questionnaire data. The number of features which could be extracted from the data was very small and concerned only company information. Moreover, there was a lot of missing - or hard to interpret - information, even regarding the interests of the user. The main problem was the extent of overlap between the stereotypes. There were five news categories and each stereotype contained in average 3.3 of these. Thus, it is clear that this classification is hardly more useful than the base rule, which says that everybody is interested about everything. This is an indication that the stereotypes are oversimplified.

At a second stage, we used a machine learning method for stereotype acquisition. Replacing the manual process by a machine learning method cannot solve the problem of the quality of information that can be extracted from the questionnaire data. However, it may provide a solution to the problem of oversimplification. A set of experiments, using C4.5, was done on the news-filtering data. The training data were extracted from the set of the 31 questionnaires. In this study there are five system-independent variables:

- The **department** in which the user is working: personnel, development, planning, finance, marketing, information support, consulting, public relations, sales.
- The type of **industry**: construction, manufacturing, financial, wholesale, retail, public services, public administration, research and education, services.
- The **size** of the company: small, medium and large.
- The **location** of the company: local, national and multinational.
- The location of the **market** for the company: local, national and international.

In many cases, the value of some of the above variables could not be decided from the questionnaires. The amount of missing information increased moving down the list of the five variables, i.e., the department type was available in all cases, while there were many cases, in which the company's market was not obvious. C4.5 handles missing information in a probabilistic manner. It fills the missing value by all possible values, attaching a weight to each one. This weight depends on the proportion of cases having this value in the training set. The news categories used in this study were the following: business development, product news, market news, company results and personnel news.

3.2 Results

Two initial experiments were run using C4.5. In the first experiment, all variables except the department, were ignored. The aim of this experiment was to see the association of news categories with the department type and compare these results with the manually constructed stereotypes of the ECRAN project. The learning task involved a simple calculation of the number of cases in which a news category was selected for each department type. These numbers are provided in Table 1. The shading of the table cells corresponds to the presence or absence of the news category in the manually constructed stereotypes. Shaded cells represent combinations appearing in the manual stereotypes. When a cell is empty it means that no cases were found in which the corresponding department type was associated with the respective news category.

Table 1. Associations between department type and news categories in the stereotypes.

department	business development	product news	market news	Company Results	personnel news
Personnel					
Development		1.0			
Planning			1.0	1.0	
Finance			1.0		
Marketing	0.55	0.45	0.92	0.92	
Information support	1.0	1.0			
Consulting	0.66	0.33	0.66	0.66	0.11
Public relations	0.33		1.0	1.0	
Sales		1.0	1.0	1.0	

The first important difference between the manually constructed stereotypes and the ones generated by C4.5 was in terms of generality. Excluding the personnel information, which appeared only once in the data, the manually constructed stereotypes defined 26 out of the 32 possible associations. Only 20 of these are verified in the training data and many of these are very weak. Thus, the automatically constructed stereotypes are more specialised and therefore seem more helpful in deciding the information that one is interested in. Furthermore, the association weights given in Table 1 could be used to prioritise the interests of the user. A similar approach was adopted in (Rich, 1983). These results should be interpreted with caution, due to the small size of the training set. A larger training set could provide more interesting and robust stereotypes.

In the second experiment, all five system-independent variables were used. Out of these the ones selected most often by C4.5 were the department and industry type, suggesting that these two variables have a larger classification power. In general, relatively small decision trees were constructed. The tree of Fig. 2 is one of the five trees that were generated.

The important problem with the induced decision trees was their low accuracy in discriminating between people who are interested in a news category and those who are not. Table 2 presents the accuracy of each of the four trees (excluding the personnel news category). For the sake of comparison, the accuracy of the default rule, classifying everybody in the majority class is presented. The majority class is usually those not interested in the news category. The exception to this rule is the market news category.

Table 2. Performance of the induced trees.

category	accuracy of stereotype	default accuracy
business development	78.6%	50.0%
products news	82.1%	60.7%
market news	92.9%	78.6%
company results	85.7%	71.4%

Despite the significant improvement over the default rule, there is still much to be desired by the decision trees. Moreover, it should be noted that these results are calculated on the training set and may give a distorted picture of the performance of the stereotypes. More thorough testing is required, involving a standard testing method, such as the n-fold cross-validation (*leave-one-out*), which is the most appropriate for small datasets.

4 Case Study II: Learning User Communities

4.1 Experimental Setting

We applied COBWEB on the task of constructing user communities for the news-filtering system (Paliouras et al., 1998). The news articles are organised into 24 news categories, e.g. economic indicators, computers, etc. During his/her registration to the news filtering system, each user specifies a subset of these news categories, which correspond to his/her personal interests. This personal list of news categories constitutes the user model, which determines what news he receives. The user model can be modified by the user, reflecting changes in his interests. The dataset for the experiment contained 1078 user models, with an average of 5.4 news categories specified in each model. These user models formed a set of training examples for the learning algorithm. Each example was represented as a binary feature vector, specifying which news categories the user was interested in. Given these training examples, COBWEB constructed classes of users with common interests, i.e., communities.

The question is whether there is any meaning in the generated communities. Since there is no personal information available about the users, the construction of stereotypical descriptions for the communities is not possible. The natural way to construct meaningful communities is by trying to identify those sets of interests on news categories that are representative for the participating users. To achieve this, we specified a metric FI_c that measures the increase in the frequency of a category "c" within a community, as compared to the default frequency of the category in the whole data set (Paliouras et al., 1998). When FI_c is negative there is a decrease in frequency and the corresponding category is not representative for the community. The definition of a representative news category for a community, is just that $FI_c > \alpha$, where α is the required extent of frequency increase. In order to see the impact on the characterisation of the communities, we varied α and measured the following two properties of the generated community descriptions:

- *Coverage:* proportion of news categories covered by the community descriptions. Some of the categories will not be covered, because their frequency will not have increased sufficiently.
- *Overlap:* amount of overlap between the constructed community descriptions. This is measured as the ratio between the total number of categories in the description and the number of distinct categories that are covered.

4.2 Results

Using COBWEB on the data set generated a concept hierarchy of which the first three layers are presented in Fig. 3. An important property of the hierarchy is the balanced split of objects in different branches. Therefore the underlying concepts are of similar strength.

Ideally, we would like to acquire descriptions that are maximally distinct, i.e., minimise the overlap, and increase coverage. We examined two different partitions of the objects, corresponding to the second and the third level of the concept hierarchy (for details see Paliouras et al., 1998). The coverage on the second level of the hierarchy is consistently lower than that on the third level. This is because the clusters on the third level are more specialised than those on the second. On the other hand, the larger the number of the communities, the larger the overlap between their descriptions. Thus, there is a trade-off between coverage and overlap, as the number of communities increases. In the case of the 15 different clusters, the extent of the overlap is significantly higher than in the 5-cluster case which gives the best results in terms of the distinctness in the descriptions. A set of very concise and meaningful concept descriptions were acquired for the 5-cluster case. Table 3 lists the news categories for the 5 clusters, together with their FI_c values.

Communities E, G and H are well-separated, corresponding to a group of people interested in the internet, economics and computers respectively. Community F, consists of people interested mainly in economics and finance, but also in computers. Some interest in computers is to be expected from the users of a system on the internet. Finally, community D serves as a

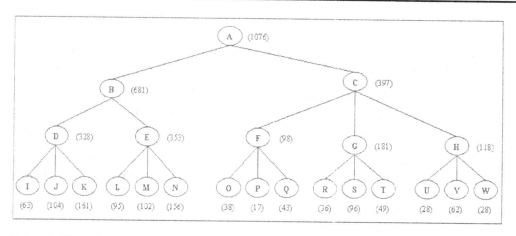

Figure 3. Hierarchy generated by COBWEB (top three levels). The numbers in brackets correspond to the size of the corresponding subset of objects.

"miscellaneous" cluster that is not homogeneous. The common feature of people in D, is that they have very specific interests, leading to sparse user models.

Table 3. Descriptions for the 5 clusters generated on the second level of the concept hierarchy

D	E	F	G	H
	Internet (0.55)	Economic Indicators (0.73)	Economic Indicators (0.58)	Computers (0.53)
		Economy & Finance (0.68)	Economy & Finance (0.61)	
		Computers (0.6)		
		Transport (0.53)		
		Financial Indicators (0.5)		

A problem with the descriptions in Table 3 is that a large proportion of the 24 news categories are not covered. In general, these are the categories that are chosen by either too few or too many users. In the former case the algorithm ignores them during learning and in the latter case, they correspond to such general interests, that they cannot be attributed to particular communities. Filtering out these two types of category is a positive feature of the FI_c metric. Coverage can increase, by moving selectively to lower levels of the COBWEB hierarchy. For instance, the children of node H give meaningful and concise communities, corresponding to categories that are related to computing, e.g. electronics and networks. However, this is not the case for all five communities in Table 3, e.g. the children of node E do not provide further meaningful subgroups in the community. The ability to select nodes at different levels of the concept hierarchy is an important advantage of the COBWEB algorithm.

5 Conclusions

This paper presented a pilot study on the acquisition of user stereotypes and communities from user-modeling data. The choice of the appropriate learning techniques, the use of stereotypes or communities, as well as the construction of meaningful communities were the major issues examined.

The notion of a stereotype and the problems of manual construction of stereotypes were first discussed. Particular emphasis was given to the characteristic features of the task of learning stereotypes and in this context the new notion of community stereotype was introduced. Experimental results, using C4.5 show that the task is solvable, but raise a number of issues. The most important one is the quality of the data. The data that were extracted from the questionnaires did not prove adequate for learning robust and general stereotypes. The lack of sufficient system-independent information led us to community modeling.

Communities can be used to improve the exploitation of a news-filtering system by its users. The construction of the communities was achieved using an unsupervised learning technique. We also proposed a metric to decide which are the representative news categories of a community. Our results are very encouraging, showing that meaningful community descriptions can be generated.

Concluding, this paper has shown that the application of learning methods to user-modeling data for the construction of stereotypes and communities is a promising research direction. We consider this work as a first step towards a methodology that can easily be integrated in a variety of news-filtering systems. A number of issues have arisen, which are of both theoretical and technical interest. Taking into account the increasing commercial interest of user modeling, especially since the advent and expansion of the WWW, we believe that this work could help considerably the construction of useful tools.

References

Benaki, E., Karkaletsis, V. and Spyropoulos, C. D. (1997). Integrating User Modeling into Information Extraction: the UMIE Prototype. In *Proceedings of the Sixth User Modeling Conference*, 55-57.

Bloedorn, E., Mani, I. and MacMillan, T. R. (1997). Machine Learning of User Profiles: Representational Issues. In *Proceedings of the National Conference on Artificial Intelligence*, 433-438.

Brajnik, G. and Tasso, C. (1994). A Shell for Developing Non-monotonic User Modeling Systems. *International Journal of Human-Computer Studies* 40:31-62.

Chiu, P. (1997). Using C4.5 as an Induction Engine for Agent Modeling: An experiment of Optimisation. In *Sixth User Modeling Conference, Workshop on Machine Learning for User Modeling*.

Fisher, D. H. (1987). Knowledge Acquisition via Incremental Conceptual Clustering. *Machine Learning* 2: 139-172.

Gluck, M. A. and Corter, J. E. (1985). Information, Uncertainty and the Utility of Categories. In *Proceedings of the 7th Conference of the Cognitive Science Society*, 283-287.

Kay, J. (1995). The um Toolkit for Cooperative User Modeling. *User Modeling and User Adapted Interaction* 4:149-196.

Paliouras, G., Papatheodorou, C., Karkaletsis, V., Spyropoulos, C., and Malaveta, V. (1998). Learning User Communities for Improving the Services of Information Providers, Lecture Notes in Computer Science, 1513 : Springer-Verlag. 367-384.

Quinlan, J. R. (1993). *C4.5: Programs for Machine Learning*, Kaufmann.

Raskutti, B. and Beitz, A. (1996). Acquiring User Preferences for Information Filtering in Interactive Multi-Media Services. In *Proceedings of PRICAI*, 47-58.

Rich, E. (1983). Users are Individuals: Individualizing User Models. *International Journal of Man-Machine Studies* 18:199-214.

Machine Learning and Knowledge Representation in the LaboUr Approach to User Modeling

Wolfgang Pohl and Achim Nick*

GMD FIT, HCI Research Department, Sankt Augustin, Germany

Abstract. In early user-adaptive systems, the use of knowledge representation methods for user modeling has often been the focus of research. In recent years, however, the application of machine learning techniques to control user-adapted interaction has become popular. In this paper, we present and compare adaptive systems that use either knowledge representation or machine learning for user modeling. Based on this comparison, several dimensions are identified that can be used to distinguish both approaches, but also to characterize user modeling systems in general. The LaboUr (Learning about the User) approach to user modeling is presented which attempts to take an ideal position in the resulting multi-dimensional space by combining machine learning and knowledge representation techniques. Finally, an implementation of LaboUr ideas into the information server ELFI is sketched.

1   Introduction

While striving to achieve user-adapted interaction, user modeling researchers have often made use of *knowledge representation* (KR) techniques: A representation formalism is used to maintain assumptions about a user within a knowledge base. The reasoning mechanisms of the formalism are used to extend this user model. The (explicit or implicit) contents of the knowledge base can be accessed by an application and be used to support its adaptivity decisions.

KR-based user modeling originated in research on (natural-language) dialog systems (Wahlster and Kobsa, 1989). User-adapted interaction, however, has long been a concern also in the area of intelligent user interfaces. Systems developed in this area typically observe system usage and determine usage regularities to form a *usage profile* (Krogsæter et al., 1994) that is to support adaptivity decisions. This procedure can be regarded as "learning from observation". Hence, it is no surprise that *machine learning* (ML) techniques have often been used to form usage profiles and support user-adapted interaction. Note that ML-based adaptivity involves user modeling: a usage profile provides an information source separate from other system knowledge and hence roughly fits the definition of a user model by Wahlster and Kobsa (1989).

In the next section, we will present examples of both KR-based and ML-based user modeling. We will examine them in order to identify a set of dimensions useful for clarifying the differences between both approaches and for characterizing user modeling systems in general. In Section 3 we describe LaboUr (Learning about the User), an approach to user modeling that attempts to combine the advantages of KR-based and ML-based user modeling. Finally, we will present

---

* This work has been supported by DFG (German Science Foundation), grant No. Ko 1044/12, DFN (German Research Network) and the German Federal Ministry of Education, Science, Research, and Technology. We thank the anonymous reviewers for their very helpful remarks.

ELFI, a system that is in real-world use as a server for information on research funding. LaboUr ideas have been implemented into ELFI in order to realize user-adaptive features.

2 Dimensions of User Modeling Systems

Several authors have spent effort on identifying categories and dimensions for characterizing several aspects of user-adaptive systems. Rich (1983) found three characterizing dimensions for user models, while Kobsa (1989) identified categories for user model contents. We will take a look at properties of user modeling components or systems from a technical point of view.

2.1 Knowledge Representation for User Modeling

Traditional user modeling systems often make use of knowledge representation techniques. KR formalisms offer facilities for maintaining knowledge bases (using representation formalisms) and for reasoning (using the inference procedures of representation formalisms). For user modeling, these facilities are typically employed as follows: Assumptions about individual characteristics of the user are maintained in a knowledge base, using a representation formalism. Since this knowledge base may additionally contain system knowledge about the application domain or meta-knowledge for inferring additional assumptions about the user from her current model (including stereotypes), it has been called user modeling knowledge base (UMKB, Pohl, 1998). If available, inference procedures of the representation formalism or meta-level inferences can be used to expand the user model. The use of (particularly logic-based) knowledge representation methods in user modeling systems has been analyzed in detail by Pohl (1998).

For a concrete example, we take the adaptive hypertext system KN-AHS (Kobsa et al., 1994), which makes use of the KR methods offered by the user modeling shell system BGP-MS (Kobsa and Pohl, 1995) to maintain assumptions about user knowledge. *Acquisition* of assumptions is based on how the user interacts with the hypertext hotwords and is controlled by heuristics like: "If the user requests an explanation [...] for a hotword, then he is [...] unfamiliar with this hotword" (cf. Kobsa et al., 1994, p.103). Assumptions are communicated to BGP-MS, which *represents* both assumptions and domain knowledge using a concept formalism, with one concept for each hotword. Once being added to the user model, an assumption may trigger meta-level *reasoning* that is based on concept relationships represented as domain knowledge in the UMKB. KN-AHS accesses both explicit and implicit user model contents to make its adaptivity *decisions*, e.g., about how to adapt the contents of hypertext nodes.

In this example, we have identified the following user modeling tasks: acquisition, representation, reasoning, and decision. Corresponding facilities can be found in many user modeling systems. Note that user model reasoning as described above has been called *secondary acquisition* by Pohl (1998), because additional assumptions are derived from existing ones. However, reasoning must be distinguished from acquisition, since it can also be used for other purposes like, e.g., consistency maintenance. Figure 1 illustrates the application of KR methods to user modeling. Acquisition and decision are performed outside the KR system, which is responsible for representation and reasoning.

Several other issues are typical of systems that use KR for user modeling. First, the separate acquisition components often employ procedures or rules which are triggered by one or few observations to construct an assumption about the user that is to be entered into the UMKB. Such

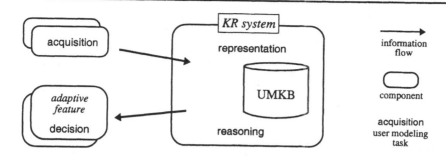

Figure 1. Using a knowledge representation system for user-adapted interaction.

an acquisition process is not incremental, i.e., it does not take observation history into account. This can lead to conflicts in the user model; the KR system needs to implement truth maintenance techniques to resolve these conflicts (Brajnik and Tasso, 1994, Paiva and Self, 1995). Second, KR-based user models mostly contain assumptions which are related to mental notions like knowledge, belief, goals, and interests and have been called *mentalistic* by Pohl (1997).

2.2 Machine Learning for User Modeling

In the early Nineties, a separate strand of research on user-adapted interaction developed in the area of intelligent user interfaces, mainly apart from the user modeling community. As an early protagonist, the system Flexcel (Krogsæter et al., 1994) discovered frequently occurring parameter settings of user commands and suggested to the user to introduce key shortcuts or menu entries for later use of the same settings. Almost at the same time, "interface agents" and "personal assistants" were introduced: Both Kozierok and Maes (1993) and Mitchell et al. (1994) describe software assistants for scheduling meetings. These employ machine learning methods (memory-based learning and decision tree induction, resp.) to acquire assumptions about individual habits of arranging meetings.

More recently, a quite large number of systems using machine learning for personalized information filtering have been described in the literature, like Syskill&Webert (Pazzani and Billsus, 1997), Letizia (Lieberman, 1995), or Amalthaea (Moukas, 1996). Let us have a closer look at Syskill&Webert. This system classifies Web pages (within one domain, e.g., biomedicine) as "hot" or "cold" according to user interests. It learns from initial classifications made by the user to make personalized recommendations. For each of a given set of words relevant to the domain, the system determines the two probabilities of the presence of the word in either "hot" or "cold" documents. These probabilities are the results of the learning process of Syskill&Webert. They are used by a Bayes classifier to determine the probabilities of a new document belonging to either category. If the probability for "hot" is greater than that for "cold", Syskill&Webert makes a positive annotation, else a negative annotation to the document.

Syskill&Webert stores learning results as triplets of the following form:

$$word \quad p(word\ present \mid hot) \quad p(word\ present \mid cold)$$

An instance of this scheme in the biomedicine domain is *genome .6 .3*. The stored set of triplets is called "user profile" by Pazzani and Billsus (1997). The format of profile entries is determined

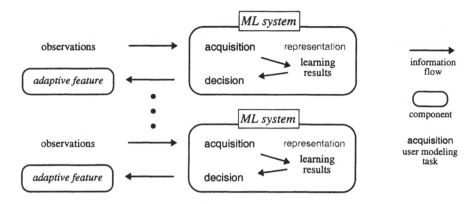

Figure 2. Using machine learning for user-adapted interaction.

by the Bayes classifier, which needs the two probabilities for classification; different learning and decision procedures would require different formats.

In general, machine learning methods process training input and offer support for decision (mainly classification) problems based on this input. Hence, ML-based user-adaptive systems work quite differently from KR-based ones. Instead of a knowledge base, learning results are the central source of information about the user. Observations of user behavior (e.g., reactions to meeting proposals or document ratings) are used to form training examples. Learning components do *acquisition* by running their algorithms on these examples. *Representation* is implicit: Formats of learning results are specific to the learning algorithm used (decision trees, probabilities, etc.) which makes them difficult to be reused for other purposes. Due to the lack of an independent representation formalism, there is no further *reasoning* based on already acquired data. However, *decisions* are directly supported, as we have seen for Syskill&Webert. Also the meeting scheduling assistants let their learning components predict the user's reaction to new meeting proposals and use this prediction for their individualized suggestions.

Figure 2 illustrates the use of machine learning for user-adapted interaction. "Representation" is grayed to indicate that representation is implicit in our terms. The figure also visualizes what we have discussed above: Learning results typically serve one specific decision process. For different adaptive features, different learning processes have to be installed.[1]

But there are not only differences in the handling of user modeling tasks. In the previous section, we observed that in systems with KR-based user modeling acquisition is non-incremental and user models are mostly mentalistic. For ML-based systems, the situation is again different. First, acquisition is incremental, i.e., it takes the history of interactions into account by processing a set of training examples, either one by one or all at once.[2] Hence, learning results (i.e., the user model of ML-based systems) are revised steadily; there is no need for special revision mechanisms. Second, as already stated, often the "user model" of ML-based systems is a us-

---

[1] However, it is possible that one adaptive feature can be exploited by several applications. E.g., text classification can be applied to e-mails, news articles, and Web pages.

[2] In the latter case, a learning method is called "non-incremental" from a technical point of view, but can be used for incremental acquisition if new observations are processed together with old ones.

age profile, i.e., it carries behavior-related information about the user. In the case of information filtering systems, however, learning results often indicate user interests in specific information content and can be regarded as (implicitly represented) mentalistic assumptions.

2.3   Characterizing User Modeling Systems

The discussion about the application of KR and ML methods to user modeling led us to a set of dimensions that can be used to compare both approaches but also to characterize user modeling systems in general. At first, we intended to take the mentioned user modeling tasks as dimensions, each with a binary scale of "supported" vs "not supported" (by the core user modeling system). However, this set of dimensions was not perfectly orthogonal: Reasoning about user model contents depends on the explicit representation of these contents. Therefore, we suggest a slightly different set of characterizing dimensions for user modeling systems. Some of them refer to user modeling tasks, while others cover other issues.

input Does the user modeling system accept *observations* of user behavior, *assumptions* (statements about the user, perhaps already formulated in the internal representation formalism), or *both*?

 Note that an answer to this question does not necessarily imply a statement about acquisition support; observations might simply be stored.

acquisition Is acquisition truly *incremental* or *non-incremental* (i.e., are user model contents modified steadily or not)?

representation Is representation *explicit* (using an accessible format with a clear semantics, potentially reusable for more than one adaptivity feature) or *implicit*?

 Note that explicit representation does not limit the input dimension to assumptions. E.g., a KR-based user modeling system can accept observations if these are coded in the available representation formalism.

aspects Information about what aspects of the user is maintained: information about user *behavior*, about *mental notions*, or about *other* user characteristics (e.g., demographic data)?

 This dimension is related to representation, but not strictly: Behavior information might be represented explicitly. E.g., Mitchell et al. (1994) discuss the transformation of decision trees into an explicit, rule-like representation. Furthermore, mentalistic assumptions like interest profiles may be represented implicitly (s.a.).

output Does the user modeling system deliver *assumptions*, *decisions*, or *both*? I.e., can applications access a user model or a learning/decision process directly?

 Note that this dimension is not strictly coupled to the input dimension; there may be user modeling processes that accept observations but are not accessible for decisions.

Table 1 shows the typical values of the above dimensions for KR-based and ML-based user modeling systems. However, many actual systems will deviate from these extremes. For example, many ML-based systems focus on user behavior, but ML-based information filtering systems implicitly represent assumptions about user interests (a mental notion).

Now we demonstrate the usefulness of these dimensions by using them to characterize a user modeling system that, at first sight, is a typical representative of neither KR-based nor ML-based user modeling. Like many other user modeling systems it uses a numerical approach to uncertainty management (see Jameson, 1996, for an overview). Such systems have also been

Table 1. Properties of typical KR-based and ML-based user modeling systems.

	input	acquisition	representation	aspects	output
KR-based	assumptions	non-incremental	explicit	mentalistic	assumptions
ML-based	observations	incremental	implicit	behavior	decisions

labeled "evidence-based" by Pohl (1998), since they explicitly maintain a degree of evidence for user model contents.

Our example is the user modeling component of the intelligent tutoring system HYDRIVE (Mislevy and Gitomer, 1996), which models a student's competence at troubleshooting an aircraft hydraulic system. HYDRIVE employs a Bayesian Network (BN); the probability distribution of network nodes are used to *explicitly represent* variables like "Electronics Knowledge" or "Strategic Knowledge", which are organized into different levels of abstraction. At the most concrete level, nodes represent "interpreted actions". Such a node stores the probabilities that an observed sequence of user activities belongs to one of a fixed number of action categories. When HYDRIVE interprets an action sequence to belong to one category, it creates an interpreted action node and adds it to the BN with the probability of this category set to 1. That is, *observation* information constitutes the *input* to the user modeling system, but it has to be coded in terms of the BN formalism. *Acquisition* is *incremental:* While interpreted action nodes only cover a limited number of observations, they have long-term effects on the formation of assumptions through propagation of probability to higher level nodes like "Strategic Knowledge". Since these mentalistic variables are the static part of the BN, mainly *mentalistic aspects* are represented in the user model of HYDRIVE. The probability distributions of these variables are the main source of adaptation; i.e., *assumptions* are the *output* of the user modeling system.

In several regards, HYDRIVE is typical of systems which use a BN for user modeling. In Jameson's overview article (1996) we found that observation-related nodes are often used for input purposes, and that most systems are dealing with notions closer to mentalistic models than behavior profiles, ranging from "short-term cognitive states and events" to "personal characteristics". In sum, by using our dimensions we found that user modeling systems with Bayesian Networks can have many typical KR-based properties. However, they share the property of incremental acquisition with typical ML-based systems; the reason is that also ML techniques implement some sort of uncertainty (using probabilities, distance measures, network weights, etc.).

3 The LaboUr Approach

According to the dimensions identified in the previous sections, what would an ideal user modeling system look like? First, it should be possible to report observations to the user modeling system. Thus, applications would not be forced to form assumptions about the user on their own. Second, acquisition should be incremental and not ignore interaction history, unless this is desired by an application. However, incremental acquisition processes should be complemented by heuristic acquisition, e.g., if quick results are needed and/or the number of observations is small.

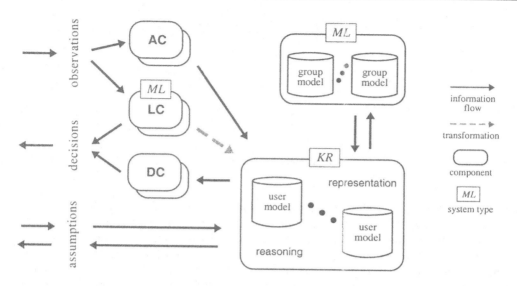

Figure 3. The LaboUr architecture.

Third, representation should be explicit, at least in cases where assumptions about the user may be useful to more than one adaptive feature and its decision process. That is, explicit representation is particularly important for a central user modeling service that is to be available to more than one application. Fourth, assumptions about the user should not be restricted to be either behavior-related or mentalistic, if both aspects are relevant to applications. Finally, the system should be able to support decisions, but ideally also allow for direct access to the user model.

We propose to integrate features of KR-based and ML-based user modeling in order to come closer to such an ideal system. A first step into this direction was made by the user model server Doppelgänger (Orwant, 1995), which uses learning methods to process information from several sources. Learning results are represented explicitly in a standardized format (all assumptions are stored using a symbolic notation with associated numerical confidence values), so that they can be used by all Doppelgänger clients. With acquisition and representation decoupled, several learning components can work on the acquisition of the same kind of data. For instance, Doppelgänger uses both hidden Markov models and linear prediction to acquire temporal patterns of user behavior, which are employed to predict future user activities.

Building upon these ideas, we proposed LaboUr (Learning about the User; Pohl, 1997), a user modeling architecture that integrates KR and ML mechanisms (see Figure 3). A LaboUr system accepts observations about the user, from which learning components (LCs) or acquisition components (ACs) may choose appropriate ones. LCs (which are ML-based) internally generate usage-related results that will be transformed into explicit assumptions, if possible. These assumptions are passed to a KR-based user modeling subsystem. ACs directly generate user model contents, which may be behavior-related or mentalistic, and do not support decisions. They can implement heuristic acquisition methods like those often used in systems with KR-based user modeling (cf. Section 2.1). In contrast to LCs, which typically need a significant

Figure 4. ELFI interface

number of observations to produce learning results with sufficient confidence, ACs can allow for "quick-and-dirty" acquisition from a small number of observations. This is useful to adaptive systems with short usage periods. LCs can be consulted for decision support based on learning results. In addition, there may be other decision components (DCs) that refer to user model contents. Besides supporting acquisition and decision processes, a LaboUr system can also offer direct access (input and output) to user models, due to its use of explicit representation facilities.

A LaboUr system may maintain several user models. In this case, ML techniques can further be used for group modeling, i.e., clustering user models into user group models. Then, individual user models may be complemented by suitable group information. LaboUr is an open user modeling architecture: Several sources of information about the user may contribute to the user model, which again can support several adaptive features or applications.

4 Applying LaboUr to ELFI

4.1 The ELFI Information Server

ELFI (ELectronic Funding Information) is a WWW-based brokering system for information about research funding. Users of ELFI are German researchers and research funding consultants working at universities and other research institutions. ELFI is described in detail by Nick et al. (1998). Here, we will only give a brief sketch of the system before focusing on adaptivity and implementation of LaboUr ideas in ELFI.

ELFI provides access to a database of funding programs and funding agencies. This information space is organized into hierarchies; for funding programs there are several hierarchies, e.g., of research topics and of funding types (like grant or fellowship). Based on these categories, users can actively specify their interest (e.g., in all fellowships in mathematics). The resulting interest profile is used for filtering unneeded information.

The interface of ELFI (see Figure 4) is divided into two parts. The left side presents one of the hierarchies (here: the research topic hierarchy) to be used as navigation tree. The checkmarks behind tree nodes can be used to specify an interest profile: a checked box shall indicate interest in a topic. The right side visualizes the contents of the current information subspace (specific funding programs or funding agencies). In Figure 4, funding programs on mathematics are listed, since this topic ("Mathematik") was selected on the left side. The user can click each list item to see a detailed view of the corresponding program.

4.2 Adaptability and Adaptivity in ELFI

As users can modify their interest profiles, ELFI is an adaptable system. However, analysis of ELFI usage showed that profile settings are often used for temporary information filtering, so that they do not yield a long-term interest profile. Second, the profile is quite coarse, since it is relative to items of the hierarchies only. Therefore, for realizing adaptive features like recommendation of particularly relevant new research programs, we needed to add facilities for acquisition of a more stable and fine-grained and user model.

Adaptivity in ELFI is based on usage log analysis. ELFI records all user interactions with the system into a log file. Currently, we are exploiting the usage log in three different ways:

- Log files are scanned for key sequences that probably indicate user interest in a certain research topic. For example, if a user subsequently makes several selections from a list of documents related to one research topic (e.g., mathematics), then she is probably interested in that topic. This kind of heuristic sequence analysis constitutes a LaboUr acquisition component (AC).
- Navigation activity (i.e., selection of items in navigation trees) is analyzed by an LC in order to find out about frequently used items and frequent transitions between items. The results can be used to generate a personalized navigation tree: frequently used items from all navigation trees are merged, with items of one tree level sorted according to frequency of use, and less frequent items placed on a lower level. Furthermore, analysis results also indicate user interest in tree items (research topics, funding agencies, etc.).
- Finally, machine learning algorithms are employed within an LC to acquire interest information based on selection of detailed views. This is problematic, since these selections only provide positive learning examples. Learning results provide an assessment of user interests with respect to detailed view contents.

All these acquisition and learning components contribute to a comprehensive model of user interests with respect to research funding. Following the LaboUr approach, an explicitly represented user model will be constructed from the results of acquisition and learning components. This model can be used to support adaptivity decisions in ELFI, e.g. the selection of especially relevant new funding information for recommendation.

5 Conclusion

In this paper, we discussed and compared the use of different techniques in user modeling systems. We distinguished systems based on knowledge representation methods from systems that use machine learning techniques. Typical representatives of both approaches were examined, and a significant difference in handling user modeling tasks could be observed. Based on this discussion, we identified dimensions that can generally be used to characterize user modeling systems. Thus, we consider this paper a contribution to basic user modeling research.

Moreover, this paper presented the LaboUr approach to user modeling that tries to integrate advantages of KR-based and ML-based user modeling. We showed how LaboUr ideas are currently being implemented into the ELFI information server, thus giving a first demonstration of the applicability of the approach. In future work, we will establish more of LaboUr into ELFI, like group model formation. Furthermore, we plan to implement a LaboUr-based user modeling service that could be utilized or even shared by the several other user-adaptive applications that are being developed in our group.

References

Brajnik, G., and Tasso, C. (1994). A shell for developing non-monotonic user modeling systems. *International Journal of Human-Computer Studies* 40:31–62.

Jameson, A. (1996). Numerical uncertainty management in user and student modeling: An overview of systems and issues. *User Modeling and User-Adapted Interaction* 5(3-4):193–251.

Kobsa, A., and Pohl, W. (1995). The user modeling shell system BGP-MS. *User Modeling and User-Adapted Interaction* 4(2):59–106.

Kobsa, A., Müller, D., and Nill, A. (1994). KN-AHS: An adaptive hypertext client of the user modeling system BGP-MS. In *Proc. of the Fourth International Conference on User Modeling*, 99–105.

Kobsa, A. (1989). A taxonomy of beliefs and goals for user models in dialog systems. In Kobsa, A., and Wahlster, W., eds., *User Models in Dialog Systems*. Berlin, Heidelberg: Springer. 52–68.

Kozierok, R., and Maes, P. (1993). A learning interface agent for scheduling meetings. In Gray, W. D., Hefley, W. E., and Murray, D., eds., *Proc. of the International Workshop on Intelligent User Interfaces, Orlando FL*, 81–88. New York: ACM Press.

Krogsæter, M., Oppermann, R., and Thomas, C. G. (1994). A user interface integrating adaptability and adaptivity. In Oppermann, R., ed., *Adaptive User Support*. Lawrence Erlbaum Associates.

Lieberman, H. (1995). Letizia: An agent that assists web browsing. In *Proceedings of the International Joint Conference on Artificial Intelligence*. Morgan Kaufmann Publishers.

Mislevy, R. J., and Gitomer, D. H. (1996). The role of probability-based inference in an intelligent tutoring system. *User Modeling and User-Adapted Interaction* 5(3-4):253–282.

Mitchell, T., Caruana, R., Freitag, D., McDermott, J., and Zabowski, D. (1994). Experience with a learning personal assistant. *Communications of the ACM* 37(7):81–91.

Moukas, A. G. (1996). Amalthaea: Information discovery and filtering using a multi-agent evolving ecosystem. In *Proceedings of the Conference on Practical Application of Intelligent Agents and Multi-Agent Technology*.

Nick, A., Koenemann, J., and Schalück, E. (1998). ELFI: information brokering for the domain of research funding. *Computer Networks and ISDN Systems* 30:1491–1500.

Orwant, J. (1995). Heterogeneous learning in the Doppelgänger user modeling system. *User Modeling and User-Adapted Interaction* 4(2):107–130.

Paiva, A., and Self, J. (1995). TAGUS – a user and learner modeling workbench. *User Modeling and User-Adapted Interaction* 4(3):197–226.

Pazzani, M., and Billsus, D. (1997). Learning and revising user profiles: The identification of interesting web sites. *Machine Learning* 27:313–331.

Pohl, W. (1997). LaboUr – machine learning for user modeling. In Smith, M. J., Salvendy, G., and Koubek, R. J., eds., *Design of Computing Systems: Social and Ergonomic Considerations (Proceedings of the Seventh International Conference on Human-Computer Interaction)*, volume B, 27–30. Amsterdam: Elsevier Science.

Pohl, W. (1998). *Logic-Based Representation and Reasoning for User Modeling Shell Systems*. Number 188 in Dissertationen zur künstlichen Intelligenz (DISKI). St. Augustin: infix.

Rich, E. (1983). Users are individuals: Individualizing user models. *International Journal of Man-Machine Studies* 18:199–214.

Wahlster, W., and Kobsa, A. (1989). User models in dialog systems. In Kobsa, A., and Wahlster, W., eds., *User Models in Dialog Systems*. Berlin, Heidelberg: Springer. 4–34.

MANAGING USER MODELS: ARCHITECTURES AND REPRESENTATIONS

Transactional Consistency in User Modeling Systems

Josef Fink

GMD FIT, German National Research Center for Information Technology,
Sankt Augustin, Germany

Abstract. It is widely accepted that the consistency of adaptive interfaces is crucial for their usability. Many threats for consistency in adaptive applications have been reported in the literature so far (e.g., consistency of adaptation methods and techniques, consistency of the user model). In this paper we argue that many, if not all, user modeling systems that have been developed so far are substantially threatening consistency by offering no adequate means for communicating consistency contexts. This is especially the case for user modeling servers, which are supposed to serve several applications in parallel. In order to prevent consistency problems in user modeling systems, we introduce basic concepts and techniques from transaction management. User modeling systems that adhere to the principles of transaction management can be expected to provide a reliable source of user information for adaptive applications, especially in real world settings.

1 Introduction

One of the central tasks of a user modeling system is the provision of user-related information to one or more applications for adaptation purposes. An interface specifies the externally available functionality of the user modeling system and an associated protocol which controls the communication between a user modeling system and one or more adaptive applications. Several interfaces and communication protocols have been proposed in the user modeling literature so far (e.g., Finin, 1989; Brajnik and Tasso, 1994; Paiva and Self, 1995; Kay, 1995; Kobsa and Pohl, 1995; Orwant, 1995; Kobsa et al., 1996; Brusilovsky et al., 1997; Kummerfeld and Kay, 1997). Despite of their differences, most, if not all, have one feature in common: Each access to a user model is treated as a request that is discrete, i.e. independent from former and subsequent accesses. The sophisticated internal functionality offered by many user modeling systems (e.g., activation and deactivation of stereotypes, drawing of inferences, preservation of model consistency and integrity) is executed autonomously and is isolated from external accesses.

This isolation practice is in sharp contrast to the cohesion between subsequent user model accesses, which can be found in many applications. Some examples from the area of adaptive hypermedia which motivate the cohesion between subsequent queries to a user model on the level of adaptations are:

- a single adaptation is triggered by several queries about a user's presumed knowledge (e.g., if one of two concepts are presumed to be known by the user then automatically provide a comparison of the two concepts (adapted from Brusilovsky, 1996));

- an adaptation is triggered by several queries about a user's presumed interests several times on a hypermedia page (e.g., if the user is presumed to be interested in historical details then automatically provide links to historical information for all points of interest (Fink et al., 1997));
- several adaptations on related hypermedia pages are triggered by several queries about a user's presumed knowledge about concepts (e.g., according to the user's presumed knowledge about the underlying concepts of a curriculum, use a traffic light metaphor on one page and, connected via a NEXT button, suggest an individual curriculum sequencing on a second page (Weber and Specht, 1997)).

The cohesion between subsequent user model accesses stems from the associated consistency context of an adaptation. Following the examples mentioned above, a consistency context can comprise of a single adaptation, several adaptations on a single hypermedia page, or several adaptations on a set of related hypermedia pages. An adaptive system needs to communicate this context to a user modeling system in order to be able to adapt in a consistent manner. The user modeling system in turn, is expected to preserve the cohesion between user model accesses by providing a unique "sphere of control" (Gray and Reuter, 1993). This means basically that internal functionality of the user modeling system and accesses from other applications that read and update the same parts of the user model are not concurrently executed.

If functionality for communicating and preserving consistency contexts is lacking, as it is the case in many user modeling systems today, then the consistency of adaptive applications is endangered. Let's exemplify this for the second example presented above. Assume that the user modeling system is queried several times for the user's presumed interest in historical information for points of interest (e.g., churches, museums, public places). The user modeling system, unaware of the coherence between subsequent calls for the user's interest, activates internal functionality (e.g., an inference) that alters this presumed interest after the first query. Subsequent queries now return a different result, leading to inconsistent adaptations on a single hypermedia page (e.g., a link to historical information is only provided for the first point of interest and not for the other points of interest or vice versa).

So far, we argued that the loss of cohesion between user model accesses can lead to consistency problems in adaptive applications. In the following chapter, we will further elaborate this with a special emphasis on related problems in user modeling systems. All user modeling systems, regardless of their architecture (e.g., embedded within the application, client/server), that offer internal user modeling functionality and at the same time no means for communicating and preserving consistency contexts cannot guarantee consistency. This is especially the case for user modeling servers which are intended to serve several applications in parallel.

In order to avoid these types of consistency problems, we introduce in Chapter 3 concepts and basic techniques from transaction management. Transactions are introduced as indivisible units of work that are used for communicating consistency contexts to a user modeling system. In Chapter 4 we summarize our findings, discuss related work, and propose directions for future developments.

2 Consistency Problems

This chapter discusses consistency problems that can occur in user modeling systems and related applications when at least two unsynchronized sequences of logically related operations (threads) that belong to different consistency contexts operate simultaneously on the same parts of a user model. Threads can be incorporated in adaptive applications and user modeling systems (e.g., graphical interfaces of the user modeling system, activation and deactivation of stereotypes, drawing of inferences, acquisition of assumptions based on user's behavior).

The following examples describe two threads that simultaneously access the same user model by calling the functions "ReadUM" and "WriteUM":

- ReadUM takes as an argument an assumption and returns yes or no, thereby indicating whether the assumption or its negation is supported by the user model. "nil" is returned by ReadUM in case of the assumption nor its negation being supported by the user model. ReadUM(KnowsMonaLisa), for example, queries the user model for the user's presumed knowledge of the concept "MonaLisa".
- WriteUM takes two arguments: The first one is the name of the assumption that is to be inserted into the user model and the second one is the associated boolean value (i.e., yes or no). WriteUM(KnowsMonaLisa, yes), for example, updates the user model with the user's presumed knowledge of the concept "MonaLisa".

Application functionality and adaptations have been widely omitted for brevity in the following examples. Local thread variables are labeled "X" and "Z". The entries in the user model reflect the state after the execution of corresponding thread functionality.

We will discuss the consistency problems "inconsistent analysis", "dirty read", and "lost update" (adapted from Saake et al., 1997). These are so-called multi-transaction anomalies (or multi-user anomalies) in the area of database and transaction management (Bernstein et al., 1987).

2.1 Inconsistent Analysis

Each of the following threads strictly preserves consistency when exclusively accessing a user model. But inconsistencies can arise if these threads run interlocked. An example of such a situation is depicted in Table 1. Thread 1, which is incorporated in an adaptive hypermedia system, queries the user modeling system for the user's presumed knowledge of the two concepts "MonaLisa" and "CharlesI". If the user model supports "Knows-MonaLisa" or "KnowsCharlesI" then a comparison of the two concepts is inserted on the current hypermedia page (this is done by calling "ProvComp(MonaLisa, CharlesI)"). Thread 2 is issued by an asynchronously running acquisition component that deduces from user's answers to a quiz that he can be presumed to know "MonaLisa", but not "CharlesI".

Table 1. Inconsistent analysis.

Threads		User Model	
Thread 1	Thread 2	Knows-MonaLisa	Knows-CharlesI
X = ReadUM(KnowsMonaLisa)		no	yes
	WriteUM(KnowsMonaLisa, yes)	yes	yes
	WriteUM(KnowsCharlesI, no)	yes	no
Z = ReadUM(KnowsCharlesI)		yes	no
if ((X = yes) or (Z = yes)) 💣 ProvComp(MonaLisa, CharlesI)		yes	no

Because both variables X and Z contain no, the *comparison* of "MonaLisa" and "CharlesI" *is not provided* by the adaptive hypermedia system. Despite the fact that each thread successfully completed its work and the user model would have supported the provision of the adaptation in its initial and its final state. Thread 2 updates an assumption in the user model that Thread 1, which is still active, has previously read. After Thread 1 resumes its work, the content of X doesn't reflect the current state of the user model anymore. Therefore, all further work that is controlled by X is probably inconsistent as well.

However, the comparison is correctly presented if these threads are sequenced by the transaction manager of the user modeling system (i.e., Thread 2 is run after Thread 1 has concluded its work). Transactions and associated components for user modeling systems will be discussed in Chapter 3.

2.2 Dirty Read

A "dirty read" is issued if the information to be read has been previously updated by another, not yet successfully completed thread. If this thread has to be rolled back for whatever reason, for example, due to a user cancellation or a system crash, then the consistency can be endangered.

An example of such an interlocked situation at running time is depicted in Table 2. Thread 1, which belongs to an adaptive hypermedia system, observed that the user requested for historical information about the "Louvre" (via a call to "ReqForHistInf(Louvre)") and updates the user model with the user's presumed interest in historical information accordingly (abbr. "IntHist"). Afterwards, the user cancels this thread, thereby initiating a rollback of all updates made to the user model so far. Thread 2 implements a simple inference rule within the user modeling system: If the user is presumed to be interested in historical information then he can also be presumed to be interested in art history (abbr. "IntArtHist").

Table 2. Dirty read.

Threads		User Model	
Thread 1	Thread 2	IntHist	IntArtHist
		no	no
if (ReqForHistInf(Louvre)) WriteUM(IntHist, yes)		yes	no
	Z = ReadUM(IntHist)	yes	no
	if (Z = yes) WriteUM(IntArtHist, yes)	yes	yes
Rollback	💣	no	yes

The *update issued by Thread 2 is based on invalid information* previously read from the user model. In addition, since Thread 2 already concluded its work, this update can't be rolled back by the user modeling system anymore. Therefore, it remains persistent in the user model and is a potential source for arbitrary inconsistencies in the future.

However, consistency is preserved if these transactions are sequenced by the transaction manager of the user modeling system (i.e., Thread 2 is run after Thread 1 has been rolled back by the user modeling system).

2.3 Lost Update

Updates can get lost if at least two threads are concurrently updating the same information in a user model. In our example, Thread 1, which belongs to an asynchronously running news filtering system, queries the user modeling system for the user's presumed interest in historical information. After some work, it updates the user model with the same information previously found in the user model and concludes. Likewise, Thread 2, which belongs to a user model inspection interface, queries the user modeling system for the user's presumed interest in historical information and displays the result. The user changes this presumed interest and finally updates the user model.

Consistency is violated from a user's point of view, if we consider for Thread 1 and 2 an interlocked situation at running time like the one depicted in Table 3:

Table 3. Lost update.

Threads		User Model
Thread 1	Thread 2	IntHist
X = ReadUM(IntHist)		yes
	Z = ReadUM(IntHist)	yes
	/* Display Z, user sets Z to no. */ if (Z <> nil) WriteUM(IntHist, Z)	no
if (X <> nil) WriteUM(IntHist, X) 💣		yes

The *update* the user initiated *gets lost* without any notification from the user modeling system. Despite the fact that both threads committed their work successfully, the update issued by Thread 2 is overwritten by Thread 1.

Like in the previous examples, consistency is preserved if these threads are sequenced by the transaction manager of the user modeling system (i.e., Thread 2 is run after Thread 1 ended).

3 Transactions

In Chapter 3.1, we introduce transactions and their properties against the background of the consistency problems we pointed out in the previous chapter. Based on that, we briefly discuss how transactions can be implemented in user modeling systems. In Chapter 3.2, we present the model of a "flat transaction" and motivate the need for more sophisticated transaction models in user modeling systems.

3.1 Transaction Properties

Transactions have been introduced in the areas of database and transaction management in order to relieve an application programmer from all aspects of concurrency and failure. A transaction is a set of logically related operations that adheres to the classical *"ACID" principle* (Gray and Reuter, 1993; Orfali et al., 1994). Against the background of user modeling, the different properties of a transaction can be described as follows:

– *A*tomicity means that a transaction is an indivisible unit of work: Either all or no accesses are processed by the user modeling system.
– *C*onsistency means that a transaction transforms a user model from one consistent state into another consistent state. If such a state can't be achieved (e.g., because of integrity constraints being violated), the user model has to be reset to the state before the transaction started.
– *I*solation means that a transaction (e.g., initiated by an adaptive application) is not affected by other, concurrently executed transactions (e.g., drawing of inferences within the user modeling system, simultaneous access of several adaptive applications) with respect to shared parts of the user model. Changes initiated by a

transaction are not visible to other transactions until this transaction has successfully ended.

- *D*urability means that once a transaction has been successfully completed all changes made to the user model are persistent, i.e. these changes survive system failures.

In database and transaction management systems, a *transaction manager* supervises the progress and state of a transaction (Gray and Reuter, 1993; Saake et al., 1997). In order to achieve this, it interacts closely with a *scheduler* that controls the relative order in which concurrent operations are executed. The overall aim of the scheduler is to maximize potential concurrency, yet preventing consistency problems that may arise from several transactions running in parallel (see Chapter 2). The synchronization of transactions preserves the properties isolation and consistency. Synchronization can be implemented by various locking strategies on data elements and associated protocols. The preservation of the transaction properties atomicity and durability is the main aim of the *recovery manager*. Its tasks include all aspects of transaction commitment and abortion including the rollback to a consistent database state after a system crash.

In order to offer transactions that adhere to the ACID principle, user modeling systems have to incorporate a transaction manager, a scheduler, and a recovery manager. The sophistication of their implementation however, depends heavily on the intended deployment scenario and the services offered. If the user modeling system is embedded in a single-user application then various internal functionality (e.g., activation of stereotypes) has to be mainly synchronized with transactions issued by the application. The scheduler and the recovery manager can be implemented in this scenario in a very rudimentary form. Synchronization can be enforced for example via one or more locks (e.g., separate locks for read and write operations) on the whole user model and recovery can be implemented by managing all user model updates in a persistent buffer until a transaction successfully commits. User modeling server however, need to implement much more sophisticated techniques in order to synchronize various internal functionality with accesses from several applications. The aforementioned lock granularity may serve as an example. It is hardly desirable that a single transaction locks the whole user model, thereby preventing all other transactions using the same model from being executed, when operating itself on a relatively small part of the user model. More fine-grained locks (e.g., on an interest partition of the user model, on an assumption about a user's interest) increase potential concurrency but raise at the same time the need for a dedicated locking manager. Its main tasks are to synchronize locking by enforcing a specific protocol (e.g., the two phase locking protocol) and handle problems that may arise from transactions incompatible locking behavior (e.g. deadlocks). For further information on this subject we refer to Gray and Reuter (1993).

From an implementation point of view, transaction management components will not have to be developed from scratch. If a database management system that offers transaction support is used as a basis for example, then the user modeling system can probably take advantage of the already available functionality.

3.2 Transaction Models

The examples presented in Chapter 2 can be modeled as "flat transactions" in the sense that all operations within a thread are on the same level and belong to the same consistency context. Flat transactions either succeed, or don't happen at all. Typically, they run only a few seconds in order to occupy shared resources (e.g., user model contents) as less as possible. The major advantages of flat transactions are simplicity and ease of use. Against the background of user modeling and user-adaptive applications, flat transactions seem to cover many basic consistency requirements, for example on the level of adaptations. However, there are scenarios that point out the limitations of flat transactions in general (Orfali et al., 1994; Saake et al., 1997), which are also relevant for user modeling systems:

- Transactions with humans in between:
  As a simple example, we can take a component of a user modeling system that allows a user to inspect and edit his user model (see Chapter 2.3). If such a tool is designed as a single flat transaction, then the whole user model is locked until the user exits. No adaptive application and no internal functionality of the user modeling system that accesses the same parts of the user model can run in the meantime. In order to avoid this, the flat transaction can be split into a query transaction and one or more update transactions. Before updating the user model, each update transaction would have to revalidate the user model contents first, before initiating the update.
- Transactions that need to be partially rolled back:
  An example can be a user-adaptive shop based on the World-Wide Web, where everything between two page requests is being modeled as a single flat transaction. If the user cancels for example the shopping transaction, then all updates to the database, the user model, and a component for learning from navigation behavior will have to be rolled back for the page of concern. However, only the rollback of the database updates and user model updates is mandatory, the rollback of the learning component updates is optional.
- Transactions that span over a long time:
  We can take a user modeling server as an example that temporarily replicates the user model or parts of it to a mobile user agent. Eventually, updated versions of the agent's user model have to be resynchronized with the server's version at a later point in time. Again, designing the whole process as a single flat transaction makes little sense, if any. The replicated parts of the central user model would be locked for the whole duration of the transaction and if any problems would occur during resynchronization, the whole transaction would have to be rolled back.

Concluding, the rigidity of ACID-based flat transactions is quite inappropriate in scenarios where flexibility is needed. Up to now, various alternatives to flat transactions have been proposed. Most of them extend the linear flow of control in flat transactions by either linearly chaining units of work (e.g., "chained transactions") or by creating nested hierarchies of units of work (e.g., "nested transactions"). More recently, sophisticated transactional models have also been proposed for long-living transactions (e.g., "Contracts", "migrating transactions", "shopping cart transactions"). The discussion of these transaction models and their reflection against the background of user modeling systems however, goes beyond the scope of this paper.

4 Discussion

The aim of this paper was to point out potential consistency problems in adaptive applications and user modeling systems that stem from unsynchronized accesses to shared parts of a user model. In order to avoid this, consistency contexts have to be communicated by adaptive applications and internal functionality of a user modeling system. The application interface of user modeling systems should provide commands like BeginOfTransaction, EndOfTransaction, and RollbackTransaction. A consistency context is communicated by BeginOfTransaction and EndOfTransaction, whereas the rollback of a user model to the state before the transaction started is communicated by Rollback-Transaction.

To the best of our knowledge, none of the interfaces and communication protocols that have been proposed in the user modeling literature so far (e.g., Finin, 1989; Brajnik and Tasso, 1994; Paiva and Self, 1995; Kay, 1995; Kobsa and Pohl, 1995; Orwant, 1995; Kobsa et al., 1996; Brusilovsky et al., 1997; Kummerfeld and Kay, 1997) puts transactional facilities and associated ACID properties at the disposal of the application developer. This is quite amazing, given the potential consistency problems pointed out in this paper and the paramount importance of consistency for the overall usability of applications (Shneiderman, 1987; Nielsen, 1993; ISO, 1995; ISO, 1996).

A static and restricted form of transaction support that focuses on the ACID properties consistency and isolation can be found in a number of systems including the PAT-InterBook system (Brusilovsky et al., 1997) and the LDAP (Lightweight Directory Access Protocol) protocol (Wahl et al., 1997), which has been recently proposed for user modeling purposes by Kummerfeld and Kay (1997). These systems offer applications the opportunity to communicate user model accesses that belong to a consistency context in a package, which, in turn, is handled by these systems in a consistent and isolated manner. Although useful in many adaptation settings, this approach is rather restricted because of the ACID properties atomicity and durability being not provided and static because of the scope of a consistency context being limited to a single package. More complex consistency contexts (e.g., adaptations on a set of related hypermedia pages) can hardly be covered by such an approach without placing considerable burden on programmers of adaptive applications.

In order to preserve consistency, internal functionality of a user modeling system that is operating on shared parts of a user model has to communicate consistency contexts as well. Examples of such internal functionality can be found in user modeling servers (e.g., activation and deactivation of stereotypes in BGP-MS (Kobsa and Pohl, 1995), integration of results from (machine) learning techniques in Doppelgänger (Orwant, 1995)). To the best of our knowledge, these user modeling servers do not communicate consistency contexts in their internal functionality.

The research area of transaction management provides a rich arsenal of concepts, techniques, and implementations that can help developers of user modeling systems in providing transactional properties and developers of adaptive systems in designing consistent applications. User modeling systems that adhere to the principles of transaction management can be expected to provide a reliable source of user information, especially in real world settings.

References

Bernstein, P. A., Hadzilacos, V., and Goodman, N. (1987). *Concurrency Control and Recovery in Database Systems*. Reading, MA: Addison-Wesley.

Brajnik, G., and Tasso, C. (1994). A shell for developing non-monotonic user modeling systems. *International Journal of Human-Computer Studies* 40:31-62.

Brusilovsky, P. (1996). Methods and techniques of adaptive hypermedia. *User Modeling and User-Adapted Interaction* 4(2):59-106.

Brusilovsky, P., Ritter, S., and Schwarz, E. (1997). Distributed intelligent tutoring on the Web. In du Boulay, B., and Mizoguchi, R., eds., *Proceedings of AI-ED'97*. Amsterdam: IOS. 482-489.

Finin, T. W. (1989). GUMS: A general user modeling shell. In Kobsa, A., and Wahlster, W., eds., *User Models in Dialog Systems*. Berlin, Heidelberg: Springer. 411-430.

Fink, J., Kobsa, A., and Nill, A. (1997). Adaptable and adaptive information access for all users, including the disabled and the elderly. In Jameson, A., Paris, C., and Tasso, C., eds., *User Modeling: Proceedings of the Sixth International Conference*. Wien, New York: Springer. 171-173.

Gray, J., and Reuter, A. (1993). *Transaction Processing: Concepts and Techniques*. San Mateo, CA: Morgan Kaufmann.

ISO. (1995). *Ergonomic Requirements for Office Work with Visual Display Terminals, Part13, User guidance*. International Standard.

ISO. (1996). *Ergonomic Requirements for Office Work with Visual Display Terminals, Part12, Ergonomic requirements for presentation of information*. Draft International Standard.

Kay, J. (1995). The um toolkit for reusable, long term user models. *User Modeling and User-Adapted Interaction* 4(3):149-196.

Kobsa, A., and Pohl, W. (1995). The user modeling shell system BGP-MS. *User Modeling and User-Adapted Interaction* 4(2):59-106.

Kobsa, A., Fink, J., and Pohl, W. (1996). *A Standard for the Performatives in the Communication between Applications and User Modeling Systems (draft)*. Available at http://zeus.gmd.de/~kobsa/rfc.ps

Kummerfeld, R., and Kay, J. (1997). Remote access protocols for user modelling. In *Proceedings and Resource kit for Workshop User Models in the Real World*. Chia Laguna, Sardinia. 12-15.

Nielsen, J. (1993). *Usability Engineering*. San Diego, CA: Academic Press.

Orfali, R., Harkey, D., and Edwards, J. (1994). *Essential Client/Server Survival Guide*. New York, Singapore: Wiley & Sons.

Orwant, J. (1995). Heterogeneous learning in the Doppelgänger user modeling system. *User Modeling and User-Adapted Interaction* 4(2):107-130.

Paiva, A., and Self, J. (1995). TAGUS-A user and learner modeling workbench. *User Modeling and User-Adapted Interaction* 4(3):197-226.

Saake, G., Schmitt, I., and Türker, C. (1997). *Objektdatenbanken – Konzepte, Sprachen, Architekturen*. Bonn, London: Thomson.

Shneiderman, B. (1987). *Designing the User Interface: Strategies for Effective Human-Computer Interaction*. New York, Tokyo: Addison-Wesley.

Wahl, M., Howes, T., and Kille, S. (1997). *Lightweight Directory Access Protocol (v3)*. Available at ftp://ftp.ietf.org/internet-drafts/draft-ietf-asid-ldapv3-protocol-09.tx

Weber, G., and Specht, M. (1997). User modeling and adaptive navigation support in WWW-based tutoring systems. In Jameson, A., Paris, C., and Tasso, C., eds., *User Modeling: Proceedings of the Sixth International Conference*. Wien, New York: Springer. 289-300.

A Computational Architecture for Conversation

Eric Horvitz[1] and Tim Paek[2]*

[1] Decision Theory and Adaptive Systems, Microsoft Research, WA, U.S.A.
[2] Department of Psychology, Stanford University, CA, U.S.A.

Abstract. We describe representation, inference strategies, and control procedures employed in an automated conversation system named the *Bayesian Receptionist*. The prototype is focused on the domain of dialog about goals typically handled by receptionists at the front desks of buildings on the Microsoft corporate campus. The system employs a set of Bayesian user models to interpret the goals of speakers given evidence gleaned from a natural language parse of their utterances. Beyond linguistic features, the domain models take into consideration contextual evidence, including visual findings. We discuss key principles of conversational actions under uncertainty and the overall architecture of the system, highlighting the use of a hierarchy of Bayesian models at different levels of detail, the use of value of information to control question asking, and application of expected utility to control progression and backtracking in conversation.

1 Introduction

Conversations are initiated to express needs or to acquire, share, or critique information. Ongoing inference about intentions is critical in conversation (Allen and Perrault, 1980). We explore the role of inference and decision making under uncertainty in conversational dialog. People engaged in conversation appear to make inferences under uncertainty about the relevance of multiple sources of information, including nonlinguistic contextual cues such as visual findings. They also make ongoing decisions about the formulation of discriminating questions and about the most appropriate level of detail at which to exchange information. We describe in this paper methods for modeling and automating conversation that leverage inference, decision making, and information gathering under uncertainty. We present a computational architecture that focuses on issues of representation, uncertain inference, and dialog control procedures for navigating among different levels of detail in conversation. We highlight basic principles in the context of an implementation of an automated conversation prototype developed at Microsoft Research named the *Bayesian Receptionist*.

The Bayesian Receptionist prototype represents a melding of several key components. Bayesian inference is employed at distinct levels of an abstraction hierarchy to infer a user's goals. Value of information procedures are employed within levels to gather additional information, and decision-theoretic strategies using threshold analyses guide the progression and backtracking in conversation based on expected utility. The system considers words and phrases as well as higher-level linguistic distinctions obtained via a natural language parse of a user's utterances. The un-

---

* We are grateful for assistance provided by Mike Barnett, Herb Clark, and Andy Jacobs.

certain reasoning machinery drives a social user interface built with the MS Agent package. The interface provides speech recognition, speech synthesis, and animations that provide an anthropomorphic presence.

2 The Receptionist Domain

The Bayesian Receptionist project centers on conversation about goals typically handled by receptionists at the front desks of buildings on the Microsoft corporate campus. Receptionists serve a vital role in facilitating daily activities at each building at Microsoft. When people interact with the receptionist, they engage in a *joint activity* (Clark, 1996; Jennings and Mamdani, 1992; Levinson, 1992). A joint activity is a task-oriented, social event with constraints on participants, setting, and most of all, reasonable or allowable contributions. Participants in a joint activity assume that they share some common set of beliefs about the activity, including assumed roles and responsibilities with other participants and the degree to which participants are attending to and understanding the content of utterances (Paek and Horvitz, 1999)

We conducted an observational study of the receptionist domain by videotaping nine hours of participants interacting with three receptionists. Through reviewing videotapes and engaging receptionists in discussions, we identified a key set of user goals, as well as key pieces of linguistic and visual information relevant to the problem of diagnosing a user's needs. Discussion with the receptionists revealed 32 mutually exclusive and exhaustive goals that make up the joint activity. The videotapes and interviews also revealed critical variables and states considered by receptionists. For example, we found that receptionists reason about the *type* of person (*e.g.,* a person visiting the campus to interview for a position). We identified 12 types of people and assessed links between person type and variables capturing appearance and patterns of behavior, as well as the different prior probability distribution over goals for people in different classes. Visual information employed by receptionists in making inferences about goals include:

- **Appearance**: the attire and type of identification badge that may be visible.
- **Behavior**: whether the user looks hurried or glances outside during the interaction.
- **Spatial configuration**: the mode of arrival and the trajectory of locomotion in the proximity of the receptionist.
- **Props**: whether the user carries some type of equipment, or was in a group of people.

In addition to visual features, we identified a set of initial utterances associated with different goals. Analysis of real-world interactions with the receptionist showed considerable linguistic variability. At times, people employed conventional phrasing such as "I'm here to see Rick Rashid." However, people frequently interacted with more telegraphic, abbreviated utterances such as "Bathroom?" to communicate the goal, "I have to use the bathroom; where is it?" and "18!" (while running toward the building exit) to relay the urgent need to order a shuttle heading to Building 18. Others have noted such use of succinct utterances in combination with contextual cues (Clark, 1996). We also found that people often used creative ad-hoc phrases, as in, "Beam me to 25 please" to indicate a need for a campus shuttle to Building 25. We even observed "contextual constructions" (Clark, 1983; Nunberg, 1979) as in "Do we do Sea-Tac airport?"

Considerable variability in dialog is possible since people take it for granted that participants in a conversation will be able to infer what they mean from their shared beliefs. We found that recep-

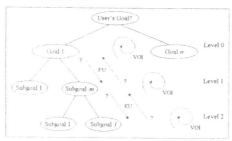

Figure 1. Schematized view of an overall model for guiding diagnosis of goals via Bayesian inference, computation of value of information (VOI), and expected utility analysis (EU) for navigation between levels of detail for progression and backtracking in conversation.

tionists are very apt at discerning what people need, relying on shared knowledge about the joint activity and the likely goals of the participants to guide the dialog. Without such knowledge it would be difficult, if not impossible, for people to communicate their goals with receptionists as efficiently as they do. Also, it became apparent that inferences about the goals of people seeking assistance depend upon integrating rich patterns of evidence beyond the utterance. Visual information, including the appearance, trajectory, and behavior of the participants, is often taken into account.

3   Hierarchical Decomposition of Conversation about Goals

Our observations of interactions, coupled with attempts to model and automate dialog as decision making under uncertainty, led us to focus on the use of a task abstraction hierarchy as an organizing representation. The task abstraction hierarchy decomposes the problem of understanding a user's goals into diagnoses at successive levels of detail. Figure 1 displays the task abstraction hierarchy used in the Bayesian Receptionist. Level 0 represents the task of discriminating the high-level goal of the user given initial observations and an initial utterance. Level 0 goals include the need to arrange a shuttle to travel to another part of campus, to enter the building, to pick something up, to drop something off, to get directions, to acquire an answer to an informational query, to acquire help with a special project, to pick up a public commuting pass, to send a fax, and to hang posters or remove posters. In order to render the set of goals exhaustive, we introduced a goal labeled *other* to refer to goals that are not explicitly considered in the high-level goal variable. Level 1 represents the refinement of the high-level goals into more specific needs. For example, the Level 1 refinements of the goal of needing a shuttle to travel to another part of campus include the need to travel as a group or as a single person to a main campus location, to the North Campus (MS Interactive Media Division), and to a non-Microsoft location. Level 2 considers the additional specification of types of shuttles for special cases, including the need for a shuttle equipped for transporting handicapped people and for express shuttles to transport senior executives. Levels more detailed than the highest level include an additional state representing the proposition that the current level is inappropriate. Inference about the belief assigned to this state is used to control backtracking in conversation.

We found several advantages to introducing a goal refinement hierarchy rather than attempting to model the problem of goal understanding to a larger problem at a single level of detail. Decomposition of a user's goals into several levels of detail allows for guiding conversation on a natural path of convergence toward shared understanding at progressively greater detail. Multiple levels also allow for the establishment of *common ground* (Clark, 1996) about uncertainties at each level and for conversation *about* comprehension of misunderstandings before progressing to the next le-

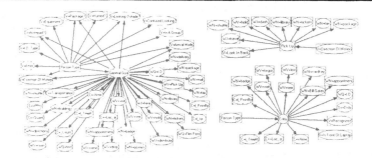

Figure 2. Bayesian networks for inference about primary high-level goals (left) and sample models for the intentions of gaining access to the building and picking up materials stored at the front desk (right).

vel of detail. That is, users can be directed, as part of a natural dialog about their goals, to implicitly or explicitly confirm or disconfirm misunderstanding at one level, reducing uncertainty to some tolerable level before progressing to the next level. Our observations suggested that such discussion about different levels of detail is common and often expected as part of natural human —human conversation. From an engineering and computational perspective, decomposing the goal understanding task into a set of nearly decomposable understanding subproblems leads to more tractable, level-specific modeling and inference. However, the introduction of multiple subproblems also introduces the need for elegant control of inference, evidence gathering, and decision making within and between the levels.

In real-time use, we employ the hierarchical decomposition to disambiguate goals by asking the most informative questions or gathering the most valuable non-linguistic evidence to identify goals at progressively more detailed levels. Given confirmation or strong belief in a speaker's goal at the current level, the system passes all of its evidence to the next more detailed level of analysis and attempts to refine its beliefs about goals at that level, until reaching a conclusion about the speaker's ultimate goals. In Sections 4 through 8, we describe details on inference, information gathering, and control policies for navigating among multiple levels of analysis.

4   Bayesian Models for Inferring a User's Communication Goals

We worked to build models for inference and decision making under uncertainty about a user's goals at each level of the task hierarchy with Bayesian networks. Bayesian networks have been useful in representing a variety of challenges centering on user modeling under uncertainty (Albrecht et al., 1997; Conati et al., 1997; Horvitz and Barry, 1995; Horvitz et al., 1998; Jameson, 1996). Bayesian-network models allow a system to fuse together the relevance of multiple classes of information allowing for inference about the goals of a user from visual information and utterances. Also, having access to probabilities at any step in a dialog allow us to guide question asking based on the computation of value of information.

We constructed and assessed by hand Bayesian networks considering linguistic and non-linguistic observations. The Bayesian networks were authored in the Microsoft Research MSBN modeling and inference system. Models were built for different levels of the task hierarchy. The non-linguistic observations in the models bring to bear contextual information, including important visual features about the appearance, location, and trajectory of locomotion of people interacting with the system. Figure 2 displays the structure of Bayesian models for the Level 0 discrimination

Figure 3. Bayesian Receptionist screen displaying a query initiating a conversation and the probability distribution over Level 0 goals inferred with a Bayesian model taking into consideration linguistic and visual cues.

problem and for two of the Level 1 subproblems centering on the goals of picking something up from the receptionist and gaining entry to the building.

In use, Bayesian networks at progressively more detailed levels of analysis are passed all of the linguistic and non-linguistic information that has been observed by the system. Figure 3 shows an initial screen of the Bayesian Receptionist considering the utterance, "I need a ride please." In addition to the linguistic information, the system considers the visual findings that the user appeared hurried, carried a notebook, and approached the automated receptionist with a trajectory characterized as "moving from inside the building to the back of the receptionist desk." The probability distribution over goals at Level 0 inferred from the visual observations and linguistic clues is displayed to the right of the screen.

5   Accessing Linguistic Evidence with Natural Language Processing

Introducing linguistic distinctions into the Bayesian models and making linguistic observations at run time posed a challenge. The taped interactions with the receptionist showed that utterances varied in syntax, length, and typicality. We first worked to identify evocative sets of words and phrases spotted in utterances, referred to as *metanyms* (Heckerman and Horvitz, 1998). To extend the ability to handle the variation in feasible linguistic inputs to the Bayesian models, we employed automated natural language processing (NLP) to also introduce higher-level linguistic abstractions as observational variables in our Bayesian models. We submitted sample utterances for different goals to a system named NLPwin (Heidorn, 1999), developed by the MS Research Natural Language Processing group to identify *syntactic*, *logical*, and *semantic* cues that can be useful for distinguishing between goals. After submitting myriad utterances of different length, typicality, and syntactic structure to NLPwin, we selected a set of frequently occurring, discriminatory cues as evidential variables in the Bayesian networks.

The textbox at the center of Figure 3 shows the user submitting the utterance, "I need a ride please." The sentence is processed in five stages of analysis. In the first stage, the system segments the input utterance into individual tokens, analyzing words by their morphological structure and looking them up in online dictionaries, including sources specifically tailored for multi-word entries. In the second stage, known as the syntactic sketch, the system parses the utterance into its syntactic components based on rules of grammar. In the third stage, known as the syntactic portrait, the system resolves attachment ambiguities by using semantic relations culled from a compiled analysis derived from online dictionary definitions. The result of the first three stages is the parse tree shown in the top panel of Figure 4. A fourth stage resolves anaphoric references and constructs the logical form of the sentence, representing predicate-argument relations in a semantic graph, by assigning sentence elements to functional roles, such as deep subjects in a semantic graph, by assigning sentence elements to functional roles, such as deep subjects (Dsub)

```
I need a ride please.
DECL1      NP1        PRON1*     "I"
           VERB1*     "need"
           NP2        DETP1      ADJ1*      "a"
                      NOUN1*     "ride"
           AVP1       ADV1*      "please"
           CHAR1      "."
-------------------------------
need1 (+Pres +T1)
|_Dsub----I1 (+Pers1 +Sing +Anim +Humn)
|_Dobj----ride1 (+Indef +Pers3 +Sing +Count)
|_Mods----please1 (+FO)
-------------------------------
2;need;VERB;0;0;-1;;;  +Pres +T1 +Economics +Sociology +Economics +So
1;I;PRON;0;0;-1;;;  +Pers1 +Sing +Anim +Humn
4;ride;NOUN;0;0;-1;;;  +Indef +Pers3 +Sing +Count +EQ +SP +EQ +TN +ON
5;please;ADV;2;Mods;-1;;;  +FO
-------------------------------
        C=_LocAt8   C=+Loc_sr8  C=+Nmm8 C=+Quant8   C=+Transportation8
```

Figure 4. Output of the natural language analysis of the query, "I need a ride please," yielding syntactic, logical, and semantic clues.

and deep indirect objects (Dind). The second panel of the output displays the logical form, concluding that the deep object (Dobj) is the indefinite, count form of the argument "ride." The final stage of NLPwin attempts to determine the most appropriate sense for words in the utterance from a list of senses, yielding semantic cues for the Bayesian models. These are listed in the third panel of the NLP analysis. As an example, an inferred sense of the noun "ride" is "+TN", short for Transportation. Linguistic distinctions noted in the parse, including the identification of semantic concepts of transportation and location are considered in the Level 1 Bayesian network.

6   Value of Information to Guide Observation and Dialog

A critical component of decision-theoretic diagnosis (Horvitz et al., 1988) is the identification of the most valuable additional observations to collect to enhance the value of actions ultimately taken in the world. Formalisms for identifying the most valuable information to collect under uncertainty hold promise for guiding automated dialog (Jameson, 1995). We have employed *value of information* (VOI) analysis to identify the best questions to ask and visual observations to make in light of the inferred probabilities of different goals at distinct levels of the goal decomposition hierarchy. VOI yields the expected utility of evaluating different pieces of previously unobserved evidence, considering the informational value and the cost of making the observation under uncertainty. To compute VOI, we consider, for each observation, the expected utility of the best decision associated with each value that the observation may take on. The analysis sums the expected utility for each value of future observation, weighted by the probabilities of seeing the different values, should that observation be made.

An exact computation of VOI requires the consideration of all possible sequences of observations. However, greedy VOI, focusing on computing the next best single piece of evidence to observe, has been found to be a good approximation (Gorry and Barnett, 1968). Within the framework of greedy VOI, a variety of approximations have been employed. Beyond an explicit decision-theoretic computation, investigators have explored an information-theoretic version of VOI based on the minimization of entropy (Gorry and Barnett, 1968; Heckerman et al., 1992), and the use of the statistical properties of large samples to develop VOI approximations.

In the Bayesian Receptionist, we harness information-theoretic VOI analysis to control information gathering to resolve the current uncertainty within levels of analysis. This approach is related to prior work on the use of VOI at multiple levels of abstraction in decision-theoretic diagnostic systems (Horvitz et al., 1989). After each new observation is evaluated, the system updates the probabilities of distinct goals within a level of the task hierarchy and recomputes the VOI. VOI continues within a level until either the expected cost of evaluating observations exceeds the expected value of the observations, there are no additional observations to make, or a higher-level decision-theoretic analysis progresses the system to the next level of detail. We now discuss the control of progression between adjacent levels of the refinement hierarchy.

7 Progression to Additional Levels of Detail

Given strong belief in a goal at some level of detail, it is typically appropriate to move on to perform inference and question asking about goals at a more detailed level of analysis. Our intuitions about the progression to additional levels of detail were developed by considering the ways people in a conversation in the context of a joint activity speak in a natural manner *about* goals and subgoals (Cohen and Levesque, 1994). At any point in a conversation, a participant may assume a goal or ask for direct confirmation about a goal or subgoal. A correct explicit guess can raise the efficiency of communication. However, a poor guess can be costly. Poor guesses, especially when coming early in a conversation, may appear unnatural and can relay an impression that the listener is rushing or is simply not considering obvious clues. Instead of communicating a guess, an agent may simply decide to assume a goal based on the probabilities of alternate goals at a level and progress to a more detailed level of discourse. Although correct action can lead to efficient conversation, erroneous decisions to progress are usually even more costly than explicit guessing as users are not given the chance to converse about the decision. We can consider such costs and benefits of alternate progression actions with a decision-theoretic analysis.

We developed and implemented methods for performing cost–benefit analysis to guide decisions about progression to the next level of detail, or to return to a previously examined level, based on inferred probabilities of goals within a level and the associated costs and benefits of progressing. As highlighted in Figure 1, at every step of the analysis, we consider the expected value of directly progressing or asking a question to confirm a goal, versus remaining at the current level of analysis and continuing to gather information based on VOI. We assess the utilities of different conversational outcomes and employ an approximate decision analysis to compute threshold probabilities for progression, seeking confirmation, or backtracking to a previously visited level. Details of the derivation of probability thresholds from a cost—benefit analysis are described in (Horvitz, 1999). Beyond derivation via consideration of the utility of outcomes, such threshold probabilities can be assessed directly.

The Bayesian Receptionist makes use of three thresholds, $p*$ *progress*, $p*$ *guess*, and $p*$ *backtrack*. If the probability of the goal with the highest likelihood does not exceed $p*$ *guess* or $p*$ *progress*, the system continues to perform VOI to gather additional information about the goals. If VOI becomes non-positive or there are no other observations to make, the system issues a request for additional information. Should the maximal likelihood goal at the current level exceed $p*$ *progress*, the system will assume the goal and move to the next level of detail. Should the maximal likelihood exceed $p*$ *guess*, but not exceed $p*$ *progress*, the system will engage the user to confirm or rule out the goal. Following a crisp disconfirmation of a goal, a probability of zero is assigned to that goal and the probability distribution for the remaining feasible goals is renormalized. The $p*$ threshold for *backtracking* is used in making a decision to return to a higher level of detail. The Bayesian models for goal disambiguation at levels more detailed than Level 0 include a *return* hypothesis. Should the probability of all subgoals decrease and the likelihood of the return hypothesis become greater than $p*$ *backtrack*, the system returns to the previous level. In such situations, the system apologizes for the misunderstanding and either continues VOI at the previous level or asks for more information if that VOI is non-positive.

Beyond the use of static utilities in the computation of the decision thresholds and VOI, we employed context-sensitive utilities. Utilities used in the computation of the threshold probabilities and VOI can be defined as functions of such observations as the user being hurried, or of observations about the conversational dialog itself such as the number of questions that have already been asked of users. The Bayesian Receptionist makes use of a special class of probability-sensitive costs for controlling VOI when deliberating about asking users questions at levels of detail that are marked as *atypical* levels of analysis. An example of an atypical level of analysis is Level 2, associated with the high-level goal of desiring a shuttle to travel somewhere on the Microsoft campus. Level 2 seeks to discover whether a person will need a special kind of shuttle, including the need for a vehicle that can transport handicapped people or a special shuttle for senior executives. Levels marked as atypical include a special goal state that represents the proposition that the level is irrelevant. Engaging users about subgoals at this level would appear unnatural in most cases. We dynamically update the expected cost used in the VOI analysis by considering the probability that an atypical level is relevant. The probability of relevance given evidence, $p(R|E)$, is the complement of the probability assigned to the state *irrelevent*. As the probability of relevance increases, the naturalness of being asked increases, making such a question less surprising, and, thus, less costly to ask. We compute the expected cost of asking as the sum of the costs for the outcomes of the level being relevant and irrelevant, weighted by the inferred probabilities as follows:

$$\text{Expected Cost} = p(R|E)\,\text{Cost}(Asking, Relevant) + 1\text{-}p(R|E)\,\text{Cost}(Asking, not\ Relevant)$$

where Cost(Asking, Relevant) is the cost of asking a question about an atypical situation when the level is relevant and Cost(Asking, not Relevant) is the cost of asking when the level is irrelevant. We use this expected cost in VOI for explicit question asking (versus those centering on the gathering of visual clues) in atypical levels of detail.

8 A Sample Conversation

Before concluding, let us complete the conversation started with the Bayesian Receptionist in Figure 3. As the dialog progresses, the system asks for additional information and notices the evocative word "shuttle" in the user's utterance. Given this observation, the probability that the user's goal is to travel somewhere by shuttle rises to 0.69. The belief in the leading hypothesis is not high enough to reach $p*$ *guess* or $p*$ *progress* so VOI is called. The system continues to gather evidence until the probability of the leading goal surpasses $p*$ *guess*. At this point, the system seeks direct confirmation, asking, "So you'd like a shuttle?" After confirmation, the system progresses to Level 1, focused on disambiguating the destination of the user and whether the user is traveling alone or in a group. The linguistic observation, "north" is noticed and added to the analysis and the probability distribution is updated. The greatest likelihood is now assigned to the goal of traveling to the North Campus alone, followed by travel to the North Campus in a group. However, the probabilities do not exceed $p*$ *guess*, so the system calls VOI. As portrayed in the upper portion of Figure 5, the VOI analysis leads to a decision to seek assistance with evaluating visual information about the presence of a group of people. The agent "observes" a group of people and integrates this evidence to update the probability distribution displayed in the center of the upper panel. The probability of this goal exceeds $p*$ *guess*, but does not exceed $p*$ *progression*, so the

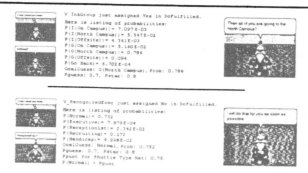

Figure 5. Upper sequence: Use of VOI to acquire visual information confirming the presence of a group, followed by update of probabilities for Level 1 goals and a decision to confirm a goal explicitly. Lower sequence: Progression to next level, use of VOI to detect if user is a recognized executive, update of probabilities of goals, and decision to forego interaction with the user about an atypical condition.

system seeks confirmation of the goal at this level of detail. Progression now occurs to Level 2 and inference is called followed by VOI. This level is labeled as an *atypical* level of refinement. Given the atypia of the level, the system computes the probability-dependent expected costs of asking the user questions and uses these costs to modulate the cost-benefit analysis in the VOI computation. Explicit questions about whether the user is an executive or is handicapped are suppressed, and the system decides to simply examine the situation with vision. As captured by the lower panel in Figure 5, visual information is acquired. The user is not recognized as an executive and inference is called. The maximal likelihood subgoal is *normal*, referring to the irrelevance of the atypical level of detail. The inferred probability of normal surpasses the $p*$ threshold and the system confirms its understanding of the user's goal at Level 1, completing the conversation.

9 Summary and Ongoing Work

We introduced an architecture for modeling dialog in joint-activity situations. Central to the architecture is the use of a goal decomposition hierarchy employing Bayesian models at increasingly detailed levels of analysis and the use of cost—benefit control procedures for navigating between levels of the hierarchy. The run-time prototype relies on the integration of several inferential components including natural language processing to provide a stream of linguistic evidence, Bayesian inference to update beliefs about the set of goals at distinct levels of analysis, value of information for asking the best questions or making the most informative observations, and decision-theoretic control policies for determining when to progress to the next level of analysis or to halt with an action. We described the operation of a prototype when populated with models built through consideration of the real-world tasks faced by receptionists at Microsoft. In our continuing work, we are pursuing the use of richer control strategies, learning of models from collected data, and extending the analysis to consider the status of a user's attention and of the mutual understanding of the semantics of concepts being communicated in conversations.

References

Albrecht, D.W., Zukerman, I., Nicholson, A.E., Bud, A. (1997). Towards a Bayesian model for keyhole plan recognition in large domains. In Jameson, A, Paris, C., and Tasso, C., eds., *Proceedings of the Sixth International Conference on User Modeling.* New York: Springer-Verlag. 365-376.

Allen, J.F., and Perrault, C. (1980). Analyzing intention in utterances. *Artificial Intelligence* 15:143-178.

Clark, H.H. (1983). Making sense of nonce sense. In G.B. Flores d'Arcais and R. Jarvella, eds., *The Process of Language Understanding.* New York: Wiley. 297-331.

Clark, H.H. (1996). *Using Language.* Cambridge University Press.

Cohen, P.R., and Levesque, H.J. (1994). Preliminaries to a collaborative model of dialogue. *Speech Communication* 15:265-274.

Conati, C., Gertner, A.S., VanLehn, K., Druzdzel, M.J. (1997). Online student modeling for coached problem solving using Bayesian networks. In Jameson, A, Paris, C., and Tasso, C., eds., *Proceedings of the Sixth International Conference on User Modeling.* New York: Springer-Verlag. 231-242.

Gorry, G.A. and Barnett, G.O. (1968). Experience with a model of sequential diagnosis. *Computers and Biomedical Research* 1:490-507.

Heckerman, D.E., Horvitz, E., and Nathwani, B.N. (1992). Toward normative expert systems: Part I. The Pathfinder project. *Methods of Information in Medicine* 31:90-105.

Heckerman, D., and Horvitz, E. (1998). Inferring informational goals from free-text queries: A Bayesian approach, *Fourteenth Conference on Uncertainty in Artificial Intelligence*, San Francisco: Morgan Kaufmann Publishers, 230-237. http://research.microsoft.com/~horvitz/aw.htm

Heidorn, G. (1999) Intelligent writing assistance. In Dale, R., Moisl, H., and Somers, H. eds., *A Handbook of Natural Language Processing Techniques.* Marcel Dekker.

Horvitz, E. Heckerman, D.E., Ng, K. and Nathwani, B.N. (1989). Heuristic abstraction in the decision-theoretic Pathfinder system, *Proceedings of the Thirteenth Symposium on Computer Applications in Medical Care.* IEEE Computer Society Press. 178-182.

Horvitz, E., Breese, J., and Henrion, M. (1988). Decision theory in expert systems and artificial intelligence. *International Journal of Approximate Reasoning, Special Issue on Uncertainty in Artificial Intelligence* 2:247-302. http://research.microsoft.com/~horvitz/dt.htm

Horvitz, E., Barry, M. (1995). Display of information for time-critical decision making. In Besnard, P., and Hanks, S , eds., *Proceedings of the Eleventh Conference on Uncertainty in Artificial Intelligence.* San Francisco: Morgan Kaufmann. 296-305. http://research.microsoft.com/~horvitz/vista.htm

Horvitz, E., Breese, J.S., Heckerman, D., Hovel, D., Rommelse, K. (1998). The Lumiere Project: Bayesian user modeling for inferring the goals and needs of software users, *Fourteenth Conference on Uncertainty in Artificial Intelligence.* San Francisco: Morgan Kaufmann Publishers. 256-265. http://research.microsoft.com/~horvitz/lumiere.htm

Horvitz, E. (1999). Principles of mixed-initiative user interfaces, In *Proceedings of Computer-Human Interaction '99*, Association for Computing Machinery Press.

Jameson, A., Schafer, R., Simons, J., and Weis, T. (1995). Adaptive provision of evaluation-oriented information: Tasks and techniques. *Proceedings of the Fourteenth International Joint Conference on Artificial Intelligence.* 1886-1895.

Jameson, A. (1996) Numerical uncertainty management in user and student modeling: An overview of systems and issues. *User Modeling and User-Adapted Interaction* 5:193-251.

Jennings, N.R., and Mamdani, E.H. (1992). Using joint responsibility to coordinate collaborative problem solving in dynamic environments. *Proceedings of the Tenth National Conference on Artificial Intelligence.* Menlo Park: AAAI Press. 269-275.

Levinson, S.C. (1992). Activity types and language. In P. Drew and J. Heritage, eds., *Talk at Work.* Cambridge University Press. 66-100.

Nunberg, G. (1979). The non-uniqueness of semantic solutions: Polysemy. *Linguistics and Philosophy* 3:143-184.

Paek, T., and Horvitz, E. (1999), A layered representation of uncertainty for managing dialogue. Manuscript submitted for publication.

One for All and All in One

A learner modelling server in a multi-agent platform

Isabel Machado[1], Alexandre Martins[2] and Ana Paiva[2]

[1] INESC, Rua Alves Redol 9, 1000 Lisboa, Portugal
[2] IST and INESC, Rua Alves Redol 9, 1000 Lisboa, Portugal
Emails: {Isabel.Machado, Alexandre.Martins, Ana.Paiva}@inesc.pt

Abstract. For the past few years several research teams have been developing intelligent learning environments (ILE) based on multi-agent architectures. For such type of architectures to be possible, the agents must have specific roles in the architecture and must be able to communicate in between them. To handle such needs, we have established a generic multi-agent architecture - the *Pedagogical Agents Communication Framework* (PACF). In PACF a set of agents were defined, their roles established, and their communication infrastructure built. Such communication infrastructure is based on a subset of the KQML language. There are two main general agents in PACF: the *Server* that acts both as a facilitator in the KQML sense and as an application-independent name server; and a Learner Modelling Server (LMS). The LMS can be used by several applications (composed by several agents) and each one can adapt the modelling strategy to its needs through the parameterisation of three configuration files: one that provides the application domain structure and the others the learner modelling strategies. Through this parameterisation the applications define how the LMS will model their learners. The LMS keeps one single database for all the learners being modelled by all the agents, allowing different applications to access to the same learner model simultaneously. These different applications can share parts of the learner models provided that they use the same domain ontology in the modelling process. This architecture has been used in a Web based distance learning scenario with two different ILEs.

1 Introduction

If we want to develop Intelligent Learning Environments (ILE) that aim to adapt the learning situations to the learners' state of knowledge, we have to maintain learner a model. Such models can be more or less complex, and can be used for either deep adaptation to the learners' preferences, state of knowledge etc., or for simple adaptation explicit in the immediate feedback provided by the environment. In both cases, the learner model itself needs to be acquired, maintained and updated along the learner interaction with the environment.

However, building such models is often left as a last job to be done in an ILE and very often remains undone. The main reason, in most cases, is that the cost of such adaptation is too high to pay the effectiveness achieved. Such high cost is due to three main reasons: first, the techniques for creating and maintaining these models are not at the finger tips of the application developers; second, very often such techniques rely on data that is difficult to acquire about the population of learners; and third even when learner models are acquired by one learning environment those models and techniques cannot be shared easily with other learning environments. In order to overcome the first problem some learner modelling shells were built so that the construction of learner modelling modules is simplified. Cases of such systems are BGP-MS (Kobsa, 1995) UM (Kay, 1995) and TAGUS (Paiva, 95). However, both systems do not allow an easy sharing of models nor they are Web oriented.

Indeed, as Web based learning environments become increasingly popular, individualisation has also became a need in such Web environments. Such individualisation has already been achieved through the use of learner modelling modules specific of some systems (see, e.g., Paiva and Machado, 1998). However, in order to use UM shells in Web scenarios we have to foster the independence between the applications and the learner modelling systems (associated with the shells). Such independence is better achieved through a client-server architecture (that is precisely the type of architectures we have on the Web). But that approach, on its own, does not guarantee us an easy online reuse of the learner models. To deal with such requirement, we need a standard communication mechanism between the server and the applications. So, in this paper we argue that such independence is better achieved with the use of a multi-agent architecture.

For the past few years, new types of architectures have been suggested for the construction of intelligent learning environments (ILEs), in particular multi-agent architectures (see, e.g., Frasson, 1996). However, one of the major problems that software developers face when following that approach is determining how the agents in the ILEs can communicate. This problem has already been subject to recent studies, in particular Ritter's protocol of communication (Ritter, 1997). However, the use of specific protocols prevents the inter-operability between agents developed by different organisations. Despite the lack of internationally accepted standards in the agent's domain, there are many situations in which a number of *de facto* standards can be used (Wooldridge, 1998). In this paper we will present a learner modelling server that is part of the PACF platform (*Pedagogical Agents Communication Framework* discussed in Martins et al., 1998). PACF adopted one of those *de facto* standards for establishing the communication between the agents - the KQML language (similar to the scenario presented by Paiva, 1996).

LMS is a learner modelling server, written in *Java*, that can be used by any application to acquire, store and maintain learner models. The application developer needs to give some configuration files to the LMS, which will take these files to perform the acquisition and maintenance of the models. The LMS, keeps the models of learners in a database, and updates these models according to the information given by the application and the configuration files provided initially. Indeed, the models are kept in a database, and then they can be shared by several applications (providing only, that they share the same ontology). The idea is that once agreed upon a common ontology, two applications can share their learner models, stored and maintained by the LMS.

This paper is organised as follows: first we will present the LMS within the PACF platform. Then we will describe in more detail the architecture and its modules, the domain and learner model composition and its parameterisation. The use of ontologies in LMS is focused and illustrated with a concrete scenario of LMS utilisation. Finally we will draw some conclusions.

2 LMS as a modelling agent in Multi-agent Platform

The LMS plays the role of a general agent in the *Pedagogical Agents Communication Framework (PACF)*. The *PACF* describes how several agents implemented as components in a multi-agent system, can interact with each other to achieve the behaviour of an Intelligent Learning Environment (see Figure 1).

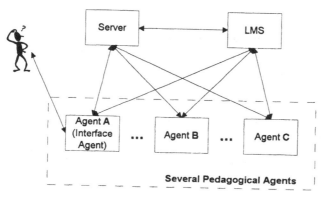

Figure 1 - The architecture of PACF

In this framework there is a set of agents that play different roles in the multi-agent learning environment. These agents can be, for example, interface agents that interact with the learner, or tutor agents that are expert in the domain. The agents must communicate exchanging messages that are called *performatives*, according to the KQML language (see Finin (1993, 1995)).

The KQML language can be understood as having three levels (Thirunavukkarasu, 1995): the *content level*, the *communication level* and the *message level*. The *content level* specifies the actual content of the message conveyed in the application's representation language, but it is in the *message level* that the actual message is built. In the framework we consider that the agents may present different capabilities and/or responsibilities in relation to the others, therefore, in order for agents to identify each other' roles, we provided a very simple agent taxonomy which gives an indication on the overall behaviour of a given agent type. Such taxonomy distinguishes two types of agents: general agents and application specific agents.

A general agent plays the same role in several different scenarios and offers the same set of functionalities in all situations. The *PACF* defines two of such general agents: the *Server* and the LMS. The *Server* acts both as a facilitator in the KQML sense and as an application-independent name server. The Server's address is known at system start-up time and the first action that all other agents perform is to register their own address and taxonomic type to that server using a KQML advertise *performative*. The server maintains a simple agent database, which is used to get agents mutually acquainted when they request to indicate another agent that is able to perform a certain task. The server supports multiple ontologies by keeping the ontology information along with each agent that complies with that ontology. This issue will be important in the sharing of the learner models.

The application specific agents are defined by each client application and their roles are specific within that application's domain. For example, an application agent that is usually found in most of the ILEs would be a domain expert agent. Another would be a tutoring agent, which task would be to interpret the data contained in the learner models (kept in the LMS) and provide adequate learning situations to the learner.

3 LMS

Within the ACF architecture the LMS plays the role of a learner modelling server. Learner modelling is the key to an individualised learning. Our main research goal was to develop a learner modelling server which could be used concurrently by multiple applications and that could also provide a reliable way of sharing the learner models between a set o applications.

3.1 The architecture of the Learner Modelling Server

With this aim in mind we based the LMS architecture on a client-server model (see Figure 2), which relies on *Java Remote Method Invocation (RMI)* protocol. With this architecture most of the learner models' manipulation is handled by the LMS, and only query results are sent back to the client applications. Although, the architecture relies on the *Java RMI* protocol, the communication between the LMS and the client applications is established by means of a subset of the KQML language. The overall communication between the LMS and the client applications is performed in the following manner:

- the client applications send a KQML *performative* to the LMS, for example, to inquire for some element of a learner model, or to require an update on a particular learner model, etc.;
- the LMS interprets the received message, performs the required actions and replies with a *performative*, which content can be the questioned value or an acknowledgement concerning a performed task.

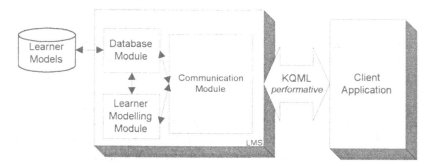

Figure 2 - The LMS architecture

To support these functionalities, the LMS architecture is modular and combines the following modules:

- the communication module - allows the communication with other agents through the use of a set of KQML *performatives*. Such performatives allow the manipulation and management of the learner models and also the establishment of the communication within the *PACF*;
- the database module – implements all the functions necessary to insert, update, delete, and select the learner models;
- the learner modelling module – executes the learner modelling cycle. It uses the parameterised learner modelling strategies to make decisions on the update of the learner models maintained by the server.

3.2 The generic Domain Model

In order to establish a basic domain model that can be used by the distinct client applications some restrictions were made:

- since the learner model aim to be used to store the learners state of knowledge with respect to a certain domain, then, we assumed that such domain is structured in *Topics*;
- while interacting with the application the learner performs *Actions* and those actions are indeed the observable behaviour of the learner that is used to infer his or her state of knowledge, preferences, etc.

With this simple structure we establish a baseline which allows the management of different domains associated to different applications, without any other different mechanism. Besides, improving the management of the domain models this generic structure makes easier the learner model sharing between the applications.

3.3 The Learner Models

For each client application the LMS stores the following information in the learner model:

- The declarative Knowledge Level associated with a particular *Topic*: $KL_{declarative}(Topic)$
- Information about some actions performed on the current *Topic*:
  - the Knowledge Level associated with each *Action* that composes the current *Topic*: $KL(Action)$;
  - the number of contacts experienced by the learner with that *Action*.

This information is stored in the database and can represent the learners' beliefs about the domain or the learners' preferences or some learners' characteristics. The content of the model, differently from the TAGUS system, (Paiva, 1995), is thus defined entirely by the application developer, using the above types of structures.

3.4 The Parameterisation of the LMS

Each client application must specify how the LMS should model its learners. This specification is done by the definition of three configuration files: a domain structure file and two learning strategy files.

The domain structure file includes the definition of all the *Topics* that are introduced by the application and all the *Actions* that can be performed by a learner in a particular *Topic*.

Besides specifying the domain structure, the application must also define a weight value associated with each *Action*. This value translates the importance of that particular *Action* within the knowledge of a *Topic*. The LMS provides a graphical environment for the definition of domain structure and for the definition of the application specific parameters (see Figure 3).

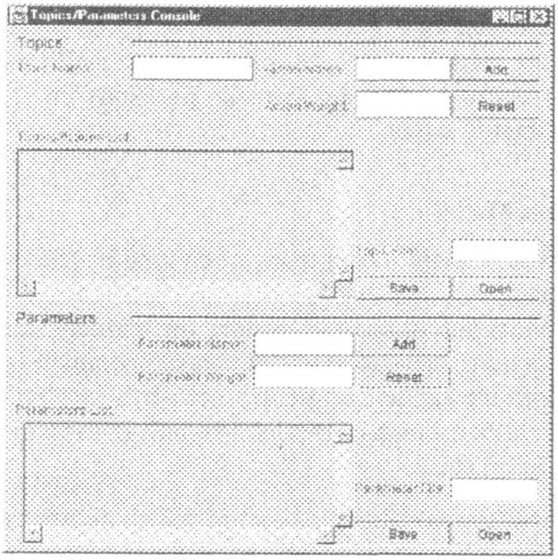

Figure 3 - Graphical environment for the definition of the domain structure and application parameters

The two learning strategy files include:

– the definition of application specific parameters, and;
– the definition of the classification and updating rules of the learner models.

The client applications have the possibility to define specific application parameters. These parameters provide the application with particular information about its learning process. Therefore, these parameters only have a meaning in that particular application. The application must define a set of rules that will assign and update values to those parameters and when defining them the application developer must also provide a default value for each of them.

The learning strategies adopted by the applications are defined through a set of rules. There are two kinds of rules: the *classification rules* and the *updating rules*. The classification rules define which learner behaviours should be included in a learner model. The syntax of the classification rules is the following:

```
CLASSIFICATION = value_l
expression_11 ... expression_1n
```

The expressions are relational expressions (using the usual relational operators: >, <, >=, <=, <> and =).

The semantic of each classification rule is expressed by the following condition:

```
if (∃i:compatible(expressionᵢ)) and (¬∃j:incompatible(expressionⱼ))
then
   CLASSIFICATION = value
```

To require an update of the learner model the client application must identify the current *Topic* and *Action*, and also define which are the correspondent updating expressions that should be used to characterise that particular learning situation. These expressions will have to match some (one) of the preconditions of a classification rule. Consequently, three distinct situations can arise, one of the preconditions of a classification rule may be:

- compatible - when it matches with one of the updating expressions and the precondition is verified;
- incompatible - when one of the updating rules invalidates the precondition, i.e., matches with one of the updating expression but is not verified;
- indifferent – when none of the updating rules matches any of the preconditions.

Therefore, one rule can be applied, in order to accomplish a request for a learner model update, if at least one of the preconditions is compatible and there is not any incompatible updating expression. This way, it is possible that there can exist several classification rules that could be applied in that particular updating request. In this case, the "winning" rule is the one that has a higher number of matches with the updating rules and if several classification rules have the same number of matches the LMS originates an internal message and no update is performed.

After finding which is the most suitable classification rule for that updating request, we have to define the set of actions that will constitute the updating rule. The updating rules will be applied to change the content of the learner models. The syntax of a updating rule is as follows:

```
CLASSIFICATION = value₁
updatе₁₁
```

The updating expressions assign values to variables (variable = aritExpression), and the aritExpression can contain the usual arithmetic operators: +, -, * and /. The semantic associated with an updating rule is:

if CLASSIFICATION = *value* then *update₁* ...*updateₙ*

The definition of both kinds of rules can be done through the use of a graphical environment (see Figure 4).

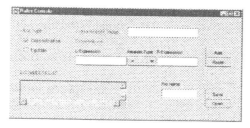

Figure 4 - Graphical environment for the definition of the classification and updating rules

The LMS configuration files are saved through the use of *Java* serializable mechanism. Through this mechanism is possible to store, in a file, *Java* objects without loosing any information associated with them.

3.5 The use of ontologies in the LMS

The learner models in LMS are maintained in a database that is accessible for any client application provided that it knows the password associated with a particular learner. So, the models stored by the LMS can be transparently shared amongst applications without the need for explicit communication between the applications, as in the case of PAT Online and Interbook (Brusilovsky, 1997). This sharing is nevertheless conditioned by the applications ontology type. The idea is that the client applications can negotiate and share the same ontology. As well as sharing the same ontology the applications need to also to share the knowledge about both domain structures, because they have to know which parts are common and can be used in the other learning strategy.

Therefore, in order for LMS to be a fully interoperable agent the learner models are structured according to the chosen domain ontology. This approach allows the agents from the different applications to interact with LMS based on a common grounded understanding of the elements that they have to specify to parameterise and use the LMS.

So far, in ILEs the use of ontologies has been centred on the description of learner models (see Mizoguchi, 1997). In here, such use is different in the sense that the ontologies are used for sharing the learner models, and thus they are domain ontologies.

4   Concrete Scenario

To illustrate this use we considered a concrete scenario in which there are two different web-based ILEs based on the PACF architecture. Both applications (ILEs) use the same LMS and interact with the general *Server*. The *Server* role is to establish the communication channels between all the agents in the platform (by indicating the remote locations of the existent agents). Both ILEs aim to teach the learners in the mathematics domain: one presents the linear functions domain and the other the quadratic functions domain. Hence, they have the same ontology type (*Mathematics*). The learner *Gil* with the password *iloveMaths* interacts with both ILEs. In the PACF platform there is an external service, which registers *Gil* within the PACF platform, and after this registration *Gil* is able to use any application on the this platform. In Table 1 and Table 2 we can see the domain structure of the two ILEs.

Linear Functions Application - Linear Functions Domain	
Topics	Actions
LinearF - y = mx + b	Identifying the functions zeros
	Graphical representation of the function
	Analytical representation of the function

Table 1 – Linear Functions Domain

Quadratic Functions Application – Quadratic Functions Domain

Topics	Actions
QuadraticF - $y = ax^2 + bx + c$	Reviewing the linear functions Introduction to the quadratic functions ...

Table 2 – Quadratic Functions Domain

Gil starts to interact with the Linear Functions Application, solving correctly an exercise about the identification of the zeros of a function. Given that information the tutor agent of this application (TutorLF) asks the LMS to update of *Gil*'s learner model. Since the communication between all agents is done through the KQML language the update request would be done through the use of a KQML *performative*. For example,

```
(tell
  :sender rmi://leeds.inesc.pt/TutorLF
  :receiver rmi://bangkok.inesc.pt/LMS
  :reply-with q1
  :language JAVA
  :content (updateTopicAction(Mathematics Gil LinearF
        identifyZeros [(Content_Type=Exercise),(Success=Correct)] ?x)))
```

Gil carries on interacting with the two applications and reaches the end of his learning process in the Linear Functions application, continuing on the Quadratic Functions topic. When the tutor agent of such application (TutorQF) detects the presence of a new learner, he will ask the LMS for information about that new learner, sending the following *performative* to LMS:

```
(ask-if
  :sender rmi://athens.inesc.pt/TutorQF
  :receiver rmi://bangkok.inesc.pt/LMS
  :reply-with q2
  :language JAVA
  :content (infoTopic(Mathematics Gil LinearF ?x)))
```

Before presenting any contents to *Gil* the TutorQF inquires the LMS about *Gil*'s knowledge level. Since the TutorQF is only interested about the *Gil's* knowledge within the *Mathematics* ontology and since it also knows the existence of another application on this ontology (and with a common domain part), it will send a performative enquiring about *Gil* state of knowledge on this particular ontology. Considering that *Gil* had already achieved a good knowledge level on the linear functions domain (both applications need to understand what means that knowledge level) the TutorQF decides not to present to *Gil* the linear functions review but the quadratic functions introduction. If *Gil* achieves a relevant performance in that particular topic the TutorQF can update the knowledge level by simply sending the following *performative* to the LMS:

```
(tell
  :sender rmi://athens.inesc.pt/TutorQF
  :receiver rmi://bangkok.inesc.pt/LMS
  :reply-with q1
  :language JAVA
  :content (updateTopicAction(Mathematics Gil QuadraticF introduction
        [(Content_Type=Explanation),(Experience=FirstTime)] ?x)))
```

With this concrete scenario we have shown some of the advantages of assigning ontologi to our domain applications, specially the immediate advantages on the sharing the learn models between those applications.

5 Conclusions

In this paper we have introduced a new approach for a learner modelling systems embedde in multi-agent architectures. This approach allows not only the reusability of the softwa components (learner modelling processes) but also the sharing of the learner models. This main feature of this approach is the communication between the agents using a subset KQML (a *de facto* standard) and the use of ontologies for the sharing of the models.

To illustrate our approach we have presented a learner modelling server for Web base learning environments that is an agent in the PACF framework. Using LMS in that multi agent framework we have presented a scenario that shows how it works with two differe applications sharing the same learner model.

References

Brusilovsky, P., Ritter, S. & Schwarz, E., "Distributed intelligent tutoring on the Web" in *Proceedin of AI-ED '97, 8th World Conference of Artificial Intelligence in Education*, Ed. B. du Boulay and Mizoguchi, IOS Press, 1997.

Finin, T., Weber, J., Wiederhold, G. & Genesereth, M., *Draft Specification of the KQML Agent Con munication Language*, University of Maryland Baltimore County, 1993.

Finin T., Labrou Y. & Mayfield, J., "KQML as an agent communication language" in Software Agen Ed. J. Bradshaw MIT Press, 1995.

Frasson, C., Mengelle, T., Aimeur, E. & Gouardères, G., "An Actor-based Architecture for Intellige Tutoring Systems" in *Proceedings of Intelligent Tutoring Systems 96 Conference*, Lecture Notes Computer Science, Springer Verlag, 1996.

Kay, J., "The UM Toolkit for Cooperative User Modeling". *User Modeling and User-Adapted Intera tion* 4(3), 149-196.

Kobsa, A. & Pohl, W., "The User Modeling Shell System BGP-MS". *User Modeling and User-Adapt Interaction* 4(1), 59-106.

Paiva, A. & Self, J., "TAGUS – A User and Learner Modeling Workbench". *User Modeling and Use Adapted Interaction* 4(3), 197-226.

Paiva, A. "Learner Modelling Agents" in *EuroAIED- Proceedings of the European Conference on Ar ficial Intelligence in Education*, Eds. P. Brna, A. Paiva & J. Self, Colibri, 1996.

Paiva, A., Machado, I., "Vincent, an autonomous pedagogical agent for on-the-job training" in *Intel gent Tutoring Systems 98 Conference,* Lecture Notes in Computer Science, Springer-Verlag, 1998.

Martins, A., Machado, I. & Paiva, A. "A KQML based communication framework for multi-agent ILE in the Pedagogical Agents Workshop of Intelligent Tutoring Systems 98 Conference, 1998.

Mizoguchi, R., Ikeda, M. & Sinitsa, K., "Roles of Shared Ontology in AI-ED Research" in *Proceedin of AI-ED '97, 8th World Conference of Artificial Intelligence in Education*, Ed. B. du Boulay and Mizoguchi, IOS Press, 1997.

Ritter, S., "Communication, Cooperation and Competition among Multiple Tutor Agents" in *Procee ings of AI-ED '97, 8th World Conference of Artificial Intelligence in Education*, Ed. B. du Boul and R. Mizoguchi, IOS Press, 1997.

Thirunavukkarasu, C., Finin, T. & Mayfield, J., "Secret Agents – A Security Architecture for the KQML Agent Communication Language" in *CIKM '95 Intelligent Information Agents Workshop*, 1995.

Wooldridge, M. & Jennings, N., "Pitfalls of Agent-Oriented Development" in *Proceedings of Autonomous Agents 98*, Eds. K. Sycara & M. Wooldridge, ACM Press, 1998.

Learning Models of Other Agents Using Influence Diagrams

Dicky Suryadi and Piotr J. Gmytrasiewicz

Department of Computer Science and Engineering, University of Texas at Arlington

Abstract. We adopt decision theory as a descriptive paradigm to model rational agents. We use influence diagrams as a modeling representation of agents, which is used to interact with them and to predict their behavior. We provide a framework that an agent can use to learn the models of other agents in a multi-agent system (MAS) based on their observed behavior. Since the correct model is usually not known with certainty our agents maintain a number of possible models and assign them probabilities of being correct. When none of the available models is likely to be correct, we modify one of them to better account for the observed behaviors. The modification refines the parameters of the influence diagram used to model the other agent's capabilities, preferences, or beliefs. The modified model is then allowed to compete with the other models and the probability assigned to it being correct can be arrived at based on how well it predicts the observed behaviors of the other agent.

1 Introduction

As research and development activities in agent-based systems progress, we can expect to see that in the future much of our computer-related works are done with the help of intelligent agents. In some systems, an agent may be working in the presence of other agents, either automated or human. These types of systems are called multi-agent systems (MAS), and are currently an active area of research. One important motivation behind the research is to find techniques that allow multiple agents to coordinate their actions so that individual rational actions do not adversely affect the overall system efficiency (Bond and Gasser, 1988). Effective coordination among agents in dynamic environments may be achieved by extending the agents' learning ability to recognize the capabilities, desires, and beliefs of other agents present in their environment (Gmytrasiewicz and Durfee, 1998).

Several papers have reported variety of techniques for constructing the models of agents. Kaminka et al. (1998) described a rule-based model for plan recognition task in the air combat simulation environment, while Carmel and Markovitch (1996) explored the use of finite automata to model the opponent agent's strategy. A series of papers reported works on recursive modeling method (RMM) for decision-theoretic agents, which uses deeper, nested models of other agents (Gmytrasiewicz et al., 1991, Vidal and Durfee, 1995, Gmytrasiewicz and Durfee, 1995, Gmytrasiewicz, 1996, Noh and Gmytrasiewicz, 1997). RMM represents an agent's decision situation in the form of a payoff matrix. In terms of belief, desire and intention (BDI) architecture, a payoff matrix contains a compiled representation of the agent's capabilities, preferences, and beliefs about the world. Beliefs about other agents are represented in terms of their own payoff matrices. These matrices form a hierarchical modeling structure, which is evaluated in the bottom-up fashion to determine the agent's action that maximize its expected utility.

Another decision-theoretic tool for constructing models of agents is an influence diagram, which represents information about an agent's capabilities, preferences, and beliefs in a more explicit form. While RMM payoff matrices can be seen to summarize the information contained in the influence diagram (Noh and Gmytrasiewicz, 1997), this type of representation may provide better insight to the learning problem as it completely specifies all known random variables in the domain and their dependence relationships.

In our work, we seek to develop a method that can be used by an agent to learn the models of other agents. Our basic paradigm is to use decision-theoretic notion of rationality to describe and predict actions of other agents. Thus, we use influence diagrams as a modeling representation for agents. Given an initial model of an agent and a history of its observed behavior, we construct new models by refining the parameters of influence diagram in the initial model. The probabilities of a model being correct can be assigned based on how well it predicts the history of behavior.

The rest of the paper starts with an overview of influence diagrams, followed by an example on how they can be used to represent decision models of agents. Next, we get into the learning problem. We present a learning method for other agents capabilities and preferences, and we provide an example on how to apply it in a particular MAS domain. Finally, we present our conclusions and directions for further work.

2   Influence Diagrams

An Influence diagram (Howard and Matheson, 1984) is a graphical knowledge representation of a decision problem. It may be viewed as an extension to a Bayesian or belief network (Pearl, 1988), with additional node types for decisions and utilities. Influence diagrams have three types of nodes: nature node, decision node, and utility node. Just as in belief networks, nature nodes are associated with random variables or features, which represent the agent's possibly uncertain beliefs about the world. Decision node holds the choice of actions an agent has, thus represents the agent's capabilities. Utility node represent the agent's preferences. The links between the nodes summarize their dependence relationships.

Evaluation of the influence diagram is done by setting the value of the decision node to a particular choice of action, and treating the node just as a nature node with a known value that can further influence the values of other nodes. An algorithm for evaluating influence diagrams can be found in Russell and Norvig (1995).

Anti-air Defense Domain.   As an example on how to use influence diagram to represent an agent's decision model, we present the anti-air defense domain, adapted from Noh and Gmytrasiewicz (1997). The scenario shown in Figure 1 depicts an MAS with two agents, in the roles of the defending units, against two incoming missiles in a 20x20 grid world. Each defending unit has only one interceptor and has to decide which of the missiles to intercept. When a missile reaches the ground, it inflicts damage in proportion to its warhead size. The goal of each unit is to minimize overall damage to the ground. To coordinate their decisions the units have to model each other to avoid redundant targeting of the same threat. Figure 2, shows an influence diagram representation that unit B1 may have to model decision-making of unit B2.

3   Learning Problem

The purpose of learning models of other agents is to have models that can predict other agents' behavior correctly, so that the predictions will lead the learning agent to arrive at the best decision

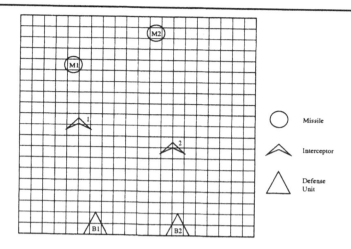

Figure 1. The anti-air defense domain.

in term of meeting the goal efficiently. The agent should already have a multi-agent reasoning system and maintain models of other agents in its knowledge base. Due to uncertainty, the agent assigns probabilities to the models, which are updated based on a history of the other agents' observed behavior. If a model is not accurate, its probability will gradually decrease. This signals the need for a better model, which can be obtained by learning.

In most situations, information about other agents only come from our observation of their behavior. Let us define a history of an agent's behavior as a set of its observed actions during a particular time frame, in which the data of the world states are known. Given only a history of behavior, how do we learn a better model? Our idea is to modify the initial model by refining parameters in influence diagram that are associated with capabilities, preferences and beliefs of other agent, based on the history of its behavior. The refinement can be done in stages with the order as above, according to the increasing level of complexity. There can be a number of modified models that can be generated. We will allow the modified models to compete with each other and other models maintained by the learning agent. The probability of each model being correct can be arrived based on how well the model predicts the history of behavior.

As we mentioned, we model the other agents as influence diagrams. From the point of view of learning, influence diagrams inherit the main feature of learning in belief networks, with additional aspects that relate to the character of decision and utility nodes. As a modeling representation tool, influence diagram is able to express an agent's capabilities, preferences, and beliefs, which are required if we want to predict the agent's behavior. Whereas learning problem in belief network is limited to learning the beliefs, influence diagram allows us to extend the description with learning the capabilities, that is, finding the correct possible value assignments for the decision node, and learning the preferences, which is finding the correct utility function.

The rest of this section describe the method we use to perform the refinement in an influence diagram. We discuss the strategy for learning the capabilities and the beliefs, but we concentrate on a method for learning the preferences.

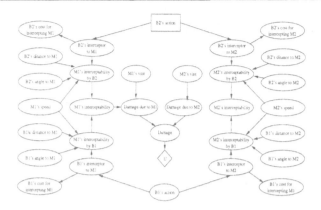

Figure 2. Decision model of defense unit B2.

3.1   Capabilities

An agent's capabilities are the alternative courses of actions it can execute to interact with the world. In an influence diagram, we represent them as possible value assignments to the agent's decision node. These values need to be exhaustive, which means that a model of other agent should cover all the possibilities of what the agent can do, even if they are not known or very unlikely. We can specify *Other* action value to represent all the unknown or unlikely actions not explicitly represented. At times, the agent may observed to be executing an action that is not explicitly present in our current model. In this case, we modify the model by specifying the action as explicit possible value of the decision node, and by updating the CPT's of the nodes that are influenced by the decision node.

For example, consider the agent as a defense unit B1 in the anti-air defense domain. It may be that initially B1 thinks that B2 is not equipped with long range interceptors. It would then model the capabilities of B2 as a set of decision node's values $\{SR\_M1, SR\_M2, Other\}$ in B1's model of B2, where SR_M1 and SR_M2 denote the actions of launching short range interceptors at missile M1 and M2, respectively. At some time, B1 could observe that B2 launches long range interceptor at one of the targets. Given this observation, B1 will modify its model of B2; the refined set of decision node's values is $\{SR\_M1, SR\_M2, LR\_M1, LR\_M2, Others\}$, where LR_M1 and LR_M2 explicitly represent the actions of launching long range interceptors at M1 and M2, which were thought unlikely before.

Conversely, sometimes the other agent's capabilities may need to be collapsed and included as part of the *Other* value. This may happen, for example, when B2 has become incapacitated and can no longer perform certain actions. From B1's perspective, it may notice that certain actions are missing from B2's history of behavior, especially when B1 believes that the missing action is the action B2 should take, if it is capable of it. To guarantee that the situation is caused only by an inaccuracy in modeling B2's capabilities, we need to identify the next preferable action given the model. If it agrees with the history of behavior, we can reason that the model still captures B2's beliefs and preferences except that somehow B2 cannot do the action that is missing from the history of behavior. B1's model of B2 is modified by removing the value of the missing action from the decision node.

3.2 Preferences

When a model of other agent cannot explain the history of its behavior, one of the possible reasons is that the agent's preferences are not accurately represented by the model. Our strategy will be to modify the model by refining the utility function so that every action in the history of behavior always maximizes utilities of the resulting states. Let $U(S)$ denote the utility of state S, which is given by a utility function.

The general structure of utility function is:

$$U(S) = f(X_1, ..., X_N) \tag{1}$$

where $X = \{X_1, ..., X_N\}$ is a set of features that directly influence the agent's preferences. In influence diagram, X is the set of parents of the utility node. The utility function f, is commonly postulated in multi-attribute utility theory (Keeney and Raiffa, 1976,Russell and Norvig, 1995) to be a weighted sum of the factors of values of features X_k, $k = 1, ..., N$. For simplicity, we assume that weighted factors depend linearly on the features X_k. We realize that this is a strong approximation, for example, in case of the utility of money, St. Petersburg paradox shows that it is not linear.

Therefore, we rewrite an agent's utility function as follows:

$$U(S) = w_1 x_1 + ... + w_N x_N \tag{2}$$

where each weight w_k corresponds to a feature X_k and represents the feature's measure of influence on the agent's utility, and x_k is the value of the feature X_k in state S. Our method of learning the agent's preferences will modify the weights w_k.

Let A^* denote an action that maximizes expected utility:

$$A^* = \arg\max_{a_i} \sum_{j=1}^{J} P(S_J | a_i, E) \times U(S_J) \tag{3}$$

where $A = \{a_1, ..., a_M\}$ is a set of the agent's alternative actions, and S_j are the possible outcome states given a, possibly non-deterministic, action a_i, with j ranging over J different outcomes. The background evidence E in the conditional probabilities represents the known data of the world which are provided in the history of behavior.

Using Equation 2 and 3, we obtain:

$$A^* = \arg\max_{a_i} \sum_{j=1}^{J} P(S_j | a_i, E) \sum_{k=1}^{N} w_k x_k^j \tag{4}$$

where x_k^j is the value of the feature X_k in the state S_j. We can show that this equation is equivalent to:

$$A^* = \arg\max_{a_i} \sum_{k=1}^{N} w_k \chi_k^i \tag{5}$$

where χ_k^i denote the expected value of feature X_k given a_i and background evidences E, given by the summation of all possible values of X_k: $(x_{k,1}, ..., x_{k,r_k})$ times their conditional probabilities:

$$\chi_k^i = \sum_{l=1}^{r_k} x_{k,l} \times P(X_k = x_{k,l}|a_i, E) \tag{6}$$

From the history of other agent's behavior, we have a set of the agent's observed actions during a given time frame. Let $D = \{D(1), ..., D(T)\}$ denotes such set, where T is the total number of actions, and $D(t) \in A, t = 1, ..., T$. The refinement of utility function is accomplished by having an initial utility function derived from the initial model, and subsequently adjusting the weights w_k based on the set D, so that $D(t)$ is equal to A^* for every situation t.

The choice of initial utility function depends on the initial knowledge the learning agent has about the other agent. In the extreme case where B1 has absolutely no knowledge on B2's preferences, it may have to put all the known features in B2's utility function and assign zero to all the weights.

To adjust the weights we follow a procedure common in neural network learning. We can render Equation 5 into neural network structure as shown in Figure 3. The network represents a

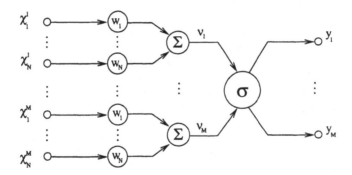

Figure 3. Network for learning the weights.

decision process at a decision situation t, where $\sigma(t)$ is the activation function that constitutes the output decision rule (Haykin, 1994):

$$y_i(t) = \begin{cases} 1 & v_i(t) > v_j(t) \ for \ all \ j \neq i \\ 0 & otherwise \end{cases} \tag{7}$$

where $i = 1, ..., M$. Let $d_i(t)$ represents the desired output value from $D(t)$ as follows:

$$d_i(t) = \begin{cases} 1 & D(t) = a_i \\ 0 & otherwise \end{cases} \tag{8}$$

Weight adjustment is done by applying a well-known gradient descent technique, namely *delta rule*(Widrow and Hoff Jr. (1960)). The idea is to minimize a cost function based on the error signal $e_i(t)$ so that each weight adjustment brings the actual output value closer to the desired value. A commonly used cost function is the *mean-square-error* criterion:

$$E(t) = \frac{1}{2} \sum_{i=1}^{M} e_i^2(t) \tag{9}$$

where $e_i(t)$ is the error signal which is defined by:

$$e_i(t) = d_i(t) - y_i(t) \tag{10}$$

According to delta rule, the weight adjustment is proportional to the product of the error signal and the input unit. In our network, we use weight sharing to indicate the symmetry of the utility computation. We settle the adjustment for a shared weight as the sum of the correction of weights for all output units. We require normalization on χ before presenting it to the network, so that the resulting weights are normalized. The normalization is given by:

$$\aleph_k^i = \frac{\chi_k^i}{\sqrt{\sum_{s=1}^{M} \sum_{t=1}^{N} (\chi_t^s)^2}} \tag{11}$$

Thus, the final rule is given by:

$$\Delta w_k(t) = \eta \sum_{i=1}^{M} e_i(t) \aleph_k^i(t) \tag{12}$$

where $k = 1, ..., N$ and η is a positive constant that determines the rate of learning. The probabilities required to compute χ^i can be determined by evaluating the influence diagram model of the agent for every a_i.

Example. For demonstration of our method, let us consider a simple situation in the anti-air defense domain. Say that B1 knows there are at most two features that influence preferences of the unit B2. That is, the set of features that can influence B2's utility is $\{Damage, Cost\}$, where the possible value assignments for $Damage$ are $(0, 100, 500)$ and $Cost$ $(0, 1000, 5000)$.

B1 initially models B2's utility in inverse proportion to $Damage$ and independent to $Cost$. Therefore, the initial assignment of weights to features is:

$$w_1 = -1.0, \ w_2 = 0.0$$

This means that B1 thinks B2 only cares about minimizing damage to the ground, and not cost of intercepting the missiles. In this example we show how these weight are modified gives observation of B2's behavior that were different from the ones predicted by the initial model.

Let $A = \{I\_M1, I\_M2\}$ is a set of B2's possible actions, where I_M1 stands for intercept missile M1, and I_M2 intercept missile M2. In this case, assume that intercepting missile M1 would require a more sophisticated and more accurate interceptor. The following conditional probability distributions for $Damage$ and $Cost$:

$$P(Damage|I\_M1, E) = (.20, .30, .50)$$
$$P(Damage|I\_M2, E) = (.10, .10, .80)$$
$$P(Cost|I\_M1, E) \ \ = (0, .30, .70)$$
$$P(Cost|I\_M2, E) \ \ = (0, .60, .40)$$

The above values reflect that using the advanced interceptor for missile M1 is more likely to reduce damage, but also more likely to result in a higher cost. The values of expected damage and cost are computed using Equation 6:

$$
\begin{aligned}
\chi_1^1 &= 0 \times .1 + 100 \times .1 + 500 \times .8 \ \ = 280 \\
\chi_2^1 &= 0 \times 0 + 1000 \times .3 + 5000 \times .7 = 3800 \\
\chi_1^2 &= 0 \times .2 + 100 \times .3 + 500 \times .5 \ \ = 410 \\
\chi_2^2 &= 0 \times 0 + 1000 \times .6 + 5000 \times .4 = 2600
\end{aligned}
$$

where χ_1^1 and χ_2^1 are expected damage and cost given M1, and χ_1^2 and χ_2^2 are expected damage and cost given M2. The next step is to normalize χ, by applying Equation 11. Using the initial weights that indicate that B2 prefers to minimize damages but does not care about the costs, B1 arrives at a prediction that B2 would choose to intercept M1 and execute the action I_M1. Therefore, the values of network outputs according to B1's model of B2 are:

$$
y_1 = 1, \ y_2 = 0
$$

In the example case, however, B2 does something B1 did not expect and intercepts missile M2. Given that, B1 observes B2 takes action I_M2, the values of desired outputs, and the error signals are:

$$
\begin{aligned}
d_1 &= 0, \quad d_2 = 1 \\
e_1 &= -1, \ e_2 = 1
\end{aligned}
$$

Using Equation 12 with the learning rate of $\eta = .1$, we have:

$$
\begin{aligned}
\Delta w_1 &= .1 \times (-1 \times 0.060 + 1 \times 0.089) = 0.029 \\
\Delta w_2 &= .1 \times (-1 \times 0.821 + 1 \times 0.561) = -0.260
\end{aligned}
$$

The weights for the utility function in B1's model of B2 become:

$$
w_1 = -0.971, \ w_2 = -0.260
$$

As the result of considering this unexpected behavior of B2, therefore, B1 adjusted the weights it uses to model B2's utility function. Intuitively, the adjusted weights indicate that B2 does not care about the damages as much as B1 initially thought, and that it cares abut the costs of the defense operation as well.

In our experiments we simulated 100 decision situations, in which the positions and the sizes of the attacking missiles were generated randomly for each situation, and B2's behavior was guided by it's preference to minimize both damages and costs in equal proportion. After these iterations, the weights were further to the values:

$$
w_1 = -0.777, \ w_2 = -0.561
$$

This result confirms our intuition in this case; as B1 observed B2's behavior, its model of B2's utility function started resembling B2's actual preferences.

3.3 Beliefs

An agent's beliefs are represented in influence diagram as the nature nodes and the probabilistic relationships that exist among them. Given that we have knowledge on other agent's capabilities and preferences, and that our model still cannot predict its behavior, it is reasonable to assume that the model may not have the correct dependence links or probability assignments. We modify the model by refining them. The obvious difficulty is to determine where to begin the refinement. In a complex model, there can be a large number of possibilities that can account for the problem. What we need is to have a method that can trace down the elements in the belief system which need refinement. Although there are some good algorithms for learning the structure and local probability distributions, such as K2 algorithm (Cooper and Herskovits (1992)), the nature of our problem prevents us to use such algorithms.

Our idea for approaching the problem is to apply similar learning method in the previous subsection, only now we set the weights fixed and learn the expected values of the features which influence the utility. By using this process, it is possible to determine which of the feature nodes that are likely to be the source of inaccuracy in the model. We let Φ denote the set of of such feature nodes. There are several strategies to modify the model that are based on exploring the possible reasons that cause the model's failure to predict the behavior.

The first strategy assumes that the reason is due to incorrect local probability distributions of the features in Φ. Based on this assumption, the model is modified by refining CPT's on the feature nodes in Φ. The second strategy assumes that the reason is due to incorrect dependence relationships involving the features in Φ. The model is modified by refining the structure of influence diagram. The alternatives are to remove links from certain parent nodes, or to add more links from other nodes. The third strategy assumes that the problem is caused, not by the features in Φ, but by their parents. It is possible that certain parent nodes have incorrect probability distributions or incorrect dependence relationships. The model is modified by performing these strategies at the level of the parent nodes of Φ. Note that this strategy has a recursive property. It allows the refinement goes bottom up until there are no more parents or the evidence nodes are reached.

These strategies attempt to narrow down the search space of possible models. However, the number of models we come up with can still be unreasonably high, and we are yet to develop a method that can decrease the number further.

4   Conclusion and Further Work

In this paper, we developed a framework that can be used by an agent to learn models of other agents in a multi-agent system. The framework makes use of influence diagrams as a modeling representation tool. We addressed three strategies to create a new model of the other agent, which are based on learning its capabilities, preferences, and beliefs, given an initial model and the agent's behavior data.

We presented a method for learning the agents' capabilities, and our ideas on how to learn the beliefs, but we concentrated on learning of the other agent's preferences. Our method attempts to modify the other agent's utility function by incorporating a neural network learning technique, which involves the presentation of the history of other agent's behavior as the training set and a series of weight adjustments. The new model for the agent is created by replacing the initial model's utility function with the one produced by our method. To assign the probability to the new model being correct, we allow it to compete with other models we have based on how well each model predicts the behavior.

We are currently working on the implementation of the learning algorithm and its integration with the agent's probabilistic frame-based knowledge base. We will provide the results from the experiment in our next paper.

References

Bond, A. H., and Gasser, L. (1988). *Readings in Distributed Artificial Intelligence*. San Mateo, CA: Morgan Kaufmann Publishers.

Carmel, D., and Markovitch, S. (1996). Learning models of intelligent agents. *AAAI/IAAI* 1:62–67.

Cooper, G. H., and Herskovits, E. H. (1992). A bayesian method for the induction of probabilistic networks from data. *Machine Learning* 9:309–347.

Gmytrasiewicz, P. J., and Durfee, E. H. (1995). A rigorous, operational formalization of recursive modeling. In *Proceedings of the First International Conference on Multi-Agent Systems (ICMAS)*, 125–132.

Gmytrasiewicz, P. J., and Durfee, E. H. (1998). Rational interaction in multiagent environments: coordination. *Submitted for publication, available at http://www-cse.uta.edu/ piotr/piotr.html*.

Gmytrasiewicz, P. J., Durfee, E. H., and Wehe, D. K. (1991). A decision-theoretic approach to coordinating multiagent interactions. In *Proceedings of the Eleventh International Joint Conference on Artificial Intelligence*, 166–172.

Gmytrasiewicz, P. J. (1996). An approach to user modeling in decision support systems. In *Proceedings of the Fifth International Conference on User Modeling*, 121–127.

Haykin, S. (1994). *Neural Network: A Comprehensive Foundation*. New York: Macmillan College Publishing Company.

Howard, R. A., and Matheson, J. E. (1984). Influence diagrams (article dated 1981). *Howard, R.A. and Matheson, J.E. (Eds.), Readings on the principles and applications of decision analysis* 2:719–762.

Kaminka, G., Tambe, M., and Hopper, C. (1998). The role of agent-modeling in agent robustness. In *Proceedings of the Conference on AI Meets the Real World*.

Keeney, R. L., and Raiffa, H. (1976). *Decisions with Multiple Objectives: Preferences and Value Tradeoffs*. New York: Wiley.

Noh, S., and Gmytrasiewicz, P. J. (1997). Agent modeling in antiair defense. In *Proceedings of the Sixth International Conference on User Modeling*, 389–400.

Pearl, J. (1988). *Probabilistic Reasoning in Intelligent Systems: Networks of Plausible Inference*. San Mateo, CA: Morgan Kauffman.

Russell, S. J., and Norvig, P. (1995). *Artificial Intelligence: A Modern Approach*. Englewood Cliffs, NJ: Prentice-Hall.

Vidal, J. M., and Durfee, E. H. (1995). Recursive agent modeling using limited rationality. In *Proceedings of the First International Conference on Multi-Agent Systems (ICMAS)*, 376–383.

Widrow, B., and Hoff Jr., M. E. (1960). Adaptive switching circuits. *IRE WESCON Convention Record* 96–104.

AWARD NOMINEE PAPERS

Interpreting Symptoms of Cognitive Load in Speech Input

André Berthold and Anthony Jameson*

Department of Computer Science, University of Saarbrücken, Germany

Abstract. Users of computing devices are increasingly likely to be subject to situationally determined distractions that produce exceptionally high cognitive load. The question arises of how a system can automatically interpret symptoms of such cognitive load in the user's behavior. This paper examines this question with respect to systems that process speech input. First, we synthesize results of previous experimental studies of the ways in which a speaker's cognitive load is reflected in features of speech. Then we present a conceptualization of these relationships in terms of Bayesian networks. For two examples of such symptoms—sentence fragments and articulation rate—we present results concerning the distribution of the symptoms in realistic assistance dialogs. Finally, using artificial data generated in accordance with the preceding analyses, we examine the ability of a Bayesian network to assess a user's cognitive load on the basis of limited observations involving these two symptoms.

1 The Challenge for User Modeling

When cosmonauts on the space station Mir communicate with ground control, their speech is monitored by psychologists for symptoms of stress (Arnold, 1997). The interpretation of the symptoms in turn influences the nature of the dialogs conducted with the cosmonauts.

Computer users do not in general stray quite as far from home as the Mir cosmonauts, nor are they subjected to the same sort of stress. But the mobility of modern computing devices has moved them ever further into the hustle and bustle of everyday life. Situational distractions can have major impact on the quality of interaction with a system—as anyone who has tried to jot down a person's address with a handheld device while standing on a street corner can testify. For user modeling research, situational distractions represent one more thing that a system can try to recognize and adapt to. Adaptation may involve, for example, a simplification of either the system's output or the required user input, in cases where situational distractions are suspected.

1.1 Scenario and Field Study

For concreteness, consider the example scenario handled by the dialog system READY (see, e.g., Jameson et al., 1999): Users are drivers whose cars need minor repairs; they request assistance from the system in natural language by phone. Our first step in studying this scenario was to get a concrete idea of the cognitive load induced by this situation and the ways in which it is

* This research is being supported by the German Science Foundation (DFG) in its Collaborative Research Center on Resource-Adaptive Cognitive Processes, SFB 378, Project B2, READY. The comments of the two anonymous reviewers strongly influenced the content of the final version.

manifested in the users' speech:[1] In a field study conducted on a winter night beside a fairly busy road, each of 8 subjects was given the task of identifying and repairing an intentionally created mechanical problem with a car. They communicated with a professional auto repairman via cellular phone. To get an idea of the information present in features of the subjects' speech, we analyzed the 8 dialogs in detail: For example, filled and silent pauses were measured and errors were classified.

In Sections 2 through 4, we will see how the data from this field study can be analyzed together with results of laboratory experiments of previous researchers so as to yield an empirical basis for a user modeling component for a dialog system. We will then check whether such a user modeling component, if given a sufficiently sound empirical basis, can make usefully accurate inferences on the basis of the limited data about a user that is available in this scenario.

1.2   Determinants of Cognitive Load

In this paper, the term *cognitive load* refers to the demands placed on a person's working memory by (a) the main task that she is currently performing, (b) any other task(s) she may be performing concurrently, and (c) distracting aspects of the situation in which she finds herself.

In the example scenario, we view the main task of the user ($\mathcal{U}$) as that of communicating with the mechanic (or a corresponding system $\mathcal{S}$). Concurrent tasks can involve looking for things, performing actions on the car, or communicating with other persons. Distracting aspects of the situation can include noises and events that interfere with one's concentration on task performance, as well as internal factors like emotional stress that have similar effects.

In the dynamic Bayesian networks that form the core of READY's user model, these types of influence on a user's continually changing cognitive load are modeled separately (see, e.g., Jameson et al., 1999; Schäfer and Weyrath, 1997). In this paper, we will simply consider the problem of assessing the total load currently placed on $\mathcal{U}$'s working memory, regardless of its origin. This load will be assumed to remain constant throughout the period during which it is being assessed.

2   Overview of Symptoms and Their Modeling

We reviewed literature from psycholinguistics and linguistics looking for evidence concerning the effects of cognitive load on features of speech. Table 1 gives a high-level summary of the results of this survey.[2]

Figure 1 shows how the relationships between these symptoms and cognitive load can be modeled with a Bayesian network.[3] To see the meaning of the variables, suppose that various factors have created a POTENTIAL WM LOAD for $\mathcal{U}$. If this load is too great for $\mathcal{U}$ to handle without

---

[1] The READY system also tries to recognize and adapt to the user's time pressure. For reasons of space, this variable will be mentioned only in passing in this paper.

[2] A much more detailed discussion of these results is given by Berthold (1998), along with references to the individual studies and results for less important features not listed here.

[3] For introductions to Bayesian networks, see, e.g., Russell and Norvig (1995) or Pearl (1988). An overview of their applications to user modeling is given by Jameson (1996).

Table 1. Summary of previous results concerning potential speech symptoms of cognitive load.

Symptoms involving output quality			Symptoms involving output rate		
Feature	Tendency[a]	Tally[b]	Feature	Tendency	Tally
Sentence fragments (number)	+	4/5	Articulation rate	−	7/7
False starts (number)	+	2/4	Speech rate	−	7/7
Syntax errors (number)	+	1/1	Onset latency (duration)	+	9/11
Self-repairs (number)	+, −, 0[c]	2, 1, 4	Silent pauses (number)	+	4/5
			Silent pauses (duration)	+	8/10
			Filled pauses (number)	+	4/6
			Filled pauses (duration)	+	1/2
			Repetitions (number)	+	5/6

[a] "+" means that the measure was generally found to increase under conditions of high cognitive load: "−" means the opposite.

[b] "m/n" means that of n relevant studies, m found the tendency indicated in the second column. (In most—but not all—cases the tendency was statistically significant.)

[c] Results concerning self-repairs show an inconsistent pattern.

difficulty, U may cope with the overload by reducing the speed of speech generation—for example, by pausing intermittently to think or to deal with distractions. (The extent to which U does this can be influenced by features of the task as well as by U's time pressure and preferences.) Any such speed reduction can be reflected in specific symptoms like the ones shown on the right in Table 1. Because of the slowing, the ACTUAL WM LOAD—which can be conceptualized as the amount of cognitive work that has to be done in a given unit of time—will be reduced.

On the other hand, U may for various reasons avoid slowing down, or may slow down only to a degree that is inadequate to reduce the ACTUAL WM LOAD to a normal level. In this case, the high ACTUAL WM LOAD is likely to be reflected in various types of defect in the utterances produced, such as the types listed in the left-hand side of Table 1 (cf. the left-hand side of Figure 1).[4]

So far, we are aware of only partial and indirect evidence in favor of the speed-accuracy tradeoff postulated in Figure 1. Concerning the relationships between the nodes for the individual symptoms and their parent nodes, useful empirical data can be extracted from the studies summarized in Table 1 and from our own field study that was sketched above. The next two sections will show how this can be done, using one example from each of the two broad categories of symptoms, starting with one that involves a decline in the quality of output.

3   Sentence Fragments as a Symptom

A *sentence fragment* can be defined as an incomplete syntactic structure I for which there exists a syntactic continuation C such that $I C$ constitutes a well-formed sentence. After articulating I,

---

[4] Baber et al. (1996), while not explicitly postulating the relationships depicted in Figure 1, discuss a number of phenomena and relationships that are consistent with this account.

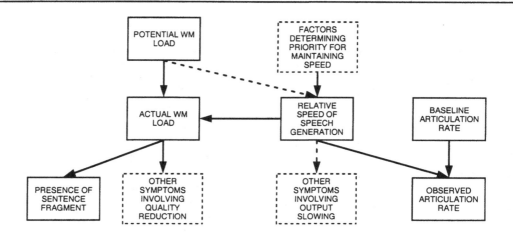

Figure 1. Simplified depiction of part of a Bayesian network for interpreting symptoms of cognitive load. (Each box with a solid border represents a node that corresponds to a single variable; each box with a dashed border denotes a group of variables that play a similar role in the network. Solid and dashed arrows denote positive and negative causal influences, respectively.)

the speaker either gives up the dialog turn or begins a new sentence N. Here are some examples from the field study:

Just a minute, I'll look. The cables ... [gives up turn]

Yes, that's ... uh, just keep repeating.

In many cases, the new sentence N begins with an alternative formulation of the content of I. In these cases, the sequence I N represents a particular type of self-repair called a *false start*. Some relevant empirical studies have looked specifically at false starts, while others have considered the broader class of sentence fragments. Since it's difficult for a system to determine automatically whether the material that follows a sentence fragment constitutes a self-repair, we will likewise ignore this distinction here and consider simply whether an utterance contains a sentence fragment.

Previous empirical results. Previous results for sentence fragments (including false starts) can be seen in the left-hand side of Table 1. The five studies in which a concurrent task was used to induce cognitive load produced the strongest effects: The concurrent task multiplied the frequency of sentence fragments by factors ranging from 1.52 to 5.50, with an average of 3.34.[5]

Distribution in the field study. Table 2 classifies the 54 sentence fragments that were found in the 628 dialog turns in our field study. The 15 fragments in the lower half of the table illustrate how sentence fragments can occur independently of cognitive load. The last category could presumably be recognized by the system and kept separate from the other categories—at least in cases where it was the system itself that interrupted the user.

---

[5] A single study by Roßnagel (1995a) that yielded similar factors in the opposite direction has yet to be explained.

Table 2. Frequency of six types of sentence fragments found in the field study dialogs.

Possibly due to high cognitive load:

- 24 turns consisting of (or ending with) a fragment
- 9 fragments followed by formulations with similar meaning
- 6 fragments followed by formulations with different meaning

Probably independent of cognitive load

- 7 sentences possibly aborted because of the arrival of new information or perceptions
- 1 sentence intended to be completed by dialog partner
- 7 sentences interrupted by the dialog partner

On the whole, though, it is not a trivial task to recognize sentence fragments automatically with a speech recognition system. The same is true of most of the other symptoms listed in Table 1.[6]

Modeling. In a Bayesian network such as that of Figure 1, observations of sentence fragments can be taken into account most straightforwardly with a single node that has two possible values: whether the most recent dialog turn of the user contained a sentence fragment or not. But what about the conditional probabilities that link this node with its parent node ACTUAL WM LOAD? Let us assume that the cognitive load induced in the five experiments that involved concurrent tasks corresponds roughly to the highest level of the variable ACTUAL WM LOAD. Assume further that the low-load condition of these experiments corresponds to the lowest level of this variable. Then the experimental results suggest the following constraints on the conditional probabilities relating ACTUAL WM LOAD (A) and PRESENCE OF SENTENCE FRAGMENT (F):

$$\frac{P(F = \text{Yes}|A = \text{Highest})}{P(F = \text{Yes}|A = \text{Lowest})} = 3.3 \qquad \frac{P(F = \text{No}|A = \text{Highest})}{P(F = \text{No}|A = \text{Lowest})} = .94$$

The second ratio, .94, reflects the fact that dialog turns that *do not* contain a sentence fragment are slightly less likely given a high level of ACTUAL WM LOAD. We found only one previous study (Roßnagel, 1995b) that yields data that can be used for the estimation of this ratio, but the exact value is actually unimportant: Given that sentence fragments occur in fewer than 10% of dialog turns, this ratio must be some number slightly less than 1.0. The consequence is that the observation of a single dialog turn *without* a sentence fragment will only slightly diminish S's estimate of U's cognitive load.

Before examining what sort of diagnostic performance these basic relationships can give rise to, let us examine a different type of symptom of cognitive load.

---

[6] Berthold (1998) discusses some of the problems involved and the possibilities offered by various approaches to speech recognition. The strategy pursued in the READY project is to determine which symptoms can play a useful role in a dialog system before making the considerable effort required to extract them automatically while using a speech recognizer. Accordingly, for system tests the properties of the input utterance are specified via a menu interface (see Jameson et al., 1999).

4 Articulation Rate as a Symptom

Among the symptoms that reflect the speaker's attempt to reduce output rate, the various types of pauses have been most thoroughly investigated (see Table 1). Though pauses also figure prominently in READY's modeling, we will look here at a less complex and less obvious symptom: the rate at which the speaker articulates syllables. To avoid overlap with the definition of pauses, we adopt the following definition:

$$\text{Articulation rate} = \frac{\text{Number of syllables articulated}}{\text{Total duration of articulated syllables}}$$

Filled pauses are left out of consideration, as are silent pauses whose length exceeds a certain threshold (here: 200 msec). The following translated example of an utterance produced by our mechanic illustrates this definition:

<uh> <P> *In the* <P> *inside under the steering wheel* <P> *to the left* <P> *there's a fuse box.*

Here, <P> stands for a silent pause; only the underlined material enters into the computation of articulation rate.[7]

Previous empirical results. Seven studies were found that measured articulation rate under conditions of varying cognitive load. As is indicated in Table 1, all of them found a tendency toward slower articulation given higher load. In the five studies that yielded specific data on average articulation rates, the rate reductions in the higher-load condition ranged from 8.8% to 19.7%, with an average of 13.6%. All of these studies induced high cognitive load by making the speaking task more difficult. We would expect the slowing to be more drastic in a condition involving a concurrent task, since this type of manipulation produced the strongest effects on sentence fragments and also in the studies on pauses.

Distribution in the field study. In a dialog situation, some dialog turns contain only a few syllables (e.g., *Yes, I can*). Measurement of articulation rate is problematic for such turns, since it would depend strongly on the properties of the syllables involved, on random variation, and on measurement error. On the basis of an initial analysis of the empirical distributions, we eliminated from consideration measurements of articulation rate for dialog turns involving 3 or fewer syllables.

The articulation rates for the 8 callers in the field study ranged from 6.3 to 7.7 syllables per second, with an average of 7.0 syllables/s. The utterances of each individual caller also varied somewhat in articulation rate, the standard deviations ranging from 1.0 to 2.1 syllables/s, with an average standard deviation of 1.35.

Modeling. In Figure 1, OBSERVED ARTICULATION RATE is viewed as being influenced by RELATIVE SPEED OF SPEECH GENERATION, but it also has a second parent node, BASELINE ARTICULATION RATE. This node is included because individual speakers differ systematically in their usual articulation rate, independently of any variations in cognitive load (cf. Goldman-Eisler, 1968). (The differences just cited in the average articulation rates of the 8 callers were presumably due both to

---

[7] By contrast, the studies counted in Table 1 for the symptom *speech rate* used a definition that was based on the total duration of each utterance.

stable individual differences and to random differences in the demands that were placed on the different callers.) Inclusion of this node in the network allows the system to learn about U's baseline rate in the course of a dialog so as gradually to become better at interpreting U's OBSERVED ARTICULATION RATE.

In sum, the potential diagnostic value of the variable OBSERVED ARTICULATION RATE lies in the tendency of speakers to slow their articulation by roughly 14% when subjected to fairly high cognitive load; but the diagnostic value may be diminished by other factors that influence articulation rate, such as individual baselines. So it is not obvious that this symptom can be of significant use for the assessment of a user's cognitive load. The next section will address this question with regard to both of the symptoms that we have discussed.

5   Assessing Potential Diagnostic Performance

Even if a network model is completely accurate, it may be of no use in practice for the modeling of individual users, because of the limitations of the available data in a dialog situation. As we have seen, the observable variables are at best noisy symptoms of the underlying variables of interest. Moreover, the number of relevant observations in a dialog may be small. To examine the data limitations in our example scenario with respect to the two symptoms discussed here, we performed the following steps:

1. Specification of the basic Bayesian network. We specified a Bayesian network with the structure shown in Figure 1 that fulfilled all of the constraints mentioned above.[8] To make possible a test simple enough to be discussed within the space limitations of this paper, we omitted all variables in the groups OTHER SYMPTOMS INVOLVING QUALITY REDUCTION and OTHER SYMPTOMS INVOLVING OUTPUT SLOWING. Moreover, the FACTORS DETERMINING PRIORITY FOR MAINTAINING SPEED were fixed at an intermediate level that reflected the assumption that users would attach roughly equal priority to output rate and output quality. We assume hypothetically for the rest of the analysis that this network is *entirely* accurate; in this way, problems arising from data limitations can be analyzed separately from those that are due to incorrect assumptions embodied in the network.

2. Definition of hypothetical users. We defined four groups of 15 hypothetical "users". Those in the first group were assumed to be experiencing somewhat below-average POTENTIAL WM LOAD (0.6 on our scale[9]); those in the fourth, very high POTENTIAL WM LOAD (1.8); and those in the second and third groups, intermediate levels (1.0 and 1.4, respectively). Within each of these groups, we defined 3 subgroups of 5 "users" with different levels of BASELINE ARTICULATION RATE: 6.75, 7.00, and 7.25 syllables/s, respectively. Recall that in our field study the average articulation rate of a speaker ranged from about 6.3 to about 7.7 syllables/s. Hence our hypothetical users do not include representatives of the extreme levels of BASELINE ARTICULATION RATE.

3. Generation of data for each user. For each such hypothetical user, we used the network to generate 10 "observations" of utterances that the user might produce in the course of a dialog. Each observation consisted of a pair of values, for the variables PRESENCE OF SENTENCE FRAGMENT and OBSERVED ARTICULATION RATE. For each user U, we generated the observations by (a) instantiating the variables POTENTIAL WM LOAD and BASELINE ARTICULATION RATE according to the definition

---

[8] A machine-readable version of this example network is available from the authors.

[9] POTENTIAL WM LOAD is indexed on a scale from 0.0 to 2.0, where 1.0 corresponds to a load that the U in question could (just barely) handle without exhibiting any decrease in the quality or speed of speech.

of that $\mathcal{U}$; (b) noting the network's resulting probability distributions for the two symptom variables; and (c) for each observation independently, using random numbers to generate values for these two variables on the basis of the probability distributions.[10] Since in our scenario about 40% of all utterances are too short to have their articulation rate measured meaningfully, for a random 40% of the utterances the OBSERVED ARTICULATION RATE was specified as "undefined".

4. Initialization of the network's prior beliefs. The network was then prepared to interpret the 10 observations of each user. For each user, we had the network start with the same a priori expectations about the unobservable variables POTENTIAL WM LOAD and BASELINE ARTICULATION RATE. These expectations corresponded to the actual distribution of these variables in the hypothetical sample (see above). In other words, we simulated a situation in which S has already accurately narrowed down its expectations with respect to these variables somewhat—a situation that could arise after the first few utterances in a dialog.

5. Interpretation of observations for each user. For each user independently, the 10 observations were interpreted one by one by the network, and S's assessments were updated accordingly. Figure 2 shows the development of S's assessments of the key variable POTENTIAL WM LOAD for the two groups of users with the lowest and highest actual levels of this variable, respectively.

On the positive side, we see that S's assessments do tend to move in the right direction: After 10 utterances there is hardly any overlap in the assessments for the two extreme groups.

At the same time, the results illustrate the reasons why a diagnostic network can fail to arrive at a precise and accurate assessment even when the data are completely consistent with its structure and probabilities:

1. The differences in the baseline articulation rates of the $\mathcal{U}$s tend to mask each $\mathcal{U}$'s actual cognitive load somewhat. In each graph, the slower-articulating $\mathcal{U}$s (represented by the gray lines) are assessed as suffering from greater cognitive load. In fact, this difference would persist even with a larger number of observations, until S encountered some observations that allowed a more precise assessment of BASELINE ARTICULATION RATE.

2. Because of the partly random variability in the data, S's assessment of a $\mathcal{U}$ often follows a zig-zag pattern instead of moving steadily toward the true value. In addition to the changes caused by the occasional sentence fragments (marked with a dot), this variability concerns the OBSERVED ARTICULATION RATE of individual utterances (not marked explicitly in the graphs).

3. Even in the whole sample of 10 utterances, a given $\mathcal{U}$'s speech may happen to show a pattern that is untypical of $\mathcal{U}$'s actual cognitive load, because of random variation (i.e., sampling error). For example, two of the $\mathcal{U}$s with low POTENTIAL WM LOAD happened to produce 3 sentence fragments in their 10 utterances, although the overall frequency of fragments even for the $\mathcal{U}$s with very high POTENTIAL WM LOAD is only about 10%.

6   Summary of Contributions and Current Work

The methodological contributions of this paper, in increasing order of novelty, are the following:

1. a way of synthesizing previously published experimental data so as to strengthen the empirical basis of a user modeling component;

---

[10] A similar method for generating hypothetical input data for a Bayesian network was applied, for example, by Henrion et al. (1996).

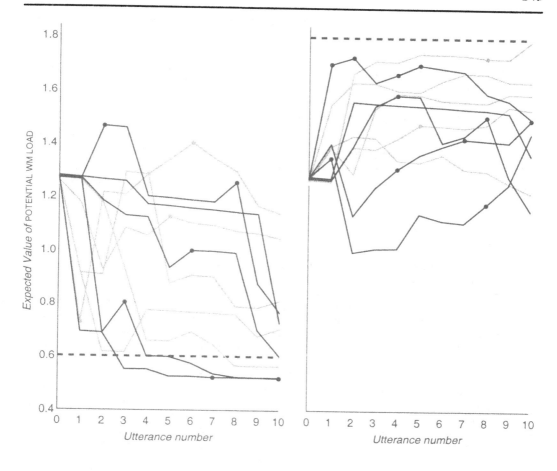

Figure 2. Test of the potential diagnostic utility of two symptoms of cognitive load. (Each jagged line traces, for one hypothetical user $\mathcal{U}$, the changes in the expected value of S's belief about $\mathcal{U}$'s POTENTIAL WM LOAD. The darker the line, the greater the BASELINE ARTICULATION RATE that was assumed for $\mathcal{U}$. Each observation that included a sentence fragment is marked with a dot. The horizontal dotted line in each graph shows the true value of POTENTIAL WM LOAD for the $\mathcal{U}$s in that graph.)

2. a way of combining such results with the results of detailed analyses of interactions in a given application domain so as to derive qualitative and quantitative constraints for a user modeling component; and
3. a method for analyzing the ways in which the diagnostic performance of a user modeling component is limited by the nature of the data available in the application scenario.

With regard to the particular problem of assessing cognitive load on the basis of speech input, the contributions are the following:

1. an overview of the most important indicators of cognitive load in speech input that have been identified so far;

2. a qualitative model of the relationships between these symptoms and theoretical variables which, though it requires specific testing, already has some degree of theoretical and empirical support;
3. an overview of the specific problems involved in the coding of sentence fragments and articulation rate;
4. several general trends concerning the diagnostic value of these two symptoms when realistically small amounts of input data are available.

The methodology is currently being applied to a different application scenario in which other interaction modalities in addition to speech are employed (Jameson, 1998). At the same time, our investigation of speech symptoms is continuing in the form of experiments whose data will be analyzed using learning algorithms for Bayesian networks with a view to arriving at a better empirical description of causal relationships such as those depicted in Figure 1.

References

Arnold, S. R. (1997). Wo das Perlhuhn trudelt. *Die Zeit* 33–34. 6 July 1997.

Baber, C., Mellor, B., Graham, R., Noyes, J. M., and Tunley, C. (1996). Workload and the use of automatic speech recognition: The effects of time and resource demands. *Speech Communication* 20:37–53.

Berthold, A. (1998). Repräsentation und Verarbeitung sprachlicher Indikatoren für kognitive Ressourcenbeschränkungen [Representation and processing of linguistic indicators of cognitive resource limitations]. Master's thesis, Department of Computer Science, University of Saarbrücken, Germany.

Goldman-Eisler, F. (1968). *Psycholinguistics: Experiments in Spontaneous Speech*. London: Academic Press.

Henrion, M., Pradhan, M., Favero, B. D., Huang, K., Provan, G., and O'Rourke, P. (1996). Why is diagnosis using belief networks insensitive to imprecision in probabilities? In Horvitz, E., and Jensen, F., eds., *Proceedings of the Twelfth Conference on Uncertainty in Artificial Intelligence*. San Francisco: Morgan Kaufmann. 307–314.

Jameson, A., Schäfer, R., Weis, T., Berthold, A., and Weyrath, T. (1999). Making systems sensitive to the user's time and working memory constraints. In Maybury, M. T., ed., *IUI99: International Conference on Intelligent User Interfaces*. New York: ACM. 79–86.

Jameson, A. (1996). Numerical uncertainty management in user and student modeling: An overview of systems and issues. *User Modeling and User-Adapted Interaction* 5:193–251.

Jameson, A. (1998). Adapting to the user's time and working memory limitations: New directions of research. In Timm, U. J., and Rössel, M., eds., *ABIS-98, Adaptivität und Benutzermodellierung in interaktiven Softwaresystemen*. Erlangen, Germany: FORWISS.

Pearl, J. (1988). *Probabilistic Reasoning in Intelligent Systems: Networks of Plausible Inference*. San Mateo, CA: Morgan Kaufmann.

Roßnagel, C. (1995a). Kognitive Belastung und Hörerorientierung beim monologischen Instruieren [Cognitive load and listener-orientation in instruction monologs]. *Zeitschrift für Experimentelle Psychologie* 42:94–110.

Roßnagel, C. (1995b). Übung und Hörerorientierung beim monologischen Instruieren: Zur Differenzierung einer Grundannahme [Practice and listener-orientation in the delivery of instruction monologs: Differentiation of a basic assumption]. *Sprache & Kognition* 14:16–26.

Russell, S. J., and Norvig, P. (1995). *Artificial Intelligence: A Modern Approach*. Englewood Cliffs, NJ: Prentice-Hall.

Schäfer, R., and Weyrath, T. (1997). Assessing temporally variable user properties with dynamic Bayesian networks. In Jameson, A., Paris, C., and Tasso, C., eds., *User Modeling: Proceedings of the Sixth International Conference, UM97*. Vienna, New York: Springer Wien New York. 377–388.

An Application-Independent Intelligent User Support System Exploiting Action-Sequence Based User Modelling

L. Miguel Encarnação[1] and Stanislav L. Stoev[2]

[1] Fraunhofer Center for Research in Computer Graphics (CRCG), Inc., Providence RI, USA
[2] Department of Computer Science, University of Tübingen, Germany

Abstract. Many software systems' usability suffers from their complexity, usually caused by the market-driven trend to bundle a huge amount of features, which are supposed to increase the product's attractiveness. This attempt, however, more often than not leads to software with poor usability characteristics, therefore requiring an extensive amount of initial effort for the users to become familiar with the system. One way to overcome this problem is by providing user-adapted usage support.

In this paper we present an experimental system for intelligent user support, which has been developed under the aspect of portability. Focusing on this goal, the system supports a variety of user- and task-modeling approaches and is independent from the hosting software application environment, thus being ready to integrate with existing and new applications. The different user-modeling approaches have been empirically evaluated and compared in a medical software application embedding our system. The results of this evaluation are briefly described in the report.

1 Introduction and Related Work

The main drawback of many software systems is their complexity, usually caused by the market-driven trend to bundle all features, which should make the product more attractive even for demanding expert users. This attempt however, often leads to software with poor usability, which not only require a large amount of initial effort for the users to become familiar with the systems. It also keeps many non-professional and even professional users from accepting new, or switching over to better software products.

Several approaches offering solutions to this problem have been described in the literature. To the most popular belong *tutoring systems*, whose basic idea is to support the user in learning the use of the application system. A second branch includes the research towards intelligent user interfaces, which has been conducted for quite a long time now. This work was driven by researchers and developers from the most distinct areas of e.g., computer science, artificial intelligence (AI), human factors, and psychology (Sullivan and Tyler, 1991, Maybury, 1993, Gray et al., 1993, Schneider-Hufschmidt et al., 1993), yet only few compelling application systems have been developed (Marks et al., 1997).

In many cases the intelligent user support has had a negative influence on the performance of the application system itself, or on the user's performance at the interface to the application system (e.g., (Woods, 1993)). In other cases, stand-alone application systems were developed as platforms for AI methods and techniques in order to demonstrate the applicability of the latter, yet condemning reasonable intelligent user support to sole academic existence. Other approaches attempt to exploit the knowledge put into graphical user interfaces at design time to automatically generate intelligent user support (Sukaviriya and Foley, 1990, Lonczewski, 1997). Here, one of the problems is that up until now only very few real-world applications have been developed on the basis of such user-interface development systems. We believe that the most promising approach is the intelligent user adapted support, which has to be flexible enough to allow an easy integration into new and existing applications.

Unlike most of the work referenced above, the ORIMUHS[1] system presented in this paper has been conceptually developed and implemented as an extension for new and existing graphical user interfaces. It offers a fair amount of intelligent user support by realizing as many components of intelligent user interfaces as possible such as; multi-modal communication (Neal and Shapiro, 1991), dynamic presentation (Castells et al., 1997), and adaptability (Dieterich et al., 1993). Yet it also strives to provide a small application programmers' interface (API) for application-independent integration with reasonably little effort, one that is flexible enough to support future enhancements towards new intelligent components or more sophisticated AI-based user support. Therefore, our approach allows the integration in real-world application systems, providing a means of introducing the different aspects of user modelling to market and industry – thus increasing its acceptance. On the other hand, it supports further research on intelligent user support – its impact and its shortcomings – in multiple 'real-world' environments, thus allowing comparative evaluations on different applications systems from various application areas.

In the next section we describe the basic concepts of our system, introducing the information we dispose of, the architecture, and the dependencies of the developed components. In Section 3 we present the user modelling methods used to evaluate the protocolled data and we outline the methods' application and usage in Section 4. Section 5 reports on results of the user modelling process, applying the techniques described in Section 3. The final section summarizes the attributes of the presented user support system.

2   System Overview

Keeping in mind the initial goal of developing an easy-to-integrate system, we attempted to define an 'as-slim-as-possible' interface between the hosting software application and our user support components. This effort resulted in the protocolling of the most basic trackable units: the user interactions with the GUI which we named *actions*. In doing so, the integration of our user support in an application system then consists of the following steps:

Application System:
- registering of the actions to be tracked.
  o adding a function notifying the HCIS.
  o assigning an ID to each action.

ORIMUHS:
- building up the action-context-concept hierarchy.
  o which unit contains which subunits.
  o assigning a LOD to each unit.
  o define for each unit the 'successful completed' criteria.
- defining correspondences between working context/concept and user support (i.e. action ID – HTML-page).
- recording the actions of the preclassified users to build the action-graphs.

---

[1] ORIMUHS stands for Object-oriented Intelligent Multimedia Help System.

We implemented the protocoling of actions by adding a function to the GUI-elements we are interested in (i.e. buttons or menu items). This functionality is hosted by the *Action Translation Module (ATM)* depicted in Figure 1. Depending on the design and implementation the application GUI, a recompilation of the application system can be limited and is sometimes even dispensable.

Once the GUI-elements are 'registered' by adding the server-notifying function, there is no need to manipulate further application code. All of the following steps, like action protocoling, action sequence evaluation, and user modelling are performed by the server ($HCIS^2$), thus not affecting the application's performance.

The HCIS is an application-independent server, communicating with the clients (the application systems) through a TCP/IP connection. It can therefore be used in a local area network (LAN) (cf. Figure 1) to serve an arbitrary number of clients simultaneously. Although the use in wide-area networks (WAN) is generally possible, security considerations make the limitation to LANs sound reasonable. The main task of the HCIS is to keep track of the performed actions and evaluate them when requested based on the evaluation methods discussed in Section 3.

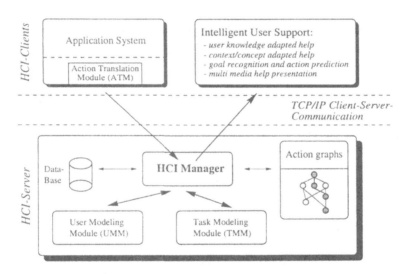

Figure 1. The architecture of the ORIMUHS system.

When a user starts working with the served application, HCIS uses his/her ID to load the available user data if the ID is unknown to the system. Otherwise a new user profile is created and initialized with default values[3]. After this initial 'handshake' with the application, the server keeps track of every interaction of interest (registered action) performed by the user (as depicted in Figure 2 of section 3.2).

The HCIS manages the action-sequence dependencies in graph-like structures, called *action graphs* (Encarnação, 1995). Such action graphs where the nodes are actions and the edges rep-

---

[2] Human Computer Interaction Server.

[3] We use a default user model for initialization and did not ask the users for rating themselves, because in most of the cases they cannot judge their own knowledge correct, thus misleading the help system.

resent connections building the action sequences, contain interactions performed by users with known levels of expertise. In this sense the graphs aim to represent the behaviour of users with similar application knowledge.

2.1 The Action Graphs

For a precise determination of the user's application knowledge a reference base is needed. Such reference model is created by protocoling the actions of users with a-priori known levels of expertise. Such models are coded in the action graphs. During the first information-gathering phase the action graphs are created adding the GUI-interactions performed by the pre-classified users to the corresponding action graph, or updating the weights of existing connections.

Once the reference action graphs have been built, the user's interactions with the application system are compared with the graphs to determine whether the user fits into a particular class of expertise or not. In this second phase the HCIS computes the expertise class of a connected user after every performed action by determining where she/he best fits in. This computation is performed for each session of the user with the application. The result is the class used to determine the adequate user support when requested, affecting the help's level of detail and presentation media. The process of updating the user-knowledge value is depicted in Figure 2 of Section 3.2.

2.2 Overlay Models

Most of today's commercial application systems are used for more than one purpose, out of which a single user usually only exploits a few. Hence, adequate user stereotypes cannot be applied to the whole application system, but have to be related to certain application purposes of the system which in return require appropriate internal representations. We therefore introduced an *overlay model* (Carr and Goldstein, 1977) paradigm to our system (Encarnação and Stoev, 1996). First, we defined lower-level units containing actions with similar meaning to the application called *contexts*. Contexts are low-level user *goals* (i.e. 'File I/O', 'Model Part', and 'Define Lights' for our CAD application system). On a higher level of abstraction, we introduced *concept* units, containing contexts as subunits. Concepts can be considered as representing the *purposes* for which an application system can be used for (i.e. 'Construction', 'Demonstration', and 'Analysis' in a CAD-System).

In contrast to traditional overlay models which only differentiate between known or unknown knowledge units, ORIMUHS' overlay modelling is able to assign levels of expertise of the corresponding user to the knowledge units. These levels of expertise are part of the user model and are computed utilizing the methods described in the next section.

3 User Modelling Strategies

Before describing the knowledge updating strategies, we introduce the user specific data the HCIS disposes of. Here we distinguish again between context- or concept-oriented data and information on the global user knowledge:

Global User Information:
- overall system knowledge:
  - o statistically calculated value.
  - o probabilistically calculated value.
- number of sessions with the application.
- number of all performed **Help, Cancel,** and **Undo** actions.

Working-Context Specific User Information:
- unit related knowledge.
- number of visits to unit.
- number of all performed **Help, Cancel,** and **Undo** when being in this unit.

The user modelling process itself, similar to the simulation of a learning process, is a dynamic process depending on the humans' learning capabilities. In order to respond to this dynamic, the user knowledge model should be updated frequently enough to represent the correct level of expertise. In our user support system a user's knowledge model is therefore updated every time he/she performs an action. This update process is depicted in Figure 2.

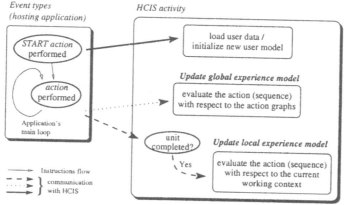

Figure 2. Updating the *global* (dotted line) and the *local* (dashed line) user expertise.

In ORIMUHS we realized two different strategies for modelling the user's knowledge in order to consider the different situations in which user support might be required or requested (Encarnação, 1997):

The *global user modelling* determines a user-expertise value related to the whole application system. It takes into account the action sequences performed by users with similar system knowledge (coded in the action-graph for this user class).

In contrast to this approach, the local strategy is based on the overlay model described above. It calculates an expertise model with respect to the given context and concept, thus reflecting not the overall system knowledge, but the expertise in particular *working contexts* (this refers to both the *contexts* and the *concepts*).

Depending on the application situation in which a user's level of expertise is computed and evaluated in order to provide user-adapted support, either one of the approaches might be feasible or a combination of both.

3.1   The Global User Model

For the calculation of the user's global expertise model we initially use two action-graph evaluation strategies. The first is the *statistical* evaluation which (statistically) computes the transmission loads between subsequent actions with respect to alternative sequences, using the action graphs as a reference base. In order to determine statistically the value u_i, representing the update of the user's expertise after performing the action a_i, we introduce the system's *confidence* in executing action a_j followed by action a_i (Encarnação, 1997, Encarnação and Stoev, 1996). This approach, based on comparison of the total number of a_i's visits with the total number of (a_j, a_i) visits, has been extended to the case where the action a_i is performed after action a_j, 'going through' action a_k. Thus we (statistically) retrieve a measure of the 'local fitting' of this action sequence in an action graph.

The *probability*-based approach is the more global one, which computes the probabilities that certain (sequences of) actions are executed. The values computed in this manner are not calculated with respect to possible alternatives, but as nearly absolute measurement. Similar to the confidence by the statistical evaluation, we introduce the probability of performing action a_i after action a_j (or $p(a_i|a_j)$). Again similar to the other approach, we extended this probability to $p(a_i, a_j, a_k)$, which denotes the execution's probability for the action sequence (a_j, a_k, a_i) (Encarnação, 1997,Encarnação and Stoev, 1996).

Both strategies can be employed to update the user's overall level of affiliation with respect to an action graph, yet should be applied according to the situation out of which the user-support need evolved: The statistical is most applicable to situations where the user has been lost in his local context, whereas the probabilistic approach is applicable to task user-support that helps to plan certain tasks.

After performing the evaluation step with all available action graphs, we obtain a suitable method for assigning a level of expertise (and thus an expertise class) to a user.

For both evaluations three actions are considered; with only two actions it would be difficult to determine the user's current working context. On the other hand, more than three actions could cause the calculations to be too expensive for the server. The server would then not be able to respond to help requests in real time when serving several applications.

3.2 The Local User Model

When considering a user model, we are often not interested in the user's overall application system knowledge, but in expertise values related to the current working context. Typically, when the help system offers user support, it should take into account the user's knowledge in the concrete situation. Otherwise the offered information might be worthless or even confusing for the user.

In order to get such information we introduce new values to the user model which represent the user's level of expertise with respect to each context or concept. These values are updated every time the user completes his/her work in that working context/concept (or short *unit*) (as shown in Figure 2).

Note that an additional unit attribute is needed in order to update the local user expertise: the unit's level of difficulty (*LOD*). This LOD is part of the unit's attributes, which consist of subunit IDs and LOD, and have to be defined by the help system's administrator.

For the update of the local user model we take into account both the current user's expertise in this context/concept, and the unit's LOD. In addition, we need to know about the user's *success* on the work in this unit before recalculating the local user's expertise. This parameter ($\in [0, 1]$) is calculated in consideration of the number of performed *Undo*, *Cancel*, and *Help* actions since entering the current unit, related to the number of subunits of the processed unit.

ORIMUHS was conceptually designed as an experimental system which supports the integration and comparative evaluation of different user modelling approaches, two of which we implemented so far:

Similar to Chin (1989), where a fuzzy logic based uncertainty management method is utilized to incrementally update the assessment for the user's expertise, we use *fuzzy rules* like the following one:

> IF user is a *Beginner* AND he/she completed a *simple*[4] working context,
>
> THEN it now seems *more likely* that she/he is an advanced user,

to update the user's expertise in the working context.

The second approach that we implemented in ORIMUHS is based on Bayesian networks. It utilizes the same input data as the Fuzzy-logic based approach, namely the current user model, the unit's level of difficulty, and the user's success on the unit's completion. The update of the user's expertise level with this method is a straight forward bottom-up evidence propagation in a Bayesian network with three nodes (ABIS, 1997). A comparison of similar user modelling strategies can be found in Jameson (1995).

4   Applying the User Model

We believe that even excellent user modelling results might lead to inappropriate and therefore confusing user support, if they cannot be applied adequately. For this reason we integrated most of the modelling strategies discussed above in the *Hypermedia Help Navigator* (*HyHN*) shown in Figure 3.

When help is requested by the user, or the system ascertains than the user needs help[5], HCIS performs following steps:

- determine the current context(s)/concept(s)[6] (using the last three performed actions);
- determine the user's expertise class (again using the last three performed actions);
- display the help assigned to the determined working context and user expertise level with the appropriate media.

Since ORIMUHS does not support the automatic generation of hypermedia documents, we developed this separate navigation interface, which is directly connected to the hypermedia user support. HyHN communicates with the HCI-Server to retrieve its information on the user model and working context (Encarnação, 1997). These user data determine how detailed the provided help should be and which kind of help presentation is appropriate for a user with the given application and working context knowledge. Additionally the user model is used in combination with the 'best fitting' action-graph to calculate a set of alternative actions (Figure 3, list box 'Alternatives'), belonging to the currently determined context/concept. This is part of the goal recognition and action prediction module described in Stoev and Encarnação (1998).

To overcome inappropriate user-modelling results, the HyHN allows the end-user to switch to the categories (*variants*) of hypermedia documents with the preferred level of detail by using

---

[4] A simple mapping is used to convert the working context's LOD to a linguistic variable.

[5] When the performed Undo and Cancel actions are protocolled, HCIS can decide to offer the user the appropriate help, which can be rejected by the user.

[6] Sometimes the systems determines more than one possible context/concept.

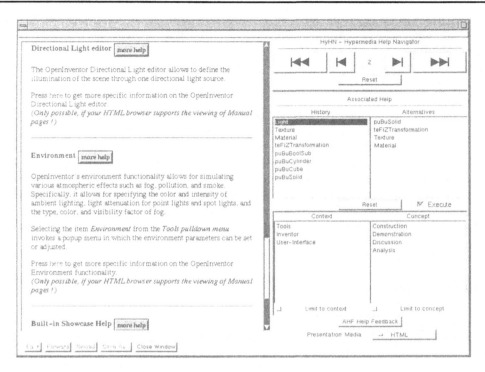

Figure 3. The *Hypertext Help Navigator.*

the arrow buttons in the upper row. In case of inappropriate goal recognition results, the correct current context and concept can be selected in the lists in the lower right corner (displayed are only units containing the last performed/selected action). To switch between the presentation media, the 'Presentation Media' button can be used which allows additional flexibility of the system with respect to the user's preferences.

The two lower selection lists display the current low-level goals (contexts) and concepts of the current (or selected) working context. They enable the end-user to retrieve less detailed, or more global information on the current (or selected) action's low-level goal or concept. In order to provide a consistent view of the entities of all realized levels of human-computer dialogue, we installed additional toggle buttons to allow the user to limit displayed sub-entities with respect to their affiliation to selected entities.

In addition to these features of HyHN and if the action which the user wants to execute next is contained in the listed set of 'alternative actions', it can be executed by double-clicking the desired item. This feature is based on the neighbourhood information embedded in the action graphs and the corresponding statistically or probabilistically computed connection weights dependent on the evaluation strategy the user or system administrator chooses to use.

The selection of alternative actions makes an indirect interaction with the application possible and helps out of (well known) situations where the users know *what* to do, but do not know *how* to do it and *where* the appropriate button or menu item is located. Based on a simple callback mechanism, this feature does not impact the portability of the system in any way, yet provides an effective tool for user support.

5 Results

The system described above is completely implemented and integrated with two software applications, *Arcade* and the *MEDStation*. The first application, *Arcade*, is a CAD-modeller (Stork and Anderson, 1995) and is an application with broad functionality, thus being important for the integration of our user support system.

The second, the *MEDStation* (Grunert et al., 1995), is developed for *CT* and *x-ray* image evaluation and diagnostic, case study and documentation, and patient data management. Through this base functionality the application system is addressing a broad community of clinical clients. This emphasizes the need for a system offering adequate user support.

To get a measure of the usability and quality of our system, we let 20 test users solve three given problems with the software applications *MEDStation*. We evaluated their interactions and then asked for a rating of the offered user support. In the first stage we used the performed actions to determine the users' levels of expertise and compared them with the users' assessment of their own levels of knowledge, i.e. affiliation with a certain user class (which could either way be quite unprecise). In 80% of the cases the system's calculated experience class corresponded to the user's self assessment. In the other 20% ORIMUHS could not clearly assign the user to the correct knowledge class (although the user belonged more often than not to the correct expertise class).

The users rated ORIMUHS' usability indirectly. We attempted to find out, whether or not our system can help users to 'explore' and apply the broad functionality of the hosting software system. In this case 65% of the users (most of them *Beginners*) stated that the *MEDStation* was not transparent enough in the first session (solving a given problem without using ORIMUHS), however being more satisfied with the *MEDStation*'s functionality at the end of the third session (with integrated intelligent user support). 35% of the users, most of which were *Advanced* or *Expert* users, found the offered user support satisfactory.

6 Conclusion

In this paper we presented a user support system which is a very useful companion for users with different application system knowledge.

Empirical user studies that were conducted within a medical application system strongly indicate that the provided user support was adapted to a satisfactory degree to all users; beginners, advanced, and even expert users. This in return gives us empirical evidence that the applied user modelling strategies produce results adequate enough, to proceed with our approach. Broader user studies will be needed to prove these initial results.

The cost-efficient integration with new and existing applications makes ORIMUHS even more appealing for commercial software products which often suffer from a lack of system transparency, a shortcoming that could be neutralized by exploiting ORIMUHS' adaptive user support.

Furthermore, we believe that our system is a useful platform for testing new methods from research areas like: user modelling, automatic help page generation, help-presentation, plan recognition, and goal prediction. Keeping this fact in mind and considering the effortless portability of ORIMUHS, seems to make the presented system interesting as a plug-in-like component for commercial software applications.

References

VEW AG. (1996). *Proc. of the 4. GI Workshop "Adaptivität und Benutzermodellierung in interaktiven Softwaresystemen" (ABIS'96), Dortmund, Germany.*

Universität des Saarlandes. (1997). *Proc. of the 5. GI Workshop "Adaptivität und Benutzermodellierung in interaktiven Softwaresystemen" (ABIS'97), Saarbrücken, Germany.*

Carr, B., and Goldstein, I. (1977). Overlays: A theory of modeling for computer aided instruction. Technical report, AI Memo 406, MIT.

Castells, P., Szekely, P., and Salcher, E. (1997). Declarative models of presentation. In *Moore et al. (1997)*, 137–144.

Chin, D. (1989). KNOME: Modeling what the User Knows in UC. In *Kobsa and Wahlster (1989)*. Springer-Verlag. 74–107.

Dieterich, H., Malinowski, U., Kühme, T., and Schneider-Hufschmidt, M. (1993). State of the art in adaptive user interfaces. In *Schneider-Hufschmidt et al. (1993)*. North-Holland. 13–48.

Encarnação, L. M., and Stoev, S. (1996). An overlay model for adaptive high-level user support in ORIMUHS. In *ABIS (1996)*.

Encarnação, L. M. (1995). Adaptivity in graphical user interfaces: An experimental framework. *Computers & Graphics* 19(6):873–884.

Encarnação, L. M. (1997). *Concept and realisation of intelligent user support in interactive graphics applications.* Ph.D. Dissertation, Eberhard-Karls-Universität Tübingen, Fakultät für Informatik.

Gray, W. D., Hefley, W. E., and Murray, D., eds. (1993). *Proc. of the 1993 International Workshop on Intelligent User Interfaces, Orlando, FL.* ACM Press.

Grunert, T., Fechter, J., Stuhldreier, G., Ehricke, H.-H., Skalej, M., Kolb, R., and Huppert, P. (1995). A PACS Workstation with integrated CASE tool and 3D-Endosonography application. In *Computer Assisted Radiology CAR 95*, 293–298. Springer.

Jameson, A. (1995). Numerical uncertainty management in user and student modeling: An overview of systems and issues. *User Modeling and User–Adapted Interaction* 5(3-4):193–251.

Kobsa, A., and Wahlster, W., eds. (1989). *User Models in Dialog Systems.* New York: Springer-Verlag.

Lonczewski, F. (1997). Providing user support for interactive applications with FUSE. In *Moore et al. (1997)*, 253–254.

Marks, J., Birnbaum, L., Horvitz, E., Kurlander, D., Lieberman, H., and Roth, S. (1997). Compelling intelligent user interfaces: "how much ai is enough?". Panel in Moore et al. (1997) (position statements).

Maybury, M. T. (1993). *Intelligent Multimedia Interfaces.* AAAI Press / The MIT Press.

Moore, J., Edmonds, E., and Puerta, A., eds. (1997). Orlando, FL: ACM SIGART/SIGCHI.

Neal, J., and Shapiro, S. (1991). Intelligent multi-media interface technology. In *Sullivan and Tyler (1991)*. ACM Press. 11–43.

Schneider-Hufschmidt, M., Kühme, T., and Malinowski, U. (1993). *Adaptive User Interfaces: Principles and Practice.* North-Holland.

Stoev, S., and Encarnação, L. M. (1998). A navigation tool for ORIMUHS based on goal recognition and action prediction. In *Report 6. GI Workshop "Adaptivität und Benutzermodellierung in interaktiven Softwaresystemen" (ABIS'98), Erlangen.* FORWISS.

Stork, A., and Anderson, B. (1995). 3D Interfaces in a Distributed Modelling Environment – 3D Devices, Interaction and Visualization Techniques. In Fellner, D., ed., *1995 Int. Workshop on Modeling, Virtual Worlds, and Distributed Graphics (MVD'95)*, 83–92. infix. URL: http://www.igd.fhg.de/˜stork/papers/mvd95/mvd95.html.

Sukaviriya, P., and Foley, J. D. (1990). Coupling a UI framework with automatic generation of context–sensitive animated help. *Proc. of the SIGGRAPH 1990 Symposium on User Interface Software and Technology (UIST'90)* 152–166.

Sullivan, J. W., and Tyler, S. W., eds. (1991). *Intelligent User Interfaces.* ACM Press.

Woods, D. D. (1993). The price of flexibility. In *Gray et al. (1993)*, 19–25.

A User-Centered Approach to User Modeling

Daniela Petrelli[1], Antonella De Angeli[2] and Gregorio Convertino[1]*

[1] Cognitive and Communication Technology Division, ITC-IRST, Italy
[2] Department of Psychology, University of Trieste, Italy

Abstract. Generally, user modeling concerns a person interacting with a standing console. This scenario does not represent the *HyperAudio* system in use: a visitor freely moves in a museum, gathering information from an adaptive and portable electronic guide. To provide designers with presumptive user behavior, data about visitor profiles and visit styles were collected through a questionnaire. The study pointed out unpredicted situations (e.g., the importance of social context) and confirmed some working hypotheses (e.g., the relevance of visit span). This paper reports on this experience, describing how to go from designer questions to guidelines for user modeling, making the best use of empirical data.

1 Introduction

The design of information systems is more and more user-centered: final users are involved from the very beginning of the planning stage. Early involvement of users has the potential for preventing serious mistakes when projecting innovative systems. Indeed, it compels designers to think in terms of utility and usability. Benefits of the user-centered approach are mainly related to time and cost saving during development, completeness of system functionality, repair effort saving, as well as user satisfaction (Nielsen, 1993). Involving users from early stages allows basing the system core on what is effectively needed. It is acknowledged that approximately 60-80% of interaction difficulties, including lack of facilities and usability problems, are due to poor or inadequate requirement specifications. Even if late evaluations are useful to assess the usability of final systems, it is unrealistic to expect that these results bring about a complete redesign.

Despite its importance, the motto *know the user* seems to be somehow neglected when planning how the system is to interpret user actions. As soon as user-modeling technology moves from research labs to real field usage, the need for a precise idea on how the interaction will evolve becomes increasingly important. The user model can manage only some dimensions (e.g., knowledge or interest) of that complex universe the human being is. Thus, these dimensions have to be the most meaningful and representative of users and uses. Moreover, an advanced sketch of the user is a key point when designing adaptive systems for completely new scenarios, such as computer augmented environments and mobile devices. This paper discusses the usefulness of a user-centered design for user modeling and reports the experience gathered in the HyperAudio project, where empirical foundation were sought to start-up an adaptive and portable electronic guide to a museum.

* We thank the HyperAudio project team for valuable suggestions throughout the design of the study, Museum staff for assistance with data collection, and all the visitors for filling out the questionnaire.

2   Know the User: Why and How [1]

To be effective in use, an information system has to be faithful to the real context. This implies that the system has to be in keeping with the employment the final users will make of it. Unfortunately, "users have infinite potential for making unexpected misinterpretations of interface elements and for performing their job in a different way than you imagine" (Nielsen, 1993). In other words, "a designer's best guess is not good enough". To cope with this, the Human-Computer Interaction community developed methodologies to design systems incrementally, in order to reach the implementation step with a design that is worth succeeding.

Adaptive systems have been proposed as a solution for usability problems (Benyon, 1993). Nevertheless, even if they greatly improve interaction, their effectiveness and their correspondence to user needs are not straightforward (Dieterich et al., 1993). Well-founded hypotheses are fundamental for a successful interaction, because they represent the basis for system reaction to user behavior. We claim that a user-centered approach enhances the probability that the model to be implemented will satisfy user needs.

Designing with a user-centered approach requires that the user be involved from the very beginning. The relative engagement and influence of users on the final design suggest splitting the approach into two classes depending on the user's role. *Consultative design* leaves decision-making power to technicians: users are simply sources of information with little to no direct influence. Designers turn to users to test their ideas and receive specific hints on the system being developed. On the opposite, *cooperative design* strongly involves selected users giving them the possibility of affecting the final system. Users have an active role: they have to understand problems and to propose solutions. A big effort is needed to create a common background, as well as to organize and lead design sessions. Here consultative design is discussed; interested readers in cooperative design can refer to Communication of the ACM, June 1993.

First of all, a user-centered approach requires understanding reality: who will use the system, where, how, and to do what. Then, the system is designed iterating a design-implementation-evaluation cycle. In this way it is possible to avoid serious mistakes and to save re-implementation time since the first design is based on empirical knowledge of user behavior. To collect it, many different techniques can be applied, among them direct observation, interviews and questionnaires. *Direct observation* is the most reliable and precise method, especially valuable for identifying user classes and related tasks. Moreover, it allows identifying critical factors, like social pressure, that can have a strong effect on user behavior when the system will be used in the field. Unfortunately, direct observation is very expensive, because it requires experimenters to observe each user individually. For this reason, it is useful when a reduced number of observations is enough to generalize behavioral predictions or when hypotheses have to be tested rather than generated. *Interviews* collect self-reported experience, opinion, and behavioral motivations. They are essential to finding out procedural knowledge as well as problems with currently used tools. Interviews cost a bit less than direct observations, because they can be shorter and easier to code. However, they still require skilled experimenters to be effective. By contrast, self-administered *questionnaires* can be handed out and collected by untrained personnel allowing to gather a huge quantity

---

[1] Here fifteen years of HCI are summarized. It is impossible go give references. Interested readers can refer to the valuable commented list of current HCI literature by Andrew Sears ("An HCI Reading List", SIGCHI Bulletin, Jan. 1998, vol. 30, n. 1) available at http://www.acm.org/sigchi/ bulletin/ .

of data at low cost. They allow statistical analyses and stronger generalizations than interviews. Questionnaires provide an overview on the current situation as well as specific answers. Which combination of these methods is worth applying depends both on requirements and budget. The ideal situation, where all of the above are used as in Vassileva (1996), is rarely justified. Nevertheless, as described in this work, the cheapest solution can give rise to interesting results.

Elaborating the outcome of the knowledge phase, designers define a first version of the system. At this stage, design techniques (e.g., task centered or scenario based) and expert reviewing (e.g., heuristic evaluation or cognitive walkthroughs) do provide satisfying solutions. Among the many methods used in HCI, probably the most suitable for systems that have a user model is parallel design. The goal is to explore different design alternatives before settling on a single proposal to be further developed. Possibly, in this way designers will propose different solutions (what to model) and different interaction strategies (what the user can control).

Then, one or more solutions can be tested with users. This step, called *formative evaluation*, aims at checking some choices and getting hints for revising the design. Techniques like paper mock-ups, prototyping and Wizard Of Oz simulations can be applied. *Paper mock-ups* are the cheapest: pieces of the system interface are drawn on paper and the interaction with a user is simulated by an experimenter. Despite its trivial appearance, this technique allows collecting reliable data which can be used for parallel reviewing. *Prototyping* allows testing some functionalities in depth (vertical prototyping) or the whole interface (horizontal prototyping). Both paper mock-ups and prototyping can be empowered by methods like focus group (i.e., many users solve a task together) or think-aloud (i.e., the user expresses verbally what he/she is doing), that clarify user behavior and understanding. They also succeed in finding misunderstandings and false presuppositions. Since no system is needed, they can be valuable tools in user modeling early testing. They can easily test the relative advantage of system self-adaptation versus user controlled adaptation (Dieterich et al., 1993), or user general understanding of interface dynamic changes. By contrast, *Wizard Of Oz simulations* require a sophisticated system to help the wizard perform as the final system will do. This technique is expensive and is justified only when a corpus of reliable interactions has to be collected (e.g., for future training or testing in dialogue systems).

At the end of the design cycle, *summative evaluation* are run. They concerns the test of the final system with effective users performing real tasks in their working environment. Therefore, a summative evaluation should be considered as the very last confirmation of the correctness of the hypotheses stated during the design process.

3   A Quick Overview of HyperAudio

The basic idea of HyperAudio arose upon observing that each museum can be coupled with a hypertext the visitor might wish to explore during the visit. Each exhibit corresponds to a sub-net. For example, a stuffed crocodile can be described by general features, evolution, life cycle etc. Entering the reptile room, approaching the crocodile, visitors explore the hypertext through their movements. Combining portable computers and physical exhibitions, coupling exhibits and hypertext structure, HyperAudio provides a new way of navigating information:

- moving in the physical space, approaching a case, the visitor implicitly selects a node of the hypertext as relevant;

- as in a "traditional" hypertext, the visitor can explicitly explore the sub-net connected to the current node (i.e., the object the visitor is facing) before moving in the physical space towards a new object.

In this way, the visit becomes a path among physical sites (rooms, objects) and semantic sites (descriptions, contents).

 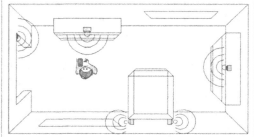

Figure1. A visitor equipped with a palmtop computer and headphones in the augmented museum.

HyperAudio stands where location aware systems and adaptive systems overlap. Exploiting position data, it provides personalized information to a user carrying a palmtop computer. The system follows the moving user and provides information at the right time (Figure 1). HyperAudio adapts to a single user, who is following a personal path in a physical context[2]. Each of these three facets (the visitor, the actual visit, and the museum) influences the process of dynamically building presentations in different ways and with different strengths (Not and Zancanaro, 1998, and Petrelli et al., 1999). A presentation is created on the fly. It is composed of an audio message (generated by assembling pieces of messages), a set of potentially interesting links, and a map or a picture valid for the discussed object. A presentation can vary in terms of: (i) the selected content; (ii) the proposed links; (iii) the language used (style and form); and (iiii) the system initiative (ranging from a fully guided tour to delivering information only upon explicit request). Selecting the proper content and links, using the most suitable language, and proposing the right level of visiting support depend on the guesswork the system makes observing visitor behavior. As described above, physical and hypertextual steps compose a visit path. The system has to interpret both steps as user input. While the link selection using a pen on the palmtop screen is explicit, moving towards, stopping, and moving away from an exhibit are signs of visitor's attitudes, but they are not straightforward. They have to be interpreted.

---

[2] HyperAudio is at the basis of a richer scenario that is being exploited, jointly with other partners, in HIPS, a European project of the Esprit I3 program, (http://marconi.ltt.dii.unisi.it/progetti/HIPS/). The HIPS consortium includes: University of Siena (Italy, coordinating partner), CB&J (France), GMD (Germany), ITC-IRST (Italy), SIETTE-Alcatel (Italy), SINTEF (Norway), University College Dublin (Ireland), and University of Edinburgh (Scotland).

4   Getting Off on the Right Foot

Good initial hypotheses are instrumental when the interaction is far from the well-known direct manipulation paradigm. When the HyperAudio project team tried to imagine visitor-system inter-action, they did not receive any support from the literature, nor from previous experiences. Moreover, the peculiar scenario further complicated the task. In a museum, the attention of a visi-tor is mainly focused on exhibits. Therefore, the time spent interacting is possibly low and distributed all along the visit. This means that HyperAudio guesses have to be based on a few details: a moving, a stop, and a single click. Thus, a reliable profile is vital. To overcome the gap between current knowledge and design needs, a case study was planned. An interdisciplinary group, involving people with background in psychology, human computer interaction, and artifi-cial intelligence, was set up. Applying a consultative design methodology, a survey study was planned. Requirements were of preliminary data on visitor's attitudes toward and behavior in museums. In that case, reliable results required a broad sample of observations. Thus, the ques-tionnaire was selected as the more suitable tool to collect relevant information on visitor profiles.

The aim of the study was to get a precise idea of how people visit museums and of what their feelings are. The final goal was to draw stereotypes (Rich, 1983) identifying the major dimensions affecting visitor behavior, feeling and attitudes. The study was not intended to be a survey of mu-seum visitors, describing for instance the average age or profession. On the contrary, here personal data are of interest if (and only if) they match a typical behavior. Age, for example, may explain variations in attitude towards technology if elderly visitors prefer human guides, while younger ones enjoy using computer guides. This information would affect interaction preferences, a major aspect of the initial user profile. Accordingly, the system is set for a completely guided tour or, alternatively, it proposes a highly interactive visit.

As a working hypothesis, we assumed that through stereotypes, we could identify visitors cate-gories by analyzing a short questionnaire (10 items at most) the user would be required to fill in at the beginning of the visit. This because we expected that visitors would be easily categorized using "classical" dimensions such as age, profession, education, specific knowledge or background. Such a categorization would allow setting important features in the user profile, such as language style (expert vs. naive), preferred interaction modalities (led by the system vs. the user), verbosity (depending on the available time). As a typical scenario, we imagined an individual visitor, going to the museum to visit it as a whole. We also assumed that the behavior should affect the dynamic part of the user model, i.e., user knowledge and user interest. Thus, jumps, skipping and staying in front of an exhibit would update the interest model, while the request for information would affect interests and knowledge. Finally, the rate of interaction would be a measure of preferred modali-ties.

5   The Questionnaire and the Case Study

The design of the questionnaire was guided by several constraints arising from field research. In particular, an accurate and quick way to collect reliable, self-reported information from visitors was needed. Questionnaire topics were defined on the basis of the literature relevant to museums. The five topic areas are listed and commented below.

- **Personal data profile** contains questions about age, sex, education, job, etc. It has the purpose of providing a sketch of the compiler.
- **Museum habits** collects information about frequency of museum visits and preferences (e.g., visiting alone or with a partner). It was introduced to complete the personal profile in the museum visit perspective.
- **Context of the current visit** moves the focus to the visit just finished. Information on general motivations for the visit was collected here.
- **Course of the current visit** was intended to clarify the use of guides (from labels to human guides) as well as the duration and the purpose of the visit.
- **Styles of visit** aims to clarify different dimensions of visiting styles, to say how people behave (e.g., stay with the companion all the time), how they feel after (e.g., afraid of having missed something important), or their attitudes towards guided tours.

The final version, as derived by a pilot study, was composed of 26 items, requiring around 10 minutes to be filled out. A page describing the purpose of the study introduced the questionnaire. For most of the items, participants were required to tick the appropriate answer from a set of given alternatives. In the "styles of visit" section participants had to express their level of agreement with 11 statements describing different behaviors or attitudes. Answers were modulated on a 5-point Likert scale. The survey was conducted from October to December 1997. Data were collected in three museums focusing on topics related to the natural sciences: *Museo Tridentino di Scienze Naturali* in Trento (Natural Science); *Museo Civico di Storia Naturale* in Verona (Natural History); *Museo dei Fossili* in Bolca (Fossil Museum). The heterogeneous sample should increase the external validity of the study, allowing to generalize findings to the class of Natural Science/History Museums. In total, 250 questionnaires were collected: 97 in Trento, 102 in Verona, and 51 in Bolca.

When leaving, visitors where asked to take part in the study by museum staff. This procedure was convenient, on the one hand, because it did not required experimenters to stay at the museum, but, on the other hand, it did not allow for any control over sampling. For instance a bias might affected the sample of Verona where teachers and professors seemed to be a preferred target. Nevertheless, we considered the whole sample reliable since we are not interested in museum statistics: we are interested in finding out if and how personal characteristics are relevant to predicting visitor behavior.

6 From Empirical Results to Briefings

Empirical results pointed out relevant and unexpected aspects that urge designers to rethink the system. In the following the main outcomes are presented and discussed. The focus is on result interpretation and on user modeling guidelines. The experiment and analysis report (Petrelli et al., 1998) is available at http://ecate.itc.it:1024/petrelli/publications.html.

6.1 Museums are Social Places

The major unexpected result regards the importance of the social dimension. This clearly emerges analyzing either self-reported behavior or preferences. Only 5% of visitors went to the museum all alone. The majority participated in a guided tour (45%), while 20% went to the museum with friends. Moreover a high percentage of people came with children (30%), showing that families are an important target for natural science museums. From these results, it appears that visiting a museum is mainly a 'social event', an experience to share with important others. Family, friends and partners play an important role in making the visit a valuable experience. This finding clearly contradicts our hypothesis stating that visiting a museum is mainly a personal experience. As a consequence, the user model has to become a group model too, because needs, expectations and behavior of groups are very different from those of individuals. Indeed, our data confirm Falk and Dierking (1992): persons tend to behave differently when visiting museums with friends or family. When visiting museums with friends, adults are mainly concerned with the nature and the content of the exhibits. Even if discussion is stated as a very important point, their attention is more focused towards what they see than towards their own social group. On the contrary, adults with their family typically focus on their children, on making the exhibition understandable and the visit enjoyable. Before the visit, they are used to gather information significantly more often than adults with friends. This finding has a strong impact on user modeling. Indeed, it is plausible that the family profile has a higher background than the most part of single visitors. Moreover, it is known that family visit depends on what attracts children and that family learning (i.e., when adults and children learn together) derives from family discussions (Borun and Dritsas, 1997). Therefore, the system has to support family discussion besides proposing a standard comment on the exhibit. The content could be organized as question-answer, because this format stimulates discussion and self-exploration. System proposals (e.g., presenting further information when a visitor remains in front of the same object) should be reduced in number and form, so as not to hamper family discussion and exploration. In terms of user modeling, a new attribute of linguistic style has to be introduced (question-answer vs. narrative presentation), and system initiative (i.e., preferred interaction modality) has to be fine-tuned.

Our data suggest also that museums play an important role in pupils learning. In the sample 36% of participants were teachers who came with the class. This experience is very different from that of being taught in a classroom: since exhibits replace the teacher as the central medium of instruction, museum learning is self-directed rather than directed by the teacher. In this context, the main purpose of a guided tour should be to have the pupils stay in the exhibits longer, learn more, and return to the museum frequently throughout their lifetimes (Falk and Dierking, 1992). Moreover, children learn well together. As a consequence, an electronic guide should take most of the group visit. It should stimulate students in working together, have them solve problems in groups, and share their solutions. Therefore, the system should shift from a guiding style to an "informal" tutoring style, proposing quizzes and problems as well as suitable explanation of the exhibits. This is of course a completely new and exciting scenario.

6.2 Guide without Dominating

Another important result is the positive attitude towards guidance. On the average, participants reported to strongly appreciate guided tours. Attitudes were found to be consistent with reported behavior. More than half of the sample (58%) used a guide during their actual visit. One of the major goals of the survey was to evince factors influencing the decision of using a guide. Such a decision appears to be correlated with familiarity with the specific museum. The more visitors are used to going to a museum, the more they will use a guide. In addition, we found that the major part of people who came to see specific objects used a guide, while people who came to visit the museum in general did not. These results are counterintuitive. Indeed, we expected that familiarity with museums should reflect an autonomous style and self-sufficiency.

Other interesting results regard the number of non-first-time visitors. It is surprisingly high (68%). This variable was found to affect the time of the visit. Contrary to our expectations, those who came to see specific objects stayed in the museum longer than those who wanted to see the museum in general did. Again these results have strong impact on user modeling. They support the idea that each visitor comes to the museum with a personal agenda in mind. Some come to get an overview, others to see specific objects, or to learn, or to relax. An accurate user model has to take these aspects into account because they change the meaning of behavior. For example, when a visitor is not coming for the first time, skipping objects has not to affect the interest model decreasing the weight of the object. Similarly, pondering an object for a long time is a sign of interest, but the system should not interrupt self-exploration with further explanations. A *beep* may be enough to signal interested visitors about available information. First-time visitors have to be considered apart because they have to be motivated and engaged if they want to learn and return. One way to stimulate first-time visitors is to create expectations (Finn, 1985). For this purpose, the system may use the very beginning of the visit, when people spend a few minutes in finding direction, to give a sketch of the possible visit. Then, each visitor would follow his/her preferences adopting a personal path and rhythm for the visit. Some visitors will have a systematic and intensive look, others will select objects to look at, and many will "cruise" the museum (Falk and Dierking, 1992). By monitoring this behavior, the system can identify relevant aspects to modify the user model.

6.3 Technology Must Be Hidden

Results show that the most liked museum visit is guided by a member of the museum staff (53%). Almost 21% of the sample prefer catalogues or books, and 19% to visit museum without any support. Only 7% reports to like using technological devices. These data lead to several important considerations. First of all visit aids are highly appreciated. Secondly, the preferred solution is still represented by human experts. This can be due to the social aspect of the situation and to the possibility of interacting with the source of knowledge to obtain the most appropriate information. It can also suggest that listening to a human guide is the easiest way (i.e. less tiring and constricting) to get information.

To conclude, the low percentage of people who prefer technological devices has to be taken into account. It can be partially explained by the reality of Italian museums, where technology is still underrepresented, or by the comparison with human guides, but it could also reflect a negative attitude towards technology in the context of a museum visit. This suggests that some visitors may never explicitly interact with the system. Thus, the user model has to take into account the possibility of facing a completely passive visitor: the system has to rely on a default setting that actively proposes a visit. This also fits the requirement that systems for public use have to be "walk-up and use", i.e., no training phase is needed to operate them. However, active users can take the initiative getting the most from HyperAudio support. For those visitors who like to interact with computers, the system has to adopt appropriate strategies, since the attraction lasts only for few minutes (Serrell and Raphling, 1992). For example, it could propose a game to measure background knowledge, a user characteristic particularly important and that is difficult to self report about.

6.4 Ask Only the Essential

Another unexpected outcome is that personal data, like age, profession, education etc., do not characterize the visitor. For example older people do not show different preferences than younger one; education is high for almost all museum visitors (91%); professional interest does not influence visit behavior. This means that personal data are not as important as expected and should be ignored in the initial questionnaire.

Secondly, a relative dislike for technology suggests reducing the explicit interaction to the very minimum, possibly even eliminating it. Filling out a questionnaire at the beginning of the interaction, a technique widely adopted in user modeling community (Fink et al., 1997, Strachen et al., 1997, Murphy and McTear, 1997 just to mention a few), does not seem to be the best solution in this context. Indeed, the negative attitude towards technology, the strong attraction of the exhibits, the small amount of time devoted to computer interaction suggests limiting system requests as much as possible. Furthermore, the four attributes that explain the most of visit and interaction variability and that the system must know to start can be inserted by museum staff when the HyperAudio guide is handed out. They are:

- **Family, school or adult**: user modeling does not only concern a single person but also has to address groups of people with a common goal. This attribute affects language style (narrative vs. question-answer) and complexity (simple terms vs. complex ones to stimulate discussion) as well as the system reaction level (high initiative of the system vs. user explicit request).
- **First-time visit**: this distinction affects content selection. For first-time visits an overview is proposed, while for following visits a deepening is preferred. This attribute also affects the dynamic part of the user model, mainly the interest, because some behavior does not have the same meaning in the two cases, e.g., skipping objects will not be interpreted as disinterest in follow-up visits, while it is one of the best guesses for a first-time visit. It also has an impact on the next attribute evaluation.
- **Foreseen visit duration**: the more time available the broader the visit can be. It affects system verbosity in terms of numbers of objects proposed or in-depth descriptions.
- **Interaction preferences**: this is an important attribute of the visitor's profile since it is used to describe passive visitors. Unfortunately it does not appear to be related to any personal or visit characteristics. Partially it can be inferred by previous attributes, for example family visitors may prefer a smooth interaction, while adults on their first-time visit could appreciate a very active guide.

Note that this questionnaire does not portray the isolated user but, better, it describes user, visit and context, the three components relevant for an effective usage of the electronic guide.

7 Conclusions

The outcome of this study has demonstrated the high level feedback that a user-centered approach can provide, even with low cost methods. The results incited designers to rethink some basic assumptions. Indeed, the idea of using stereotypes had to be set aside in favor of a broader view, where user, visit, and context were the key points. It is worth noting that no prototype was developed for the study. Hence the whole system could be easily redesigned. A sketch of the current user model implementation is given in Sarini and Strapparava (1999), in the poster section of this volume. Given the very interesting results, we are going to follow the user-centered design approach exploring games to measure background knowledge through paper mock-ups.

References

Benyon, D. (1993). Adaptive Systems: A Solution to Usability Problems. *User Modeling and User-Adapted Interaction* 3(1):65-87.

Borun, M., and Dritsas, J. (1997). Developing Family-Friendly Exhibits. *Curator* 3: 178-196.

Communication of the ACM (1993). Participatory Design. 36(4).

Dieterich, H., Malinowsky, U., Kuhme, T., and Schneider-Hufschmidt, M. (1993). State of the Art in Adaptive User Interaction. In Schneider-Hufschmidt, M., Kuhme, T., and Malinowsky, U., eds., *Adaptive User Interfaces: principles and practice*. Amsterdam: Elsevier Science Publishers, 13-48.

Falk, J., and Dierking, L. (1992). *The Museum Experience*. Ann Arbor, MI: Whalesback Books.

Fink, J., Kobsa, A., and Nill, A. (1997). Adaptable and Adaptive Information Access for All Users, Including the Disabled and the Elderly. In *Proceedings of the 6th International Conference on User Modelling*, 171-173.

Finn, D. (1985). *How to Visit a Museum*. New York, NY: Harry Abrams Pub.

Nielsen, J. (1993). *Usability Engineering*. San Diego, CA: Academic Press.

Not, E., and Zancanaro, M. (1998). Content Adaptation for Audio-based Hypertexts in Physical Environments. In *Proceedings of the 2nd Workshop on Adaptive Hypertext and Hypermedia* (proceedings available at http://wwwis.win.tue.nl/ah98/Proceedings.html), at Hypertext'98.

Murphy, M., and McTear, M. Learner Modelling for Intelligent CALL. In *Proceedings of the 6th International Conference on User Modelling*, 301-312.

Petrelli, D., De Angeli, A., and Convertino, G. (1998). *Analysing Visiting Preferences and Behaviour in Natural Science Museums*. IRST Technical Report. ref. n. 9812-01.

Petrelli, D., Not, E., Sarini, M., Stock, O., Strapparava, C., and Zancanaro, M. (1999). HyperAudio: LocationAwareness+Adaptivity. In *Companion of CHI'99, Human Factors in Computing Systems*. (in press).

Rich, E. (1983) . Users are individuals: individualizing user models. *International Journal of Man-Machine Studies* 18:199-214.

Sarini, M., and Strapparava, C. (1999). User Modelling in a Museum Exploration Adaptive System. In *Proceedings of the 7th International Conference on User Modelling*.

Serrel, B., and Raphling, B. (1992). Computers on the Exhibit Floor. *Curator*, 35(3): 181-189.

Strachen, L, Anderson, J., Sneerby, M., and Evans, M. (1998) Pragmatic User Modelling in a Commercial Software System. In *Proceedings of the 6th International Conference on User Modelling*, 189-200.

Vassileva, J. (1996). A Task-Centered Approach for User Modeling in a Hypermedia Office Documentation System. *User Modeling and User-Adapted Interaction* 6:185-223.

The Emergence of Student Models from an Analysis of Ethical Decision Making in a Scenario-Based Learning Environment

Mike Winter[1] and Gord McCalla[1]*

[1] ARIES Laboratory, Department of Computer Science, University of Saskatchewan, SK, Canada

Abstract. Too often, professional ethics issues are trivialized in software engineering education. To begin to remedy this situation, we have built two interactive, adaptive learning *scenarios* that place students in the role of a software project manager confronting many critical project decisions, each with an ethical dimension. As students move through a scenario, making and justifying their decisions, their behaviour can be monitored and used both to adapt the scenario to each student as they proceed, and in post hoc analysis to identify different classes of ethical behaviour. In this paper we discuss five different classes of student behaviour that emerged from the analysis of protocols collected during the use of these scenarios in a third year undergraduate software engineering class. We speculate that the existence of these general *student models* can be used in several ways to further enhance the learning of ethics

1 Introduction

Professional ethics issues are often seen to be an irrelevant afterthought to students learning to become software professionals. Yet, the importance of preparing students to be ethical computer professionals in their practice, and to be aware of the social impact of their work, is widely acknowledged (eg. Appel, 1998; Gotterbarn and Riser, 1997). One of the main purposes of our research is to make ethics seem less 'academic' to computer science students. Key to this goal is the realization that making ethical decisions in the software development process isn't an afterthought to the process; it's an integral part of it. It is important for students to realize that connection and to understand they are not just technicians without moral responsibilities.

We have designed two goal-based scenarios (following the idea of Schank and the Community Partnering Development Team, *http://www.ils.nwu.edu/projects/cper/overview.html*) to be used by students to practise making ethical decisions in a realistic context. In each scenario, a student takes on the role of a manager of a large software project, and is then confronted with a series of difficult situations, each requiring him/her to make a decision with an ethical dimension. These scenarios were used in a third year software engineering course at the U. of Saskatchewan. From an analysis of the data collected during this use, several classes of

* We would like to express our gratitude to John Cooke and Judy Thomson who helped with the experiment, and acknowledge the Natural Sciences and Engineering Research Council of Canada for funding this research. We would also like to thank the Basser Department of Computer Science at the University of Sydney, Australia, who acted as sabbatical hosts for Gord McCalla during the time this paper was written.

student behaviour were identified. In this paper we describe these *student models* and speculate as to their potential uses.

2 The Ethics Scenarios

Two goal-based scenarios (accessible via the Web) have been developed. As students individually interact with a scenario, they move through different situations, each confronting them with a decision that must be made about the software development process. The ethical issues in each situation are confounded and contextualized by other issues such as looming deadlines, people management concerns, unexpected opportunities to further the project, etc. In each situation, students are able to consult the relevant section from the ACM Software Development Code of Ethics (http://www.computer.org/tab/seprof/code.htm), thus helping them to reify abstract Code concepts. The students' choices at each decision point determines the path they take through the scenario. Different choices lead to different consequences, in the short or long term, leading each individual to have a different experience in using the system. The goal is to give students a realistic feeling for the true complexities they will face in the real world of software development, if they are to maintain an ethical stance. As they make their way through a scenario, students are asked to justify their decision in each situation with a paragraph explaining why they did what they did. It forces them to reflect on the ambiguities inherent in each situation and to relate ethical issues to concrete reality, thus consolidating and deepening their understanding of the issues. At the end of the overall scenario there is a final outcome provided to the students based cumulatively on their previous decisions and a recap of all their decisions is provided for them to browse. Students are also given a chance to comment on the entire scenario, and add commentary on each of the choices they made earlier, should they wish.

In scenario one, students take on the role of being the new head of a small team of programmers and software engineers at Denodyne Systems, and are charged with guiding the team as it overhauls the company's MedXFile medical database system. From this starting premise, each student has to deal with a variety of crises as the development team struggles to release a finished product by the release date. Some of the crises include electronic harassment, a major yet rare bug, an angry user group, and the need to look through the project team's e-mail to try to stem an information leak. Scenario two (not shown) is structured similarly, but explores the issues that arise in building an embedded system application.

A truncated version of a typical student's interaction with scenario one is shown in Figure 1. The system's output is in plain text, with a bold label indicating each new situation; the student's input is italicized; and ".....″ is used to indicate that text has been left out of a situation in this paper for the sake of brevity. Only the initial setup, abbreviated versions of the first and second situations, and the start of the third situation are shown, to give a flavour for the style of interaction.

SETUP

You are the new head of a small group of programmers and software engineers at Deno-dyne Systems in Calgary, which is in the market of producing medical database products. ..... At your first management meeting, you are told the situation at Denodyne, and receive the following talk from Mr. D, the general manager of the company: "You know we're counting on you ....."

ILLICIT_CODE

..... After meeting with the entire team, you are approached by one of the team members. He says, " ..... I hang out with a few guys from Phrack, and we trade software and games and stuff, and one of them gave me a disk from work with some stuff on it. There was some source code and new structures on there from a version of their program that he had taken home to work on. This code could really help us in development ..... We could change it around a bit so that no one would ever know where it came from. It's done all the time. They would do the same to us if they could. You can't copyright an algorithm, so it's not illegal, and it's no different from using a system library or some code off of the net."

This could really give you a leg up on development; do you allow the code to be used in your project?

Choice: *NO*

Justification: *This is obviously unethical and I don't think it is worth it to risk the company's reputation. If the boss doesn't like it, I'm sure I can find a job somewhere else.*

READ_EMAIL2

You decide not to use the Phrack source code. You realize that while it may not be illegal, it probably isn't ethical to use someone else's intellectual property. You're also worried that using outside source code might cause more problems than it's worth to try and integrate it into your software. ..... A week later, Mr. D calls you into his office and presents you with an advertisement in the business pages of the local newspaper. He says "Look at this; somehow Phrack found out how we're coding the new features we're planning to implement. ..... Do what you have to do to find the person [responsible for the leak] and get rid of him or her."

Talking to your network manager later, he tells you that the company routinely logs all e-mail and internet use statistics for trouble-shooting purposes. It would be pretty likely that you could find out who was leaking the information if you went through the e-mail. .....

Do you look through the e-mail or not?

Choice: *NO*

Justification: *This is also unethical and workers would turn to hate me for invading their privacy. I tend to agree with them and would not like it if someone did this to me.*

SPYING4

You decide not to read through the e-mail ..... if you read through e-mail that's generally considered private, morale would go down even lower than it is. However, when Mr. D finds out about this, he is furious with you. .....

Figure 1. A Truncated Version of a Typical Interaction with Scenario One

Scenarios are structured in an underlying discrimination graph. Discrimination graphs seem to be both simple and well suited for rapidly prototyping new scenarios, but ultimately a structure such as a Bayes Net (as used by Mislevy and Gitomer, 1996, for example), might allow for more sophisticated analysis. The discrimination graph for scenario one is shown in Figure 2. Situations are represented by nodes. Each situation contains a textual description of an ethical dilemma. The situation normally starts with a synopsis of the reasons that may have motivated the student to decide as they did in the previous situation. The text then moves on to outline the new situation, at the end of which the student is asked to choose among (possibly several) alternatives, thereby opening up different paths in the graph. Branches in Figure 2 represent the alternative paths. To control unconstrained growth in the graph, a process of 'folding in' of some of the paths happens. Thus, different students may temporarily take a different path, but come back together again at some later point.

The path that a student follows is not always determined by their choice at the immediate decision point. Thus, in the last two situations of scenario one, a linear weight function that accesses all previous decisions (kept in a logfile for each user) is applied to choose a follow-up situation. It can reward unethical behavior in some ways. For example, if a student has chosen not to fix a major bug (the BUGFIX situation), they get a major boost in getting the product out on time. The weight function punishes unethical behaviour in other situations. For example, if a student has spied on the workers (the SPYING situation), the negative morale that results is counted against them. The weights and the threshold value are then cumulated to come up with a final decision about which follow up situation is appropriate. It would be easy, of course, to modify the weight function in order to explore the effects on students of different reward systems, thus allowing the creation of essentially "malevolent" or "benevolent" worlds that differently reward ethical vs. unethical behaviour.

3 The Experiment

We conducted an experiment in the use of the scenarios in a third year software engineering class (Cmpt. 370) at the University of Saskatchewan. In the experiment the 95 students in the class were asked to go through both scenarios, working on their own. The students' decisions, rationales, and end-comments were all recorded, analyzed, and later used to stimulate a classroom discussion. The discussion was extremely vigorous. It was focussed by the specific issues that emerged from the students' shared experience in using the scenarios, and it was animated by the different decisions they had made at various important junctures in the scenarios.

There were two different phases of analysis done. The first, used to facilitate in-class discussion, recorded how the students collectively responded to each ethical situation. The decisions made by the students in each of these situations were counted, and the justifications for each choice summarized. The numbers next to each decision point in Figure 2 indicate the percentage of students who took that path in the experiment. This material was used to encourage in-class discussion, for example around similarities and differences in student decisions and justifications in the two situations involving privacy (READ_EMAIL and SPYING). The second phase of analysis looked at each student's behaviour over a whole scenario, to see if standard patterns of behaviour, *student models*, occurred.

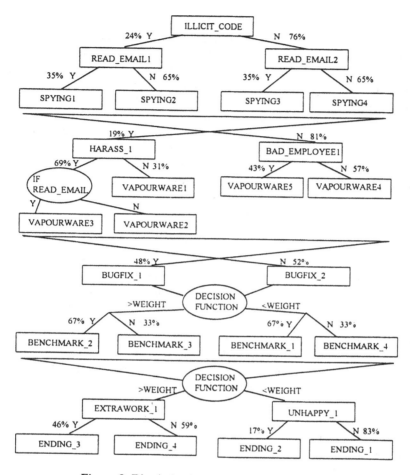

Figure 2. Discrimination Graph for Scenario One

4 The Student Models

The second phase of analysis categorized students on the basis of the paths they had taken through a whole scenario. Clear patterns only emerged from scenario one, so this became the focus of the analysis. Student decisions in HARASS_1 and the alternative BAD_EMPLOYEE1 were ignored; as were their decisions at the EXTRA_WORK and UNHAPPY alternatives. In each case, these situations partitioned the students into two distinct groups confronting two distinct situations, thus making it illogical to compare their decision making. Therefore, only the 6 situations that all students shared "in common" (ILLICIT_CODE, READ_EMAIL, VAPOURWARE, SPYING, BUGFIX, and BENCHMARK) were used. If any two students responded identically, they were put in the same group. Each group was further augmented by comparing the justifications of students in the group to the justifications of students who had taken similar paths (with one decision made differently). If the justifications were similar, the students with small differences in their paths were added to the main groups.

Overall, 91 of the 95 students in the class tried scenario one. Of these, 82 finished the scenario all the way through, 19 of them multiple times. For the students who tried the scenario more than once, we chose for analysis the chronologically earliest run through in which the students had fully justified their decisions, feeling this was most representative of their real feelings. We were able to categorize 67 of the students who completed the scenario into 5 different student models; the remaining 15 did not fit into any equivalence class. These students may, in fact, be part of other as yet undefined student models. However, we either did not find a consistency of behaviour among their decision making, or the numbers of students in that unknown model were not sufficient to form a critical mass. The descriptions of these student models follows.

Student model A: *straight and narrow*
Number of users: 21
Common paths taken: No/No/No/No/Yes/No; No/No/No/Yes/Yes/No

People in this model tended to make the 'safe' decisions, never taking any risks, or making any decisions that could be perceived as unethical. Figure 1 is an example of a straight and narrow student. Their behavior may be construed as being very concerned with ethical issues that involve the end users and workers in the software firm, but deficient in terms of the user's responsibility to the firm he or she is employed with. Although it should be noted that the students in this model often took the stance that they would do a certain action to facilitate good software development, they were reluctant to break any perceived behavioural taboos. They also thought that the bond of trust between themselves and the software developers was one of the most important facets of the software development process.

Student model B: mission critical dominant
Number of users: 13
Common paths taken: No/Yes/No/No/Yes/No; Yes/Yes/No/No/Yes/No

The most interesting characteristic of students in student model B is their understanding of the special nature of the 'mission-critical' elements of the software being developed. The most obvious place where this concern manifested itself was the VAPOURWARE situation where students were encouraged to claim the software would be done by its release date, even if this meant releasing it with bugs. Students in model B pointed out that rushing the development of the software to try to meet an impossible deadline was sure to lead to more problems in the long run, including potentially serious risks for end users of the system. An interesting situation where people in this group acted differently from others in similar student models was the READ_EMAIL situation. Everyone in this model was of the opinion that if an employee is using email on company time then the company has a right to look at it, but they then thought that increased surveillance of the employees (SPYING) was counterproductive and unethical.

Student model C: opportunistic
Number of users: 9
Common paths taken: Yes/No/No/Yes/Yes/No; Yes/No/No/Yes/Yes/Yes

The behavior of the main group of students in this model was similar to that of the second biggest sub-group in student model A. The major difference was in their handling of the ILLICIT_CODE situation. The students in this model were of an opportunistic mindset when confronting whether to use the source code from the rival company. The thought seemed to be that if the company was careless enough to hand over their important source code, the company was absolved of responsibility for using it. The urgency of the situation was also a deciding factor for many of the students. They were strongly opposed to any sort of violation of personal privacy of the workers (READ_EMAIL, SPYING). The other situation where they differed from those in student model A was in the VAPOURWARE situation. Where the students in model A generally claimed the release date would be met in order to show confidence in their workers, the students in student model C thought that a bit of constructive dishonesty was necessary to keep enough customers in place so that the company would stay afloat. The students in this group were more cutthroat than those in some of the other models. A small subgroup in this model also thought it necessary (and of minor ethical concern) to edit the testing logs to give the company an added competitive advantage (BENCHMARK). The majority of the students in this model tended to think that this action was very unethical.

Student model D: public relations dominant
Number of users: 14
Common paths taken: No/No/Yes/Yes/Yes/No; No/No/Yes/No/Yes/No

The students in this model are an interesting combination of those in student model C and student model E. Students in model D were reluctant to read workers' e-mail (in the READ_EMAIL situation) for reasons of privacy, but thought that increased surveillance (in the SPYING situation) was so essential to the completion of the project that they had to do it. Students in model D were not as driven by ethical concerns as in some of the other models, but were more concerned about the public relations consequences of their actions. It should be noted, however, that even though they assured their users of a successful early completion of the project, they all thought it was necessary to fix the major bug in the program (BUGFIX), and that it wasn't right to alter the test logs to give themselves a competitive advantage (BENCHMARK).

Student model E: business dominant
Number of users: 10
Common path taken: No/Yes/No/Yes/Yes/No

This student model originally seemed to be a subgroup of student model B, but the students' responses were of quite a different calibre from those of model B. The main difference in the two groups was the willingness of students in model E to release the software with a few bugs while reassuring the user group that the product would be out on time (VAPOURWARE). This didn't show the concern about the 'mission-critical' nature of the project that the students in model B did. It should be noted that most people in this group then chose to fix the major bug that was discovered (BUGFIX), but a significant subgroup did not. This group was also very business oriented. In their justifications, there were not that many concerns about the ethics of actions, but mainly about the business consequences of each move.

5 Use of the Student Models

The existence of such student models is interesting in its own right, but could also be useful in several ways. One of the main uses of these student models would be to enhance the system's decision making using stereotypes based on the student models, in a long-standing user modelling tradition going back at least to Rich (1979). For example, after the SPYING situation is presented, a user who has answered "No/No/No" would be un-ambiguously identified as a straight and narrow stereotype (model A). This person has the strength of being highly ethical (or at least behaving in such a way), but perhaps unre-alistically so. Such a person might be confronted with further situations where a prior ethical decision has, itself, led to negative consequences. For example, a "type A" person refusing to read e-mail to catch a leak of project information to a competitor (READ_EMAIL), might be presented with a follow up situation where Denodyne loses the contract to that competitor, and all project members lose their jobs. Such challenges to a student's vested beliefs might lead them to a more subtle understanding of the issues, and the ability to identify and respond appropriately to ethical concerns they later meet in the real world.

Another use of the student models is for a class instructor to use them to categorize the students in his/her class. This can be done merely by observing common paths taken when using the scenarios (confirmed by a quick look at the qualitative information provided by the students). The most commonly occurring student models can then be the focus of the actual discussion in class, and the unethical or unrealistic aspects of each type of student explicitly discussed. Further, comparisons among the student models can be prepared in advance by the instructor to stimulate discussion. For example, it would be possible to point out to the students, should there be enough of them in each model, the way that the public relations dominant thinkers in model D are similar to and different from the op-portunistic students in model C and the business dominant students in model E. All three classes of students thus see natural variations of their own behaviour patterns and gain a broader perspective.

Finally, the student models make it possible for students to take particular roles when interacting with a scenario. For example, students diagnosed as straight and narrow thinkers (model A) in their first pass through scenario one could take an opportunistic stance (model B) in a subsequent run through scenario one or in scenario two. This would broaden their experience and prepare them for a more complex real world than they imagine exists. It is possible in assigning roles to create artificial student models, for example the "spawn of Satan" who always behaves totally unethically. This would allow students who are already leaning towards unethical behaviour to be better acquainted with the ultimate consequences of being unethical. In fact, we postulate that many of the 19 students who used the scenario more than once in the experiment, may have assigned themselves different roles each time through.

6 Comparison to the Literature

The use of paper-based scenarios is a long-standing one in ethics teaching, and their use primarily in the classroom has proven to be effective (Stevens et al, 1993) (Ascher, 1986). In fact, the inspiration for some of the situations in the scenarios here was taken from Kallman and Grillio (1996), and various online sources. Perhaps the most similar to our work is the ethical board game developed by Lockheed Martin (http://www.lmco.com/cxcth/dilbcrt.html) in which groups of employees form teams and then are presented with ethical scenarios and a range of responses. The teams then discuss the effects of all possible decisions and debate their merits.

Our research extends the use of scenarios by computationalizing and individualizing them for one-on-one student-system interaction. Technically oriented students are given a familiar technological environment in which they personally must make decisions that they recognize as important, but which have non-obvious consequences. This provides a realism and a personal relevance that is hard to achieve in a pure classroom approach or even in the group-based gaming approach of Lockheed Martin. Our approach will work best, however, with a combination of individual use and classroom follow-up, as we showed in the experiment.

Our analysis, inducing student models from observed student behaviour, is also non-standard. In other ethics experiments, subjects are given on paper several small scenarios with action plans, and are then asked to rank their approval of the action on a Likert scale of 'strongly disagree' to 'strongly agree', with five intermediate steps (Abratt et al, 1992)(Stevens et al, 1993). A more complex example is given in Reidenbach and Robin (1988) in which students rate various scenario/action pairs on a thirty point sliding scale with various ethical considerations divided into categories (i.e. deontological, utilitarian, etc.). Regression analysis is then performed on the responses, and the scores are compared across the groups in various categories. The most comprehensive attempt to measure moral development is in Colby and Kohlberg (1987) who describe a fifteen year long longitudinal study to categorize people into various moral 'stages'. This is done by doing an intensive qualitative analysis of the rationales subjects give for making various choices in response to ethical scenarios. This approach, while attractive for its depth of analysis, is impractical for measuring changes in ethical stance brought on by students using one or two goal-based scenarios over a short period of time.

Most of these methods use previously existing groups, and then rate their responses, but for our methods, we wanted to discover groups with similar ethical value systems based on observed actions in the scenarios. Our approach has allowed us to compare actual paths through the computational scenarios. This seems to be a more useful way of categorizing groups of people who think similarly, in particular because we can then reason about subtle differences in behaviour based on the actual decisions taken relative to the specific situations involving computer software. We also then set up the useful possibility of the system itself automatically classifying future students as they use the scenarios, not after the fact.

7 Conclusion

In this research we have shown that it is possible to design goal-based scenarios that allow students to actually experience the complexities of making ethical decisions in realistic situations. Frequently, unanticipated consequences result from decisions taken, based not just on one action but possibly the cumulative effect of many actions. Judging by the positive response of students who used the scenarios in an experiment carried out in a software engineering class and the enthusiastic follow-up discussion in class, the scenarios were a success in stimulating students to think more deeply about ethical issues and to realize their importance. As this paper has shown, the experiment also has allowed the delineation of several different classes of student behaviour, what we have called "student models", that can be used in a number of ways to further enhance the scenarios and their use.

The scenarios have been used again in a fourth year ethics class at U. of Saskatchewan in January, 1999, with similar enthusiasm on the part of the students. Preliminary analysis shows similar student models emerging, as well, although with fewer students taking a straight and narrow approach (model A) than in the first experiment. Further analysis will be carried out to confirm this. This analysis will also look at the data from both experiments in order to see if other student models emerge, in either scenario.

Overall, we believe this research shows that providing students with a realistic means of exploring abstract issues in a concrete setting allows the issues to be perceived by the students as both relevant and appropriately subtle and hard, not something trivial. It allows "soft" issues to be seen as integrated with technical concerns, and raises topics like ethics to "first class" status for technically oriented students.

References

Abratt, R. N., Higgs, D. and Nicola, S. (1992). An examination of the ethical beliefs of managers using selected scenarios in a cross-cultural environment. *Journal of Business Ethics*, 11: 29-35.

Appel, F. (1998). Including the social and ethical implications of computing in the computer science curriculum. *ACM Computers and Society*, 28: 56-57.

Ascher, M. (1986). Ethical conflicts in the computing field - an undergraduate course. *ACM Computers and Society*, 16: 19-22.

Colby, A. and Kohlberg, L. (1987). *The Measurement of Moral Judgement: Volume 1, Theoretical Foundations and Research Validation*. Cambridge: Cambridge University Press.

Gotterbarn, D. and Riser, R. (1997). Ethical activities in computer science course: goals and issues. *ACM Computers and Society*. 27: 10-15.

Kallman, E. A. and Grillio, J. P. (1996). *Ethical Decision Making and Information Technology: An Introduction with Cases*. New York: Mc-Graw Hill.

Mislevy, R.J., and Gitomer, D.H. (1996). The role of probability-based inference in an intelligent tutoring system. *User-Modeling and User-Adapted Interaction*. 5: 253-282.

Reidenbach, E. R. and Robin, D. P. (1988). Some initial steps toward improving the measurement of ethical evaluations of marketing activities. *Journal of Business Ethics*. 7: 871-879.

Rich, E. (1979). User modeling via stereotypes. *Cognitive Science*. 3: 329-354.

Stevens, R.E., Harris, J. O. and Williamson, S. (1993). A comparison of ethical evaluations of business school faculty and students: a pilot study. *Journal of Business Ethics*. 12: 611-619.

Predicting Users' Requests on the WWW

I. Zukerman, D.W. Albrecht and A.E. Nicholson
School of Computer Science and Software Engineering
Monash University
Clayton, VICTORIA 3168, AUSTRALIA

Abstract. We describe several Markov models derived from the behaviour patterns of many users, which predict which documents a user is likely to request next. We then present comparative results of the predictive accuracy of the different models, and, based on these results, build hybrid models which combine the individual models in different ways. These hybrid models generally have a greater predictive accuracy than the individual models. The best models will be incorporated in a system for pre-sending WWW documents.

1 Introduction

Users typically have to wait for information they require from the World Wide Web (WWW). The eventual aim of this project is to develop a system that reduces a user's expected waiting time by pre-sending documents s/he is likely to request (Nicholson et al., 1998,Albrecht et al., 1999). This requires the development of models which can anticipate a user's requests on the WWW. In this paper, we consider several such models (Sections 4 and 5), and compare their predictive power and their efficiency in terms of time and space consumption (Section 6). Our models are based on observing the behaviour patterns of many users, rather than modeling the requirements of an individual user. This is due to the constantly changing population of casual visitors to most WWW sites, in particular the site from which we gather our data (the School of Computer Science and Software Engineering at Monash University). Our models are generated by considering different combinations of two main features of our observations: the order in which documents are requested and the structure of the server site. These combinations yield four basic Markov models: Time, Space, Second-order Time, and Linked Space-Time (Section 4). The best of these models are then combined to yield hybrid models (Section 5).

In the next section we describe related research. We then describe the features of our domain, followed by our prediction models. Finally, we discuss our results, which motivate our hybrid models, and present concluding remarks.

2 Related Work

The recent growth in the WWW and on-line information sources has inspired research on agents that help users derive the most benefit from the vast quantities of available information. These agents may be broadly classified into *recommender systems*, which recommend information items that are likely to be of interest to the user, and *action systems*, which go one step further, performing actions on the user's behalf. Examples of recommender systems are WebWatcher (Joachims et al., 1997) and Letizia (Lieberman, 1995); examples of action systems are those described in (Bestavros, 1996,Balabanović, 1998). Both types of systems require a prediction model which anticipates a user's preferences, including documents a user may find interesting, or his/her future actions. These models are generally obtained by applying machine learning techniques to identify these preferences or future actions based on the preferences or actions of (1) the users themselves (Davison and Hirsch, 1998,Joachims et al., 1997,Lieberman, 1995), (2) a group of similarly-minded users (Alspector et al., 1997), or (3) the general population (Bestavros, 1996,Albrecht et al., 1998).

Our system, which predicts web pages of interest to a user based on behaviour patterns of the general population, is most closely related to Bestavros'. However, Bestavros' system features one prediction model only – a Time-Markov model that predicts the probability of a future document request. In contrast, we are interested in comparing the accuracy of different predictive models. The prediction of the next request, rather than a future request, is the simplest basis for this comparison. The most accurate model will then be used to predict future requests.

3   The Domain

Analysis of information obtained from our WWW server yields the following features. (1) We can observe only one type of action performed by a user, namely a document request in the WWW (and our aim is to predict the user's next request). (2) It is extremely difficult to obtain a perspicuous representation of the domain. Typically there are huge numbers of documents located on a server and many links between them (there are also links to and from pages in external locations); the existence, location and size of documents are subject to continual change, as are the links between documents. (3) There is no obvious clear objective that applies to all users — some users may be browsing, others may be seeking specific information; also, there may be many ways to achieve an objective, since there may be many paths from a document to the desired information. (4) The sequence of requests from a user observed by the server providing the documents is only a partial record of the user's movements through the internet, since not all the user's movements to external locations are observed. (5) Finally, most WWW browsers and proxy servers cache documents received by a user. Thus, a user's requests for previously supplied documents that are still in the cache will not be observed.

The server logs the document requests which were satisfied, where a request takes the form {client referer requestedDoc time size}. The client is the internet server site that made the request. The referer is the current internet location of the user requesting the document, which may have one of the following values: (1) the http address of a local location, i.e., a (previously requested) web page on our server site; (2) the http address of an external location, i.e., a web page on another internet site; or (3) empty (represented by ' - '), because the information has not been provided. The requestedDoc is the http address of the document being requested by the client. The time indicates when the request was received (measured in seconds elapsed since the startup of the system). The size is the number of bytes in the requested document. The requests are grouped into sessions, so that each session contains the temporal sequence of requests from a single client. This grouping supports the development of request models based on the temporal sequence of requested documents, i.e., Markov models (Section 4).

During pre-processing we perform the following actions to reduce the distortion of prediction models due to server traffic generated by certain WWW phenomena, the existing client-server protocol, or the configuration of the WWW at the server site. (1) We remove data generated by search engines and sessions identified as originating from a web-crawler client. (2) We remove instances of self-referring documents, since the requested document is already in the client's cache. (3) We infer implicit document requests within our server site; these are requests which were not logged by our current data-logging protocol (since the requested document is already in the client's cache), but must have occurred to enable a particular sequence of events to take place. Inferred requests can be incorporated into our document prediction model (see Section 4.2 for an example), but not into our time prediction model (Section 4.1), since we do not know when an inferred request was made. (4) Finally, we take into account documents embedded in a main document, e.g., images embedded in text. These embedded documents are automatically requested by the main document within a few seconds after the main document is requested. Embedded documents must be identified when building a prediction model, since on one hand, they can almost never be pre-sent before they are requested (hence their incorporation in prediction models does not enhance these models, while slowing down the computations), and on the other hand, these documents must be pre-sent when pre-sending any document which contains them.

Our web site has over 200 personal pages plus hundreds of pages which contain coursework, research and administration information. These documents are organized in a complex lattice with many links connecting between pages of different types. The results presented in this paper are based on logs of web-page requests recorded by our server over a 50-day time window. After pre-processing, the following data were obtained: 1,095,730 document requests, where 59,486 clients requested 17,332 documents from 21,692 referer locations. The data include 14,023 referers which are also requested documents, and 103,972 different referer/document combinations.

4   Prediction Models

The models described in this section predict the document requested next. That is, they estimate $P(D_{R_1}, T_{R_1}|\text{previous requests})$, where D_{R_1} is the next document requested, and T_{R_1} is the time D_{R_1} is requested. In order to make the prediction problem computationally tractable, we assume that the distribution of the time for requesting a document is independent of the actual document that is requested, that the next document requested depends only on the previous documents requested, and that the time of the next request depends only on the time of the last request, T_R. This last assumption over-simplifies our domain, since the size of a document affects both its transmission time and the user's reading time, thereby influencing the time of the next request. In the future, we intend to factor the size of a document into the estimation of the time of the next request. According to our assumptions

$$P(D_{R_1}, T_{R_1}|\text{previous requests}) = P(D_{R_1}|\text{previous documents}) \times P(T_{R_1}|T_R) \ .$$

The estimation of $P(T_{R_1}|T_R)$ is described in Section 4.1 and that of $P(D_{R_1}|\text{previous documents})$ in Section 4.2.

4.1   Next document is requested at a particular time

For our current database (based on 50 days of data), the time between successive requests from a client ranges from 0 to 4,100,910 seconds ($\sim$ 47 days): $0 \leq T_{R_1} - T_R \leq 4,100,910$.

Figure 1(a) shows the cumulative frequency distribution of the inter-arrival time between consecutive requests (plotted against a log scale). This distribution indicates that approximately 90% of document requests from a client are made within 122 seconds of the previous request, 95% are made within 874 seconds, and 99% within 343,412 seconds. As shown in Figure 1(a), a combination of three functions provides a good fit for the data (these functions were found using a weighted least-squares method). Therefore, we use the probability function in Figure 1(b) to estimate the probability of receiving a request at a particular time.

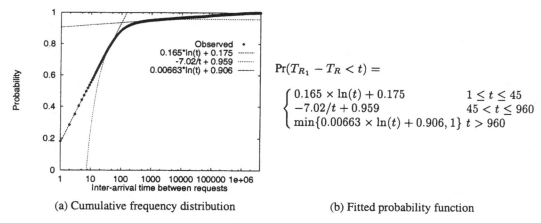

$$\Pr(T_{R_1} - T_R < t) =$$

$$\begin{cases} 0.165 \times \ln(t) + 0.175 & 1 \le t \le 45 \\ -7.02/t + 0.959 & 45 < t \le 960 \\ \min\{0.00663 \times \ln(t) + 0.906, 1\} & t > 960 \end{cases}$$

(a) Cumulative frequency distribution   (b) Fitted probability function

Figure 1. Document requests at a particular time: (a) the cumulative frequency distribution plotted against a log scale of the inter-arrival time between requests (i.e., $T_{R_1} - T_R$) and fitted with three functions; and (b) the fitted probability function for $T_{R_1} - T_R$.

4.2 A particular document is requested next

In our earlier work, we considered a *Time Markov* model, which predicts a user's next request based only on the document that was requested last (Nicholson et al., 1998). Further analysis of the data logs of access to our site points to the importance of the structure of the site for building accurate prediction models. In this section, we introduce three additional prediction models, *Space Markov, Second-order Time Markov* and *Linked Space-Time Markov* (also called *Linked Markov*), and give a graphical representation for all four models. The Time and Second-order Time Markov models consider temporal information only; the Space Markov model considers structural information; and the Linked model combines temporal and structural information.

The **Space Markov model** was motivated by the observation that normally people follow links on web pages. Hence, in this model, the probability of a client requesting a document depends only on the referring document, which has a link to the requested document. In the **Second-order Time Markov model**, the probability of a client requesting a document depends on both the last requested document and the document requested before that. Finally, in the **Linked Space-Time Markov model**, the probability of a client requesting a document depends on both the last visited document and the referring document of the last visited document. Like the Second-order Time Markov model, this model considers two information items, but these items may be obtained from a single request record.

We use a graphical representation for each document prediction model, where the graph represents the probability that a document D_i is requested after an event E_{i-1}. The graph corresponding to each model contains a vertex for each event E_{i-1} and each requested document D_i observed in the training data. If a client's request for D_i was preceded by event E_{i-1} during a session, then there is an arc in the graph from E_{i-1} to D_i. In this case, we say that D_i is a successor of E_{i-1} ($D_i \in succ(E_{i-1})$). For the Time Markov model, the event of interest is the last document requested (D_{i-1}), with an arc from D_{i-1} to D_i indicating that document D_i was requested after D_{i-1}. For the Space Markov model, E_{i-1} is the referring document of D_i (D_{Ref_i}), with an arc from D_{Ref_i} to D_i indicating that D_i was reached through a link from D_{Ref_i}. For the Second-order Time Markov model, E_{i-1} is a tuple which contains the last two documents requested,($\{D_{i-2}, D_{i-1}\}$), with an arc from $\{D_{i-2}, D_{i-1}\}$ to D_i indicating that a request for document D_i was preceded by a request for D_{i-1} which in turn was preceded by a request for D_{i-2}. Finally, for the Linked Space-Time Markov model, E_{i-1} is a tuple that contains the last document requested and its referer ($\{D_{Ref_{i-1}}, D_{i-1}\}$), with an arc from $\{D_{Ref_{i-1}}, D_{i-1}\}$ to D_i indicating that a referral from $D_{Ref_{i-1}}$ to D_{i-1} was followed by a request for D_i.

Each arc from event E_{i-1} to D_i has an associated weight, $w(E_{i-1}, D_i)$, which is the frequency of an event-document pair across all sessions. Thus, after observing an event E, the probability that the next requested document is D can be computed as follows.

$$\Pr(D_{R_1} = D | E) = \frac{w(E, D)}{\sum_{D_j \in succ(E)} w(E, D_j)} .$$

To illustrate these models and the manner in which they are built, consider a fragment of training data from a client who visits the documents in the WWW site shown in Figure 2(a) in the order indicated in Figure 2(b). The document to the left of each arrow is the referring document, the document to the right of the arrow is the next document, and the time stamp indicates when the requests were made. Note that the first and last requests have no referring documents, because the client's browser has not supplied this information to the server. For this example, we assume that D6 and D7 were always visited whenever D3 was visited, and these visits were performed shortly after visiting D3. Hence, D6 and D7 are considered embedded documents of D3, forming one document with D3. This is not the case for D8, which is visited sometime after D3, and not every time D3 is visited. After applying the pre-processing operations described in Section 3 to this sequence of requests, we obtain the extended log in Figure 2(c), where the steps inferred from those actually logged appear in boldface, i.e., the referrals **D2** → **D1** and **D8** → **D1**, and the embedded documents, i.e., *D3;D6;D7*, appear in italics. This extended log is used to build the graphs corresponding to our four models as follows.

The graph corresponding to the Time Markov model (Figure 2(d)) is built by following the sequence of documents to the right of the arrow, viz D1, D2, **D1**, *[D3;D6;D7]*, D8, **D1**, D4, D5.[1,2] The graph that represents the Space Markov model (Figure 2(e)) is built using the $\{$referer, document$\}$ pairs in each line, viz − →D1, D1→D2, **D2**→**D1**, D1→*[D3;D6;D7]*, *[D3;D6;D7]*→D8, **D8**→ **D1**, D1→D4, − →D5. This graph, which represents structural information in the WWW server site, is the same as the graph in Figure 2(d) when the links in the current site are followed; the graphs differ when there is no referral log for a requested document, as in the first and last lines in Figure 2(c), or when the referer is an external location. The graph that represents the Second-order Time Markov model (Figure 2(f)) is built using event-document pairs, where the events are composed of two consecutive documents to the right of the arrow, which in turn precede the next document, i.e., $\{$D1, D2$\}$ **D1**, $\{$D2, **D1**$\}$ *[D3;D6;D7]*, $\{$**D1**, *[D3;D6;D7]*$\}$ D8, $\{$*[D3;D6;D7]*, D8$\}$ **D1**, $\{$D8, **D1**$\}$ D4, $\{$**D1**, D4$\}$ D5. Finally, the graph that represents the Linked Markov model (Figure 2(g)) is built from $\{$preceding-referer, preceding-request$\}$ events, which precede the next requested document, viz $\{$− → D1$\}$ D2, $\{$D1→D2$\}$ **D1**, $\{$**D2**→**D1**$\}$ *[D3;D6;D7]*, $\{$D1→*[D3;D6;D7]*$\}$ D8, $\{$*[D3;D6;D7]*→D8$\}$ **D1**, $\{$**D8**→**D1**$\}$ D4, $\{$D1 → D4$\}$ D5.

To illustrate the calculation of the probability of requesting a particular document after observing an event, let us reconsider the Time Markov model in Figure 2(d), and assume that

---

[1] This graph also contains weights for the arcs, which are obtained from frequency counts of pairs of consecutively requested documents in the training data. Similar frequency counts may be obtained for the other models, but are not required for this exposition.

[2] The inferred links are drawn in thick lines in the graphs representing the Time and Space Markov models.

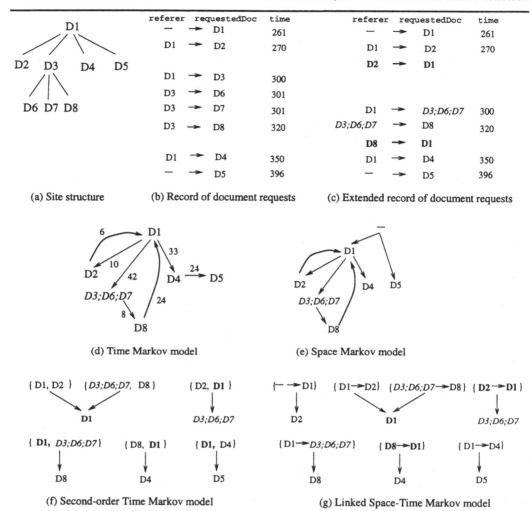

Figure 2. Sample Time, Space, Second-order Time and Linked Space-Time Markov models.

document D1 has just been requested. The model would then assign a zero probability to the next requested document being D8, D5 or a document not seen in training, and it would predict $\Pr(D_{R_1} = D2|D1) = \frac{10}{10+42+33} = 0.12$, $\Pr(D_{R_1} = \{D3; D6; D7\}|D1) = \frac{42}{10+42+33} = 0.49$, and $\Pr(D_{R_1} = D4|D1) = \frac{33}{10+42+33} = 0.39$.

5   Results

The results presented in this section were obtained from 50 days of data logged by our server. All the models were tested using 80% of the sessions for training and 20% for testing, with results showing averages from 10 runs. Differences noted in the results for the various prediction models are significant at the 5% level.

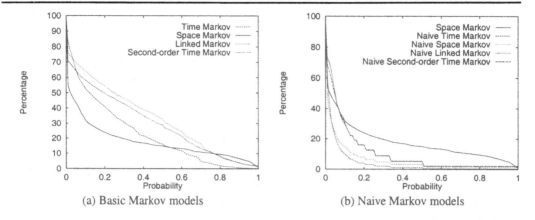

(a) Basic Markov models   (b) Naive Markov models

Figure 3. Comparison of the prediction probabilities obtained with: (a) the basic Markov models, and (b) the naive Markov models.

The prediction models were assessed in terms of the probability with which they predict the actual next request. Figure 3(a) compares the prediction probabilities obtained with our four Markov models. The x-axis shows the probability with which a model predicts the next request made by the user. The y-axis shows the average percentage of predictions whose probability is greater than or equal to the probability shown on the x-axis. For example, the Linked Markov model predicts the actual next request with probability greater than or equal to 0.5 32.9% of the time, while the Second-order Time Markov model predicts the next request with probability greater than or equal to 0.5 29.0% of the time.

The results in Figure 3(a) indicate that the predictive performance of the Time Markov model is better than that of the other models when the probability of this prediction is low (≤ 0.06). When the prediction probability is between 0.06 and 0.77, the Linked model has the highest predictive accuracy. The relative performance of the Space Markov model improves from a prediction probability of 0.06 to 0.77, at which point it overtakes the Linked Markov model. This means that the Space Markov model is more accurate than the other models when its predictions have a high probability (> 0.77). Still, the overall performance of the Linked Markov model is better than that of the other models.

Since the predicted probabilities shown in Figure 3(a) seem quite low, we validate our models by comparing these probabilities with the predictions made by the naive counterparts of our models. The naive version of a model predicts the request which follows an event using a uniform distribution; that is, each of the n successors of a vertex which represents this event is predicted with a probability of $1/n$. This probability differs for each vertex, since each vertex may have a different number of successors. Figure 3(b) compares these naive predictions with those obtained using the Space Markov model, which generally gives the lowest predictions of all the basic Markov models.[3] For probabilities greater than 0.08, the Space Markov model is clearly a

---

[3] The variation in the predictive performance of the naive models is due to differences in the number of vertex successors typically found in the graph corresponding to each model. For instance, 92% of the vertices have 5 or less successors in the Second-order model, 6 or less successors in the Linked model, 9 or less in the Space model, and 15 or less in the Time Markov model. Although these branching factors seem low, each graph has many vertices with hundreds of successors.

better predictor than all the naive models, indicating that our models, which incorporate request frequency information into the arc weights, improve upon the naive predictions.

Hybrid Prediction Models Each prediction model is sometimes unable to make a prediction because the current situation was unseen during training ("% seen" column in Figure 4(b)). This adversely affects its predictive performance. We have designed two hybrid models, `maxHybrid` and `orderedHybrid`, to address this problem.

The `maxHybrid` model consults all the Markov prediction models, and makes its own prediction using the model which made a prediction with the highest probability, i.e., the model which has the most confidence in its most likely prediction.

The `orderedHybrid` model consults the Markov models in the following order, which was determined based on the relative performance of these models: Linked, Second-order, Time and Space. The first model which can make a prediction is selected.

Finally, as seen in Figure 3(a), when the Space Markov model predicts the actual next request with a high probability, its predictive performance is better than that of the other Markov models. This is the basis for the `spaceLinkedHybrid` model, which combines the Space and Linked Markov models as follows:

If the maximum prediction made by the Space Markov model is > 0.77, then use its predictions, otherwise use those of the Linked Markov model.

The results obtained with these hybrid models are shown in Figure 4(a) compared to the overall best of the individual prediction models, the Linked Space-Time Markov model. The predictive accuracy of the `orderedHybrid` model is higher than that of the other models until the probability reaches 0.39, at which point the `maxHybrid` model starts performing better than the other models. For probabilities greater than 0.5 all the hybrid models perform significantly better than the Linked Markov model.

We postulate that the `maxHybrid` model performs better when the prediction probability is relatively high (> 0.39), because such a probability indicates that the basic Markov model which was selected has some information about the user's behaviour. In contrast, a "highest" prediction probability that is relatively low indicates that all the candidate models are rather uninformed. In this case, the `orderedHybrid` model performs better because it primarily relies on the Linked Markov model, which is the best of the basic models (other models are consulted only when the Linked Markov model cannot make a prediction). As expected, the relative performance of the `spaceLinkedHybrid` model improves as the prediction probabilities increase. Still, even for high probabilities, its performance falls below the performance of the `maxHybrid` model. In summary, due to the improved predictive accuracy of the `maxHybrid` model in the higher probability ranges, we consider it the best prediction model for a document pre-sending system.

6 Discussion

The two main features of our domain are the spatial structure of the server site and the order in which documents are requested. The results in the previous section show that the Linked Markov model, which combines these two features, gives better predictions overall than the Markov models which incorporate only one of these features. The inability of the basic models to make a prediction some of the time motivated the development of the `orderedHybrid` and `maxHybrid` models, while the good performance of the Space Markov model when its predictions have a high probability motivated the `spaceLinkedHybrid` model. As shown in the previous section, the `maxHybrid` model is the most suitable for a document pre-sending system.

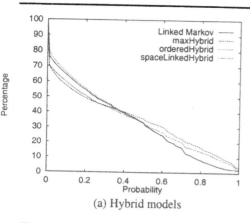

Markov Models			
model	#vertices	#arcs	% seen
Time	17,298	125,897	91.1
Space	25,000	103,972	60.3
Linked	101,110	271,022	78.6
Second-order	123,227	287,924	73.3

Hybrid Models			
model	#vertices	#arcs	% seen
maxHybrid	266,635	788,815	91.5
orderedHybrid	266,635	788,815	91.5
spaceLinkedHybrid	126,110	374,994	78.9

(a) Hybrid models   (b) Model size

Figure 4. (a) Comparison of the prediction probabilities obtained with hybrid models. (b) Features of the prediction models: maximum number of vertices and arcs, and average percentage of test data for which a model is able to make a prediction.

We now examine how the following factors affect the predictive performance of our models: time and space resources required, coverage of the test data, and model selection policy (for the hybrid models).

The computation time required by the prediction models is as follows. The training time for each of the four basic Markov models is about 700 seconds of CPU time on a SGI Indy R5000. All the prediction models make fast predictions in the testing phase, from 1.6 to 2.0 ms/request.[4]

We measure the size of the prediction models by the number of vertices and arcs in their graphical representations (Figure 4(b)). While the larger models tend to have a better predictive performance than the smaller ones, size is not the only determining factor. For instance, the Linked Markov model is the best of the basic Markov models, even though it is not the largest.

The average percentages of the "seen" test data, i.e., the data for which the models are able to make a prediction, are shown in Figure 4(b). Increasing this percentage can improve predictive performance, e.g., the maxHybrid model compared to the Linked Markov model. However, as shown by the relatively poor performance of the Time Markov model, a high proportion of seen data does not in itself improve the predictive accuracy of a model.

The maxHybrid model and the orderedHybrid model, which have the same number of vertices and arcs and the same percentage of seen data, have the best predictive performance under different circumstances. The dynamic model selection performed by the maxHybrid model yields better results for higher prediction probabilities, while the static selection performed by the orderedHybrid model (based on the previous relative performance of the basic models) yields better results for lower probabilities.

In summary, the predictive performance of the models is affected by the following inter-related factors: (1) domain features – temporal order and spatial structure; (2) size – number of vertices and arcs in the models' graphical representations; and (3) coverage of test data – percentage of seen data. The model selection policies applied by the hybrid models also affect the performance of these models.

---

[4] We would expect the models with the lowest branching factor to be the fastest, however the Second-order model is the slowest due to the way in which the database lookup was implemented.

7 Conclusion and Future Work

We have compared prediction models that take into account two factors in isolation or in combination: (1) the order in which documents are requested, and (2) the structure of the server site. We have shown that the combination of these factors in the Linked Markov model yields the greatest predictive power among the basic prediction models. Further, combining more than one prediction model in a hybrid model overcomes the problem of unseen data to some extent, resulting in models that are better than the individual models. This improvement is achieved through the use of more space and time resources, however the space requirements are not prohibitive and the predictions can still be made in milliseconds.

We are currently investigating the incorporation of our best prediction model, the maxHybrid model, into a document pre-sending system (Albrecht et al., 1999). In the future, we intend to extend the best models to predict a user's future requests (rather than the next request). Such predictions are required to pre-send documents that are not immediately needed by a user, but may be required later on.

Finally, we plan to identify user profiles based on a classification developed using unsupervised learning techniques (such as those used by Albrecht et al. (1998) to classify actions). To this effect, we will consider attributes such as inter-request time, type of document requested, whether the referer is internal or external to our site, time of day, and depth of the document in the server site document hierarchy. The resulting classification will support the tailoring of prediction models to different types of user, which should yield improved predictive performance.

Acknowledgments

This research was supported in part by grant A49600323 from the Australian Research Council.

References

Albrecht, D. W., Zukerman, I., and Nicholson, A. E. (1998). Bayesian models for keyhole plan recognition in an adventure game. *User Modeling and User-Adapted Interaction* 8(1-2):5–47.

Albrecht, D. W., Zukerman, I., and Nicholson, A. E. (1999). Pre-sending documents on the WWW: A comparative study. In *IJCAI99 – Proceedings of the Sixteenth International Joint Conference on Artificial Intelligence*.

Alspector, J., Koicz, A., and Karunanithi, N. (1997). Feature-based and clique-based user models for movie selection: A comparative study. *User Modeling and User-Adapted Interaction* 7(4):279–304.

Balabanović, M. (1998). Exploring versus exploiting when learning user models for text recommendation. *User Modeling and User-adapted Interaction* 8(1-2):71–102.

Bestavros, A. (1996). Speculative data dissemination and service to reduce server load, network traffic and service time in distributed information systems. In *Proceedings of the 1996 International Conference on Data Engineering*.

Davison, B., and Hirsch, H. (1998). Predicting sequences of user actions. In *Notes of the AAAI/ICML 1998 Workshop on Predicting the Future: AI Approaches to Time-Series Analysis*.

Joachims, T., Freitag, D., and Mitchell, T. (1997). WebWatcher: A tour guide for the World Wide Web. In *IJCAI97 – Proceedings of the Fifteenth International Joint Conference on Artificial Intelligence*, 770–775.

Lieberman, H. (1995). Letizia: An agent that assists web browsing. In *IJCAI95 – Proceedings of the Fourteenth International Joint Conference on Artificial Intelligence*, 924–929.

Nicholson, A. E., Zukerman, I., and Albrecht, D. W. (1998). A decision-theoretic approach for pre-sending information on the WWW. In *PRICAI'98 – Proceedings of the Fifth Pacific Rim International Conference on Artificial Intelligence*, 575–586.

SHORT PAPERS

Cognitive Representation of Common Ground in User Interfaces

Derek Brock and J. Gregory Trafton*

U.S. Naval Research Laboratory, Washington, DC, USA

Abstract. We argue that Clark's theory of participant representations of common ground in joint activities between people is relevant to the design of human-computer interaction. Features of common ground can be shown to exist in current interaction models suggesting that computers as sophisticated information processors can be legitimately construed as participants in the interactive process. Software, though, is rarely designed to explain itself or to demonstrate a knowledgeable awareness of the user's concerns. We describe an effort to provide a principled basis for this capacity in the form of an embedded cognitive simulation representing an application's task and user related common ground. **Keywords:** *common ground, cognitive modeling, joint activities, task model tracing*

Modern user interfaces continue to have fundamental shortcomings, many of which are directly related to the limits of their abilities to communicate well with users. For instance, users are rarely given the direct means to find out what a program knows about its domain of activity or, more importantly, what it has done in the course of a series of interactions that may be unclear or confusing. As another example, applications rarely devote functionality to the job of anticipating users' concerns or recognizing what they are trying to do. User interfaces are seldom designed to present such information, much less to keep track of it. One consequence is that users are often on their own when it comes to puzzling out a program's various features and abilities. In complex, feature-rich systems, this can be a barrier to successful or timely task performance.

Communicative shortcomings in user interfaces are easily identified but are notoriously difficult to solve in a comprehensive sense. One reason for this may be the enormous complexity of such problems and another may be the general lack of a coherent theoretical framework. In his 1996 book *Using language*, Herbert Clark (1996b) advances an insightful proposal about the nature of communication between people. Specifically, he argues that "language use is really a form of *joint action*" in which participants – people – act with intentions and in coordination with each other to accomplish goals that are part of their broader ends in *joint activities*. Clark describes joint activities as a basic category that encompasses all participatory circumstances in which conventional language plays a role. More to the point, he notes, "If we take language use to include such communicative acts as eye gaze, iconic gestures, pointing, smiles, and head nods – and we must – then all joint activities rely on language use." To coordinate joint activities, some form of signaling is required. For Clark, language in its linguistic sense is simply one of many possible signaling systems, some highly organized and others spontaneously improvised.

Clark argues that all joint activities advance through the accumulation of common ground – the knowledge, beliefs, and suppositions that participants believe they share about an activity.

* This work was conducted at the U.S. Naval Research Laboratory with sponsorship from the Office of Naval Research.

Common ground has been widely studied in discourse, so Clark's broader claim that it is an essential underpinning of all joint activities follows naturally from his argument that language use is a form of joint action. At any moment, an individual's common ground can be thought of as being made up of three parts, all three of which have important empirical characteristics. For instance, in many joint activities, a telling aspect of *initial common ground* is each participant's knowledge of relevant conventions – standard ways of doing things and a sense of what is expected. In their representation of the *current state of a joint activity* people often depend greatly upon "external representations" – features of and in the immediate physical environment that are taken to be germane to the activity. And, as people keep track of the *public events so far* in a joint activity, they do so mostly in the form of annotated records and characterize events colloquially in terms of their significance.

The basic thesis of this paper is that much of Clark's theory of the nature of joint activities is applicable to the design of human-computer interaction (see also Clark, 1996a). Models of communication between humans have often been proposed as a basis for models of human-computer interaction (for a survey, see Pérez-Quiñones, 1996), but little or no work has explicitly studied the idea of using common ground as both a way to interpret the demands of the interactive process and as an analytical basis for its design. Computers, though, as sophisticated information and display processors, inherently use programmatic representations of meaning and process for the coordination of interactions and presentation of information. These representations are functionally elements of common ground for the purpose of participatory activities with people. Accordingly, we find that human-computer interaction can be usefully viewed as a form of joint activity – albeit with its own language (signaling system) and affordances (cf. Clark's use of the term "availability") – well suited to the application of communicative principles identified in Clark' theory.

In joint activities, each participant's purpose in keeping track of common ground is to know enough of what the other participants know to jointly succeed at coordinating the activity itself. In other words, a participant in a joint activity presumes to model both the activity itself and the understanding maintained by the activity's other participants. Between a user and a computer, the same ideas apply. Common ground's full potential is achieved only to the extent that the computer can successfully simulate two skills that are ultimately cognitive in nature: the skill of keeping track of both the activity itself and the user's understanding of the activity, and the skill of making use of this representation to coordinate its participation in the joint activity.

The effort we describe here focuses cognitively on the accumulation of common ground in joint activities between users and computers. Our working system is an application embedded with a cognitively modeled representation of its domain-related common ground. The application is a complex, non-trivial, resource allocation task in a probabilistic military setting. The embedded representation of common ground is modeled in ACT-R (Anderson and Lebiére, 1998). Our working strategy has not been to computationally model common ground in a conversational sense but to work at the higher, more schematic level of a task analysis. By this, we simply mean we have modeled information about the task (the joint activity) that the application should be aware of and that may be of use to the user.

Our application domain is very roughly that of a military mission planning tool. Many of the factors the user must consider in planning a mission are interdependent, and to further complicate matters there are several probabilistic risks of failure in carrying out a mission. The application user interface utilizes a standard point-and-click paradigm and is composed of several dialog-box style windows in which the user can review and select destinations, equip and allocate tanks, and subsequently evaluate the success or failure of a mission.

Our cognitive modeling effort utilizes a model tracing paradigm (Anderson, 1987) we call "task model tracing." The emergence of unified theories of cognition (Newell, 1990) in cognitive science has given researchers an invaluable tool for exploring the ramifications of simulated cognition in applied settings such as user interfaces. ACT-R's adaptive processing strengths with regard to memory and learning (Anderson and Lebiére, 1998) have proven to be a good fit with our line of inquiry. In task model tracing, as the application responds to user input, it also drives the cognitive model, effectively "tracing" each interaction. As the model runs, it reasons independently about changes in the state of the system and implications of the user's input.

Applications are rarely if ever designed to explain themselves. By cognitively modeling an application's task domain, we can provide a requisite basis for implementing this capacity. Our approach has been to represent knowledge gleaned from an analysis of portions of our task. ACT-R provides us with a principled means for accounting for salience in a non-deterministic world as well as a proven framework for the job of representing a task analysis in the user's terms (Anderson, 1987). These features constitute a form of user modeling. The system provides the user with a direct means for consulting the application about the task (confirming the common ground) by augmenting the user interface with an additional dialog-box style window in which the user can request a "situation analysis" with a button click. This produces an annotated report of the current context and an advisory list of situationally relevant information and actions the user may wish to take next. The system is also able to carry out any of the actions it proposes at the user's discretion. When an action requires the system to make a choice for the user, ACT-R's theory of memory retrieval correctly identifies the most salient choice based on the composition of both its recency and number of mentions. The model also makes note of when it or the user does an action and demonstrates sensitivity to the meaning and occurrence of previous interactions though its choice of terms.

How then does our work demonstrate an advance in the joint activity of human-computer interaction? Our model instantiates a cognitively-based, participatory representation of each of the three parts of common ground for the application at any moment. Its initial common ground – the underlying representations of the task and the user's likely concerns – inform the application's accumulation of common ground during the task. And through its presentations, the system's representation of the current state of the activity serves to reinforce the user's own accumulating representation with its advisory knowledge and selectively annotated record of the task's public events so far.

References

Anderson, J. R., and Lebiére, C. (1998). *The Atomic Components of Thought*. Lawrence Erlbaum.

Anderson, J. R. (1987). Production system, learning, and tutoring. In *Production System Models of Learning and Development*. MIT Press.

Clark, H. H. (1996a). Arranging to do things with others. In *Conference Companion of the Conference on Human Factors in Computing Systems—CHI'96*. Association for Computing Machinery.

Clark, H. H. (1996b). *Using Language*. Cambridge University Press.

Newell, A. (1990). *Unified Theories of Cognition*. Harvard University Press.

Pérez-Quiñones, M. A. (1996). *Conversational Collaboration in User-Initiated Interruption and Cancellation Requests*. Ph.D. Dissertation, The George Washington University.

A Collaborative Approach to User Modeling within a Multi-Functional Architecture

Pablo R. de Buen[1]*, Sunil Vadera[2], Eduardo F. Morales[3]

[1] Instituto de Investigaciones Eléctricas, Cuernavaca, México
[2] University of Salford, UK
[3] ITESM-Campus Morelos, México

Abstract. This paper describes a pragmatic collaborative user modeling approach based on three main components: a multi-functional knowledge base, an open user model, and a set of rules (i.e., the adapting criteria).

1   Introduction

One of the challenges of developing adaptive systems is to design architectures that can tailor the support given to the users, without restricting them from following their own preferred path. The cost of allowing greater flexibility is, however, (i) having less control and certainty about what the user is doing, or (ii) the need for augmenting the representation of the domain in order to take into account the different valid paths a user can follow. An alternative solution to this trade-off between control and flexibility is to involve the user in the process Self (1994). The user model, that is the main basis of the system decisions, can be built collaboratively with the user and can support the co-management of the dialogue (i.e., not requiring the system to make all the decisions). Additionally, the user model can be inspectable, promoting the reflection of the user upon its contents Self (1988) Bull and Pain (1995).

This paper presents a collaborative user modeling approach implemented in a multi-functional system called LacePro (Learning, Applying, and Consulting Established Procedures), which provides users with both alternatives: a directive system with adaptive characteristics, and a flexible system in which the user can define her own approach. This is within a collaborative environment in which the user provides the information the user model requires, has the possibility to inspect the user model at any time, and can reject or accept the system's suggestions.

2   LacePro

LacePro is a system in which professional engineers can learn, apply and consult established procedures. The architecture of LacePro enables a user to combine these three

* This work was developed under the support of CONACYT (Mexican government's council for science and technology).

tasks in order to satisfy her own requirements under a given situation. For instance, depending on how familiar she is with a procedure, a user can start applying the procedure to solve a problem, and then move to the consulting mode to inspect specific information, or move to the tutoring mode in order to have a full tutoring session about that procedure. When learning a procedure, she can select to receive a full tailored session that includes explanation of the steps and theoretical concepts, examples and evaluations; or she can choose to learn the procedure by solving problems or by navigating by her self through the domain knowledge; or by a combination of these two methods. To enable this flexibility, LacePros' architecture keeps the procedural structure of procedures. In LacePro, the domain knowledge is represented by a set of goal networks in which the nodes represent the steps of the procedure, and the links represent the flow of the procedure. Those theoretical concepts required to understand the basis of a step are stored in concept nodes that are linked to the step nodes.

In this representation, a step can be a procedure. The structure of the nodes contains all the information required to perform the tasks related with learning, applying and consulting the procedures. It also includes information about the user, which corresponds to an overlay user model (for more details about this representation consult De Buen et al. (1998)). The same single representation of procedures is used in LacePro for the tutoring, consulting and problem solving tasks. This makes it easy for the system (and user) to switch from one mode to another as desired. Additionally, in this way the user model can be shared by these three modules.

3   Adaptability in LacePro

Since the users of LacePro are professionals, the following conditions were considered for its design: (a) in general, people will use LacePro's tutoring capacity in order to learn a procedure that will enable her to solve a real problem (not just to learn a subject because it is part of a curriculum); and (b) it is expected that a person that uses LacePro (e.g., an engineer) will have some familiarity with the domain (at least she must have learned the general basis of the domain at school); this, in general, will ease the communication between the system and the user.

Based on the above conditions, a collaborative approach was selected. Two major considerations behind LacePro's collaborative approach are: (i) in principle, the system will consider as true all what the user says (e.g., that she knows a step or concept), and (ii) most actions proposed by the system (e.g., what to explain) can be accepted or rejected by the user.

In LacePro, the user model is comprised of three elements: (i) an overlay model over the network of the procedure, (ii) the characteristics of a user, and (iii) the structure of the procedure network, which can be traced to model a user's incorrect solution. These elements can be inspected by the user. This enables the user to know, at any moment, what the system has registered in relation to what she knows and/or has performed correctly. By accessing this information, the user may have a better understanding of the origin of the system's recommendations and, thus, have additional information for deciding whether to accept or reject them.

The user model is used to support the system in the following tasks: (a) to define whether or not to recommend an agenda for learning a procedure, before a user tries to solve a problem with that procedure; (b) to select the contents of this agenda; (c) to tailor the information that will be presented to the user when explaining the steps of a procedure and the theoretical concepts of the domain; and (d) to locate and remediate user errors.

4 Scenarios and Empirical Evaluation

LacePro's architecture was evaluated in two ways: (i) analysing the behaviour of the system under different scenarios (simulated data), and (ii) through an empirical study with twenty engineers. For these evaluations, a prototype of LacePro containing three real procedures for the wind design of structures was used. The scenarios (described in detail in De Buen (1998)) demonstrated the multi-functionality and adaptability features of the architecture. The empirical study showed that engineers liked this open and flexible approach.

5 Conclusions

The flexibility provided by both the multi-functionality and the collaborative user modeling approach of LacePro produce an environment, that, on the one hand, is able to satisfy the user requirements (by providing the applying, tutoring and consulting tools she requires) and preferences (e.g., enabling her to select how to combine these tools) and; on the other hand, can support her by proposing an agenda and the available information that best fits her state of knowledge and the characteristics of the procedure being used. In this collaborative approach, the system works as a proposer-assistant, and the user, who has access to the user model at any time, takes most of the decisions based on what the system recommends. Thus, LacePro's user modeling becomes an additional tool for the user, who has the flexibility to use it in the way she prefers.

References

Bull, S., and Pain, H. (1995). 'Did I say what I think I said, and do you agree with me?': Inspecting and questioning the student model. In *Proceedings of the World Conference on Artificial Intelligence in Education*, 501–508.

De Buen, P., Vadera, S., and Morales, E. (1998). A multi-functional knowledge based system to learn, apply, and consult procedures. *Expert Systems with Applications* 15(3/4):265–275.

De Buen, P. (1998). *An Adaptive Multi-Functional Framework To Learn, Apply and Consult Procedures, Doctoral dissertation*.

Self, J. (1988). Bypassing the intractable problem of student modelling. In *Proceedings of the Intelligent Tutoring System Conference (ITS-88)*, 18–24.

Self, J. (1994). The role of student models in learning environments. *IEICE Transactions on Information and Systems* E77-D(1):3–8.

Reader, Writer and Student Models to Support Writing

Susan Bull and Simon Shurville[*]

School of Languages, University of Brighton, U.K.

Abstract. We present a triad of user models to support writers. A reader model gathers information about the target readership. Its construction by the user helps them focus on expectations of their readers. A writer model is inferred from answers to brief questions, and holds information on writing strategies. This enables advice to be tailored to the user's preferred way of writing. A student model is inferred from on-line Help viewed, and from information given by the user. This enables additional Help to be suggested. The models are designed to improve the performance of on-line writing environments by serving appropriate, individualised advice, as needed.

1   Introduction

There is much interest in helping students write appropriately for their academic discipline, as evidenced by literature on research on writing, and implications for the classroom (Grabe and Kaplan, 1996; Kroll, 1990), and texts for students (Jordan, 1996; Swales and Feak, 1994). There are also an increasing number of Online Writing Labs (OWLs), many containing detailed advice, according to course requirements (Cogdill, and Kilborn, 1997; Jordan-Henley, 1998; Williams and Liem, 1996). It would be useful to supplement static material in OWLs, based on users' writing strategies and characteristics of the target readership. We describe SCRAWL, a user model with this aim, comprising a student, reader and writer model. SCRAWL may be used with any web-based Help; the reader and writer models may also be used independently.

2   The SCRAWL Models

Since writing is open-ended, traditional student models are insufficient here. Student contributions to a student model have been used to improve its accuracy (Beck et al, 1997; Bull and Pain, 1995; Dimitrova and Dicheva, 1998; Kay, 1995). The SCRAWL models develop this approach, with differing levels of student-contribution according to the role of the model. The 3 SCRAWL models take account of Student Concerns; Reader Attitudes; and Writer Leanings. The Student Model (SM) has two components, containing information about areas of concern. SM^{system} is a system maintained, inferred model. $SM^{student}$ comprises a learner's contributions: it supplements SM^{system} with a student's *stated* beliefs. The Reader Model (RM) is also created by the student, in answer to questions about the target readership. This supports reflection on the requirements for the audience of the written product, by considering readers' likely attitudes. This model is also a checklist for use on completion of a document. The Writer

---
[*] We thank Elspeth Broady. Tony Hartley and Raf Salkie for their support.

Model (*WM*) is co-constructed by user and system. It is in part inferred from user responses to questions, in part from user amendments to the inferences. *WM* represents a user's orientation to writing, enabling support according to their preferred way of writing–the writer leanings.

2.1 The Student Model

SM^{system} is related to Help Pages viewed. Each time a student views a Help Page, 1 is added to the score for that page. SM^{system} assumes Help viewed several times describes a difficulty. Help viewed just once indicates the learner may need further support, or they understand the material since using Help. (Thus on the first viewing no implication is derived.) The representation of difficulty level increases with viewing frequency, from 'potentially difficult', through 'difficult', to 'very difficult'. From this information SCRAWL offers easier access to pages, by selection from an individualised menu. SCRAWL may suggest additional web pages that may be helpful. $SM^{student}$ is complementary to SM^{system}: it enables users to contribute to their *SM*. The potential contents of $SM^{student}$ are determined by Help topics available, defined by the student's tutor. The actual $SM^{student}$ is constructed by the user selecting from alternatives. Whereas SM^{system} is fully inferred, $SM^{student}$ is *given* by the learner, and is not dependent on viewing frequency. When a student no longer has problems with an issue in either part of *SM*, they may remove it. The lack of a representation indicates a topic is irrelevant, or the learner has no problems. Alternatively they may hold a misconception of which they are unaware, so did not seek Help. The system cannot detect such cases; these must be picked up by the tutor.

2.2 The Reader Model

RM prompts for information about readership, e.g. whether the readers are knowledgeable about the subject; whether they will be sympathetic or critical to the argument, etc. Advice is offered based on the answers, in the form of questions for the author to consider, e.g.:
  Your readers are not experts   • Is it clear *what* is important? • Is it clear *why* it is important?
  • Have you defined your terms? • Have you provided adequate examples?
An advantage of *RM* is that it encourages reflection on aspects of writing that can be easily forgotten, despite their importance. *RM* can be brought into use as appropriate for an individual, e.g. at the start for planners, and also later for discovery writers. A second advantage is that *RM* can later be used by the writer as a checklist, to ensure important issues have been included in the document, and the level or detail of content is appropriate for their readers. *RM* remains accessible for viewing throughout writing. It may be modified by the author at any time, as may be useful, for example, if a student is revising a previous document for wider circulation.

2.3 The Writer Model

Authors have varied writing strategies, defined by Chandler (1995) as *architect, bricklayer, oil painter, water colourist*. These distinctions were investigated by Wyllie (1993) in the context of word processing, with an additional category: *sketcher*. The strategies are briefly defined thus:
  Architects usually plan first. They tend not to correct slips as they write, but edit later.
  Bricklayers usually rework sentences & paragraphs to form a foundation before proceeding.
  Oil painters do not usually plan, but write down ideas as they occur to them, revising later.
  Water colourists usually write a single draft which requires little revision.

Sketchers tend to form a rough plan at the beginning, which is later revised.

WM helps writers build a model of their approach to writing by asking 8 questions:

1 Does writing help you to organise your thoughts? 2 Do you correct slips as you write?
3 Do you complete a draft at the first attempt?   4 Do you start with the easiest part?
5 Do you find the screen restrictive?   6 Do you consciously choose strategies?
7 How much do you *revise* your text at the *end* ?   8 How much do you *plan* at the *beginning*?

SCRAWL then offers a series of suggestions to the user, based on their writing strategies, e.g.:

> Because you usually 'discover' your text as you write, try also to think about your readers
> while writing. Make sure your developing text satisfies the needs of *these* readers.

Individualised advice based on writing strategies is useful, as writers may prefer one set of approaches over others (Snyder, 1993). It may be difficult to change strategies (Wyllie, 1993), or users may be writing in a familiar genre, with developed, effective strategies (Torrance, 1996).

3   Summary

SCRAWL's triad of user models complements static information provided by OWLs. *SM* offers Help about aspects of writing, according to a student's difficulties. *SM^{system}* is inferred, and thus the most familiar kind of user model. *SM^{student}* is built entirely by the student. *WM* enables suggestions according to a user's writing strategies. It is built cooperatively by user and system. *RM* models target readers, advising the writer according to likely expectations of their readership. It is created by the user, in response to system prompts. *RM* is unusual as it is not a model of the current user—it models how the recipients of the user's undertakings might view the outcome of their efforts. Creating this model and receiving advice aims to help authors focus, thus contributing to the individualised Help received by a user based on *SM* and *WM*.

References

Beck, J., Stern, M. and Woolf, B.P. (1997) Cooperative Student Models, in B du Boulay and R Mizoguchi (eds), *Artificial Intelligence in Education*, IOS Press, Amsterdam, 127-134.

Bull, S. and Pain, H. (1995) 'Did I say what I think I said, and do you agree with me?': Inspecting and Questioning the Student Model, in J. Greer, *World Conference on AI in Education*, Washington.

Chandler, D. (1995) *The Act of Writing*, University of Wales, Aberystwyth.

Cogdill, S. and Kilborn, J. (1997) *LEO: Literacy Education Online*, http://leo.stcloud.msus.edu

Dimitrova, V. and Dicheva, D. (1998) 'Who is Who': the roles in an intelligent system for foreign language terminology learning, *British Journal of Educational Technology* 29(1), 47-57.

Grabe, W. and Kaplan, R.B. (1996) *Theory and Practice of Writing*, Addison Wesley Longman, NY.

Jordan, R.R. (1996) *Academic Writing Course*, Addison Wesley Longman Ltd., Harlow, Essex.

Jordan-Henley, J. (1998) *RSCC Online Writing Lab*, http://www2.rscc.cc.tn.us/~jordan_jj/OWL/

Kay, J. (1995) The UM Toolkit for Cooperative User Modelling, *User Modeling and User Adapted Interaction* 4.

Kroll, B. (ed) (1990) *Second Language Writing, Research Insights for the Classroom*, CUP, NY.

Snyder, I. (1993) Writing with Word Processors: a research overview, *Educational Research* 35(1).

Swales, J. and Feak, C. (1994) *Academic Writing for Graduate Students*, Michigan University Press.

Torrance, M. (1996) Strategies for Familiar Writing Tasks, in G. Rijlaarsdam, H. van den Bergh and M. Couzijn, *Theories, Models & Methodology in Writing Research*, AUP, 283-298.

Williams, S. and Liem, T. (1996) *The Writing Center*, http://www.hamilton.edu/academic/Resource/

Wyllie, A. (1993) *'On the Road to Discovery'*, MA Dissertation, University of Lancaster, UK.

Tailoring Evaluative Arguments to User's Preferences

Giuseppe Carenini[1] and Johanna Moore[2]*

[1] Intelligent Systems Program, University of Pittsburgh, U.S.A.
[2] HCRC, University of Edinburgh, U.K.

Abstract. Computer systems that serve as personal assistants, advisors, or sales assistants frequently need to argue evaluations of domain entities. Argumentation theory shows that to argue an evaluation convincingly requires to base the evaluation on the hearer's values and preferences. In this paper we propose a framework for tailoring an evaluative argument about an entity when user's preferences are modeled by an additive multiattribute value function. Since we adopt and extend previous work on explaining decision-theoretic advice as well as previous work in computational linguistics on generating natural language arguments, our framework is both formally and linguistically sound.

1 Introduction

Computer systems that serve as personal assistants, advisors, or sales assistants frequently need to generate evaluative arguments for domain entities. For instance, a student advisor may need to argue that a certain course would be an excellent choice for a particular student, or a real-estate personal assistant may need to argue that a certain house would be a questionable choice for its current user. Argumentation theory indicates that to argue an evaluation convincingly requires to base the evaluation on the hearer's values and preferences. Therefore, the effectiveness of systems that serve as assistants or advisors in situations in which they need to present evaluative arguments critically depends on their ability to tailor their arguments to a model of the user's values and preferences. In this paper we propose a computational framework for generating evaluative arguments that could be applied in systems serving as personal assistants or advisors. In our framework, as suggested by argumentation theory, arguments are tailored to a model of user's preferences. Furthermore, in accordance with current research in user modeling, we adopt as model of user's preferences a conceptualization based on multiattribute utility theory (more specifically an additive multiattribute value function (AMVF)).

2 Background on AMVF

An AMVF is a utility model based on a *value tree* and on a set of *component value functions*, one for each attribute of an alternative. A value tree is a decomposition of the objective to maximize the value of the selection for the decision maker into an objective hierarchy in which the leaves correspond to attributes of the alternatives. The arcs of the tree are weighted depending on the

* This work was supported by grant number DAA-1593K0005 from the Advanced Research Projects Agency (ARPA). Its contents are solely the responsibility of the authors and do not necessarily represent the official views of either ARPA or the U.S. Government.

importance of an objective in achieving the objective above it in the tree. Note that the sum of the weights at each level is equal to 1. A component value function for an attribute expresses the preferability of each attribute value as a number in the $[0, 1]$ interval. Formally, an AMVF has the following form:

$$v(a) = v(x_1, ..., x_n) = \sum_{i=1}^{n} w_i v_i(x_i) \tag{1}$$

- $(x_1, ..., x_n)$ is the vector of attribute values for alternative a
- For each attribute i, v_i is the *component value function*, which maps the least preferable x_i to 0, the best x_i to 1, and the other x_i to values in $[0,1]$
- w_i is the *weight* for attribute i, and $0 < w_i < 1$ and $\sum_{i=1}^{n} w_i = 1$

3   The Framework and a Sample Argumentative Strategy

Our framework for generating evaluative arguments is based on previous work in artificial intelligence on explaining decision-theoretic advice (Klein and Shortliffe, 1994), and on previous work in computational linguistics on generating natural language evaluative arguments (Elhadad, 1995) . On the one hand, the study on explaining decision-theoretic advice produced a rich quantitative model that can serve as a basis for strategies to select and organize the content of decision-theoretic explanations, but was not concerned at all with linguistic issues. On the other hand, the work in computational linguistics produced a well-founded model of how argumentative intents (i.e., whether a proposition favors or disfavors the alternative) can influence sophisticated linguistic decisions, but it produced weak results as far as the selection and the organization of the argument content is concerned.

From Klein and Shortliffe (1994) we adopted and adapted two basic concepts for content selection and organization: s − compellingness and notably−compelling?. An objective can be compelling in arguing for an alternative either because of its strength or because of its weakness in contributing to the value of an alternative. So, if x measures how much the value of an objective is contributing to the overall value difference of an alternative from the worst case[1] and y measures how much the value of an objective is determining the overall value difference of an alternative from the best case, a possible definition for s − compellingness is the greatest of the two quantities x and y. Informally, an objective is s−notably−compelling? if it is an outlier in a population with respect to s − compellingness.

Elhadad's techniques for performing sophisticated linguistic decisions based on argumentative intent used a model of user's preferences different from an AMVF. So, in order to adopt his work, we have to show how argumentative intents can be computed from an AMVF-based model of user's preferences. Basically, two subintervals of the interval $[0, 1]$, $[0, k_-]$ and $[k_+, 1]$ must be defined (e.g., $[0, 0.4]$ and $[0.6, 1]$). Then we consider the value of an alternative for an objective to correspond to a negative, positive or neutral argumentative intent depending on whether it belongs to $[0, k_-]$, $[k_+, 1]$ or $[k_-, k_+]$ respectively.

We sketch now a sample argumentative strategy for the communicative goal of evaluating a single entity. The strategy is based on the notions of
s − compellingness and notably−compelling?
defined previously. First, we introduce some terminology: *Root* is the objective the argument is

---

[1] a_{worst} is an alternative such as that $\forall o\; v_o(a_{worst}) = 0$, whereas a_{best} is such as that $\forall o\; v_o(a_{best}) = 1$.

$User = user - b, Entity = house - b15, k = -1, k_- = 0.4, k_+ = 0.6, v(house - b15, user - b) = 0.741$

```
I would strongly suggest house-b15. It is spacious. It has a large lot-size (800 sqf),
many rooms (7) and plenty of storage space (200 sqf). Furthermore, since it offers an
exceptional view and appears nice, house-b15 quality is excellent. Finally, house-b15 has a
fair location. Although it is far from a shopping area, it has access to a park (2 miles).
```

Figure 1. Sample concise and fluent natural language evaluative argument

about; *MainArgIntent* is either + or - and determines whether the generated argument will favor or disfavor the entity; *ArgItent* is a function that when applied to the value of an objective returns its argumentative intent (which is either +, - or neutral); the *Express* function indicates that an objective must be realized in natural language with a certain argumentative intent.

Argumentation Strategy

argue(Root, entity, user-model, MainArgIntent, k, k_-, k_+)
;; *content selection and assignments*
  Eliminate all objectives o_i for which $s - notably - compelling?(o_i, siblings(o_i), a, Root)$ is false.
  $MainFactorInFavor \leftarrow$ most compelling objective o such as that $o \in children(Root)$ and
  $\qquad\qquad ArgItent(v_o(entity)) = MainArgIntent$
  $ContrastingSubObjectives \leftarrow$ all o_i such as that $o_i \in children(Root)$ and
  $\qquad\qquad ArgIntent(v_{o_i}(entity)) \neq MainArgIntent$
  $RestInFavor \leftarrow$ all o_i such as that $o_i \in children(Root)$ and
  $\qquad\qquad o_i \neq MainFactorInFavor$ and $ArgItent(v_{o_i}(entity)) = MainArgIntent$
;; *Steps for expressing the content.*
Express(Root, MainArgIntent) ;; (e.g., "I strongly suggest this entity")
Argue($MainFactorInFavor$, entity, user-model, MainArgIntent, k, k_-, k_+)
For all $o_i \in ContrastingSubObjectives$, Express($o_i$, ArgIntent($v_{o_i}(entity)$)) ;;ordered by compellingness
For all $o_i \in RestInFavor$, Argue(o_i, entity, user-model, MainArgIntent, k, k_-, k_+) ;;ordered by compellingness

This strategy is based on guidelines for presenting evaluative arguments suggested in argumentation literature (Mayberry and Golden, 1996). The main factor in favor of the evaluation is presented in detail, along with possible counter-arguments (i.e., $ContrastingSubObjectives$), that must always be considered, but not in detail. Finally, further supporting factors must be presented in detail. As specified in the strategy, details about a factor are presented by recursively calling the function $argue$ on the factor. Figure 1 shows a sample argument generated by the strategy when it is applied to a user model based on a value tree consisting of 15 objectives.

As future work, we plan to empirically evaluate our framework. We also intend to extend it to more complex models of user preferences and to generating arguments that combine language with information graphics.

References

Elhadad, M. (1995). Using argumentation in text generation. *Journal of Pragmatics* 24:189–220.

Klein, D. A., and Shortliffe, E. H. (1994). A framework for explaining decision-theoretic advice. *Artificial Intelligence* 67:201–243.

Mayberry, K. J., and Golden, R. E. (1996). *For Argument's Sake: A Guide to Writing Effective Arguments.* Harper-Collins, College Publishers. Second Edition.

A Student Model to Assess Self-Explanation while Learning from Examples

Cristina Conati[1] and Kurt VanLehn[1, 2*]

[1] Intelligent Systems Program, University of Pittsburgh, U.S.A.
[2] Department of Computer Science, University of Pittsburgh, U.S.A.

Abstract. The SE-Coach is a tutoring system that supports students in applying the learning strategy known as self-explanation - the process of clarifying to oneself the solution of an example. In this paper, we describe the student model used by the SE-Coach to assess the students' self-explanations and to provide hints to improve them. The assessment is based on the student's prior physics knowledge and on the student's studying actions. We describe a version of the user model based on a Bayesian network, and a simplified version that is more efficient but handles only examples with no inferential gaps in the solution.

1 Introduction

The benefits of learning from examples strongly depend on how students study them. Many studies indicate that self-explanation - generating explanations to oneself while studying an example - can improve learning, and that guiding self-explanation can extend these benefits.

We have developed a tutoring module, the SE (Self-Explanation) Coach, that trains students in the application of this general learning skill. The SE Coach is part of the Andes tutoring system for university physics (Conati et al., 1997a). Within Andes, the SE Coach ensures that students generate appropriate self-explanations to understand each component of a physics example.

In this paper, we describe the student model that allows the SE Coach to decide when and how to elicit further self-explanations. We discuss the differences between the current student model, which efficiently handles examples without inferential gaps in the solution, and a more general model based on a Bayesian network (Conati et al., 1997), which provides principled assessment for a wider range of examples but that can have inadequate response times.

2 The SE-Coach's Bayesian student model

The SE-Coach provides the students with an interface, called the Workbench, to read and study examples (Conati and VanLehn, 1999). In the Workbench, the example text and graphics are covered with gray boxes, corresponding to single units of information. The boxes disappear when the student moves the mouse pointer over them. This allows the SE-Coach to track what the student is looking at and for how long, a crucial piece of information to assess whether a student is self-explaining or simply reading. The

* This research is sponsored by ONR's Cognitive Science Division under grant N00014-96-1-0260.

Workbench also provides tools to build self-explanations for each example item. These tools include 1) a Rule Browser and templates to explain which physics rules justify an example item, and 2) A Plan Browser to explain which goal a given item achieves in the solution plan underlying the example.

Every student action, including viewing times, is recorded in the SE-Coach's student model. The model is a Bayesian network that includes 1) a representation of the example solution (the *solution graph*), automatically generated from a set of physics rules (Conati et al., 1997a), and 2) nodes reflecting reading and self-explanation actions (see Figure 1).

Example 1

Jake is lowered from an heli-copter, with an acceleration of 2m/s².

Jake's mass is 80Kg.

Find the tension in the rope to which Jake is attached.

Solution

We apply Newton's 2nd law to solve the problem.

We choose Jake as the body....

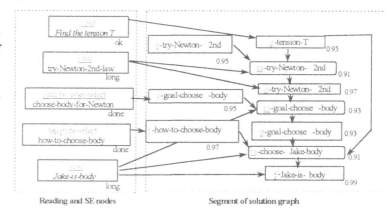

Reading and SE nodes   Segment of solution graph

Figure 1. Segment of student model after the student reads and explains the solution lines on the left.

The solution graph consists of fact and goal nodes (f- and g- nodes in Figure 1) representing the solution items, linked through 1) rule (r-) nodes representing the rules that generated each item and 2) rule application (ra-) nodes representing the actual application of the rules.

Reading and self-explaining actions provide only indirect evidence that the student knows a solution item or a physics rule. The links and the probability tables in the Bayesian network encode the probabilistic relations between interface actions and knowledge of solution items and physics rules (Conati et. al, 1997b). The evidence provided by reading and self-explanation actions is propagated in the Bayesian network. Lack of self-explanation is identified with low probability of rule application nodes, and triggers the intervention of the SE-Coach to elicit additional explanations from the student (Conati et. al, 1997b).

3 Simplified student model

The student model needs to be updated every time the student uncovers a different example item. The available implementations of the Bayesian update algorithm proved to be too slow for this task. In order to be able to evaluate the SE-Coach with real students, we developed a simplified version of the student model, which works only for examples with no inferential gaps in the solution. Like the general model, the simplified model is based on the solution graph, and generates its predictions from the student's prior knowledge and student's studying actions. However, it does not use propagation of evidence in the Bayesian network to assess self-explanation. In the simplified model, an element in the solution graph is considered self-explained if and only if 1) the student has spent enough time reading one of the example items mentioning that element and 2) the student knows the rules necessary to self-explain the element.

When the student uncovers an example item, the corresponding node in the student model is marked as "not-read", "read" and "read-for-SE", depending on how much time the student has spent on the item. When the student fills in a rule template to self-explain an example item, the SE-Coach updates the probability of the corresponding rule node in the student model. The update formula takes into account the prior probability of the rule and how many attempts were made to fill in the template correctly.

When the student decides to close an example, the student model returns pointers to solution items that need more self-explanation. In particular it returns items that correspond to facts or goals derived from rules with probability below a certain threshold (0.75 in the current version). We do this because it is unlikely that correct self-explanation has occurred if the student is missing the relevant physics knowledge, no matter how much time the student spent on the solution item. The model also returns pointers to solution items related to physics rules with high probability, but with insufficient reading time for self-explanation.

It is important to notice that students do not have to use the Workbench tools to have their self-explanations acknowledged. If a rule has a high prior probability, and the student has spent enough time on a solution item derived from that rule, the student model assumes that the student self-explained the item correctly. Asking students to always use the Workbench to make their explanations explicit would allow more accurate assessment, but may also burden the students who are natural self-explainers with unnecessary work, compromising their motivation to use the system.

4   Future work

We are currently evaluating the accuracy of the simplified student model. The data for the evaluation come from a laboratory experiment that we conducted with 57 college students who were taking introductory physics (Conati and VanLehn, 1999). We plan to evaluate the accuracy of the student model by analyzing whether the probabilities assessing the knowledge of students in the experimental group are predictive of the students' post-test results. We also plan to use log data files from the experiment to test the performance of the Bayesian network model with an improved update algorithm that may provide acceptable response times.

References

Conati, C., Gertner, A., VanLehn, K., & Druzdzel, M. (1997a). On-line student modeling for coached problem solving using Bayesian networks. In Jameson, A., Paris, C, and Tasso, C. (Eds.), *User Modeling: Proc. of the Sixth International conference, UM97*. New York: Springer 231-242.

Conati, C., Larkin, J., and VanLehn, K. (1997b). A computer framework to support self-explanation. In *Proc. of the Eighth World Conference of Artificial Intelligence in Education* 279-286.

Conati, C., and VanLehn, K. (1999). Teaching meta-cognitive skills: implementation and evaluation of a tutoring system to guide self-explanation while learning from examples. To appear In *Proc. of the Ninth World Conference of Artificial Intelligence in Education*.

Modeling Cognition-Emotion of Users for Improved Interaction With Software Systems

Christine Lisetti

Department of Information Systems and Decision Sciences, University of South Florida, USA

Abstract. In this article, a strong case for the need to include emotions in the user model is developed and documented.

1 Introduction

New theories of cognition emphasize the tight interface between affect and cognition. Given the increasing use of computers which support the human user in many kinds of task, issues in affective computing (Picard, 1997) – " computing that relates to, arises from, or deliberately influences emotions" – necessarily begin to emerge. Indeed, there is now plenty of evidence in neuroscience and psychology about the importance of emotional intelligence for the overall human performance in tasks such as rational decision-making, communicating, negotiating, and adapting to unpredictable environments. As a result, people can no longer be modeled as pure goal-driven, task-solving agents: they also have emotive reasons for their choices and behaviour which (more often than not) drive rational decision-making (Mandler, 1975). We presently propose that user models need to include affective phenomena and model *both* the user cognitive *and* affective processing resources .

In the remainder of this article, we document why the interface between affect and cognition needs to be acknowledged in user modeling.

2 User Modeling, Affect and Cognition

As a result of recent findings, emotions are now considered as associated with adaptive, organizing and energizing processes. We mention a few already identified phenomena of interaction between affect and cognition, which we expect will be further studied and manipulated by building intelligent interfaces which acknowledge such an interaction. We also identify the relevance of these findings about emotions for the field of User-Modeling.

- *Organization of memory and learning*: we recall an event better when we are in the same mood as when the learning occured (Bower, 1981). Hence eliciting the same affective state in a learning environment can reduce the cognitive overload considerably. User models concerned with reducing the cognitive overload (Kalyuga et al., 1997) – by presenting information structured in the most efficient way in order to eliminate avoidable load on working memory – would strongly benefit from information about the affective states of the learners while involved in their tasks.

- *Focus and attention*: emotions restrict the range of cue utilization such that fewer cues are attended to (Derryberry and Tucker, 1992);

- *Perception*: when we are happy, our perception is biased at selecting happy events, likewise for negative emotions (Bower, 1981). Similarly, while making decisions, users are often influenced by their affective states. Reading a text while experiencing a negatively valenced emotional state often leads to very different interpretation than reading the same text while in a positive state. User models providing text tailored to the user need to take this affective information into account to maximize the user's understanding of the intended meaning of the text.

- *Categorization and preference*: familiar objects become preferred objects (Zajonc, 1984). User models which aim at discovering the user's preferences (Linden et al., 1997), also need to acknowledge and make use of the knowledge that people prefer objects that they have been exposed to, even when they were shown these objects subliminally.

- *Goal generation and evaluation*: patients who have damage in their frontal lobes (cortex communication with limbic system is altered) become unable to feel, which results in their complete dysfunctionality in real-life settings where they are unable to decide what is the next action they need to perform (Damasio, 1994), whereas normal emotional arousal is intertwined with goal generation and decision-making.

- *Decision making and strategic planning*: when time constraints are such that quick action is needed, neurological shortcut pathways for deciding upon the next appropriate action are preferred over more optimal but slower ones (Ledoux, 1992). Furthermore people with different personalities can result in very distinct preference models (Myers-Briggs Type Indicator). User models of personality (Paranagama et al., 1997) can be further enhanced and refined with the user's affective profile.

- *Motivation and performance*: an increase in emotional intensity causes an increase in performance, up to an optimal point (inverted U-curve Yerkes-Dodson Law). User models which provide qualitative and quantitative feedback to help students think about and reflect on the feedback they have received (Bull, 1997), could include affective feedback about cognitive-emotion paths discovered and built in the student model during the tasks.

- *Intention*: not only are there positive consequences to positive emotions, but there are also positive consequences to negative emotions – they signal the need for an action to take place in order to maintain, or change a given kind of situation or interaction with the environment (Frijda, 1986). As described later in this paper, pointing to the positive consequences – the functional attributes – of the emotions experienced during interaction with a specific software could become one of the roles of the user modeling agents.

- *Communication*: important information in a conversational exchange comes from body language (Birdwhistle, 1970), voice prosody, facial expressions revealing emotional content (Ekman and Friesen, 1984), and facial displays connected with various aspects of discourse (Chovil, 1991).

- *Learning*: people are more or less receptive to the information to be learned depending on their liking (of the instructor, of the visual presentation, of how the feedback is given, or of who is giving it). Moreover, emotional intelligence is learnable (Goleman, 1995), which opens interesting areas of research for the field of user modeling as a whole.

Given the strong interface between affect and cognition on the one hand (Leventhal and Scherer, 1987), and given the increasing versatility of computers agents on the other hand, the attempt to enable our tools to acknowledge affective phenomena rather than to remain blind to them appears desirable. In a future paper, we will present the prototype of a user-model which combines the results of our current research project to partially model the user's emotional states (see Lisetti et al., 1998 for a explanation of the overall architecture, and Lisetti and Schiano, 1999, and Lisetti and Rumelhart, 1998 for extracting information based on facial expressions , and Lisetti, 1997 for identifying relevant emotional components).

References

Birdwhistle, R. (1970). *Kinesics and Context: Essays on Body Motion and Communication*. University of Pennsylvania Press.

Bower, G. H. (1981). Mood and Memory. *American Psychologist* 36(2).

Bull, S. (1997). See Yourself Write: A Simple Student Model to Make Students Think. In *User Modeling: Proceedings of the Sixth International Conference UM97*.

Chovil, N. (1991). Discourse-oriented facial displays in conversation. *Research on Language and Social Interaction* 25:163–194.

Damasio, A. (1994). *Descartes' Error: Emotion, Reason, and the Human Brain*. New York: Grosset/Putman Book.

Derryberry, D., and Tucker, D. (1992). Neural Mechanisms of Emotion. *Journal of Consulting and Clinical Psychology* 60(3):329–337.

Ekman, P., and Friesen, W. (1984). *Unmasking the Face. A Guide to Recognizing Emotions From Facial Cues*. Englewood CLiffs, NJ: Prentice Hall.

Frijda, N. H. (1986). *The Emotions*. New York: Cambridge University Press.

Goleman, D. (1995). *Emotional Intelligence*. New York, NY: Bantam Books.

Kalyuga, S., Chandler, P., and Sweller, J. (1997). Levels of Expertise and User-Adapted Formats of Instructional Presentations: A Cognitive Load Approach. In *User Modeling: Proceedings of the Sixth International Conference UM97*.

Ledoux, J. (1992). Emotion and the Amygdala. In *The Amygdala: Neurobiological Aspects of Emotion, Memory, and Mental Dysfunction*, 339–351. Wiley-Liss, Inc.

Leventhal, H., and Scherer, K. (1987). The Relationship of Emotion to Cognition: A Functional Approach to a Semantic Controversy. *Cognition and Emotion* 1(1):3–28.

Linden, G., Hanks, S., and Lesh, N. (1997). Interactive Assessment of User Preference Models: The Automated Travel Assistant. In *User Modeling: Proceedings of the Sixth International Conference UM97*.

Lisetti, C., and Schiano, D. (1999). Facial Expression Recognition: Where Human-Computer Interaction, Artificial Intelligence and Cognitive Science Interact. *Pragmatics and Cognition* To Appear.

Lisetti, C., and Rumelhart, D. (1998). Facial Expression Recognition Using a Neural Network. In *Proceedings of the Eleveth International FLAIRS Conference*. Menlo Park, CA: AAAI Press.

Lisetti, C. L., Rumelhart, D. E., and Holler, M. (1998). An Environment to Acknowledge the Interface between Affect and Cognition. In *Working Notes of the 1998 AAAI Spring Symposium Series on Intelligent Environments. Technical Report SS-98-02*. Menlo Park, CA: AAAI Press.

Lisetti, C. L. (1997). Motives for Intelligent Agents: Computational Scripts for Emotion Concepts. In Grahne, G., ed., *Proceedings of the Sixth Scandinavian Conference on Artificial Intelligence (SCAI-97)*. Helsinki, Finland: Amsterdam: IOS Press Frontiers in Artificial Intelligence and Applications.

Mandler, G. (1975). Mind and Emotion. New York, NY: Wiley.

Minsky, M. (1981). A Framework for Representing Knowledge. In Haugeland, J., ed., *Mind Design: Philosophy, Psychology, Artificial Intelligence*, 95–128. Cambridge, MA: MIT Press.

Paranagama, P., Burstein, F., and Arnott, D. (1997). Modelling the Personality of Decision Makers for Active Decision Support. In *User Modeling: Proceedings of the Sixth International Conference UM97*.

Picard, R. W. (1997). *Affective Computing*. Cambridge, MA: M.I.T. Press.

Zajonc, R. (1984). On the Primacy of Affect. *American Psychologist* 39:117–124.

Adapting the museum: a non-intrusive user modeling approach.

P. Marti[1], A. Rizzo[1 3], L. Petroni[1], G. Tozzi[1], M. Diligenti[2]

[1] University of Siena Multimedia Laboratory Via dei Termini 6I-53100 Siena
[2] University of Siena Department of Information engineering Via Roma, 56 I-53100 Siena
[3] Istituto di Psicologia CNR Viale Marx, 135 I – 00137 Roma

Abstract. Technology within museums can improve human cognition by supporting the experiential mode more than the analitic one. In order to exploit this powerful concept our approach is based on empathy and "mimesis". This work explores issues of audio-guide adaptivity based on physical navigation and information browsing. The goal is to design an augmented reality system that is able to transform the museum into an intelligent environment, which can integrate individual needs and collective behaviors. Physical movements within the museum are used to classify visitors. This dynamic classification utilizes a non-intrusive user modeling approach, wherein the museum acts as an interface.

1 Introduction.

The aim of this project is to mediate a museum visit in an experiential and empathic mode (Norman, 1993). The mediation aim to be dynamically personalized and used by the system as a base of learning in order to adapt itself to each new visitor. The main hypothesis is that the spatial movements of the visitors inside the rooms are an important source of information for developing an implicit user modeling approach. Anticipating the physical behavior that visitors will adopt in each consecutive room and integrating this data with the information regarding the individual's preferences, the system can adapt an engaging and personalized visit. The complexity of this approach has been resolved in our prototype by adopting an hybrid architecture, using a socio-semiotic classification implemented by means of artificial neural networks integrated with a self-organizing algorithm. This dynamic user modeling generates an adaptive audio path from a hypertext related to each work of art. An evaluation phase, based on the user-centered approach, has been carried out in the HIPS project, which provides museum visitors with PDAs offering audio headphones, motion tracking and wireless data transmission.

2 Non-intrusive user modeling.

Detailed field surveys have shown how visitors tend to navigate an exposition space in homogeneous modes. Adopting a socio-semiotic perspective, Veron & Lavasseur (Veron et al., 1983) classify visitors in four main categories: ant (long visit, sequential, complete, physically next to works of art); butterfly (half-term duration, selective, less sequential); fish (quick visit, superficial, away from the work of art); grasshopper (short visit, with a few stops, non-sequential). From the field studies phase, conducted by means of non-partecipative observation, it has emerged how the modalities mentioned above are also found inside the "Museo Civico" of Siena, which is an historical building adapted to museum. The detection of the physical behavior of visitors within a museum, taking into account the time, movements and trajectory, can facilitate the acoustic mediation generated by the system. The variables that have to be analyzed to carry out this kind of classification are difficult to account for using static and discrete models. A prototype has been developed in which physical user modeling is proposed, managed by a recurrent neural network (Giles et al. 1994) based on concrete examples from field observation, following the categories proposed by Veron & Levasseur. The variables considered in the first prototype include: the organization of physical space in cells, the time spent in each cell, and the association of time values and i.d. number of the cells. Some of the museum's artworks have a larger affordance, because of their importance, dimension or position. This aspect is carried out normalizing the array, which represents the time spent in the field of action of an artwork, by a prominence factor.

2.1   Physical space and collective tracks.

Structural and organizational similarities between rooms simplify the process of monitoring visitors' behavior as they pass from room to room. In the prototype an initial clustering of the rooms based on the topological parameters is proposed. The subsequent subjects navigating the rooms will dynamically improve this classification. To attain this goal a module of the prototype consists of a self-organization algorithm (Learning Vector Quantization) (Kohonen et al., 1992), which calculates an 11 dimensional vector. The first 7 elements concern the topological and general parameters of the room (dimension, number and period of the work of arts, prominence) and the other 4 update the clustering, calculating in a dynamic way the statistics of the physical user model's relation to the rooms. This aspect enables the physical user model to anticipate visitor behavior, with respect to the characteristics of the museum, and rooms' navigation statistics.

2.2   Audio adaptive presentation and collaborative machine learning.

An experimental set is designed to investigate the conformity between the navigation of the physical space and the information space within a museum. In the prototype (Fig.1), an auditory presentation not supported by a visual display is provided to subjects, in order to explore the possibility of expanding the interaction with the environment. The descriptions of the artworks have been segmented in small blocks, each of them labeled with one of four possible topics (generalist, historical, anecdotal, and artistic). In the prototype the hypertext corresponding to each description has been represented in a matrix of nodes and links between nodes. Each link is weighted by a value. The blocks have been organized in a hypertextual structure, setting links between them on the basis of logical relationships. The information space is managed by a specific learning algorithm based on the deposit of the tracks of each visit. At the entry of the action field of an artwork, the system receives the physical user model type to which the user belongs, integrated with his topic preferences statistically updated at the end of each artwork hypertext browsing. Each user type is assigned a different threshold value for generating the audio path. The learning algorithm updates the weights over the connections according to visitors' reactions to the adaptive path proposed for each artwork.

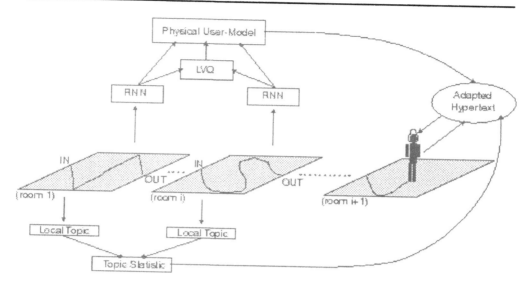

Figure 1. Prototype design.

3 Prototype evaluation.

Iterative design guides the development steps. Using a user-centered approach each module of the prototype has been tested in the real context inside the museum and in reconstructed scenarios. The results shows how the subjects' reactions to the proposed path change critically taking into account (or not) the right classification of the subject's strategies for browsing the physical space: the amount of information skipping, and of explicit requests for more information significantly increase if the physical user-model has been altered.

References

Giles C. L., Khun G.M. and Williams R.J. (1994) "Special Issues on Dynamic Recurrent Neural Networks", *IEEE Trans. on Neural Networks*, 5,2.

Norman D. A. (1993) *Things that make us smart*. Reading, MA: Addison-Wesley.

Kohonen T.,Kangas J., Laaksonen J. and Torkkola K. (1992), "LVQ_PAK: A program package for the correct application of Learning Vector Quantization algorithms" *Proc. IJCNN'92, Int. Joint Conf. on Neural Networks*, Vol. I, pp. 725-730, IEEE Service Center.

Veron E. and Levasseur M. (1983) *Ethnographie de l'exposition*, Paris: Bibliothèque Publique d'Information, Centre Georges Pompidou.

ARGUER: Using Argument Schemas for Argument Detection and Rebuttal in Dialogs

A.C. Restificar[1], S.S. Ali[2], and S.W. McRoy[1]

[1] Electrical Engineering and Computer Science
[2] Mathematical Sciences
University of Wisconsin-Milwaukee, Milwaukee, WI, USA

Abstract

This paper presents a computational method for argumentation on the basis of a declarative character-ization of the structure of arguments. The method can be used to implement a computational agent that is both able to detect arguments and to generate candidate arguments for rebuttal. The method makes no a *priori* assumptions about *attack* and *support* relations between propositions that are advanced by the agents participating in a dialog. Rather, using the method, these relations are dynamically established while the dialog is taking place. This allows incremental processing since the system need only consider the current utterance advanced by the dialog participant, along with the prior context, to be able to continue processing.

1   Introduction and Motivation

Argument detection is an important task in building an intelligent system that can understand and engage in an argument. An intelligent dialog system (IDS)(Bordegoni *et al.* (1997)) is an interactive system that tailors its responses according to the user's needs and intentions. In an IDS, it is necessary to detect whether an utterance given by the user is an argument against an utterance advanced by the system, because two agents, *e.g.* the system and the user, may not always agree. Each of them may attempt to resolve issues either by attacking an agent's claim or by defending its position. Thus, an IDS must be able to determine whether a proposition advanced by an agent in a dialog attacks a claim currently held by the other agent, supports it, or does neither. An IDS must also be able to generate rebuttals (utterances that attack or support previous utterances). Finally, an IDS must be able to process arguments incrementally, while the dialog is taking place. This work extends our prior work on detecting and correcting misunderstandings during the course of a dialog (McRoy and Hirst (1995), McRoy (1995), and McRoy (1998)).

The method that we describe here, which is used in our system ARGUER, uses argument schemata that match the deep meaning representation of propositions that have been advanced in a dialog. In contrast to Birnbaum *et al.* (1980), we present a general computational method of establishing relations between propositions. Argument schemata characterize important patterns of argument that are used to establish whether propositions *support* or *attack* other propositions. These patterns are instantiated by propositions expressed by the agents during a dialog, as well as related beliefs that the agents might hold. To account for disagreements, separate models of the agents' beliefs are maintained, both for the system and the user. Hence, a proposition believed by the system might not necessarily be believed by the user. To generate a correct and convincing response, the system considers both its own beliefs and those beliefs held by the user. In addition to allowing for incremental processing of arguments, this method is *symmetric* because it can be used for interpretation or generation of arguments. This is important because the system can have the role of observer or participant.

*This work was supported by the National Science Foundation, under grants IRI-9701617 and IRI-9523666 and by a gift from Intel Corporation.

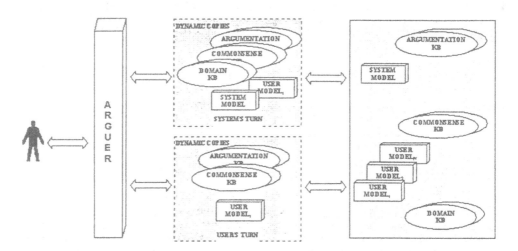

Figure 1: Architecture of ARGUER

2 Argument Detection and Rebuttal

The architecture of ARGUER is depicted in Figure 1. The system has access to the Domain Knowledge Base (KB) (domain knowledge), Argumentation KB (argumentation knowledge, *i.e.* knowledge about the structure of arguments), and the Commonsense KB. (The underlying knowledge representation used by ARGUER is SNePS Shapiro and Rapaport (1992), which provides facilities for reasoning, truth-maintenance and knowledge partitioning.) The system is presumed to be the domain expert. During turn-taking (the dotted boxes in Figure 1 represent the extensions of the knowledge base used for each turn), the system has access to the users' belief models (because it is the system's models of the users). Depending on whose turn it is, the system attempts to interpret whether the current utterance attacks or supports previous claims (which may be any prior utterance).

When the user inputs an utterance, the system will attempt to interpret the user's utterance as an attack or support on a prior utterance of the system. It does so by asking, *What does the user's utterance attack?* and second, *What does the user's utterance support?* All reasoning to answer these questions occurs in an extension of the user's belief model that includes the argumentation and common sense knowledge (which are presumed to be shared knowledge).

When the system generates a reply, it will attempt to attack or support the previous utterances of the user. Otherwise, the system will attempt to provide utterances that support its prior utterances. To generate a response, the system will reason with an extension of its knowledge including domain, argumentation, and common sense knowledge, along with a relevant set of the user's beliefs (Ali *et al.* (1999)). (The latter is determined by considering applicable argument schemata).

Figure 2 is an example dialog that includes an argument. In the figure, S1 and S2 are utterances of the system. U1 is the user's utterance. To detect that U1 attacks S1, the system makes use of the argument schema rule: *If X is an utterance implying Y, then NOT Y is an attack to X* (which is in the Argumentation KB). A rule in the common-sense KB allows the system to derive that requiring something of an agent (which follows from the imperative form of S1) implies that there is a need for that thing by the agent. S1 implies Y ("There is a need for a blood pressure check.") Thus, using the above argument schema rule, *(NOT Y)* ("there is no need for a blood pressure check") is an attack to X ("system requires the user to have a blood pressure check").

This argument schema can also be used to generate a rebuttal. Suppose the user said S1. Using the argument schema rule describe above, Y is instantiated as "there is a need for a blood pressure check". This, in turn, allows the system to select *(NOT Y)* as an attack to X to make the utterance U1 to rebut S1.

S1 Have your blood pressure checked.
U1 There is no need.
S2 Uncontrolled high blood pressure can lead to heart attack, heart failure, stroke or kidney failure.

Figure 2: An Example Argument

3   Related Work

This work deals with issues closely related to understanding arguments in an interactive environment, more specifically, in a dialog. Recent work in interactive argumentation systems include IACAS (Vreeswijk (1995)) and NAG (Zukerman *et al.* (1998)). IACAS allows the users to start a dispute and find arguments. However, it does not address the issue of maintaining separate belief models for each participant in a dialog. NAG, on the other hand, uses tagged words from the input and uses Bayesian networks to find the best set of nodes that can be formed as an argument for a proposition. Neither system, however, addresses argument detection; they deal with issues different from the ones that concern us. Chu-Caroll and Carberry (1995) focus on a different, but related, problem within dialog, the collaborative construction of a plan. This work considers the problem of deciding whether the system should accept or reject a user's proposal, on the basis of its consistency with the system's beliefs and the evidence offered by the user. Unlike ARGUER's approach to deciding whether some evidence supports a belief, which relies on domain-independent schemata, their system's approach relies on domain-specific patterns of evidence. Other approaches to argumentation, like ABDUL/ILANA (Birnbaum *et al.* (1980)) and HERMES (Karacapilidis and Papadias (1998)), do not address the issue of how attack and support relations between propositions may be established computationally. Alvarado's OpEd (Alvarado (1990)), although designed to understand arguments, is limited to processing editorial text and does not address issues that arise in dialog.

References

Syed S. Ali, Angelo C. Restificar, and Susan W. McRoy. Relevance in argumentation. 1999. In submission.

S. Alvarado. *Understanding Editorial Text: A Computer Model of Argument Comprehension.* Kluwer Academic, 1990.

L. Birnbaum, M. Flowers, and R. McGuire. Towards an AI Model of Argumentation. In *Proceedings of the AAAI-80*, pages 313–315, Stanford, CA, 1980.

M. Bordegoni, G. Faconti, T. Y. Maybury, T. Rist, S. Ruggieri, P. Trahanias, and M. Wilson. A Standard Reference Model for Intelligent Multimedia Representation Systems. *The International Journal on the Development and Applications of Standards for Computers, Data Communications and Interfaces*, 1997.

Jennifer Chu-Caroll and Sandra Carberry. Generating Information-Sharing Subdialogues in Expert-User Consultation. In *Proceedings of the 14th IJCAI*, pages 1243–1250, 1995.

N. Karacapilidis and D. Papadias. Hermes: Supporting Argumentative Discourse in Multi-Agent Decision Making. In *Proceedings of the AAAI-98*, pages 827–832, Madison, WI 1998.

Susan W. McRoy and Graeme Hirst. The repair of speech act misunderstandings by abductive inference. *Computational Linguistics*, 21(4):435–478, December 1995.

Susan W. McRoy. Misunderstanding and the negotiation of meaning. *Knowledge-based Systems*, 8(2–3):126–134, 1995.

Susan McRoy. Achieving robust human-computer communication. *International Journal of Human-Computer Studies*, 48:681–704, 1998.

S. C. Shapiro and W. J. Rapaport. The SNePS Family. *Computers and Mathematics with Applications*, 23, 1992.

G. Vreeswijk. IACAS: An Implementation of Chisholm's Principles of Knowledge. In *Proceedings of the 2nd Dutch/German Workshop on Nonmonotonic Reasoning*, pages 225–234, 1995.

I. Zukerman, R. McConachy, and K. Korb. Bayesian Reasoning in an Abductive Mechanism for Argument Generation and Analysis. In *Proceedings of the AAAI-98*, pages 833–838, Madison, Wisconsin, July 1998.

Information Services Based on User Profile Communication

Annika Waern, Charlotte Averman, Mark Tierney and Åsa Rudström

Swedish Institute of Computer Science
Human Computer Interaction and Language Engineering Laboratory

1 Introduction

Web-based, user-adaptive information services impose a difficult requirement on user modeling: the inference schema for user modeling and user-adapted information retrieval must be maintained over time. There are two reasons for this: 1) the information itself may change; and 2) the user group is largely unknown from the start, and may change during the usage of the system. To address these problems, we view profile structures and information classifications as means of *communication* as well as means for automatic information retrieval. Users communicate their information needs, and editors communicate the structure and content of available information. Our focus is to provide tools in which such communication can be efficiently accomplished. These tools are then used to enhance the day-to-day information retrieval in terms of information filtering and search.

In this paper, we propose a design for web information services based on user profile communication. We illustrate the approach by an example application, in which conference and workshop calls are collected and distributed to interested users. We present the results of an initial study of this system, which points towards the most important characteristics of this collaboration. Finally, we discuss future extensions for the system.

2 ConCall: Conference and Workshop Call Reminder Service

ConCall (Waern et al, 1998) is an agent-based system that implements the EdInfo ideas[1] (Höök, Rudström and Waern, 1997). The ConCall service is accessed over the web and supports the collection, filtering and browsing of conference and workshop calls. Using ConCall, the user can review calls and set up reminders for deadlines. To avoid uninteresting calls, the user sets up a user profile (essentially a filter) to retrieve a personal selection of calls and organize them in a personal manner. A user is provided with several ways of maintaining the user profile including a system-inferred candidate profile based on user interaction with the calls.

An immediate concern for the design of the ConCall user profiling was that it should be open-ended and adaptive, but yet be as simple as possible to maintain. To achieve an open-ended design, we required that neither users nor editors should be bound to any predefined ontology in the formulation of filters and the structuring of calls. Users and editors are essentially free to define their own classification schemas, although some synchronization is needed.

The filtering mechanism for the first version of ConCall relies on a particular type of meta-data annotation that we have chosen to name *buzzwords*. The buzzwords for a conference call are simply a set of terms that have been chosen by the editor as a useful

---

1 The EdInfo project is funded by The Swedish research Institute for Information Technology (SITI AB) and the Swedish board for Technical Development (NUTEK).

characterization of the call. Similarly, user profiles consist of buzzwords selected from the set of editor buzzwords or invented by the users. Technically, buzzwords are treated as keywords; they form an additional parameter of the representation of calls.

The long-term aim of the ConCall system, as a demonstrator for EdInfo, is to use it as a platform in which tools for buzzword handling can be evaluated. These tools should enable users and editors to utilize buzzwords not only for information filtering and retrieval, but also as an open-ended communication channel.

3   User Study

The initial user studies of ConCall focussed on creating suggestions for how the filter component could be enhanced to increase communication between users and editors. The first study covered two aspects: 1) the actual set of tools that would be useful for users, and 2) the possible usage of ConCall as a peer-to-peer recommendation system rather than as a service provided by an editor.

Essentially, we wanted to know what user tools were needed for structuring calls, if users wanted to act as editors (sending recommendations) and if users wanted other users to act as editors (receiving recommendations from peers). We also sought some information on the actual quality of the service, i.e. if users were able to set up their filters so that interesting calls were retrieved. The adaptive functionality behind the candidate profile was not subject of evaluation in this study, since its mechanisms must be tuned to actual user behavior to provide useful adaptations. A secondary purpose of the study was to gather log information from usage, which will be used for this tuning.

The study was conducted through questionnaires, interview questions, and logging of user behavior during test runs with the system. The test group consisted of 11 participants, all familiar with calls for paper/participation. The buzzwords used were provided by editors only, and not tuned to the users' needs since this was the first test performed.

A number of the functionalities examined in the study were shown to be of high interest to the participants. In particular, participants liked the reminder service, and would like to see the possibility to get recommendations, in particular from friends and colleagues.

4   ConCall Extensions Based on Results of Study

Since conference calls usually are distributed on a peer-to-peer basis, it seems obvious that ConCall would benefit from a scenario where anyone can add conference calls, as well as read them. It is technically very simple to do this extension. In practice, however, the success of this approach requires that some people actually will provide the calls in the appropriate structure, and seek appropriate buzzword annotations for calls. The study showed that there were individuals that are willing to take on this task. However, a critical success factor is that good editor tools are available. One way we aim to address this issue is to include tools for information extraction of call properties as well as potential buzzwords. Editors would also benefit from buzzword management tools, and tools for identifying and maintaining user groups.

A more elaborate extension is to increase the support for collaborative filtering [CACM 1997]. Users may benefit from being able to review each other's profiles, or being presented with a typical profile for a group of users. Our study showed that an important factor here is whom you want to send the information to or receive information from.

The possibility to set up different filters for different types of information is most likely a necessary extension, as the same buzzword may mean radically different things in different contexts. Categorization also allows for better feedback to editors concerning possible annotations for calls. These categories will have a "buzz" flavor, and change over time, in contrast with most existing information services.

There were two additional wishes from users that we see as less useful additions. Users expressed a wish to increase the expressive power of profiles by adding types to buzzwords, so that the search for the buzzword is limited to a certain type of information ("Hawaii" is a location buzzword, "Johnson" is a program committee buzzword). However, it is unclear if this will have any large effects in practice: very few buzzwords are likely to be ambiguous in the sense that they mean widely different things if occurring in different context in the same call.

Finally, users expressed a wish to be able to grade the importance of buzzwords. This is a natural wish, but it is very unclear how such gradings should affect the behavior of the system. Should there be a threshold value for the overall importance of a call that determined if it would be sent to a particular user, or should the information be used locally to sort calls in order of importance? Here, we believe that further studies are needed to determine how users envision the optimal behavior of a system.

5 Final remarks

The ConCall service shows that edited adaptive information services indeed are possible without imposing large and complicated novel tasks on editors. Edited adaptation provides added value for the individual user as well as for the editor, who obtains better means to organize information to suit the needs of the users. The initial study of ConCall shows that there is a clear need for tools for the handling of filters. In particular, the study shows that such tools should enable *recommendations*, so that the individual, be it a user or an editor, can receive recommendations from peer users and editors. Furthermore, the study shows that recommendations from friends and colleagues are valued higher than any other types of recommendation.

References

Höök, K., Rudström, Å., and Waern, A. (1997) Edited Adaptive Hypermedia: Combining Human and Machine Intelligence to Achieve Filtered Information. In Milosavljevic, Brusilovsky, Moore, Oberlander and Stock (Eds.), proceedings of the *Flexible Hypertext Workshop*. Macquarie Computing Report No. C/TR97-06, Macquarie University, Australia. Also available at http://www.sics.se/~kia/papers/edinfo.html

Waern, A., Tierney, M., Rudström, Å., and Laaksolahti, J. (1998) *ConCall: An Information Service for Researchers Based on EdInfo*. SICS Technical Report, T98:04, ISSN 1100-3154, October 1998.

Case-based User Profiling in a Personal Travel Assistant

Pawel Waszkiewicz[1], Padraig Cunningham[1], and Ciara Byrne[2]

[1] Department of Computer Science, Trinity College, Dublin, Ireland
[2] Broadcom Research Ireland Ltd., Dublin, Ireland

Abstract. This paper presents an architecture for a Personal Travel Assistant (PTA) which can elaborate on a users travel request and evaluate travel offers. Information on user behaviour is stored in a case base in the form of a Case Retrieval Net. This lazy approach has the advantages that it is incremental, extendible and allows flexible reuse of the information.

1 The FIPA PTA Scenario

FIPA is a standards organisation concerned with specifying generic agent technologies. FIPA has proposed a set of prototype applications (FIPA (1997)) in which proposed standards can be tested. One of these applications is a travel scenario where agents assist a user both during pre-trip planning and during travel. The travel scenario is being implemented as part of the FACTS (FIPA Agent Communication and Services) (FACTS (1998)) project which attempts to validate the work of FIPA and other standards bodies by building demonstrator systems.

In the travel scenario envisaged, there will be three different types of agent: Personal Travel Agents (PTA) which represent the interests of an individual user or organisation, Travel Broker Agents (TBA) which broker travel services, and Travel Service Agents (TSA) which represent a particular travel service or have expertise in a particular area, e.g. Danish hotels. A user requests a trip by giving the PTA the trip details and specifying some preferences, such as preferred airline. The PTA then negotiates with the TBA over the details. The TBA composes a trip from several different elements (e.g. flight, hotel, etc.) supplied by the TSAs. This paper focuses on the design of the PTA and in particular on the pre-trip planning phase. We have identified two tasks which the PTA can learn to perform for the user during this phase: adding extra user preferences to a travel request (Task 1) and evaluating a travel offer (Task 2).

2 User Modeling in the PTA

The PTA stores a user profile as a collection of cases. Case Base Reasoning (CBR) was chosen as the learning method because it is an incremental learning system, cases can be acquired easily and the decisions of the agent can be easily explained to the user. CBR is a form of lazy learning. Lazy learning systems often use local approaches (problems are solved by reference to nearby examples in the problem space) which can lead to highly adaptive behaviour not usually found in eager algorithms (Aha (1997)). Case information is stored in a Case Retrieval Net (Lenz et al. (1998)). Two types of entity appear in a Case Retrieval Net(CRN): cases and information entities (IE). An information entity is a basic knowledge item such as a single feature-value pair. Each case is connected to a number of IEs which describe its features. Similarity links exist between

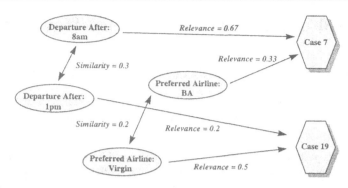

Figure 1. Partial Case Retrieval Net

IEs which have the same feature name and indicates the similarity of a particular pair of values, e.g. how similar a 1-star hotel is to a 3-star hotel. Relevance links between a case and an IE which specifies the importance of that feature in the case (See Figure 1). A spreading activation process is used in order to retrieve cases. IEs which describe the features of a new trip are activated. Activation is spread through similarity links to neighbouring IEs. Finally, cases activations are calculated from the activation of the IEs linked to the case and the relevance of each active IE. The cases with the highest activations are retrieved.

3   PTA Tasks

The PTA acquires profile information by observing the users actions when planning a trip. This information is converted into cases which are stored in a CRN. A minimal amount of direct user feedback will also be used. Figure 2 shows the flow of data through the system when the user requests a trip. The travel preferences supplied by the user are used to query the case base, and one or more cases similar to the new case are retrieved. Travel preferences defined in these cases are extracted. Preferences from several different cases may be combined. The travel preferences specified by the user and those extracted from the case base are merged. The PTA then constructs a trip request message from this information, gets user approval and sends it to the TBA. A new case is created from the travel request.

Task 2 involves evaluating an offer sent by the TBA whose features do not exactly match the preferences specified by the user. Some basic details in the offer and the request sent by the PTA, e.g. destinations, are compared to make sure that they match. If there is a mismatch between these details, then the offer is rejected immediately. Otherwise, the rest of the users preferences are compared with the offer details and the differences between them are identified. This information is passed to the retrieval module which retrieves cases in which there were similar discrepancies. If the offer is categorised as being of interest (depending on whether the offer was accepted in the retrieved cases), then it is passed to the user for evaluation. Otherwise it is rejected.

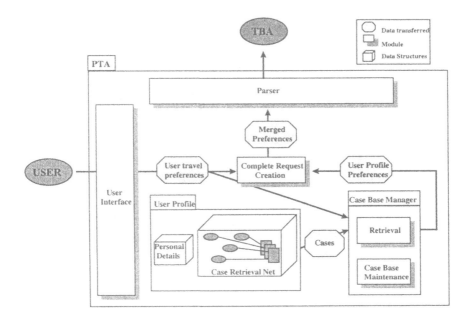

Figure 2. System Diagram

4 Conclusions and Future Work

The PTA is currently being implemented. We feel that the case-based approach to user profiling is suitable in this domain, in particular because of the use of the CRN. The CRN offers several advantages as a method of storing a user profile: it is easy to extend, flexible and content-sensitive. A new case feature can be added to the CRN without making any major changes to its structure. The CRN can be adapted to address more than one problem (i.e. adding preferences and deciding whether to reject an offer) without having to modify the basic case representation or retrieval method. Finally, the CRN allows very flexible specification of similarity functions. The weights on relevance links can be adjusted to implement context-dependent similarity measures where, for example, each case evaluates its input differently. Potential disadvantages include the need to automatically calculate relevance weights and construct similarity metrics. These issues will be investigated as the work proceeds.

References

Aha, D. W. (1997). Editorial on lazy learning. *Artificial Intelligence Review* 11:7–10.
ACTS Project AC317. (1998). *FIPA Agent Communication Technology and Services: Project Summary*.
Foundation for Intelligent Physical Agents. (1997). *Draft Specification, Part 4, Personal Travel Assistance*.
Lenz, M., Auriol, E., and Manago, M. (1998). Diagnosis and decision support. In M. Bartsch-Sporl, H. D. B., and Wess, S., eds., *Case-Based Reasoning Technology: From Foundations to Applications*, volume 1400 of *Lecture Notes in Computer Science*. Springer-Verlag.

DOCTORIAL CONSORTIUM PAPERS

User Models and Regression Methods in Information Retrieval From the Internet

Jacek Brzezinski *

Institute for Applied Artificial Intelligence School of Computer Science,
Telecommunications and Information Systems
DePaul University, Chicago, USA

Abstract. This research focuses on learning a semantic representation of the user's information needs from a database of relevant documents and queries the in the presence of hierarchically structured semantic classes and lexical databases. The resulting user model will be enhanced by regression methods applied to capturing the syntactic structure of the documents.

1 Introduction

In traditional Information Retrieval (IR) documents are retrieved by literally comparing words from a query with words from documents. However, the natural language ambiguity makes these methods inaccurate. Internet search engines, in response to a query, often provide a long list of documents that share terms with a query but are not relevant to the users' information needs. We propose an approach that tries to overcome the problems of natural language ambiguity through the combination of evidence from four sources: queries, an external categorization hierarchy, a set of relevant documents, a lexical database such as Wordnet (see, e.g. Miller, 1990). The resulting knowledge base will constitute a user model. User models will serve as a source of semantic context information for expanding queries and filtering tasks. We will apply regression methods to model relations between the semantics and the structure of related documents. The model generation process will not require an explicit feedback from the user.

2 Problem statement

Most users submit short, abbreviated queries to search engines. As a result they receive a long list of "hits". The retrieved documents share terms with a query but due to the polysemy in natural language, the documents may not be related to the user's information needs. Also, because of the synonymy property of natural language, many relevant documents do not share terms with a query, so those documents will not be retrieved. The system we are working on is a client side agent that helps a user to retrieve relevant information from the Internet by performing three basic functions: unsupervised generation of user models for query expansion and filtering of incoming documents.

---

* This research has been inspired by the members of my Ph.D. committee: Dr. S. Lytinen (DePaul University), Dr. G. Knafl (DePaul University), Dr. B. Mobasher (DePaul University).

We propose an alternative for the "bag-of-words" approach to Information Retrieval (IR) in which evidence from text documents is represented by a high dimensional vectors of weights (see, e.g. Salton, 1989). Despite the proven robustness of the vector space methods, it is often difficult to infer that two different terms are semantically close. The co-occurrence statistic methods find relationships between terms that are local to the corpora. Instead, we apply regression methods for modeling senses of terms in the presence of hierarchically structured semantic classes. The regression modeling is intended to capture the syntactic structure of the documents, whereas the external databases will be used to classify semantics of the context.

3   Overview of the system

We are interested in developing user models in an unsupervised fashion. In our system we will apply the unsupervised approach proposed by Morita and Shinoda (1984) for collecting relevant documents without an explicit relevance feedback. The collected documents will be subjected to a semantic analysis based on three sources of information: a lexical database, a classification hierarchy e.g. YAHOO (http://www.yahoo.com), The Library of Congress Classification System (http://geography.miningco.com/library/) etc., and a database containing queries submitted by a user.

We will use Wordnet as a lexical resource. Wordnet can be thought of as an extension of a thesaurus. Each lexical item belongs to one or more "synonym sets" (synsets). Synsets are then connected by several types of links: hypernym, hyponym, meranym etc. Wordnet will be used for finding synsets for terms from the relevant documents. Classification hierarchies, included in the system, are the source of domain knowledge and will be used for semantic tagging of relevant documents. The semantic tags are sets of topics, organized in hierarchies of increasing specificity, associated with a term or a passage. The regression modeling will be used learn relations between the semantic tags and sets of terms present in the relevant documents. Those models will be utilized to automatically categorize terms or sets of terms with respect to a hierarchically structured response variable. The resulting user model is intended to be a low dimensional semantic representation of the relevant documents accompanied with a model of systematic relations between terms and structured classes. The model will be used for semantically precise query expansion and document filtering.

References

Miller G., (1990) WORDNET: An Online Lexical Database. *International Journal of Lexicography* 3 (1)

Morita M., Shinoda Y. (1984). Information Filtering Based on User Behavior Analysis and Best Match Text Retrieval. In Croft B., van Rijsbergen C. J., eds.,*Proceedings of the Seventeenth Annual International ACM SIGIR Conference on Research and Development in Information Retrieval.* ACM 272–281.

Ott L., R. (1988) *An Introduction to Statistical Methods and Data Analysis.* Duxbury Press. Fourth Edition.

Rich E. (1983) Users are individuals: individualizing user models. *International Journal of Man-Machine Studies.* 18:199–214.

Salton G. (1989) *Automatic Text Processing. The Transformation, Analysis, and Retrieval of Information by Computer.* Addison-Wesley Publishing Company. 313–326.

User Modeling in Mixed-Initiative Hypertexts

Berardina De Carolis

Department of Informatics, University of Bari, Italy

Abstract. This thesis proposes an approach to the generation of hypertexts in mixed-initiative situations in which the points of view of both the user and the system are taken into account. The system, besides planning the content of each "hyperdialogue" section at the appropriate level of detail, has the capability of dealing with changes in the interaction context that require reaction, and proactively provides advice to the user accordingly.

1 Thesis Synopsis

The interaction with a mixed-initiative hypertext can been seen as a form of dialogue in which the user asks for information using the links in a hypertext node and the system answers this query by taking into account the user attitudes and feedback, and by ensuring that the global goal of the communication is achieved through the sequence of dialogue sections. In situations in which the system has a strong communicative goal, such as tutoring or instructing, in addition to adapting the information content of each hyperdialogue section, the system can proactively generate context-dependent advice; this is done when the interaction context requires the system to take the initiative in the dialogue. Establishing a hypertext node content, in this case, requires a dynamic approach to planning to: a) consider both the User and the System's points of view; b) plan the discourse at the sufficient and appropriate abstraction level, to achieve the communicative goal of a specific hyperdialogue section; c) react to changes in the context during interaction by updating the user model and planning the subsequent hyperdialogue section. In my Ph.D. thesis, a method for generating mixed-initiative hypertexts, which fulfils these requirements, has been developed. This method combines a deliberative with a reactive approach: a discourse planner plays the role of a mediator between the system's and the user's points of view, and reacting rules are employed to handle changes in the context situations that require revising the system behavior.

To consider the points of view of both the user and the system, several attitudes have to be included in the two models: knowledge and beliefs, pro-attitudes regarding intentions and goals, and ability to "domain actions" (by the user) and "communicative actions" (by the system). These attitudes are scored in relation to the level of detail with which information was presented to the user.

While planning, several methods are employed to adapt the information content of the explanation: i) through the PRECOND field of planning operators, that may contain conditions on the user's and the system's mental states; ii) by using mediation strategies between the system goals and the user interests. In particular, the generator checks the system goals; if the effect to be achieved is part of them, then the generator checks the system's propensity to talk about that topic to that particular category of user. The following situations may hold:

a.   *the system's propensity to talk is high*. The generator checks the intention of the user: a1) if this is **high** too, it plans for that topic at the lowest level of abstraction, by including a great amount of details; a2) if this is *low*, it plans for that topic at the highest level of abstraction and sets as 'expandible' those steps that admit a further abstraction level, by rendering them as links in the page;

b.   *the system's propensity to talk is low*. The generator checks, again, the user intention: b1) if this is **high,** it plans as for the case a2; b2) if this is *low*, it plans for that topic at the highest level of abstraction without setting as expandible those steps that admit a further abstraction level.

If the effect to be achieved is not part of the system's goals, then the generator plans for the required information according to the user level of interest in knowing about that topic or in doing that action. In addition to this type of adaptivity, Dy-GeNet also considers the user feedback inferred from link selections, to generate context-dependent advice. When the user selects a link in a previously generated page, the planning process is activated to generate and execute a "relevant" plan. This is the reactive part of the system: each subgoal, or link in the hypertext, is associated with a process that allows planning, executing or recovering a portion of the plan. This process is based on a set of reacting rules that set up the most relevant abstract plan for the given interaction context; this plan will then be refined and executed by the Hypertext Generator. The result of this process is to decide whether or not to include the system advice, and if so, to use it in order to suggest or remind the user to view some related topic or some skipped steps (De Carolis, 1999).

2 Conclusions and Future Work

The need to use a reactive approach in the generation of interactive explanations has been raised by other authors (Moore and Swartout, 1992; Andrè and Wahlster, 1998). My dissertation proposes an approach to the generation of mixed-initiative hypertexts that combines reactive planning, dynamic hypertext generation and modeling of the mental state of the two participants to the dialogue. The described work is almost completed and tested on a medical application domain. However, the planner itself needs to be tested in other domains; in addition, more work on the agent's mental state is needed to refine the reasoning mechanism (at the moment, most of the reasoning is left to the planner. Finally, an evaluation study is needed in order to check the user acceptance of the system.

References

Andrè, E., and Wahlster, W. (1998). *Intelligent Multimedia Interface Agents*. ECAI 98 Tutorial, Brighton.

De Carolis, B. (1999). Generating Mixed-Initiative Hypertexts: a Reactive Approach. In *Proceedings of IUI 99*, ACM, Redondo Beach, CA.

Moore, J. D., and Swartout, W. J. (1992). A Reactive approach to Explanation: Taking the User's Feedback into Account. *NLG in AI and CL*, C. Paris, W. Swartout and W. Mann (eds), Kluwer Academic Publishers, 3-47.

Temporary User Modeling
for Adaptive Product Presentations in the Web

Tanja Joerding

Department of Computer Science, Dresden University of Technology, Germany

Abstract. This work proposes a temporary user modeling approach that enables the immediate adaptation of product presentations in the Web to the individual customer at runtime by using a machine learning algorithm. We focus on the question of how monitored user interactions can be preprocessed to get example data for the learning algorithm and how existing decision tree or decision list algorithms fit the requirements of the new application field of electronic shopping.

1 Introduction

In the area of electronic shopping static product presentations in the Web cannot always meet the expectations of all customers. There are various hardware and software preconditions, customers have different preferences for multimedia elements, and they are interested in different information concerning the product.

First approaches of adaptive product catalogues with conventional user modeling techniques are not convincing. Customers are not motivated to answer questions and they are often distrustful to give private data. Most of the user modeling techniques, like e.g. rule-based systems or collaborative filtering, are not flexibel enough in that changing preferences of the customer are not taken into account.

2 Temporary User Modeling

This work focuses on a temporary user modeling approach, that monitors the behaviour of the customer and that realizes adaptive presentations without storing user data for other sessions. The customer can remain anonymous but uses a system that recognizes his needs and preferences and that adapts the product presentations immediately. The development of temporary user models consists of three steps:

Monitoring interactions. To get information about the customer, we use only implicit knowledge acquisition by monitoring the behaviour of the customer on the side of the client. These are interactions with single presentation elements, e.g. if the customer follows a certain link, starts audio or video players, interrupts the downloading of images, saves or prints an image or text, or takes a step in virtual reality worlds. Because of the permanent observation the system gets up-to-date information and it is unnecessary to annoy the customer with explicit questions.

Preprocessing data. Using a set of general rules, the system evaluates for every presentation element whether the customer was interested in it or not, e.g. if a video seleted by a link was played for more than 5 sec, then the interest of the customer in the video is assumed to be positive. The evaluated presentation elements are then used as example data for an incremental learning algorithm.

Learning preferences. To learn the preferences of the customer, we use at present an incremental algorithm based on CDL4 (Shen, 1996). This algorithm considers three attributes for every presentation element: type of medium, content description, and downloading time. Example data looks like the following tuple (audio, {car, VW-Golf, engine}, 3sec, negative). The result of the algorithm is a decision list that can be interpreted as a list of rules, e.g. if the presentation element gives information about "cars" and the kind of medium is not "video", then the customer may be interested. The chosen algorihm works incrementally, i.e. when the customer moves from one product presentation to another one, the algorithm receives the interaction data of the customer and updates its rule base. This means that the user model for each customer consists of individual temporary changing rules. If there are contradictory data, the algorithm prefers more recent data over older data. These properties are important because many customers navigate only for a short time in a catalogue. Additionally, while navigating in the product catalogue, the preferences of the customers can change.

3   Future Work

At present, we have implemented a first prototype system named TELLIM (inTELLIgent Multimedia) and have applied the system to a small jumble sale for selling second-hand cars (Joerding and Meissner, 1998), (Joerding and Michel, 1999).

It remains to evaluate the approach of temporary user modeling. As a first step in this direction we will consider the preprocessing of monitored user interactions to answer the following questions: Do the interaction possibilities fit the needs of the customers? Is it possible to use general rules to infer the interest of the customer? Are the implemented rules adequate? How can we get more detailed evaluations? Is it helpful to replace binary variables by fuzzy ones?

In a next step we will look at the learning algorithm and work on the following questions: What are the specific requirements of the learning task? What existing decision tree or decision list algorithms can be applied? Are there adequate algorithms that can process fuzzy values? How can we evaluate their usefulness by user studies?

References

Joerding, T., and Meissner, K. (1998), Intelligent Multimedia Presentations in the Web: Fun without Annoyance. In: *Proccedings of the Seventh International World Wide Web Conference*, Brisbane, Australia, 649-650.

Joerding, T., and Michel, S. (1999), Personalized Shopping in the Web by Monitoring the Customer. In: *Proceedings of The Active Web - A British HCI Group Day Conference*, Stafford, UK.

Shen, W.M. (1996), An Efficient Algorithm for Incremental Learning of Decision Lists. *Technical Report, USC-ISI-96-012*, Information Sciences Institute, University of Southern California, http://www.isi.edu/~shen/papers_by_date.html

User models for helping the helper in peer help networks

Vive Kumar

Department of Computer Science, University of Saskatchewan, Canada
Email: vive.kumar@usask.ca

Abstract. *My Ph.D. thesis investigates customised, personalised, and just-in-time help extended to the helper in peer help networks deployed in learning, tutoring, training, and workplace environments. A system called Helper's Assistant that supports peer help networks is being built as part of my thesis that relies on user models to help the helper.*

1 Introduction

Increasingly, communities of computer users are interconnected through the Internet or Intranets. For instance, while on the job, most of the workers in a national banking organisation are interconnected through their computers. Similarly, in a University environment, most of the students are connected through networked computers either from their workplaces (computer labs) or from their homes. Such communities of networked users form what we call "peer help networks". These users possess different degrees of work expertise and request for different types of assistance while performing computer-oriented tasks.

Normally, when users issue a help request, they provide a brief question. In I-Help (Greer et al, 1998), a helpee supplies a question and a help topic from a precompiled list of topics. Using this information and other user model data I-Help identifies a ready, able, and willing helper. Finally, I-Help establishes communication between the chosen helper and the helpee using a chat tool. My research augments this scenario whereby the chosen helper is assisted with an expanded form of help request, a pedagogically sound help plan, and a personalised means to deliver help.

2 User Models to Help the Helper

A system called "Helper's Assistant" is being built on top of I-Help to help the helper (Kumar et al, 1999). It is conceivable that the more the help request information the better the quality of help received from the help system. To that effect, the first step provides the helper with a comprehensive "help-context". The initial help request is augmented with relevant information from the helpee's and helper's user models, a topic hierarchy, a concept network, and possibly queries to the helpee.

The second step in assisting the peer helper involves the generation of a "help-plan". Help plans in Helper's Assistant provide the means to select appropriate help resources and pedagogical strategy. A help plan is derived from a precompiled structure called "help-plan-network" depending on various factors such as helper's preference, helpee's preference, relevance of help material, and distributed accessibility of help tools.

The third step in assisting the peer helper concerns the delivery of help according to the help plan. Depending on the type of help request, the preferences of the helpee, and the preferences of the helper, help can be delivered in different types, modes, and forms. For instance, the preferences of the helpee or the helper, related to the type of help response (pointer, short answer, analogy, clue, etc.), the mode of help response (offline, online, just-in-time), and the form of help response (manual or automated) can be deduced from the helpee's user model.

In addition to these three major steps, Helper's Assistant also incorporates means to offer usage-based statistical assistance to the helper. It will use an unconventional user model called "collaboration model" that stores the knowledge involved in the selection of help components that enables multi-user interaction. Each collaboration model is comprised of a variety of collaboration attributes. There are three types of collaboration models being designed: Helpee-helper model, Helper-System model, and Helpee-System model.

The collaboration attributes of a helpee-helper model represent type of help context, type of helpee's preferences, type of helper's preferences, and the success rates for each participant. To illustrate, a vector containing four values corresponding to the help context type, helpee preferred help response type, helper preferred help response type, and the success-rate of the help session can form an instance of helpee-helper collaboration attribute. Using various combinations of help context type and helper/helpee preferences, one can generate a variety of helpee-helper collaboration attributes. A set of such attributes constitutes a helpee-helper collaboration model that can be populated with values from the case library of help sessions. Over a period of time, the collaboration model can help the researcher or system administrator infer pedagogical rules that can select appropriate help plans for a given set of context type, helper preferences, and helpee preferences.

In a similar fashion, the collaboration attributes of the helper-system and helpee-system collaboration models represent type of help context, help tool preferred by the helpee/helper, and the success rates of help sessions. For example, a vector containing three values corresponding to the help context type, use of relative-debugger tool, and the success-rate for this vector, forms an instance of a collaboration attribute. Collaboration models help the researcher or system administrator evaluate the quality of selection of peer helpers, help plans, and help tools with respect to a given type of help context.

References

Greer J.E., McCalla G.I., Collins J.A., Kumar V.S., Meagher P., Vassileva J. (1998), Supporting Peer Help and Collaboration in Distributed Workplace Environments, *International Journal of AI and Education.* 9 (to appear in printed form, available on the WWW at: http://cbl.lccds.ac.uk/ijaicd/).

Kumar V., McCalla G., & Greer J. (1999). Helping the peer helper. International conference on Artificial Intelligence in Education. Le Mans, France (to appear).

A System to Assess Students' Competence That Re-uses a Pencil and Paper Tool

Stéphanie Jean

Department of Computer Science, Université du Maine, France

Abstract. PÉPITE is a multidisciplinary project in computer science and didactics for mathematics. It aims to develop a computerized environment able to model the reasoning process of 15 year-old students in elementary algebra. This work is based on a didactical analysis whose result is a validated pencil and paper diagnosis tool. The aim of the PÉPITE project is to automate this tool.

1 Basis of the project

We propose an approach of assessment that re-uses a validated pencil and paper diagnosis tool built by educational researchers of the project (Grugeon, 1997). This tool combines a set of pencil and paper tasks with a diagnosis matrix linking questions and dimensions of analysis. This very fine description of the student's behavior requires a higher level description: the cognitive profiles, which are built by transversal analysis of the diagnosis matrix. These profiles describe students' algebraic competence qualitatively. They can be used by teachers to form groups in classes relying on students' knowledge and not just on marks, or in a Computer Supported Learning Environment proposing activities, advice and explanations adapted to the student's knowledge.

The PÉPITE project aims to automate this pencil and paper diagnosis tool.

2 The Student Interface

PÉPITEST offers students an *adaptation* of the pencil and paper tasks to the computer and collects their answers, with 22 different exercises. The design of the student interface plays a significant role in the quality of the diagnosis. Taking into account HCI issues and adapting them to the AI-Ed domain ensures us better results in the analysis by allowing students to behave as they usually do and therefore by furnishing more reliable answers. So PÉPITEST proposes several carefully designed tools to replace students' usual pencil and paper tools.

PÉPITEST is now completed. It has been tested with 75 students. The main results are as follows. For each question of the test, we have found every kind of answer proposed in the model of algebraic competence: PÉPITEST does not reduce the range of the students' productions. Even if students had difficulties in producing algebraic expressions, PÉPITEST didn't prevent students from writing them. Thus it shows the test's completeness in relation with the model of competence.

Educational researchers can fill in the diagnosis matrix from students' answers to PÉPITEST problems. The teacher of the class could thus confirm the manually obtained profiles.

3   The Diagnosis

PÉPIDIAG interprets and codes students' productions, from the data furnished by PÉPITEST. The difficulty in establishing this diagnosis comes from the variety of exercises and from the variety of students' answers. Each question corresponds to a set of answers usually given by students (this is the result of the didactical research) which corresponds to a code in the diagnosis matrix. The system has to interpret the students' answers to associate them with the right code. This association is quite easy to do with closed questions but can be very difficult with totally open questions where the students mix natural language and mathematics.

A first prototype of PÉPIDIAG already exists. We have obtained these initial results: PÉPIDIAG is able to analyze each multiple-choice answer and every simple algebraic expression answer automatically. We can analyze 75 percent of the students' answers to PÉPITEST problems, partially automating the diagnosis.

We ran PÉPIDIAG on every student answer in our corpus and the system filled the diagnosis matrixes. In order to correlate this partial diagnosis with human assessment, we chose 5 students with different levels of competence and we asked an expert to manually fill in the diagnosis matrix. PÉPIDIAG and the human assessor were quite in agreement.

PÉPIDIAG has now to be fully developed to analyze all the questions in order to obtain full profiles.

4   The Profiles

PÉPIPROFIL, the teacher interface, establishes the students' profiles from the filled matrix by transversal analysis (which corresponds to an algorithm) and presents them to the users (teachers or researchers). PÉPIPROFIL is completed. In our evaluation of PÉPIPROFIL we obtained two main results: With a manually filled matrix, PÉPIPROFIL computes the same profile as a teacher does. From the partial matrixes yet filled by the system, PÉPIPROFIL builds partial profiles that are confirmed by the teachers. Tests are planned for the presentation of the profiles to the teachers.

5   Conclusion

The three modules of PÉPITE are now completed to a large extent. Our validation criteria are clearly defined: Validating PÉPITEST consists of verifying that we obtain equivalent answers to the pencil and paper test and also that data obtained from the software allows us to build profiles equivalent to the pencil and paper profiles. We evaluate PÉPIDIAG and PÉPIPROFIL by comparing the automatic profiles to human assessors' ones.

From the beginning, we integrated teachers and educational researchers in our design team. This multidisciplinary and user-centered approach allows us to propose a test adapted to students (producing more reliable data) and to build profiles really adapted to teachers' needs.

References

Grugeon, B., (1997). Design and Using of a Multidimensional Structure of Analysis in Elementary Algebra, In *Recherches en Didactique des Mathématiques* 17(2): 167–210. (In French)

Towards Building An Interactive Argumentation System

Angelo C. Restificar

Electrical Engineering and Computer Science
University of Wisconsin-Milwaukee

Abstract. This research aims to apply agent models and user-adapted interaction techniques to construct a computational model of argumentation that would enable a system to process utterances (even if agents make claims with which the system disagrees), and to generate appropriate responses. The study is expected to cover issues in areas that include natural language processing, argumentation theory, user modeling, knowledge representation, and commonsense and non-monotonic reasoning.

1 Introduction

Dealing with issues involved in argumentation can lead to a better understanding of how a conflict may be resolved. In a human-computer collaborative situation, for example, people will not always agree with what the system tells them; they might need to be convinced. The system must be able to detect whether the user is agreeing or disagreeing with the system and be able to construct a convincing supporting argument or rebuttal when the need arises. Agent models and user-adapted interaction techniques would facilitate the processing of tasks involved in such problems.

2 Proposed Approach and Relevant Issues

The objective of this research is two-fold: (1) to be able to formulate an effective and efficient computational, and well-founded theoretical framework for natural language-based interactive argumentation systems and (2) to be able to demonstrate and validate such framework by building the argumentation system. The approach involves the use of agent models and user-adapted interaction techniques to process utterances and generate appropriate responses.

In structuring the knowledge base, the beliefs of agents participating in a dialog will have separate models. The models are essentially knowledge-bases that contain the system's initial "idea" of the participants. The models are updated dynamically as the dialog progresses. This approach allows the system to reason about, store updated views of the participants, and draw inferences without believing in what the participants believe.

The research will address important issues involving interactive argumentation systems. It will attempt to combine formal techniques in argumentation (Vreeswijk, 1997; Loui and Norman, 1993) and those that focus on generating effective arguments (Grasso, 1998; Zukerman et al., 1998; Reed et al., 1996). Issues involving model acquisition, knowledge representation, and inferencing techniques in a natural language-based argumentation framework using dynamic belief models will be addressed.

A basic issue in argumentation is argument detection. During the course of an ongoing conversation between participating agents, it is important to determine how to detect an argument to be able to effectively handle the interaction. Moreover, in the context of a dialog, utterances may only correspond to portions of an entire argument. Determining what the argument is, which part of the argument to attack, or which argument to use as a basis for rebuttal, are relevant issues.

The underlying principle for detecting arguments will be to find a general case of an argument schema into which the meaning representation of an utterance can be matched. An argument schema corresponds to how an argument maybe structured. Arguments can be detected and generated via these argument schemata. If a matching schema is found, the corresponding variables are instantiated, thereby establishing attack or support relations between propositions (see Restificar et al., 1999). The use of argument schemata for argument detection and rebuttal allows argument relations between propositions to be established dynamically. Moreover, the method is incremental in that it allows processing of each piece of the utterance and uses only a part of the argument to continue.

Rebutting an argument involves choosing an effective strategy. The strategy may be affected by factors that include input from the user model, the strength and soundness of the argument, and the way the corresponding utterance is generated. A user model is envisaged to play an important role in choosing an effective strategy for constructing rebuttals. The information in the model can be utilized in deciding whether an argument to be presented is convincing enough for a particular user. An effective argument must take into consideration the user model which contains the system's model of the user's characteristics, background, and beliefs. In addition, a user's response would allow the system to make inferences about the user. These inferences can then be used to revise and update the user model. Hence, a user model is envisaged to influence how arguments will be constructed and is itself influenced by the information that can be inferred by the system about the user during the course of the interaction.

References

Grasso, F. (1998). Exciting Avocados and Dull Pears: Combining Behavioural and Argumentative Theory for Producing Effective Advice. In *Proceedings of the 20th Annual Meeting of the Cognitive Science Society*.

Loui, R. P., and Norman, J. (1993). Rationales and Argument Moves. *Artificial Intelligence and Law*.

Reed, C., Long, D., and Fox, M. (1996). An Architecture for Argument Dialogue Planning. In Gabbay, D., and Olhbach, H. J., eds., *Practical Reasoning: Proceedings of the First International Conference on Formal and Applied Practical Reasoning (FAPR'96)*, volume 1085 of *LNAI*. Springer-Verlag.

Restificar, A., Ali, S., and McRoy, S. (1999). ARGUER: Using Argument Schemas for Argument Detection and Rebuttal in Dialogs. In *present volume*.

Vreeswijk, G. (1997). Abstract argumentation systems. *Artificial Intelligence* 90(1-2):225–279.

Zukerman, I., McConachy, R., and Korb, K. (1998). Bayesian Reasoning in an Abductive Mechanism for Argument Generation and Analysis. In *Proceedings of the Fifteenth National Conference on Artificial Intelligence (AAAI-98)*, 833–838.

Evaluating Instructional Hypermedia: A User Modelling Perspective

Judi R. Thomson

Department of Computer Science, University of Saskatchewan, Canada

Abstract. The goal of this research is to define a semi-automated method called Applying Patterns to Hypermedia Instructional Design (APHID) for the development of instructional hypermedia applications using established software engineering and instructional design principles. Resulting applications are evaluated using techniques common to user modelling and adaptive hypermedia.

1 Applying Patterns to Hypermedia Instructional Design (APHID)

The APHID method is based on the notion that design patterns can be used to describe instructional design principles and subsequently used to guide the design of instructional hypermedia applications. The research spans several fields including software engineering, instructional design, hypermedia design, and user modelling. Of interest to the user modelling conference is the novel application of user modelling techniques to the validation of the hypermedia applications produced using the prototype APHID environment.

One important aspect of the instructional process is sequencing information for presentation to learners (Merrill, 1998). Within a hypermedia application, instructional design is accomplished, in part, by carefully planning the learner's sequence through the material. Most hypermedia development processes provide no mechanism for including the sequencing of conceptual information in the application design. The APHID method documents the structure associated with the concepts in the domain of instruction as a concept map. Instructional design is represented as organizational patterns on the concept map. Both are used during the creation phase to automatically generate instructional hypermedia applications that are tailored to a specific instructional goal. Because the creation process is not completely controlled by the instructional designer, it is paramount that validity and usability of the hypermedia applications generated by APHID be established. A significant portion of this research is to evaluate the applications produced using the APHID environment.

2 Evaluating Hypermedia

Most effective software validation exercises include some evaluation of the software by users (Nielsen & Mack, 1994). Validation of user interactions with hypermedia is limited by what can be observed either directly or through some sort of monitoring. One observable characteristic of hypermedia users is the path they take through an application. A record of user browsing behaviour through a hypermedia application allows comparison of different users and classification of those users into groups.   A user who is classified into one particular group is likely to benefit from pages viewed by other users who also belong to that group.

Much of the present work on user interactions with hypermedia comes from user modelling researchers who wish to create adaptive hypermedia. One method of classifying users relies on a longest common subsequence algorithm for determining the similarity of one path through the hypermedia to another path (Sun & Ching, 1995). Different users of the same hypermedia application should have similar paths through the hypermedia, if their purposes and skill levels are relatively equal. A second method considers not the path through the hypermedia, but the material viewed by the user (Yan, Jacobsen, Garcia-Molina & Dayal, 1996). Each page the user accesses, along with the approximate time spent on the page is represented as part of a vector. The vectors from different users are clustered and the clusters are used as classifications for the users. When these techniques are used to adapt hypermedia applications for individuals the hypermedia is assumed to be correct. Once the individual user's preferences (or purpose) are identified, a correct adaptation can be supplied.

A slightly different perspective allows the same algorithms to be used to evaluate the hypermedia application. If the purpose of a group of users is assumed, their browsing patterns should be similar to one another if the application is constructed properly. In the case of an APHID-created application, the purpose is assumed, therefore users with similar backgrounds and abilities should browse through the hypermedia application using a similar pattern. The application of previously mentioned techniques to browsing logs should result in most users falling in the same cluster if the application is correctly constructed.

For this research, a controlled experiment using browsing pattern analysis will be performed to determine if APHID-created hypermedia applications are valid. The users will be selected to be homogeneous (all from the same beginning computer science class). These users should have similar browsing patterns (both in terms of pages viewed and in terms of order) and those patterns should match the desired patterns predicted by the APHID environment.

It is hoped that users who self-report an increase in knowledge after using the hypermedia application will be the same users who exhibit browsing patterns that match the patterns predicted by APHID.   Second, we hope to show that users working with a properly constructed instructional application exhibit similar (and predictable) browsing patterns.   Future applications created with APHID can then be validated simply by analyzing user browsing patterns.

References

Merrill, M. D. (1998, March/Apr). Knowledge Analysis for Effective Instruction. *CBT solutions*, pp. 1-11.

Nielsen, J., & Mack, R. (1994). Usability Inspection Methods: An Executive Summary. In J. Nielsen & R. Mack (Eds.), *Usability Inspection Methods* (pp. 1-23). John Wiley & Sons.

Schwabe, D., Rossi, G., & Barbosa, S. D. J. (1996). Systematic Hypermedia Applications Design with OOHDM. Hypertext 96.

Sun, C.-T., & Ching, Y.-T. (1995). Hypermedia Browsing Pattern Analysis. *International Journal of Educational Telecommunications, 1*(2/3), 293-308.

Yan, T. W., Jacobsen, M., Garcia-Molina, H., & Dayal, U. (1996, 10/05). From User Access Patterns to Dynamic Hypertext Linking. Fifth International World Wide Web Conference. Paris, France.

Learning Bayesian Networks With Hidden Variables for User Modeling

Frank Wittig*

Department of Computer Science, University of Saarbrücken, Germany

Abstract. The goal of the research summarized here is to develop methods for learning Bayesian networks on the basis of empirical data, focusing on issues that are especially important in the context of user modeling. These issues include the treatment of theoretically interpretable hidden variables, ways of learning partial networks and combining them into one single compound network, and ways of taking into account the special properties of datasets acquired through psychological experiments.

1 Goals

Although Bayesian networks have frequently been employed for user modeling tasks, techniques for learning the networks from data have so far rarely been applied in this context. Yet these learning techniques offer a promising way of deriving satisfactory answers to the question "Where do the numbers come from?". Possible sources of data include (a) records of naturally occurring user behavior and (b) the raw data of psychological experiments. The latter type of data is especially interesting for user modeling research in that it raises some issues that are more or less specific to situations in which a human agent is being modeled.

I aim to achieve the following specific goals:

1. Identify, develop, and extend existing methods for gathering empirical data and for learning appropriate (perhaps very complex) Bayesian networks for user modeling. These networks should be not only technically correct but also interpretable.
2. Offer explicit guidance to future user modelers who want to apply such learning methods.
3. In the specific example domain that I am working in, strengthen the empirical basis of the Bayesian networks for the READY system (see, e.g., Berthold and Jameson, 1999).

2 Issues and Current Status

First, appropriate algorithms for the learning task have to be identified. For user modeling, an especially important case of learning Bayesian networks is the case where the structure—which may include hidden variables such as the user's working memory load—is known, whereas the entries in the conditional probability tables (CPTs) are unknown. There exist several methods for handling this case, including Gibbs sampling (see Heckerman, 1995) and the APN approach

---

* This research is being supported by the German Science Foundation (DFG) in its Collaborative Research Center on Resource-Adaptive Cognitive Processes, SFB 378, Project B2, READY.

(Russell et al., 1995). Currently, I'm learning rather simple networks on the basis of data from a psychological experiment that was recently conducted in the READY project, in which a user's execution of different types of instructions with or without a concurrent secondary task was studied. So far, I have received the best results with an implementation of the APN algorithm with directions chosen by the Polak-Ribière method as described by Russell et al. (1995).

A second issue concerns the problem of learning probabilities in such a way that the learned networks will be interpretable. Normally, learning algorithms do not take into account the meaning of the variables in question. They yield a network that performs more or less well when applied to particular cases. But the CPTs associated with the nodes—especially with those for the hidden variables—are sometimes inconsistent with the intended theoretical interpretation of the variables in question. I am looking for ways of influencing the learning process so that the theoretical meaning of the key variables is maintained. One possible solution to this problem is to introduce constraints on the CPT entries before learning takes place. (The use of such constraints may also greatly increase the efficiency of the learning.)

The known learning algorithms do not consider the special situation of learning from a dataset that contains data from a limited number of persons. The typically large individual differences between experimental subjects have to be taken into account when the results of the learning are generalized to other persons. A first approach that I have tried is to introduce variables (e.g., "average speed of execution") that capture important individual differences. Since the values of these variables can be computed straightforwardly on the basis of the raw data, these variables can serve as observable variables for the purpose of learning, although they would not be observable in an application situation.

In most realistic scenarios, it will be impossible to gather data for entire networks at once, because the complete networks are in general too complex. This is an especially important problem in the present context, because psychological experiments are typically designed to investigate only a few variables at a time. Therefore, an interesting problem is that of learning partial networks and putting these parts together into one single compound Bayesian network. During the learning phase it should be possible to fix some CPTs in advance and to restrict the learning process to the other CPTs.

The evaluation of the learned Bayesian networks can be accomplished in at least two ways: In a traditional cross-validation, the dataset is partitioned into a learning set and a test set and the learned Bayesian networks are evaluated in terms of their accuracy on the test cases. A complementary type of evaluation checks whether a learned network can actually make useful inferences about a user on the basis of the limited input data that is typically available (see Berthold and Jameson, 1999).

References

Berthold, A., and Jameson, A. (1999). Interpreting symptoms of cognitive load in speech input. In Kay, J., ed., *User Modeling: Proceedings of the Seventh International Conference, UM99*. Vienna, New York: Springer Wien New York.

Heckerman, D. (1995). A tutorial on learning with Bayesian networks. Technical Report MSR-TR-95-06, Microsoft Research. Revised November 1996.

Russell, S., Binder, J., Koller, D., and Kanazawa, K. (1995). Local learning in probabilistic networks with hidden variables. In Mellish, C. S., ed., *Proceedings of the Fourteenth International Joint Conference on Artificial Intelligence*. San Mateo, CA: Morgan Kaufmann. 1146–1152.

INVITED PRESENTATIONS

User Knowledge, Multimedia Dialogue, and the Missing Axiom Theory

Alan W. Biermann

Department of Computer Science
P. O. Box 90129, Duke University
Durham, N. C. 27708-0129, USA
(awb@cs.duke.edu)

The missing axiom theory of dialogue (Smith and Hipp, 1994; Smith et al., 1995) asserts that an interaction takes place in order to achieve a goal, and it employs theorem proving mechanisms to try to prove that the goal has been achieved. If the system proves the goal assertion, no significant dialogue will take place. However, if it fails, then it attempts to isolate key assertions, "missing axioms," which, if they could be proven, would enable the proof of the target goal. Then the system opens dialogue with other participants, humans or machines, to try to achieve these necessary subgoals. If these subgoals can be achieved, the complete proof of the dialogue goal will be possible and the interaction can terminate successfully.

When the dialogue system discovers a missing axiom, it examines its model of other resources to obtain a guess as to which one may be able to provide the desired information. If there is indication that one source or another, human or machine, may be able to provide the needed help, the system undertakes a subdialogue to attempt to fill the void. The interaction may be successful leading to an increment in the top level proof; it may fail leading the system to seek other sources of information.

The system may not find any resource that is likely to supply a missing axiom. In this case, it can examine its own logical rule base and try to break this subgoal into parts that are simpler and more likely to be answerable by sources.

An example of these mechanisms occurs in the case of an individual who may wish to go via airplane to another city. Suppose the system has information from previous interactions that the individual has a reservation and a ticket and has packed for the trip. But suppose the person does not have a means to get to the airport. Then theorem proving would achieve the target goal except for the transit to the airport which would become the key missing axiom. Thus dialogue would not occur on any of the topics related to the reservation and ticket but would focus on the issue of getting to the airport. However, user modelling might fail to indicate that anyone at hand can provide taxi information or otherwise help obtain the proposed transit. However, an internal rule might exist indicating that the taxi subgoal can be achieved if the taxi phone number and a telephone can be obtained, and these subgoals might be shown by the user model to be achievable. The resulting dialogue with the user whose goal is to reach another city might thus become "You need to find a phone book and telephone and call a cab." In fact, a net-based system might have both available as resources and proceed to use them to achieve the subgoal. In this case, the user might be presented with "Go to the front door and a Yellow Cab should arrive in ten minutes."

An issue that arises in this theory is how to decide which missing axiom (subdialogue) to attack next. The user may have a method for solving goals and prefer to initiate dialogue. In the example, one might assert that a friend will provide a ride to the airport. The system must provide machinery to enable change of initiative when this is necessary. A system which dogmatically followed the above algorithm when the user can steer around difficulties would be undesirable. The solution is to have a mechanism (Guinn, 1996) that estimates the likelihood that the user can better control the dialogue than the machine and which appropriately adjusts initiative to maximize total dialogue efficiency. A part of this mechanism can be a negotiation feature which presents the partial proof tree to the user and argues for a particular strategy. Simultaneously, it examines a partial proof from the user model and judges whether it should have the user take control.

The mode of the interactions is another issue of concern. The individual communications between the machine and other participants should account for the special characteristics of those participants as the interactions occur (Biermann and Long, 1996; Biermann et al. 1997). A user at one moment might prefer an audio spoken interaction because display screens are not currently visible. At another moment, video interactions might be preferred because of audio disturbances. The dialogue machine should track these needs and provide interactions appropriate to the moment.

A final issue concerns the millisecond-by-millisecond details of the interaction. What are the appropriate timings for socially acceptable dialogue? What back-channel responses should occur and what are their meanings? What pauses will occur and what are their meanings? What mechanisms communicate initiative, focus, and engagement? How can these aspects of the interaction be programmed into a machine?

In summary, the talk will cover user modelling for the purposes of dialogue efficiency and control, for individual utterance optimization, and for dialogue engagement. At all levels, the missing axiom theory provides the context for the approach. The talk will discuss these topics and a series of dialogue systems implemented to test and learn about them. It will conclude with a listing of research challenges for the community in the coming years.

References

Alan W. Biermann, Curry Guinn, Michael S. Fulkerson, Greg Keim, Zhang Liang, Douglas Melamed, K. Rajagopalan, Goal-Oriented Multimedia Dialogue with Variable Initiative, in *Foundations of Intelligent Systems*, Zbigniew W. Ras and Andrzej Skowron (Eds.), Springer, Berlin, pages 1-16, 1997.

Alan W. Biermann and Philip M. Long, The Composition of Messages in Speech-Graphics Interactive Systems, *Proceedings of the 1996 International Symposium on Spoken Dialogue*, Philadelphia, Penna., October 2-3, pages 97-100, 1996.

Curry I. Guinn, Mechanisms for Mixed-Initiative Human-Computer Collaborative Discourse, *Proceedings of the 34th Annual Meeting of the ACL*, Santa Cruz, June 24-27, 1996.

Ronnie W. Smith and D. Richard Hipp, *Spoken Natural Language Dialog Systems* , Oxford University Press, New York, 1994.

Ronnie W. Smith, D. Richard Hipp, and Alan W. Biermann, An Architecture for Voice Dialog Systems Based on Prolog-Style Theorem Proving, *Computational Linguistics*, Vol. 21, No. 3, pages 281-320, 1995.

User Modeling: The Long and Winding Road

Gerhard Fischer

Center for LifeLong Learning and Design (L^{3}D), Department of Computer Science
and Institute of Cognitive Science
University of Colorado, Boulder, CO, USA

Abstract. The long and winding road of user modeling is grounded in different episte-mological assumptions exploring different dimensions of the problem. User-modeling research has explored different domains, identified important distinctions underlying different approaches within user modeling research, and created a number of challenging research problems. These issues are explored in the context of high-functionality applications and how our research over the last ten years has addressed the problems of making high-functionality applications more usable, more useful, and more learnable with a variety of different user modeling approaches.

1. Introduction

User modeling is one of a number of research areas that intuitively seem to be winning propositions and worthwhile investments based on their obvious need and potential payoff. One area comparable to user modeling is software reuse. The approaches seem to be appealing, natural, theoretically justifiable, desirable, and needed (e.g., reuse can be justified by the fact that complex systems develop faster if they can build on stable subsystems). But in reality, progress in these areas has been slow and difficult, and success stories are rare.

The research area has

- explored different domains such as: natural language dialog, human computer interaction, intelligent assistants, information retrieval, and high-functionality applications;

- identified important distinctions such as: adaptive versus adaptable components, explicit versus implicit modeling techniques, user models versus task models, canonical versus individual models, and long-term versus short-term models;

- created a number of challenging research problems, such as how to: (1) integrate different modeling techniques; (2) capture the larger (often unarticulated) context and what users are doing (especially beyond the direct interaction with the computer system); (3) identify user goals from low-level interactions; (4) reduce information overload by making information relevant to the task at hand; (5) support differential descriptions by relating new information to known information and concepts; and (6) reach a better balance for task distributions between systems and users.

Some of these challenges will be illustrated in the context of the work that we have done to make high-functionality applications more usable, more useful, and more learnable.

2. High-Functionality Applications

High-functionality applications (HFAs) (such as Unix, MS-Office, Photoshop, Eudora, etc.) are used to model parts of the world and not just to implement algorithms. They are complex systems because "reality is not user friendly". If you ask a 100 different people what features they would like to have in a particular application, you end up with a very large number of features. The design of HFAs must address two problems: (1) the unused functionality must not get in the way and (2) unknown existing functionality must be accessible or delivered at times when it is needed.

We have conducted a variety of empirical studies to determine the usage patterns of HFAs, their structure, their associated help and learning mechanisms. All of these studies have led us to the identification of the qualitative relationships between usage patterns of HFAs as illustrated in **Figure 1**.

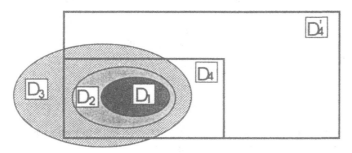

The ovals represent users' knowledge about the system's information space. D_1 represents concepts well known, easily employed, and used regularly by a user. D_2 contains concepts known vaguely and used only occasionally, often requiring passive help systems. D_3 represents concepts users *believe* to exist in the system, some of which lie outside the actual information space. The rectangle D_4 represents the actual infor-

Figure 1: Levels of Users' Knowledge about a System's Information Spaces

mation space of a system. As the functionality of HFAs increases to D_4', little is gained for users unless there are mechanisms to help them relate the additional functionality to their needs.

The area of D_4 that is not part of D_3 is of specific interest to research in user modeling. This is system functionality, whose existence is unknown to users. For the "D_4 and not D_3" domain, information access (the user-initiated location of information when they perceive a need for an operation) is not sufficient, but information delivery (the system volunteering information that it inferred to be relevant to the users' task at hand) is required. Active help systems and critics are required to point out to users functionality that may be useful for their tasks and to help users to avoid to get stuck on suboptimal plateaus.

Figure 1 shows usage patterns of HFAs without taking the users' tasks into account. There is no reason for users to worry about additional existing functionality in D_4, if this functionality is not relevant to their tasks. However, if the system *does* provide functionality in D_4 related to users' tasks, it is desirable to avoid having users unable to perform the task or do so in a suboptimal or error-prone way because they do not know about this functionality. In **Figure 2** the gray rectangle T represents the information that is relevant to the users' task at hand, and the dots represent different pieces of functionality. *Passive* intelligent support systems supporting information access can help users to explore pieces of functionality that are contained in D_3

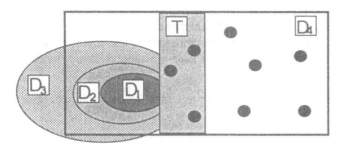

Figure 2: Functionality and its Relevancy to the Task at Hand

and T, whereas *active* intelligent systems supporting information delivery are needed for the functionality contained in T and not in D_3. The functionality in D_4 outside of T is often offered by push systems such as "Did You Know" (DYK) systems [Owen, 1986] or Microsoft's "Tip of the Day" [Horvitz, 1997], which throw decontextualized concepts at users.

"Experts" and Expertise in HFA. "Experts" (users who know everything about a system) no longer exist in HFAs. Being an "expert" is at best an attribute of a specific context, rather than a personal attribute. The different spaces of expertise (determined by individual interest) are illustrated in **Figure 3**. In this *multi-kernel model*, {D_1, U_i} means the area of functionality that is well known to a particular user U_i; for example: U_1 knows about the equation editor; U_2 about mail-merge functionality; U_3 uses a bibliography system for references, and U_4 knows about collaborative writing tools.

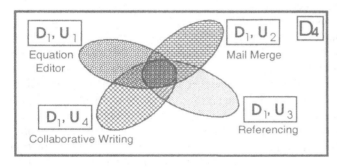

Figure 3: Distributed Expertise in HFAs

3. How Our Research Address the Problems Created by HFAs

Our research related to user modeling has attempted to address the challenges created by HFAs. *Active help systems* [Fischer et al., 1985] were an early attempt to analyze the behavior of users and infer higher-level goals from low-level operations [Horvitz, 1997; Nardi et al., 1998].

HFAs, as argued above, came into existence as environments that are useful for a large number of different users (see **Figure 3**). In order to reduce their complexity, HFAs have often migrated to a collection of domain-oriented subsystems each with their own templates, forms, and their own associated wizards thereby being able to provide additional support for user modeling and assistance not available in more general systems.

In our own research, we have taken this approach further by developing *domain-oriented design environments* [Fischer et al., 1998]. These are environments which model specific domains (such as computer networks, user interfaces, kitchens, and voice dialog design [Sumner et al., 1997]) by allowing designers to engage in authentic tasks from their own respective work practices. Domain-oriented design environments make computers invisible and enable designers to communicate with domain-specific concepts, representations and tools. The domain orientation of these environments makes HFAs more usable, more useful, and more learnable by bringing the objects closer to the conceptual world of their users. In support of user modeling, domain-oriented design environments provide

- *specification components* [Nakakoji, 1993] to allow users to enrich the description of their tasks, and

- *critiquing components* [Fischer et al., 1998] to analyze and infer the task at hand in order to be able to detect and identify the potential for a design information need and then present stored knowledge for designers. We have used the artifact (including its partial construction and partial specification) combined with domain knowledge in the design environment as an index to infer high-level goals from simple user actions. The existence of the specification component has allowed us to complement generic critics (which can be defined at design time) with specific critics whose behavior is dependent on the information provided by individual users at use time.

Domain-oriented design environments integrate a number of components, and the research built around them has tried to developed principles and arguments for the trade-off between adaptive and adaptable approaches [Fischer, 1993; Thomas, 1996]. **Figure 4** shows a screen image from the Voice Dialog Design Environment [Sumner et al., 1997], which supports adaptation mechanisms to allow users to select specific rule sets for critiquing and to determine the intervention strategy for the intrusiveness of the critics ranging from active behavior (every step is immediately critiqued) through intermediate levels to passive behavior (users have to explicitly invoke the critiquing system). Similar solutions can be found in modern spelling correction programs. The need to customize and tailor critiquing systems to individual users' objectives has also been explored in the domain of business graphs and use of color [Gutkauf, 1998].

Domain-oriented design environments pose a number of challenging problems for user modeling. Contrary to Intelligent Tutoring Systems [Burton & Brown, 1982], they model (open-ended) domains in support of self-directed learning and user-directed activities within a domain. They are able to exploit domain models for user modeling [Hollan, 1990; Mastaglio, 1990]. At design time (when the system is developed), domain models including generic critiquing knowledge and support for specification, and end-user adaptation is provided. In these open-ended systems, the task that users engage in cannot be anticipated: they have to be inferred or articulated at use time. Design environments support both adaptable and adaptive components and tune system behavior to the specific needs of individual users and their tasks [Gutkauf, 1998; Nakakoji, 1993].

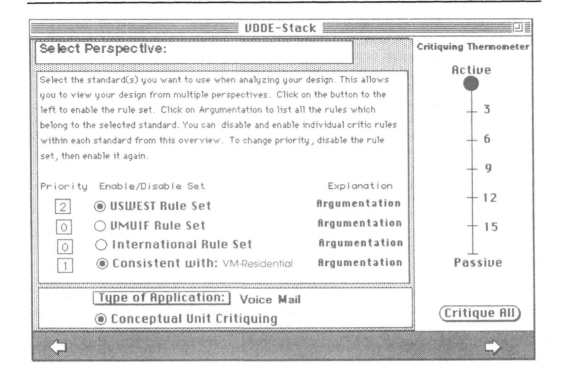

Figure 4: Adaptation Mechanism to Control Different Critiquing Rule Sets
and Different Intervention Strategies

HFAs create challenging *learning problems* that are representative for numerous complex systems. As illustrated with the above figures, nobody learns these systems completely, but users acquire some base functionality and learn additional functionality on demand. User-modeling techniques can effectively support learning on demand [Fischer, 1991] by helping users to identify opportunities to learn additional functionality relevant to their task at hand and to avoid people becoming stuck on suboptimal plateaus. User modeling techniques based on logged user data can support the organization-wide learning of HFAs [Linton et al., 1998].

4. User Modeling and Human-Computer Collaboration

Some of the beginnings of the long and winding road of user modeling were derived from the need and desire to provide better support for human-computer collaboration. Collaboration in this context is defined as *"a process in which two or more agents work together to achieve shared goals"* [Terveen, 1995]. Some fundamental issues (such as shared goals, shared context, control, (co)-adaptation, (co)-evolution, and learning) can be derived from this definition. Human-computer collaboration can be approached from two different perspectives: an emulation and a complementing approach. The emulation approach is based on the metaphor that to improve human-computer collaboration is to endow computers with "human-like abilities". The complementing approach is based on the fact that computers are not human and that human-centered design should exploit the asymmetry of human and computer by developing new interaction and collaboration possibilities [Suchman, 1987].

Historically, the major emphasis in user modeling has focused on the human emulation approach (see for example, [Kobsa & Wahlster, 1989], and the section "user and discourse modeling" in [Maybury & Wahlster, 1998]). However, based on the limited success of the emulating approach, the interest has shifted more and more to the complementing approach [Bobrow, 1991; Fischer, 1990]. There is growing evidence that the problems of user modeling in the complementing approach are more tractable, more feasible, and more desirable, as evidenced by their increasing influence in the design of commercial high-functionality applications [Horvitz, 1997]. As the complexity of commercially available HFAs grows, and as we see more computational assistants (such as agents, advisors, coaches, and critics) appear in widely available commercial applications, a detailed, state-of-the-art analysis and understanding of how people learn, work and collaborate with and around HFAs will provide us with new requirements for the design of user modeling components.

In the long and winding road that is not only behind us but also before us, our understanding of the trade-offs, the promises, and the pitfalls between adaptive and adaptable systems, between push (information delivery) and pull (information access) technologies, and between contextualized information representation and serendipity will hopefully lead us to new ideas and new insights in the design of future human-centered systems supported by adequate user modeling techniques.

Acknowledgments. I would like to thank the members of the Center for LifeLong Learning and Design (L³D) who have contributed to the ideas and perspectives expressed in this paper. A special *thank you* goes to my former students who, in their Ph.D. theses, explored important issues in user modeling as they occur in high-functionality applications, domain-oriented design environments, and critiquing systems.

References

Bobrow, D. G. (1991) "Dimensions of Interaction," *AI Magazine,* 12(3), pp. 64-80.

Burton, R. R. & Brown, J. S. (1982) "An Investigation of Computer Coaching for Informal Learning Activities." In D. H. Sleeman & J. S. Brown (Eds.), *Intelligent Tutoring Systems,* Academic Press, London - New York, pp. 79-98.

Fischer, G. (1990) "Communication Requirements for Cooperative Problem Solving Systems," *Information Systems,* 15(1), pp. 21-36.

Fischer, G. (1991) "Supporting Learning on Demand with Design Environments." In L. Birnbaum (Ed.) *International Conference on the Learning Sciences (Evanston, IL),* Association for the Advancement of Computing in Education, pp. 165-172.

Fischer, G. (1993) "Shared Knowledge in Cooperative Problem-Solving Systems - Integrating Adaptive and Adaptable Components." In M. Schneider-Hufschmidt, T. Kuehme, & U. Malinowski (Eds.), *Adaptive User Interfaces - Principles and Practice,* Elsevier Science Publishers, Amsterdam, pp. 49-68.

Fischer, G., Lemke, A. C., & Schwab, T. (1985) "Knowledge-Based Help Systems." In L. Borman & B. Curtis (Eds.), *Proceedings of CHI'85 Conference on Human Factors in Computing Systems,* ACM, New York, pp. 161-167.

Fischer, G., Nakakoji, K., Ostwald, J., Stahl, G., & Sumner, T. (1998) "Embedding Critics in Design Environments." In M. T. Maybury & W. Wahlster (Eds.), *Readings in Intelligent User Interfaces,* Morgan Kaufmann, San Francisco, pp. 537-561.

Gutkauf, B. (1998) *Improving Design & Communication of Business Graphs through User Adaptive Critiquing,* Ph.D. Dissertation, Mathematics and Computer Science, Universität-GH Paderborn, Paderborn, Germany.

Hollan, J. D. (1990) "User Models and User Interfaces: A Case for Domain Models, Task Models, and Tailorability." In *Proceedings of AAAI-90, Eighth National Conference on Artificial Intelligence,* AAAI Press/The MIT Press, Cambridge, MA, p. 1137.

Horvitz, E. (1997) "Agents with Beliefs: Reflections on Bayesian Methods for User Modeling." In C. P. A. Jameson, C. Tasso (Ed.) *Proceedings of the Sixth International Conference on User Modeling (UM'97),* Springer Wien-New York, Sardegna, Italy, pp. 441-442.

Kobsa, A. & Wahlster, W. (Eds.) (1989) *User Models in Dialog Systems,* Springer-Verlag, New York.

Linton, F., Charron, A., & Joy, D. (1998) *OWL: A Recommender System for Organization-Wide Learning,* at http://www.mitre.org/technology/tech_tats/modeling/owl/Coaching_Software_Skills.pdf.

Mastaglio, T. (1990) *A User-Modelling Approach to Computer-Based Critiquing,* Ph.D. Dissertation, Department of Computer Science, University of Colorado at Boulder, Boulder, CO.

Maybury, M. T. & Wahlster, W. (1998) *Readings in Intelligent User Interfaces,* Morgan Kaufmann, San Francisco.

Nakakoji, K. (1993) *Increasing Shared Understanding of a Design Task Between Designers and Design Environments: The Role of a Specification Component,* Ph.D. Dissertation, Department of Computer Science, University of Colorado at Boulder, Boulder, CO.

Nardi, B. A., Miller, J. R., & Wright, D. J. (1998) "Collaborative, Programmable Intelligent Agents," *Communications of the ACM,* 41(3), pp. 96-104.

Owen, D. (1986) "Answers First, Then Questions." In D. A. Norman & S. W. Draper (Eds.), *User-Centered System Design, New Perspectives on Human-Computer Interaction,* Lawrence Erlbaum Associates, Inc., Hillsdale, NJ, pp. 361-375.

Suchman, L. A. (1987) *Plans and Situated Actions,* Cambridge University Press, Cambridge, UK.

Sumner, T., Bonnardel, N., & Kallak, B. H. (1997) "The Cognitive Ergonomics of Knowledge-Based Design Support Systems." In S. Pemberton (Ed.) *Proceedings of CHI 97 Conference on Human Factors in Computing Systems,* ACM/Addison-Wesley, pp. 83-90.

Terveen, L. G. (1995) "An Overview of Human-Computer Collaboration," *Knowledge-Based Systems Journal, Special Issue on Human-Computer Collaboration,* 8(2-3), pp. 67-81.

Thomas, C. G. (1996) *To Assist the User: On the Embedding of Adaptive and Agent-Based Mechanisms,* R. Oldenburg Verlag, München/Wien.

User Modeling in Adaptive Interfaces

Pat Langley*

Adaptive Systems Group
DaimlerChrysler Research and Technology Center
1510 Page Mill Road, Palo Alto, CA 94304 USA
LANGLEY@RTNA.DAIMLERCHRYSLER.COM

Abstract. In this paper we examine the notion of adaptive user interfaces, interactive systems that invoke machine learning to improve their interaction with humans. We review some previous work in this emerging area, ranging from software that filters information to systems that support more complex tasks like scheduling. After this, we describe three ongoing research efforts that extend this framework in new directions. Finally, we review previous work that has addressed similar issues and consider some challenges that are presented by the design of adaptive user interfaces.

1   The Need for Automated User Modeling

As computers have become more widespread, the software that runs on them has also become more interactive and responsive. Only a few early users remember the days of programming on punch cards and submitting overnight jobs, and even the era of time-sharing systems and text editors has become a dim memory. Modern operating systems support a wide range of interactive software, from WYSIWYG editors to spreadsheets to computer games, most embedded in some form of graphical user interface. Such packages have become an essential part of business and academic life, with millions of people depending on them to accomplish their daily goals.

Naturally, the increased emphasis on interactive software has led to greater interest in the study of human-computer interaction. However, most research in this area has focused on the manner in which computer interfaces present information and choices to the user, and thus tells only part of the story. An equally important issue, yet one that has received much less attention, concerns the *content* that the interface offers to the user. And a concern with content leads directly to a focus on *user models*, since it seems likely that people will differ in the content they prefer to encounter during their interactions with computers.

Developers of software for the Internet are quite aware of the need for personalized content, and many established portals on the World Wide Web provide simple tools for filtering information. But these tools typically focus on a narrow class of applications and require manual setting of parameters, a process that users are likely to find tedious. Moreover, some facets of users' preferences may be reflected in their behavior but not subject to introspection. Clearly, there is a need for increased personalization in many areas of interactive software, both in supporting a greater variety of tasks and in ways to automate this process. This suggests turning to techniques from machine learning in order to personalize computer interfaces.

---

* Also affiliated with the Institute for the Study of Learning and Expertise and the Center for the Study of Language and Information at Stanford University.

In the rest of this paper, we examine the notion of *adaptive user interfaces* – systems that learn a user model from traces of interaction with that user. We start by defining adaptive interfaces more precisely, drawing a close analogy with algorithms for machine learning. Next, we consider some examples of such software artifacts that have appeared in the literature, after which we report on three research efforts that attempt to extend the basic framework in new directions. Finally, we discuss kinships between adaptive user interfaces and some similar paradigms, then close with some challenges they pose for researchers and software developers.

2   Adaptive User Interfaces and Machine Learning

For most readers, the basic idea of an adaptive user interface will already be clear, but for the sake of discussion, we should define this notion somewhat more precisely:

> An adaptive user interface is a software artifact that improves its ability to interact with a user by constructing a user model based on partial experience with that user.

This definition makes clear that an adaptive interface does not exist in isolation, but rather is designed to interact with a human user. Moreover, for the system to be adaptive, it must improve its interaction with that user, and simple memorization of such interactions does not suffice. Rather, improvement should result from generalization over past experiences and carry over to new user interactions.

The above definition will seem familiar to some readers, and for good reason, since it takes the same form as common definitions of machine learning (e.g., Langley, 1995). The main differences are that the user plays the role of the environment in which learning occurs, the user model takes the place of the learned knowledge base, and interaction with the user serves as the performance task on which learning should lead to improvement. In this view, adaptive user interfaces constitute a special class of learning systems that are designed to aid humans, in contrast with much of the early applied work on machine learning, which aimed to develop knowledge-based systems that would replace domain experts.

Despite this novel emphasis, many lessons acquired from these earlier applications of machine learning should prove relevant in the design of adaptive interfaces. The most important has been the realization that we are still far from entirely automating the learning process, and that some essential steps must still be done manually (Brodley and Smyth, 1997; Langley and Simon, 1995; Rudström, 1995). Briefly, to solve an applied problem using established induction methods, the developer must typically:

- reformulate the problem in some form that these methods can directly address;
- engineer a set of features that describe the training cases adequately; and
- devise some approach to collecting and preparing the training instances.

Only after the developer has addressed these issues can he run some learning method over the data to produce the desired domain knowledge or, in the case of an adaptive interface, the desired user model.

Moreover, there is an emerging consensus within the applied learning community that these steps of problem formulation, representation engineering, and data collection/preparation play a role at least as important as the induction stage itself. Indeed, there is a common belief that, once they are handled well, the particular induction method one uses has little effect on the outcome (Langley and Simon, 1995). In contrast, most academic work on machine learning still focuses on refining induction techniques and downplays the steps that must occur before and after their invocation. Indeed, some research groups still emphasize differences between broad classes of learning methods, despite evidence that decision-tree induction, connectionist algorithms, case-based methods, and probabilistic schemes often produce very similar results.

We will adopt the former viewpoint in our discussion of adaptive user interfaces. As a result, we will have little to say about the particular learning methods used to construct and refine user models, but we will have comments about the formulation of the task, the features used to describe behavior, the source of data about user preferences, and similar issues. This bias reflects our belief that strategies which have proved successful in other applications of machine learning will also serve us well in the design of adaptive interfaces.

3 Examples of Adaptive User Interfaces

We can clarify the notion of an adaptive user interface by considering some examples that have appeared in the literature during recent years. Many of these systems focus on the generic task of *information filtering*, which involves directing a user's attention toward items from a large set that he is likely to find interesting or useful. Naturally, the most popular applications revolve around the World Wide Web, which provides both a wealth of information to filter and a convenient mechanism for interacting with users. However, the same basic techniques can be extended to broader *recommendation* tasks, such as suggesting products a consumer might want to buy.

One example comes from Pazzani, Muramatsu, and Billsus (1996), who describe SYSKILL & WEBERT, an adaptive interface which recommends web pages on a given topic that a user should find interesting. Much like typical search engines, this system presents the user with a list of web pages, but it also labels those candidates it predicts the user will especially like or dislike. Moreover, it lets the user mark pages as desirable or undesirable, and the system records the marked pages as training data for learning the user's preferences. SYSKILL & WEBERT encodes each user model in terms of the probabilities that certain words will occur given that the person likes (or dislikes) the document. The system invokes the naive Bayesian classifier to learn these probabilities and to predict whether the user will find a particular page desirable.

This general approach to selection and learning is often referred to as *content-based filtering*. Briefly, this scheme represents each item with a set of descriptors, usually the words that occur in a document, and the filtering system uses these descriptors as predictive features when deciding whether to recommend a document to the user. This biases the selection process toward documents that are similar to ones the user has previously ranked highly. Other examples of adaptive user interfaces that embody the content-based approach include Lang's (1995) NEWSWEEDER, which recommends news stories, and Boone's (1998) Re:Agent, which suggests actions for handling electronic mail. Of course, content-based methods are also widely used in search engines for the World Wide Web, and they predominate in the literature on information retrieval, but these typically do not employ learning algorithms to construct users models.

Another example of an adaptive interface is Shardanand and Maes' (1995) RINGO, an interactive system that recommends movies a person might enjoy. To this end, the system requires the user to rate a series of sample movies, from which it constructs a simple profile. RINGO then finds other people who have similar profiles to the current user and recommends films that they liked but that the current user has not yet rated. This general approach is usually called *social* or *collaborative filtering*, since it makes predictions about items based on feedback from many different users. Unlike content-based methods, collaborative approaches require no explicit descriptions of the objects or products being recommended, which appears to make them well suited for subjective domains like art, where users base their decisions on intangible features that are difficult to measure. Collaborative filtering is used by a number of vendors on the World Wide Web, including AMAZON.COM, to sell books and other items.

Although researchers typically contrast content-based and collaborative filtering, the two approaches are not mutually exclusive. For example, Balabanovic (1998) describes FAB, a system that retains profiles both for individual users and for topics, and that combines their predictions to give both content-based and collaborative behavior. Basu, Hirsh, and Cohen (1998) report a different approach that uses rule induction over both user preferences and item descriptions to give combined recommendations. Such work builds on the intuition that the two approaches have different inductive biases, so that taking both content and social factors into account will produce better filtering systems.

Systems for information filtering and recommendation are probably the most common examples of adaptive user interfaces, but they are certainly not the only types possible. Some problems involve more than just selecting from among a large set of documents or products; they require generative systems that actually create new knowledge structures to satisfy the user's goals. Hinkle and Toomey (1994) describe one such advisory system, CLAVIER, that proposes loads and layouts for aircraft parts to be cured in a convection oven. The system draws on previous layouts stored in a case library, preferring candidates that include currently needed parts and ones that have cured well in the past. A graphical interface presents a suggested load and layout to the user, who can then replace parts or rearrange their positions, producing yet another case for the library. CLAVIER has been in continuous use since 1990, generating two to three loads per day and nearly eliminating problems caused by incompatible loads.[1]

Another intriguing adaptive interface comes from Hermens and Schlimmer (1994), who developed an interactive aide for filling out repetitive vacation forms. Their system uses rules to predict likely values for various fields in the form based on the values of earlier fields, but these are defaults that the user can always override. Once the user completes the form, the program treats the new entries as training data and invokes an induction algorithm to revise its existing rules. Three administrative staff used the system during an academic year, and inspection of user traces showed that it reduced keystrokes by 87 percent over this period. Although this work did not focus on user modeling per se, Schlimmer and Hermens (1993) took a very similar approach in another adaptive interface for note taking. This system learns a grammar that predicts the order and content of a user's notes, aiming to reduce keystrokes and help them better organize their thoughts on a topic.

The Calendar Apprentice (Dent et al., 1992) also directly addresses issues of personalization, in this case aiding a secretary who must schedule meetings for a professor. The system proposes default values for the day, time, duration, and location of a meeting, which the user can either accept or replace with her own choices. Again, each such decision provides data for learning a user model, although the induction process occurs every night rather than in true online fashion.

---

[1] Although the CLAVIER work did not emphasize issues of personalization, one can still view the system as developing a user model from feedback.

The system learns a distinct set of rules for each of the four attributes that it aims to predict; thus, it recasts the scheduling task as a set of separate classification decisions, an issue to which we will return later. A departmental secretary used the Calendar Apprentice on a regular basis for some years to schedule a faculty member's meetings.

This sample certainly does not exhaust the list of adaptive user interfaces present in the literature. The most popular topics remain information-filtering tasks like sorting electronic mail and finding interesting web pages, but the number of applications is certain to grow as people become increasingly reliant on the World Wide Web and as developers realize the potential of machine learning to construct accurate user models.

4   New Directions in Adaptive Interfaces

Although a variety of research and development efforts have shown the potential of adaptive user interfaces, there remains considerable room for extending their flexibility and their interaction style. Here we describe three ongoing projects designed to explore new directions in the automated construction of user models. The first effort takes a novel approach to the task of making recommendations, whereas the other two deal with a different class of problems not typically addressed in research on adaptive interfaces.

4.1   A Conversational Approach to Recommendation

Most work on information filtering and recommendation systems follows an approach originally developed for document retrieval: the user enters some topic or keywords and the system responds with an ordered list of candidates. This scheme makes sense for situations in which the user wants multiple items, as when reading news stories or finding Web pages, but seems much less appropriate for recommendation tasks in which he wants a single item, as when selecting a hotel, movie, or restaurant. Ordered lists also have drawbacks when the user must rely on auditory presentations, as when he is driving an automobile.

In response, we are developing a conversational interface, the *Adaptive Place Advisor*, designed to recommend places of interest, such as restaurants or hotels, that the user might want as his destination. Rather than accepting keywords and returning a long list of choices, the system carries out a dialogue with the user that helps him decide on a target location. More specifically, the advisor asks the user a series of questions, each designed to reduce the number of acceptable candidates, and the user's answers provide constraints that narrow the search. The current version focuses on recommending places to eat, and it draws on a database of nearly one thousand restaurants in the San Francisco Bay Area, each described in terms of fields like cuisine, price range, city, and parking availability. The system also gives sample values of each field on request, and it lets the user replace suggested questions and even change answers he has given earlier in the dialogue. Elio and Haddadi (1998) present a detailed design for this conversational interface.

We can view the Adaptive Place Advisor as a tool for the interactive construction of database queries, with the system recommending fields that should be specified and the user giving their values. Another interpretation is that the system and user pursue an interactive process of constraint satisfaction, with the former suggesting variables and the latter setting their values. But we hope users will treat the system simply as a knowledgeable advisor that helps them select effectively from a large set of restaurants. The current version of the Place Advisor includes a graphical interface, displayed in Figure 1, that shows system questions (restaurant attributes) on

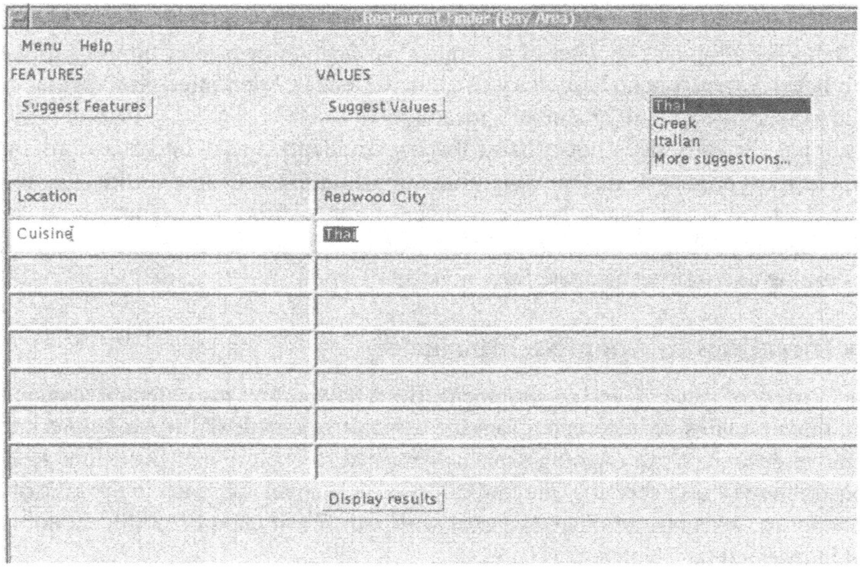

Figure 1. Graphical display for the Adaptive Place Advisor, showing a state after the system has asked two questions and received answers from the user.

the left and user answers (selected values) on the right. The box at the bottom presents additional information about a restaurant, such as its name and address, but only after the dialogue has reduced the candidate set to a few restaurants.

In future versions, we intend to replace this graphical display with a spoken interface that can handle a reduced subset of English. This extension should be tractable, since user responses will typically be limited to short answers and queries rather than unconstrained continuous speech. The next version will also include a mechanism for modeling the user, not at the level of complete items, but at the finer-grained level of the questions he prefers and the answers he tends to give. Our approach here involves collecting statistics about the questions the user is willing to answer, as well as his answers to each question, possibly conditioned on answers to previous ones. As the system gains experience with a user, it should come to suggest options that he finds attractive, thus reducing the need for interaction. The overall aim is not only to recommend restaurants that the user finds desirable, but to improve the efficiency of the communication process, as happens when people get to know each other. Of course, this is an empirical prediction that we must test with actual users, but we are confident that some version of the conversational approach will prove effective.

4.2   An Adaptive Route Advisor

Another limitation of previous work on adaptive user interfaces has been its emphasis on 'choice' problems like selecting web pages or books. Adaptive advisors for more complex decision-making tasks, when they occur, typically decompose the problem into a number of separate one-step classification problems, as in Dent et al.'s Calendar Apprentice and Hermens and Schlim-

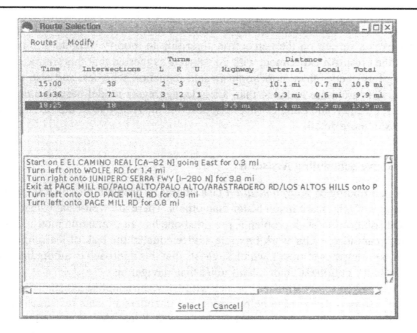

Figure 2. Graphical display for the Adaptive Route Advisor, showing summaries of the two initially proposed routes, a third candidate generated from the first in response to the user's request for 'more highway', and turn-by-turn directions for this route.

mer's form-filling assistant.[2] We have developed another advisory system, the *Adaptive Route Advisor*, that deals more directly with such a complex task: generating and selecting routes between a driver's current location and his destination. Like standard navigation aides, our system carries out a best-first search over a digital map to find an optimal route, then displays the result both graphically and with turn-by-turn directions.

However, the Adaptive Route Advisor differs from its predecessors in some essential ways. First, rather than optimizing paths along a single dimension, it finds the route that is best according to a weighted combination of features including the estimated driving time, number of intersections, number of turns, distance along different road types, and familiarity of segments. The weights on this evaluation function constitute the system's user model, with higher scores reflecting greater importance to the driver. Second, as illustrated in Figure 2, the system always presents the user with at least *two* routes, one the optimum according to the current model and the others found by varying its weights and penalizing overlaps with the first route. Moreover, the user can ask the system to improve a given route along some dimension, which leads it to generate another candidate using different weights.

Although desirable in their own right, these features also let the Adaptive Route Advisor collect data on user preferences in an unobtrusive manner. Whenever the driver selects a route, the system assumes that he likes that alternative more than the others displayed. If the current

---

[2] Hinkle and Toomey's layout advisor is a clear exception to this trend, but such efforts are rare compared to work cast in terms of simple choice tasks.

user model predicts this decision, no changes are necessary, but if the prediction is incorrect, the system invokes a variant on the perceptron algorithm to modify weights in directions that tend to correct the error. An experiment with 24 subjects suggested that this simple approach to driver modeling fares better than more sophisticated induction schemes, and also showed that personalized models are more accurate than a single, aggregate model based on data from all subjects. Rogers, Fiechter, and Langley (in press) describe the Adaptive Route Advisor and these empirical results in more detail.

4.3 An Interactive Scheduling Assistant

We can view route finding as an *optimization* task, that is, a problem in which there are many solutions, but some of which are much better than others. There are well-established algorithms for finding good solutions to such problems, provided one has an evaluation metric or objective function to order candidates. Our work on route advice equated the task of learning this metric with the task of building a user model, which suggests that this approach to automated modeling might prove useful for optimization problems other than navigation.

In fact, we have taken a very similar approach with INCA, an adaptive assistant for interactive scheduling. The system is designed to help incident commanders allocate resources in response to emergencies that involve hazardous materials. To this end, it includes a knowledge base which specifies actions that constitute legal responses to spills and fires for various types of materials. INCA differs from the Route Advisor in that, rather than generating candidates from scratch, it retrieves schedules from a case library that are similar in terms of their situation and the resources they require.

After retrieving likely schedules from memory, the system shows the top few candidates to the user, who selects one for improvement. If desired, he can also specify the criterion (related to the spill, the fire, and the health hazard) along which improvement should occur and the type of revision (adding a job, as well as changing its start time or duration). INCA carries out a limited beam search through a repair space to generate new schedules that are better according to an evaluation metric. The system then presents a small set of successors to the user, who selects one of these schedules (as shown in Figure 3) and asks for further improvements. This process continues until the user finds a proposed schedule that he considers acceptable.

INCA's differences from the Adaptive Route Advisor – starting from a retrieved case and searching through a repair space – do not keep it from using the same approach to user modeling. The system's users still select one candidate from a set of options, and this still gives feedback about which schedules they prefer over others. Moreover, INCA also uses a weighted combination of features to direct search through the space of schedules, and it calls a modified perceptron algorithm to revise weights when the user decides to revise a candidate not ranked best by the current model. The fact that this approach to data collection and user modeling fits so well into two otherwise different frameworks recommends it as a promising approach to adaptive interfaces for optimization tasks. Gervasio, Iba, and Langley (in press) describe the INCA system in more detail, along with some encouraging results on synthetic subjects.

Before moving on, we should contrast our work on routing and scheduling advice with other approaches to adaptive interfaces for complex decision-making tasks. As we noted earlier, most work in this area transforms a multi-step problem into a number of single-step tasks. This makes excellent sense for applications in which the steps are relatively independent, such as Hermens

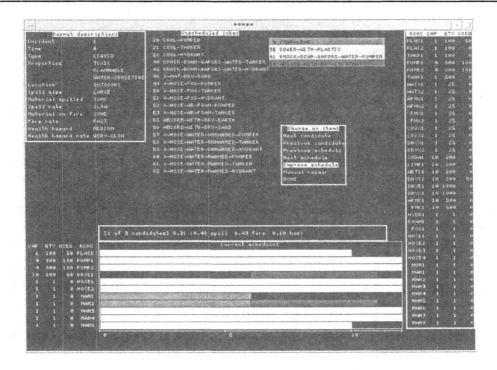

Figure 3. The graphical display for INCA, showing the incident description (top left), unscheduled and scheduled jobs (top center), resources (right), user menu (center), and a current schedule (bottom).

and Schlimmer's form-filling domain. But such a decomposition seems less suited for optimization problems, where different criteria interact, as in Dent et al.'s Calendar Apprentice. Again, the previous system most akin to INCA and the Adaptive Route Advisor is CLAVIER, since it treats each layout as a single item that it evaluates as a whole.

5   Relation to Other Paradigms

Although the notion of adaptive user interfaces is relatively recent, this approach to interactive software has some clear relatives in the literature. Perhaps the closest in spirit has been work on *programming by demonstration*, a paradigm that aims to construct personalized interfaces by observing the user's behavior. One example is Cypher's (1991) EAGER system, which learns iterative procedures from observation in a HyperCard setting, then highlights the actions it anticipates for the user's approval. In general, systems in this framework focus on quite constrained tasks that support online learning from very few training cases, but they carry out induction every bit as much as ones that use less domain-specific learning algorithms. A more significant difference is their emphasis on learning macro-operators, which can reduce the effective length of solutions, rather than learning (as in most adaptive interfaces) to order alternatives, which can reduce the effective branching factor. A collection by Cypher (1993) contains a representative sample of work on programming by demonstration.

Another older yet kindred paradigm is *intelligent tutoring systems*, which sometimes draw on techniques from machine learning to personalize instruction. For instance, O'Shea (1979) embedded simple learning methods in his quadratic tutor in order to model its student's skills and thus influence instructional sequences. Langley and Ohlsson's (1984) ACM drew on methods for learning search-control knowledge to model individual student errors in arithmetic, and more recently, Baffes and Mooney (1995) have adapted techniques for theory revision to develop personalized student models using data on programming errors. More generally, Anderson's (1984) technique of *model tracing* relies on careful observation of student behavior in the same way as adaptive user interfaces, giving advice only when the student diverges from acceptable paths. The main difference between the two paradigms is their application of user models, with tutoring systems aiming to change student behavior and adaptive interfaces trying to support more effective decision making.

A third tradition, known as *learning apprentices*, also holds much in common with adaptive user interfaces. This framework was originally proposed as a method for creating knowledge-based systems for complex problem-solving tasks. Rather than deal directly with the serious problem of credit assignment, this approach collected traces of an expert's decisions in the domain and learned to imitate his behavior. For instance, Mitchell, Mahadevan, and Steinberg (1985) used this technique to form search-control rules for VLSI design, transforming a multi-step learning problem into a set of independent supervised induction tasks. More recently, Sammut, Hurst, Kedizer, and Michie (1992) have used a very similar approach, which they call *behavioral cloning*, to learn control knowledge for domains such as flying an airplane. Learning apprentices and adaptive interfaces differ mainly in their perspectives, with the former emphasizing how domain experts can ease the process of machine learning and the latter how machine learning can reduce user effort.

Of course, there exist other approaches to user modeling that do not rely on machine learning. Some researchers favor manual construction of models for 'stereotypical' users, as Rich (1979) did in her early work on book recommendation. In this framework, the interactive system assigns a user to membership in some predefined class based on his behavior or his answers to questions. This process is more akin to classification or categorization than to induction, although the system can still use the inferred class to make predictions about the user's preferences or behavior. Nor are the two approaches mutually exclusive, since a system could use a predefined class description as an initial user model and then use learning to fine tune it based on additional behavior traces.

Another paradigm constructs a new model for each user, but accomplishes this feat by extracting explicit preferences rather than through induction over user traces. Linden, Hanks, and Lesh (1997) describe one such system, the *Automated Travel Assistant*, that addresses the selection of airline flights. Their formulation shares some important features with the Adaptive Route Advisor, in that it casts user models as weights on numeric criteria and presents users with choices in order to better identify their concerns. However, their system uses these choices to elicit generic preferences directly from the user, rather than learning them from training data, and there is no evidence that it retains the user model across different travel tasks.

We should also consider the place of adaptive interfaces in the context of research on human cognition. There exists a large literature on this topic that describes computational models for many domains, including most of those we have considered here. However, nearly all computational models of cognition focus on the *process* of human thought and decision making. This contrasts with work on adaptive user interfaces, which deals primarily with the *content* of human decisions. Such systems construct cognitive models that predict future behavior, but these models lay no claim to operate on the same representations, or draw on the same mechanisms, as does the human cognitive architecture. Nevertheless, if one's goal is more effective software, user models of this sort have practical advantages over the more detailed process models that predominate in cognitive science.

6   Challenges in Adaptive User Interfaces

We proposed earlier that many of the lessons mastered from the study of machine learning should carry over directly to work on adaptive user interfaces. This suggests some clear challenges to which any designer must respond if he hopes to create a viable system that learns user models from interaction traces. However, adaptive interfaces also differ in some important respects from applications of machine learning like data mining, leading to other challenges that appear unique to this new class of artifacts.

As in other applications of machine learning, the developer of an adaptive user interface must first find a way to recast the problem of user modeling in terms of a standard induction task, typically some form of supervised learning. This includes selecting some level of aggregation at which to make predictions and deciding on the classes the system will predict. Most work on information filtering and recommendation treats documents and products as single items, attempting to place them into two classes, such as interesting and uninteresting, but the Adaptive Place Advisor shows one can model users at finer grains as well, including the level of conversational actions. Similar issues arise for more complex decision-making tasks. For example, Hermens and Schlimmer treated form filling as a set of separate prediction tasks, as Dent et al. did for scheduling meetings, whereas INCA and the Adaptive Route Advisor handled schedules and routes as complete entities.

An adaptive interface developer must also decide how to encode user data and user models, as such representation engineering can be an important factor in making induction tractable. As we have seen, most adaptive systems for information filtering represent documents in terms of the words they contain, though some recommendation systems use a more constrained attribute-value scheme, as illustrated by the Adaptive Place Advisor. In essence, the distinction between content-based and collaborative filtering revolves around the best way to represent user data and models. One key to designing a successful adaptive interface is to select descriptors that can predict user behavior, but to include as few such descriptors as possible, since irrelevant features can reduce the learning rate. For example, in both INCA and the Adaptive Route Advisor, we decided on a few global features that we felt would most concern users, rather than a larger set that would be more complete.

A third challenge in applied machine learning concerns the collection of training cases. Fortunately, by their very definition, adaptive user interfaces are designed to *interact* with people, and traces of such interaction give a ready source of data to support learning. However, one can implement this data collection in very different ways. Some adaptive interfaces require users to give explicit feedback about system suggestions, such as by rating candidate items. Others rely on implicit feedback based on interactions that would occur naturally even if no user modeling were involved, such as requesting improved schedules in INCA and answering questions posed by the Adaptive Place Advisor. Billsus and Pazzani (in press) have incorporated a fine example of this idea into NEWS DUDE, an adaptive interface that reads news stories and lets listeners interrupt items they do not want to hear. This means that the system knows which words the user has encountered by the time he interrupts a story, which it uses to constrain the learning process. In general, users should favor adaptive interfaces that collect data on their preferences in unobtrusive ways, other things being equal.

One difference between adaptive user interfaces and other applications of machine learning is the embedded nature of the induction process. This characteristic suggests the need for *on-line* learning, in which the knowledge base is updated each time a user interaction occurs. This contrasts with most work in data mining, which assumes that all data are available at the outset. Because adaptive user interfaces collect data during their interaction with humans, one naturally expects them to improve during that use, making them 'learning' systems rather than 'learned' systems. This is not a strict requirement, in that the interface could collect data during a session, run the induction method offline, and then incorporate the results into the knowledge base before the next session, but the online approach seems most desirable, and thus places constraints on system design.

Because adaptive user interfaces construct models by observing their user's behavior, a final challenge is to support *rapid* learning. The issue here in not CPU time, but rather the number of training cases needed to generate an accurate model of user preferences. Most data-mining applications assume large amounts of data, typically enough to induce accurate knowledge bases even when the model class includes many parameters. In contrast, adaptive interfaces rely on a precious resource – the user's time – which makes the available data much more limited. This suggests relying on induction methods that achieve high accuracy from small training sets over those with higher asymptotic accuracy but slower learning rates. Other factors being equal, an adaptive interface that learns rapidly should be more competitive than ones that learn slowly.

7 Concluding Remarks

In this paper, we considered the notion of adaptive user interfaces and explored its relation to machine learning. We reviewed a variety of systems that invoke induction algorithms to automatically construct user models from interaction traces, designed for tasks ranging from information filtering to generating layouts and schedules. We also described three research efforts on new types of adaptive interfaces. One of these systems, the Adaptive Place Advisor, supports a conversational recommendation process and models users at a finer grain than typically done. Two other prototypes – the Adaptive Route Advisor and INCA – provide assistance on optimization tasks – route selection and crisis scheduling – and model user preferences as a numeric evaluation function. We also discussed some related research paradigms and examined five challenges that arise when developing any system of this sort.

Clearly, we have only started to explore the design space of adaptive interfaces, and there undoubtedly exist other ways in which we can make them more effective. But these improvements will only come from developing prototypes for particular domains, running experimental studies with human subjects, and evaluating their ability to personalize themselves to the user's needs. Fortunately, we should be able to borrow many tools and heuristics about the design and evaluation of complex systems from the parent fields of machine learning and human-computer interaction. This suggests that the study of adaptive user interfaces will mature rapidly, now that scientists and engineers have started to recognize their considerable potential.

Acknowledgements

We thank our collaborators on the research efforts described in this paper, including Renée Elio, Claude-Nicolas Fiechter, Melinda Gervasio, Afsaneh Haddadi, Wayne Iba, Seth Rogers, Cynthia Thompson, and Lei Wang. An earlier version of this survey appeared in the *Proceedings of the 21st Annual German Conference on Artificial Intelligence*, and the development of INCA was funded by the Office of Naval Research under Grant No. N00014-94-1-0505.

References

Anderson, J. R. (1984). Cognitive psychology and intelligent tutoring. *Proceedings of the Sixth Annual Conference of the Cognitive Science Society*, 37–43. Boulder, CO: Lawrence Erlbaum.

Baffes, P. T., and Mooney, R. J. (1995). A novel application of theory refinement to student modeling. *Proceedings of the Thirteenth National Conference on Artificial Intelligence*, 403–408. Portland, OR: AAAI Press.

Balabanovic, M. (1998). Exploring versus exploiting when learning user models for text recommendation. *User Modeling and User-Adapted Interaction* 8: 71–102.

Basu, C., Hirsh, H., and Cohen, W. (1998). Recommendation as classification: Using social and content-based information in recommendation. *Proceedings of the Fifteenth National Conference on Artificial Intelligence*, 714–720. Madison, WI: AAAI Press.

Billsus, D., and Pazzani, M. (in press). A personal news agent that talks, learns and explains. *Proceedings of the Third International Conference on Autonomous Agents*. Seattle: ACM Press.

Boone, G. (1998). Concept features in Re:Agent, an intelligent email agent. *Proceedings of the Second International Conference on Autonomous Agents*, 141–148. Minneapolis, MN: ACM Press.

Brodley, C. E., and Smyth, P. (1997). Applying classification algorithms in practice. *Statistics and Computing* 7: 45–56.

Cypher, A. (1991). EAGER: Programming repetitive tasks by example. *Proceedings of the Conference on Human Factors in Computing Systems*, 33–39. New Orleans: ACM.

Cypher, A. (Ed.). (1993). *Watch What I Do: Programming by Demonstration*. Cambridge, MA: MIT Press.

Dent, L., Boticario, J., McDermott, J., Mitchell, T., and Zaborowski, D. (1992). A personal learning apprentice. *Proceedings of the Tenth National Conference on Artificial Intelligence*, 96–103. San Jose, CA: AAAI Press.

Elio, R., and Haddadi, A. (1998). *Dialog management for an adaptive database assistant* (Technical Report 98-3). Daimler-Benz Research and Technology Center, Palo Alto, CA.

Gervasio, M. T., Iba, W., and Langley, P. (in press). Learning user evaluation functions for adaptive scheduling assistance. *Proceedings of the Sixteenth International Conference on Machine Learning*. Bled, Slovenia: Morgan Kaufmann.

Hermens, L. A., and Schlimmer, J. C. (1994). A machine-learning apprentice for the completion of repetitive forms. *IEEE Expert* 9: 28–33.

Hinkle, D., and Toomey, C. N. (1994). CLAVIER: Applying case-based reasoning to composite part fabrication. *Proceedings of the Sixth Innovative Applications of Artificial Intelligence Conference*, 55–62. Seattle, WA: AAAI Press.

Lang, K. (1995). NEWSWEEDER: Learning to filter news. *Proceedings of the Twelfth International Conference on Machine Learning*, 331–339. Lake Tahoe, CA: Morgan Kaufmann.

Langley, P. (1995). *Elements of Machine Learning*. San Francisco: Morgan Kaufmann.

Langley, P. (1997). Machine learning for adaptive user interfaces. *Proceedings of the 21st German Annual Conference on Artificial Intelligence*, 53–62. Freiburg, Germany: Springer.

Langley, P., and Ohlsson, S. (1984). Automated cognitive modeling. *Proceedings of the Fourth National Conference on Artificial Intelligence*, 193–197. Austin, TX: Morgan Kaufmann.

Langley, P., and Simon, H. A. (1995). Applications of machine learning and rule induction. *Communications of the ACM* 38: 55–64.

Linden, G., Hanks, S., and Lesh, N. (1997). Interactive assessment of user preference models: The Automated Travel Assistant. *Proceedings of the Sixth International Conference on User Modeling*, 67–78. Chia Laguna, Sardinia: Springer.

Mitchell, T. M., Mahadevan, S., and Steinberg, L. (1985). LEAP: A learning apprentice for VLSI design. *Proceedings of the Ninth International Joint Conference on Artificial Intelligence*, 573–580. Los Angeles, CA: Morgan Kaufmann.

O'Shea, T. (1979). A self-improving quadratic tutor. *International Journal of Man-Machine Studies* 11: 97–124.

Pazzani, M., Muramatsu, J., and Billsus, D. (1996). SYSKILL & WEBERT: Identifying interesting web sites. *Proceedings of the Thirteenth National Conference on Artificial Intelligence*, 54–61. Portland, OR: AAAI Press.

Rich, E. (1979). User modeling via stereotypes. *Cognitive Science* 3: 329–354.

Rogers, S., Fiechter, C., and Langley, P. (in press). An adaptive interactive agent for route advice. *Proceedings of the Third International Conference on Autonomous Agents*. Seattle: ACM Press.

Rudström, A. (1995). *Applications of machine learning*. Licentiate thesis, Department of Computer and Systems Sciences, Stockholm University, Sweden.

Sammut, C., Hurst, S., Kedizer, D., and Michie, D. (1992). Learning to fly. *Proceedings of the Ninth International Conference on Machine Learning*, 385–393. Aberdeen, Scotland: Morgan Kaufmann.

Schlimmer, J. C., and Hermens, L. A. (1993). Software agents: Completing patterns and constructing user interfaces. *Journal of Artificial Intelligence Research* 1: 61–89.

Shardanand, U., and Maes, P. (1995). Social information filtering: Algorithms for automating 'word of mouth'. *Proceedings of the Conference on Human Factors in Computing Systems*, 210–217. Denver, CO: ACM Press.

Adaptive Learning Systems in the World Wide Web

Gerhard Weber

Department of Psychology, University of Education Freiburg, Germany

Abstract: With the steadily growing demand for further education, the World Wide Web is becoming a more and more popular vehicle for delivering on-line learning courses. A challenging research goal is the development of advanced Web-based learning applications that can offer some amount of interactivity and adaptivity in order to support learners who their start learning with different background knowledge and skills. In existing on-line learning systems, some types of adaptivity and adaptability require different types of user models. This paper briefly introduces ELM-ART, an example of a substantial adaptive learning system on the WWW. It uses several adaptive techniques and offers some degree of adaptability. The adaptive techniques are based on two different types of user models: a multi-layered overlay model that allows for sophisticated link annotation and individual curriculum sequencing; and an episodic learner model that enables the system to analyze and diagnose problem solutions and to offer individualized examples to programming problems. The last section gives an overview of empirical results with adaptive learning systems and discusses the problems concerned with the evaluation of complex learning systems in real-world learning situations.

1 Introduction

The World Wide Web is becoming an increasingly popular vehicle for delivering on-line learning courses (Khan, 1997). The benefits of Web-based education are clear: classroom independence and platform independence. An application installed and supported in one place can be used by learners from any place in the world. They only have to be equipped with any kind of Internet-connected computer.

With the steadily growing demand for further education in all areas of life, intranet-based corporate training constitutes another application area of Web-based learning systems. This is accompanied with catchwords like "learning on the job" and "learning on demand". Many companies are already using or planning server-based training courses delivered to an employee's desktop via an intranet. Principally, there is no difference between server-based learning systems via the WWW or via intranets, although the variety of users in an intranet will not be as large as in WWW-based learning systems. In both cases, different levels of background or prior information will require adaptive and adaptable learning systems that are able to take into account that existing knowledge in order to provide an individually tailored training course for the particular learner.

The problem is that most of the existing Web-based learning systems consist of a network of static hypertext pages. A challenging research goal is the development of advanced Web-based learning applications which can offer some interactivity and adaptivity. Adaptation is especially important for Web-based learning for at least two general reasons. First, most Web-based applications are to be used by a much wider variety of users than any standalone application. A Web application which is designed with a particular class of users in mind may not suit other users. Second, in many cases the user is "alone" working with a Web "tutor" or "course" (probably from home). The assistance that a colleague or a teacher typically provides in a normal classroom situation is not available.

2 Adaptation in Web-based Learning Systems

Existing Web-based learning systems use different types of adaptation techniques (Brusilovsky, 1996). These comprise adaptive presentation and adaptive navigation support, curriculum sequencing, intelligent analysis of students' solutions, interactive problem solving support, and example-based problem solving support. In the future, adaptive collaboration support, specially designed for the context of Web-based education, may complete this list.

The goal of *adaptive presentation* is to adapt the content of a hypermedia page to the user's goals, knowledge, and other information stored in the user model. In a system with adaptive presentation, the pages are not static but adaptively generated or assembled from different pieces for each user. For example, with several adaptive presentation techniques, expert users may receive more detailed and deep information, while novices receive additional explanations.

The goal of *curriculum sequencing* (also referred to as instructional planning technology) is to provide the student with the most suitable, individually planned sequence of knowledge units to learn and sequence of learning tasks (examples, questions, problems, etc.) to work with. In other words, it helps the student to find an "optimal path" through the learning material.

The goal of *adaptive navigation support* is to support the student in hyperspace orientation and navigation by changing the appearance of visible links. In particular, the system can adaptively sort, annotate, or partly hide the links of the current page to simplify the choice of the next link. Adaptive navigation support can be considered as an extension of curriculum sequencing technology into a hypermedia context. It shares the same goal - to help students to find an "optimal path" through the learning material. At the same time, adaptive navigation support is less directive than traditional sequencing: it guides students implicitly and leaves them with the choice of the next knowledge item to be learned and next problem to be solved.

Intelligent analysis of student solutions deals with students' final answers to educational problems (which can range from a simple question to a complex programming problem) no matter how these answers were obtained. Unlike non-intelligent checkers which can tell no more than whether the solution is correct, intelligent analyzers can tell exactly what is wrong or incomplete and which missing or incorrect piece of knowledge may be responsible for the error. Intelligent analyzers can provide the student with extensive error feedback and update the student model.

The goal of *interactive problem solving support* is to provide the student with intelligent help on each step of problem solving - from giving a hint to executing the next step for the student. The systems which implement this technology can watch the actions of the student, understand them, and use this understanding to provide help and to update the student model.

In an *example-based problem solving* context, students solve new problems taking advantage of examples from their earlier experience. In this context, an ITS helps students by suggesting the most relevant cases (examples explained to them or problems solved by them earlier). An example from the domain of teaching programming is ELM-PE (Weber, 1996b). Example based problem solving does not require extensive client-server interaction and, therefore, can be used easily in adaptive learning systems on the Web.

All these adaptation techniques require at least a rudimentary type of user modeling. While presentation adaptation and simple types of curriculum sequencing can be based on (typically rough) stereotype user models, adaptive navigation support and dynamic types of curriculum sequencing require at least overlay user models. The most sophisticated adaptation techniques (intelligent analysis of student solutions, interactive problem solving support, and example-based problem solving) require more advanced AI-techniques that typically are used in intelligent tutoring systems (e.g., rule-based or case-based reasoning).

3   User Modeling and Adaptation in ELM-ART

The introductory LISP course ELM-ART (ELM Adaptive Remote Tutor) is an example of a substantial an adaptive WWW learning system which uses different types of adaptivity and adaptability. It consists of an electronic textbook enhanced with significant interactive features (e.g., tests and quizzes, interactive programming support and program evaluation, and interaction with tutors or other learners via a chat room). This section explains how adaptivity and adaptability work in ELM-ART and describes the different types of knowledge representation and the underlying student modeling.

ELM-ART distinguishes two different types of knowledge representation. On the one hand, the electronic textbook with all the lessons, sections, and units is based mainly on domain knowledge and deals with acquiring this knowledge. On the other hand, the episodic learner model, ELM, deals with the procedural knowledge necessary to solve particular programming problems.

3.1   The Multi-layered Overlay Model

Knowledge about units to be learned from the electronic textbook is represented in terms of a conceptual network. Units are organized hierarchically into lessons, sections, subsections, and terminal (unit) pages. Terminal pages can introduce new concepts, present lists of test items to be worked at, or offer problems to be solved. Each unit is an object containing slots for the text unit to be presented with the corresponding page and for information that can be used to relate units and concepts to each other. Slots store information on prerequisite concepts, related concepts, and outcomes of the unit (the concepts that the system assumes to be known if the user worked through that unit successfully). Additionally, each unit can have a list of test items or a programming problem to be solved by the learner.

The user model related to this declarative conceptual domain knowledge is represented as a multi-layered overlay model. The first layer describes whether the user has already visited a page corresponding to a concept. The second layer contains information on which exercises or test items related to this particular concept the user has worked at and whether he or she successfully worked at the test items up to a criterion or solved the programming problem. The third layer describes whether a concept could be inferred as known via inference links from more advanced concepts the user already worked at successfully. Finally, the fourth layer describes whether a user has marked a concept as already known. Information in the different layers is updated independently. So, information from each different sources does not override others.

The multi-layered overlay model supports both the adaptive annotation of links and individual curriculum sequencing. Links that are shown in an overview on each page or in the table of contents are visually annotated according to five learning state of the corresponding concept. (1) A concept is annotated as 'already learned' if enough exercises or test items belonging to that concept or the programming problem have been solved successfully. (2) The concept is annotated as 'inferred' where the concept is not 'already learned' and it was inferred as learned from other concepts (third layer). (3) The concept is annotated as 'stated as known by the user' in case the user marked this concept as already known and there is no information that the concept is 'already learned' or 'inferred'. (4) A concept is annotated as 'ready and suggested to be visited' where it is not assigned to one of the first three learning states and all prerequisites to this concept are assigned to one of the first three learning states. (5) A concept is annotated as 'not ready to be visited' if none of the other four learning states hold. Link annotation is used as a hint only. That is, a learner can visit each page even if it is not recommended to be visited.

Individual curriculum sequencing in ELM-ART means that the system's suggestion of the next page to visit is computed dynamically according to the general learning goal and the learning state of the concepts as described above. The next suggested page will belong to the concept that is not assigned to one of the first three learning states and that is the next one ready to be learned.

3.2   The Episodic Learner Model

The system's knowledge consists of both common LISP domain knowledge (described above) and episodic knowledge about a particular learner. Both types of knowledge are highly interrelated. That is, on the one hand, the system is able to consider individual, episodic information for diagnosing code and for explaining errors in addition to using the common domain knowledge. On the other hand, when explaining individual errors and examples from the learner's individual learning history, the system can combine episodic information with information from the domain knowledge

The representation of the domain knowledge used in episodic modeling consists of a heterarchy of concepts and rules (Weber, 1996a). Concepts comprise knowledge about the programming language LISP (concrete LISP procedures as well as superordinate semantic concepts) and schemata of common algorithmic and problem solving knowledge (e.g., recursion schemata). These concept frames contain information about plan transformations leading to semantically equivalent solutions and about rules describing different ways to solve the goal stated by this concept. Additionally, there are bug rules describing errors observed by other students or buggy derivations of LISP concepts which, e.g., may result from confusion between semantically similar concepts.

The individual learner model consists of a collection of episodes that are descriptions of how problems have been solved by a particular student. These descriptions are explanation structures (in the sense of explanation-based generalization, Mitchell, Keller, & Kedar-Cabelli, 1986) of how a programming task has been solved by the student. That is, stored episodes contain all the information about which concepts and rules were needed to produce the program code the students offered as solutions to programming tasks. Episodes are not stored as a whole. They are distributed into snippets (Kolodner, 1993) with each snippet describing a concept and a rule that was used to solve a plan or subplan of the programming task. These snippets are stored as episodic instances with respect to the concepts of the domain knowledge. In this way, the individual episodic learner model is interrelated with the common domain knowledge.

To construct the learner model, the code produced by a learner is analyzed in terms of the domain knowledge on the one hand and a task description on the other hand. This cognitive diagnosis results in a derivation tree of concepts and rules the learner might have used to solve the problem. These concepts and rules are instantiations of units from the knowledge base. The episodic learner model is made up of these instantiations. In ELM, only examples from the course materials are pre-analyzed and the resulting explanation structures are stored in the individual case-based learner model. Elements from the explanation structures are stored with respect to their corresponding concepts from the domain knowledge base, so cases are distributed in terms of instances of concepts. These individual cases—or parts of them—are used in ELM-ART for two different adaptation purposes. First, episodic instances can be used during further analyses as shortcuts if the actual code and plan match corresponding patterns in episodic instances. The ELM model and the diagnosis of program code is described in more detail in (Weber, 1996a). Second, cases are used by the analogical component to show similar examples and problems for reminding purposes (Weber, 1996b).

3.3   Adaptable Features in ELM-ART

Some users like to be able to adapt a system to their own needs. In particular, this is true for more experienced users and those with previous experience and knowledge in the learning domain. Perhaps the most important feature that ELM-ART offers a user is the possibility to inspect and to edit his or her own user model as already mentioned above. In this way, the user can cooperate with the learning system in refining the learner model. That is why we can call the multi-layered user model a collaborative (Brusilovsky, 1996) or cooperative (Kay, 1995) learner model.

We think that in the WWW context and especially in a lifelong education context, collaborative student modeling becomes very important. Students accessing a WWW course may range from complete novices in the subject being taught to students who missed just a few aspects of the course. A Web-based learning system should not assume, as many on-site learning systems do, that all students have no knowledge of the subject. Instead, it has to provide an interface for advanced students to communicate their starting knowledge. Therefore, ELM-ART not only offers a cooperative student model but also offers pre-tests for each section. Students can show in the pre-tests how much they already know and the system will infer, from the successfully solved test items, which concepts the learner already knows. Then, the system will annotate these concepts as already known and will guide the learner to those pages that have to be learned or re-learned by the student.

Other adaptable features of ELM-ART comprise the possibility to determine the color of link annotation, to switch off or on link annotation and guiding, to suppress warnings, and to read the texts alone, without the exercises being presented.

4   Evaluation of Adaptive Learning Systems

Over the last two years, more and more results of empirical investigations have been reported. Most of them show only moderate (or even no) effects of single adaptation techniques. E.g., the empirical study on the effects of link annotation and individual guiding with ELM-ART (Weber & Specht, 1997) showed only some hint of how these adaptive techniques may influence the learning process. Subjects who had no previous experience with any programming language tried to learn longer with ELM-ART when they were guided by the system using a NEXT button. These results can be easily interpreted when one looks at the navigation behavior of the complete beginners more closely. All but one of the beginners had no experience in using a WWW browser. That is, these subjects profited from being guided directly by the system when using the NEXT button. Without such a button, they had to navigate through the course materials on their own. Learning to navigate through hypertext in addition to learning the programming language may have been too difficult. So individual adaptive guidance by the system is especially helpful for the complete beginners. Most subjects who were also familiar with at least one other programming language were familiar with Web browsers. They were more pleased with the link annotation and stayed with the learning system longer when links were annotated adaptively.

Crucial to a learning situation is how successful and how fast learners complete the course. As ELM-ART directly stems from the on-site learning environment ELM-PE (Weber and Möllenberg, 1995), comparing results of learning with ELM-ART to previous results from learning with ELM-PE will give an idea of how well one can learn with a web-based learning system. In ELM-PE, students used the system to solve programming tasks in parallel to the traditional classroom course. ELM-PE offered automatic diagnosis of problem solutions and the individual presentation of example solutions based on the episodic learner model. In ELM-ART, presentation of the texts and all explanations were given by the system in addition to all adaptive features mentioned above. Results from the final programming tasks (three tasks on recursive programming) show that students learning with ELM-ART were more often successful in solving the third, most difficult programming problem. Interestingly, this effect not only holds for learners with previous programming knowledge but also for the very beginners. This may be interpreted as a hint that adaptive techniques in combination with interactive feedback and knowledge-based problem solving support may result in a more successful learning situation.

The main problem with most studies investigating the effects of adaptive link annotation and individual curriculum sequencing not showing up clear effects may stem from the very specific learning situations. Most of these studies were done with learners that were introduced to a totally new domain. That is, the best learning strategy of the learners was to follow the pages of the course from the beginning to the end like reading a book from the first to the last page. This was the same sequence of pages that link annotation and guiding suggested.

In the beginning it was argued that adaptive techniques like link annotation and guiding will be most effective in further education and especially in re-learning situations. What we need are empirical investigation of learning situations where learners with totally different background knowledge of the learning domain are compared. A first example of such an investigation was done by Specht (1997) with his adaptive statistics tutor AST. In a re-learning situation, students first had to answer an introductory questionnaire. In the Experimental Group, students were only guided to pages where they had shown gaps in the introductory questionnaire while students in the Control Group had to follow their own path through the course. The results show that students from the Experimental Group much faster worked through the re-learning situation and answered the questions more successfully in the final questionnaire. I expect that further investigations in similar learning situations will support these preliminary results.

References

Brusilovsky, P. (1996). Methods and techniques of adaptive hypermedia. *User Modeling and User-Adapted Interaction, 6*, 87-129.

Kay, J. (1995). The UM toolkit for cooperative user models. *User Models and User Adapted Interaction, 4*, 149-196.

Khan, B. H. (1997). *Web-based instruction.* Englewood Cliffs, NJ: Educational Technology Publications.

Mitchell, T. M., Keller, R. M., & Kedar-Cabelli, S. T. (1986). Explanation-based generalization: a unifying view. *Machine Learning, 1*, 47-80.

Kolodner, J. L. (1993). *Case-based reasoning.* San Mateo, CA: Morgan Kaufmann.

Specht, M. (1997). *Adaptive Methoden in computerbasierten Lehr/Lernumgebungen.* Dissertation: Universit%œt Trier.

Weber, G. (1996a). Episodic learner modeling. *Cognitive Science, 20*, 195-236.

Weber, G. (1996b). Individual selection of examples in an intelligent programming environment. *Journàl of Artificial Intelligence in Education, 7*, 3-31.

Weber, G. & Möllenberg, A. (1995). ELM programming environment: A tutoring system for LISP beginners. In K. F. Wender, F. Schmalhofer, & H.-D. Böcker (Eds.), *Cognition and computer programming* (pp. 373-408). Norwood, NJ: Ablex Publishing Corporation.

Network Supported Active Social Learning Activities

Tak-Wai Chan

Department of Computer Science and Information Engineering
National Central University
Taiwan

Networks will essentially connect all the people, all the content and all the computing power in the world. As a result, a learning society will emerge and a learning ecology will evolve. If we want to find out the biggest impact of networks on education, then the answer must be that the network changes the way we learn, including when, where, what, how and why we learn. In particular, we hypotheses that *network supported active social learning activities* will take the key role in accelerating all these changes and opening the door for advancing learning technology development.

Active social learning is a national project in Taiwan with around 50 team members from various universities and research institutes. It covers disciplines of learning software technology (agent technology, natural language processing, machine learning, component technology, virtual reality), education, cognitive psychology, and advanced network and hardware. The project focuses on four active social learning models. The first model, omnipresent and highly interactive classroom learning, extends the meaning of classroom learning with handheld computers and both short and long distance wireless communication. This work investigates how learning happens within and outside traditional classroom and enhances interactions among teachers and students. The second model is *structural knowledge learning*. This model actually is the scaling up traditional computer aided instruction systems and intelligent tutoring systems to support learning decomposed knowledge units in a safe way on the network. Structural knowledge learning includes two sub-models, subject-based learning and target-based learning. The third model, *task-based learning*, addresses learning and abilities required in next century. Task-based learning includes four sub-models, theme-based learning, project-based learning, mission-based learning, and creative problem solving. While the structural knowledge learning stresses on knowledge acquisition, task-based learning intends to promote students to organize teams to accomplish some tasks by using and integrating what they have learnt in a creative way and with the support of resources available on the network. The fourth model is *virtual community based learning* supported by a cyber city called EduCities. This model encourages a student to serve others, such as playing the roles of peer tutors and police, and thus learn to be a good cyber citizen. There are various activities in EduCities that help build a learning society, including parents, volunteers, professors, etc.

Besides explaining our vision of active social learning project, I shall pose some challenges on student modeling research. For example, in the view of supporting such a variety learning activities in a cyber community, to further our research, shall we have to re-define student modeling? How student modeling can be extended to community modeling that can incorporate students' and teachers' input? What are the uses of all these works in the first place? In a way, this talk gives a glimpse of my answer and action towards a vision I gave in a talk in AIED95 some years ago, but it actually raises more questions than answers.

Recent User Modeling Research in Germany

Alfred Kobsa

GMD FIT and University of Essen, Germany

A special interest group of the German Society of Informatics (GI) on User Modeling and Adaptivity in Interactive Dialog System has been founded in 1996 (ABIS Homepage). Annual workshops have been held since 1994 in academic and industrial environments (ABIS Homepage). Most subareas of user modeling and user-adaptive systems are well represented in Germany, with the following clusters being particularly active research areas:

Student modeling and student-adaptive tutoring systems: KBS Homepage, Multibook Homepage, Trier Educational Software Server.

Adaptive multimedia product presentation: Jörding 1999, Popp & Lödel 1996, Rössel 1998, Timm & Rosewitz 1998.

Interest-sensitive mobile tourist guidance systems: Deep Map Homepage, Fink et al. 1999, HIPS Homepage, Oppermann & Specht 1998, LaboUr Homepage.

Machine learning for user modeling: ML4UM Homepage, Joachims & Mlademic (1998), LaboUr Homepage, Pohl & Nick 1999, PAN Hompage, READY Homepage.

ABIS Home page: http://fit.gmd.de/GI/fg2.3.3.html

Deep Map Homepage: http://www.villa-bosch.de/eml/englisch/projekte/deepmap/vision.html

Fink, J., Kobsa, A., and Nill, J. (1999): Adaptable and Adaptive Information Provision for All Users, Including Disabled and Elderly People. *New Review of Multimedia and Hypermedia*, in print.

HIPS Homepage (GMD site): http://fit.gmd.de/hci/projects/hips/

Joachims, T. and Mlademic, D. (1998): Browsing-Assistenten, Tour Guides und adaptive WWW-Server. Künstliche Intelligenz 3/98, 23-29.

Jörding, T. (1999); Temporary User Modeling for Adaptive Product Presentations in the Web. UM99.

KBS Hyperbook Homepage: http://www.kbs.uni-hannover.de/hyperbook/

LaboUr Homepage: http://fit.gmd.de/~labour/

ML4UM Homepage: http://fit.gmd.de/ml4um/

Multibook Homepage: http://www.kom.e-technik.tu-darmstadt.de//Research/mmbook/

Oppermann, R. and Specht, M. (1998): Adaptive support for a mobile museum guide. Available at http://www.egd.igd.fhg.de/~imc98/Proceedings/imc98-SessionMA3-2.pdf

Pohl, W and Nick, A. (1999): Machine Learning and Knowledge-Based User Modeling in the LaboUr approach. In this volume.

Popp, H. and Lödel, D. (1996): Fuzzy Techniques and User Modeling in Sales Assistants. User Modeling and User-Adapted Interaction 5(3-4), 349-370.

PAN Homepage: http://www.dfki.de/~bauer/PAN/

Rössel, M. (1998): Pragmatische Benutzermodellierung im Adaptiven Multimedialen Präsentationssystem AMPRreS. ABIS-98, 67-75.

READY Homepage: http://w5.cs.uni-sb.de/~ready/

Trier Educational Software Server: http://cogpsy.uni-trier.de:8000/TLServ-e.html

Timm, U. J. and Rosewitz, M. (1998): Benutzermodellierung in der Elektronischen Produktberatung. ABIS-98, 105-112.

The Canadian TeleLearning Network of Centres of Excellence and Its Potential for User Modelling Research

Gordon McCalla[1]

Department of Computer Science, U. of Saskatchewan,
Saskatoon, SK, S7N 5A9, CANADA

TeleLearning is one of Canada's Networks of Centres of Excellence (TL·NCE), a geographically distributed, but conceptually focussed, network of researchers and client communities from across Canada who are collectively working on the development, application, and evaluation of advanced technologies to support human learning (http://www.telelearn.ca). The underlying research philosophies are based on collaborative learning and knowledge building, using the most advanced communications and information technology. Over 130 researchers from education, the social sciences, computer science (including the presenter of this talk), and engineering from 30 universities are working with client communities to achieve the Network's mission. Among the goals of TL-NCE are (i) to develop new models of learning, learning environments, and pedagogies to better meet the needs of the workplace and the nation; (ii) to develop and transfer new technologies that can manage, sustain and constructively direct networked learning; (iii) to understand the nature of effective TeleLearning communities at all levels.

In this talk, I will discuss TL-NCE and its current and potential need for user modelling. TL-NCE is a rich environment in which to explore user modelling, both by providing interdisciplinary perspectives to the research effort and by supplying client groups from industry, government, and educational organizations to field test new user modelling ideas and to extend the technologies developed in research labs into the community. Moreover, the potential application of user modelling techniques to TL-NCE cuts across a wide range of TeleLearning areas, for example, (i) to ensure appropriate metaphors and interface options for different types of users (learners and teachers); (ii) to enable adaptive course generation, teaching strategies, and content selection; (iii) to adaptively support collaboration, group formation, and role assignment; (iv) to adaptively configure TeleLearning communication environments; (v) to dynamically find appropriate peer helpers and support their interaction; (vi) to provide input to socio-economic modelling based on models of individuals and groups. In some of these areas, such user modelling research is being actively pursued; but in most of them user modelling is neither being investigated nor deployed. The non-trivial challenge facing the user modelling researchers in TL-NCE is to demonstrate to our social science and humanities colleagues and our industrial partners the value-added that can be provided by user modelling and other artificial intelligence techniques.

---

[1] Visiting Scholar, 1998-99 at Basser Department of Computer Science, University of Sydney, Sydney, NSW 2006, AUSTRALIA

User Modeling Research in Japan

Riichiro Mizoguchi

ISIR, Osaka University, Japan

This abstract overviews user modeling research in Japan. Not only modeling methods including learning algorithms but visualization for adaptive interaction and human modeling for plant operator have been extensively done. Modeling in learning support is also active. The activities are classified into the following five major categories.

1. User modeling for adaptive interface
   Command sequence prediction (Motoda 1997)
2. User modeling for information search
   Visualization for adaptive interaction(Lokuge 1995)(Sugimoto 1997)(Sugimoto 1998)
3. Learner modeling for individual adaptation
   Logic-based induction(Kono 1994)(Ikeda 1994) and opportunistic group formation for CSCL(Ikeda 1997)
4. Human modeling(General)
   4.1 Plant operator modeling(Furuta 1993)(Naito 1995) (Ujita 1995) (Yoshimura 1997)
   4.2 Speaker modeling in spoken dialog(Yamada 1993)
5. Idea creation support(Hori 1994)(Fujita 1997); Many others in Japanese.
   Visualization using a Multi-Dimensional Scaling, called MDS-kNN has been extensively used (Kakusho 1983).

Reference

Fujita, K.and S. Kunifuji (1997) A realization of a reflection of personal information on distributed brain-storming environment, Springer's LNCS 1274, 166-181.
Furuta, K. and S. Kondo (1993) An approach to assessment of plan man-machine systems by computer simulation of an operator's cognitive behavior, Int. J. of Man-Machine Studies, 39,3, 473-493.
Hori, K. (1994) A system for aiding creative concept formation, IEEE Trans. On SMC, 24, 6, 882-894.
Ikeda, M. and R. Mizoguchi (1994) FITS: A Framework for ITS -- A Computational Model of Tutoring, J. of AI in Education, Vol. 5, No.3, 319-348.
Ikeda, M., S. Go and R. Mizoguchi (1997) Opportunistic Group Formation--A Theory for Intelligent Support in Collaborative Learning --, Proc. of AI-ED-97,167-174, Kobe, Japan.
Kakusho, O and R. Mizoguchi (1983) A new algorithm for non-linear mapping with applications to dimension and cluster analyses, Pattern Recognition, 16, 1, 109-117.
Kono, Y., M. Ikeda, and R. Mizoguchi (1994) THEMIS: A Nonmonotonic Inductive Student Modeling System, J. of AI in Education, Vol. 5, No.3, 371-413.
Lokuge, I. and Ishizaki, S. (1995) GeoSpace: An interactive visualization system for exploring complex information spaces, Proc. CHI'95, 409-414.
Motoda, H. and K. Yoshida (1997) Machine learning techniques to make computers easier to use, Proc. of IJCAI97, 1622-1631, Nagoya, Japan.

Naito, N., J. Itoho, K. Monta and M. Makino (1995) An intelligent human-machine system based on an ecological interface design concept, J. of Nuclear Engineering and Design, 154, 97-108.

Sugimoto, M., N. Katayama and A. Takatsu (1997) COSPEX: A system for constructing private digital libraries, Proc. of IJCAI97, 738-744, Nagoya, Japan.

Sugimoto, M., K. Hori and S. Ohsuga (1998) A system for visualizing viewpoints and its application to intelligent activity support, IEEE Trans. SMS, 28C, 1, 124-136.

Ujita, H., R. Kawano and S. Yoshimura (1995) An approach for evaluation expert performance in emergency situations, J. of Reliability Engineering and Systems Safety, 47, 163-173.

Yamada, K., R. Mizoguchi, et al. (1993) Model of Utterance and Its Use in Cooperative Response Generation, Proc. of East-West International Conference on Human-Computer Interaction (EWHCI '93), 252-264.

Yoshimura, S. and N. Hasegawa (1997) Operator behavior model with learning mechanism, Proc. of Time and Space in Process Control, 191-194, Italy.

POSTER PRESENTATIONS

Ivon Arroyo, Joseph Beck, Klaus Schultz, Beverly Park Woolf,
A useful prediction variable for student models: cognitive development level

Jim Carter,
The affective adaptation of hypermedia based on personality characteristics

David Chin, Matha Crosby, Asanga Porage and Rita Vick,
The effectiveness of user models in reducing cognitive load

Amos David and David Bueno Vallejo,
The user's main objective and relevance feedback for personalising the system's solution

D Djian, K Tsui, B Remael,
Detecting user presence and state of mind in a multi-modal user interface

Mattias Forsberg, Kristina Hook, Martin Svensson,
How to design for social navigation

Trude Heift and Paul McFetridge,
The role of the student model in the analysis of student input

Nicola Henze and Wolfgang Nejdl,
Student modeling in an active learning environment using bayesian networks

Jatinder Hothi and Wendy Hall,
The StaDy UM: constructing a user model framework for educational adaptive hypermedia

Martin Kurze,
Modeling the user in virtual environments - more than just geometry

E Millan, J Agosta and J Perez de la Cruz,
Simplifying the problem of the specification of the parameters in bayesian student modeling

Matthias Rauterberg and Morten Fjeld,
An automatic task modelling approach based on empirical data

Marc Roessel,
Concept and realization of the right support at the right time: the intelligent tour guide

Mia Stern, Joseph Beck and Beverly Park Woolf,
Naive Bayes Classifiers for User Modeling

Marcello Sarini and Carlo Strapparava,
User modelling in a museum exploration adaptive system

Barry Smyth, Paul Cotter and Gregory O'Hare,
Surfing the digital wave - generating personalised TV programme guides using collaborative,
content-based recommendation techniques

Junichi Suzuki and Yoshikazu Yamamoto,
Metadata management in personalizing web presentations

Stefanie Thies,
User modelling for collaborative critiquing

AUTHOR ADDRESSES

Agosta, J.M.
Knoledge Industries
334 Arbor Drive
South San Francisco,
CA 94080. USA
johnmark@kic.com

Albrecht, D.W
School of Computer Science and
Software Eng., Monash University
Clayton - VICTORIA 3168
AUSTRALIA
dwa@csse.monash.edu.au

Ali, Syed S.
Elect. Eng. and Computer Science
University of Wisconsin-Milwaukee
3200 N. Cramer Street
Milwaukee WI 53211
syali@uwm.edu

Ardissono, Liliana
Dipartimento di Informatica
Universita di Torino
C.so Svizzera 185
10149 Torino - Italy
liliana@di.unito.it

Arroyo, Ivon
School of Education and
Computer Science Department
University of Massachusetts,
Amherst
ivon@cs.umass.edu

Averman, Charlotte
Swedish Inst. of Computer Science
Human Computer Interaction and
Language Engineering Laboratory

Bartell, Brian T.
Conceptual Dimensions, Inc
San Diego CA
USA

Beck, Joseph E.
School of Education and
Computer Science Department
University of Massachusetts,
Amherst
beck@cs.umass.edu

Belew, Richard K.
Dept. of Computer Science and
Engineering
University of California
San Diego CA
USA

Berthold, Andre
Department of Computer Science
University of Saarbrucken
Germany
berthold@coli.uni-sb.de

Berthouze, Luc
Intelligent Systems Division
Electrotechnical Laboratory
Japan
berthouz@etl.go.jp

Bianchi-Berthouze, Nadia
Intelligent Systems Division
Electrotechnical Laboratory
Japan
bianchi@etl.go.jp

Biermann, Alan W.
Department of Computer Science
P.O Box 90129 Duke University,
Durham, N.C 27708-0129 U.S.A
awb@cs.duke.edu

Billsus, Daniel
Dept. of Information and Computer
Science
University of California
Irvine, CA - USA
dbillsus@ics.uci.edu

Brock, Derek
U.S. Naval Research Lab.
Washington, DC
USA

Brzezinski, Jacek
Institute for Applied AI
School of Computer Science,
Telecommunications and
Information Systems
DePaul University, Chicago,
USA
jbrzezin@condor.depaul.edu

Bull, Susan
School of Languages
University of Brighton
Falmer, Brighton, East Essex
BN1 9PH
UK
s.bull@brighton.ac.uk

Bushey, Robert
SBC Technology Resources, Inc
Austin, TX
USA
Bob_Bushey@tri.sbc.com

Bynre, Ciara
Broadcom Research Ireland Ltd
Dublin
Ireland

Carenini, Giuseppe
Intelligent Systems Program
University of Pittsburgh
USA
carenini@cs.pitt.edu

Chan, Tak-Wai
Department of Computer Science
and Information Engineering
National Central University
Taiwan

Cohen, Robin
Department of Computer Science
University of Waterloo
Waterloo, ON
Canada
rcohen@dragon.uwaterloo.ca

Conati, Cristina
Intelligent Systems Program
University of Pittsburgh
USA
conati@isp.pitt.ed

Convertino, Gregorio
Cognitive and Communication
Technology Division
ITC-IRST
Italy

Cottrell, Garrison W.
Dept. of Computer Science and
Engineering
University of California
San Diego CA
USA

Cruz, J.L Perez de la
Dept. de Lenguajes y Ciencias de
la Computacion. E.T.S.I de
Informatica.
Campus Univeritario de Teatinos.
Malaga 29080. Spain
eva@lcc.uma.es

Cunningham, Padraig
Department of Computer Science
Trinity College
Dublin
Ireland
Padraig.Cunningham@cs.tcd.ie

De Angeli, Antonella
Department of Psychology
University of Trieste
Italy
deangeli@univ.trieste.it

de Buen, Pablo R.
Instituto de Investigaciones
Electricas
Cuernavaca
Mexico
debuen@iie.org.mx

De Carolis, Berardina
Department of Informatics
University of Bari
Italy
nadja@aos2.di.uniba.it

Deelman, Tomas
SBC Technology Resources, Inc
Austin, TX
USA

Diligenti, M.
University of Siena
Dept. f Information Engineering
Via Roma
561-53100
Siena

Djian, David
BT Laboratories, MLB 1/PP 12
Martlesham Heath
Ipswich IP5 3RE, U.K
djiand@info.bt.co.uk

du Boulay, Benedict
School of Cognitive & Computing
Sciences
University of Sussex
Brighton
BN1, 9QI
UK

Encarnacao, L. Miguel
Fraunhofer Center for Research
in Computer Graphics (CRCG), Inc
Providence RI, USA

Fink, Josef
GMD FIT
German National Research Center
for Information Technology
Sankt Augustin
Germany
josef.fink@gmd.de

Fisher, Gerhard
Center for LifeLong Learning and
Design
Department of Computer Science
and Institute of Cognitive Science
University of Colorado, Boulder, CO,
U.S.A

Fleming, Michael
Department of Computer Science
University of Waterloo
Waterloo, ON
Canada
mwflemin@neumann.uwaterloo.ca

Forsberg, Mattias
PharmaSoft AB, Box 1237
S-751 42 Uppsala, Sweden
mattias.forsberg@pharmasoft.com

Gaines, Brian R.
Knowledge Science Institute
University of Calgary
Alberta
Canada T2N 1N4
gaines@cpsc.ucalgary.ca

Gmytrasiewicz, Piotr J.
Dept. of Computer Science and
Engineering
University of Texas at Arlington
piotr@huckle.uta.edu

Goy, Anna
Dipartimento di Informatica
Universita di Torino
C.so Svizzera 185
10149 Torino
Italy
goy@di.unito.it

Heift, Trude
Department of Linguistics
Simon Fraser University
Burnaby, B.C Canada V5A 1S6
heift@sfu.ca

Henze, Nicola
University of Hannover
Lange Laube 3,
30159 Hannover
henze@kbs.uni-hannover.de

Hook, Kristina
SICS, Box 1263
S-164 28 Kista, Sweden
kia@sics.se

Horvitz, Eric
Decision Theory and Adaptive
Systems
Microsoft Research
WA
USA
horvitz@MICROSOFT.com

Jameson, Anthony
Department of Computer Science
University of Saarbrucken
Germany
jameson@cs.uni-sb.de

Jean, Stephanie
Department of Computer Science
Universite du Maine
France
Stephanie.Jean@lium.univ-lemans.fr

Joerding, Tanja
Department of Computer Science
Dresden University of Technology
Germany
tj4@inf.tu-dresden.de

Johnson, C.W.
Department of Computer Science
University of Glasgow
Glasgow - Scotland
johnson@dcs.gla.ac.uk

Joy, Deborah
The MITRE Corporation
Bedford MA
USA

Karkaletsis, Vangelis
Institute of Informatics and
Telecommunications, National
Centre for Scientific Research
(NCSR) "Demokritos"
15310 Aghia Paraskevi Attikis
Greece
vangelis@iit.demokritos.gr

Kato, Toshikazu
Dept. of Industrial and System Eng.
Chuo University
Tokyo - Japan
kato@etl.go.jp

Kobsa, Alfred
GMD FIT
German National Research Center
for Information Technology
D-53754 St. Augustin
Germany
kobsa@zeus.gmd.de

Koedinger, Kenneth R.
School of Computer Science
Carnegie Mellon University
Pittsburgh, PA
USA
ken.koedinger@CS.CMU.EDU

Kuepper, Detlef
GMD FIT
German National Research Center
for Information Technology
D-53754 St. Augustin
Germany
ADJN.Kuepper@t-online.de

Kumar, Vive
Department of Computer Science
University of Saskatchewan
Canada
vive.kumar@usask.ca

Kurze, Martin
T-Berkom GmbH
Goslarer Ufer 35
10589 Berlin, Germany
kurze@berkom.de

Langley, Pat
Intelligent Systems Laboratory
Daimler-Benz Research and
Technology Center
1510 Page Mill Road, Palo Alto, CA
94304 USA
langley@rtna.daimlerbenz.com

Lau, Tessa
Dept. of Computer Science &
Engineering
University of Washington
Seattle, WA
USA

Lesh, Neal
MERL-A Mitsubishi Electric
Research Laboratory
lesh@merl.com

Linton, Frank
The MITRE Corporation
Bedford MA
USA
linton@mail11.mitre.org

Lisetti, Christine
Department of Information Systems
and Decision Sciences
University of South Florida
USA
lisetti@coba.usf.edu

Litman, Diane J.
AT&T Labs - Research
Florham Park, NJ
USA
diane@research.att.com

Luckin, Rosemary
School of Cognitive & Computing
Sciences
University of Sussex
Brighton - BN1, 9QI
UK
rosel@cogs.susx.ac.uk

Machado, Isabel
INESC
Rua Alves Redol 9
1000 Lisboa
Portugal
Isabel.Machado@inesc.pt

Mark, Mary A.
School of Computer Science
Carnegie Mellon University
Pittsburgh, PA
USA
mmbt@cs.cmu.edu

Marti, P.
University of Siena
Multimedia Laboratory
Via dei Termini
6I-53100 Siena
Italy

Martins, Alexandre
IST and INESC
Rua Alves Redol 9
1000 Lisboa
Portugal
Alexandre.Martins@inesc.pt

Mauney, Jennifer Mitchell
Mauney Consulting
Austin, TX
USA

McCalla, Gordon
Department of Computational
Science 1C101 Engineering Building
University of Saskatchewan
Saskatoon, Saskatchewan
Canada S7N OWO
Mccalla@cs.usask.ca

McFetridge, Paul
Department of Linguistics
Simon Fraser University
Burnaby, B.C Canada V5A 1S6
mcfet@sfu.ca

McRoy, Susan W.
Electr. Eng. and Computer Science
University of Wisconsin-Milwaukee
3200 N. Cramer Street
Milwaukee - WI 53211
mcroy@uwm.edu

Millan, E.
Dept. de Lenguajes y Ciencias de
la Computacion. E.T.S.I de
Informatica.
Campus Univeritario de Teatinos.
Malaga 29080. Spain
eva@lcc.uma.es

Mizoguchi, Riichiro
ISIR, Osaka University
Japan
miz@ei.sanken.osaka-u.ac.jp

Moore, Johanna
HCRC
University of Edinburgh
UK
jmoore@cs.pitt.edu

Morales, Eduardo F.
ITESM-Campus Morelos
Mexico

Morales, Rafael
School of Artificial Intelligence
University of Edinburgh
United Kingdom
R.Morales@ed.ac.uk

Nejdl, Wolfgang
University of Hannover
Lange Laube 3,
30159 Hannover
nejdl@kbs.uni-hannover.de

Nicholson, A.E
School of Computer Science and
Software
Engineering, Monash University
Clayton
VICTORIA 3168
AUSTRALIA
annn@csse.monash.edu.au

Nick, Achim
GMD FIT
HCI Research Department
Sankt Augustin
Germany
achim.nick@gmd.de

Paek, Tim
Department of Psychology
Stanford University
CA
USA

Pain, Helen
School of Artificial Intelligence
University of Edinburgh
United Kingdom
helen@aisb.ed.ac.uk

Paiva, Ana
IST and INESC
Rua Alves Redol 9
1000 Lisboa
Portugal
Ana.Paiva@inesc.pt

Paliouras, Georgios
Institute of Informatics and
Telecommunications, National
Centre for Scientific Research
(NCSR) "Demokritos"
15310
Aghia Paraskevi Attikis Greece
paliourg@iit.demokritos.gr

Pan, Shimei
Computer Science Department
Columbia University
New York, NY
USA

Papatheodorou, Christos
Division of Applied Technologies
National Centre for
Scientific Research (NCSR)
"Demokritos" 15310
Aghia Paraskevi Attikis Greece
papatheodor@lib.demokritos.gr

Pazzani, Michael J.
Dept. of Information and Computer
Science
University of California
Irvine, CA, USA

Petrelli, Daniela
Cognitive and Communication
Technology Division
ITC-IRST
Italy
petrelli@irst.itc.it

Petroni, L.
University of Siena
Multimedia Laboratory
Via dei Termini
6I-53100
Siena - Italy

Pohl, Wolfgang
GMD FIT
HCI Research Department
Sankt Augustin
Germany
Wolfgang.Pohl@gmd.de

Restificar, Angelo C.
Electrical Engineering and Computer
Science
University of Wisconsin-Milwaukee
3200 N. Cramer Street
Milwaukee
WI 53211
angelo@miller.cs.uwm.edu

Rich, Charles
MERL-A Mitsubishi Electric
Research Laboratory
rich@merl.com

Rizzo, A.
University of Siena
Multimedia Laboratory
Via dei Termini
6I-53100
Siena
Istituto di Psicologia
CNR Viale Marx
135I-00137
Roma

Rudstrom, Asa
Swedish Institute of Computer
Science
Human Computer Interaction and
Language Engineering Laboratory
asa@sics.se

Sarini, Marcello
Istituto per la Ricerca
Scientifica e Tecnologica,
I - 38050 Povo/Trento, Italy

Schaefer, Hans-Peter
The MITRE Corporation
Bedford MA
USA

Schultz, Klaus
School of Education and
Computer Science Department
University of Massachusetts,
Amherst
schultz@cs.umass.edu

Shaw, Mildred L. G.
Knowledge Science Institute
University of Calgary
Alberta
Canada T2N 1N4

Shurville, Simon
School of Languages
University of Brighton
Falmer, Brighton, East Essex
BN1 9PH
UK
sjs16@itri.bton.ac.uk

Sidner, Candace L.
Lotus Development Corporation
csidner@lotus.com

Spyropoulos, Constantine D.
Institute of Informatics and
Telecommunications, National
Centre for
Scientific Research (NCSR)
"Demokritos"
15310
Aghia Paraskevi Attikis Greece
Costass@iit.demokritos.gr

Stern, Mia K.
Center for Knowledge
Communication,
Department of Computer Science
University of Massachusetts
Amherst, MA 01003
stern@cs.umass.edu

Strapparava, Carlo
Istituto per la Ricerca
Scientifica e Tecnologica,
I - 38050 Povo/Trento, Italy
strappa@itc.it

Stoev, Stanislav L.
Department of Computer Science
University of Tubingen
Germany
sstoev@gris.uni-tuebingen.de

Suryadi, Dicky
Dept. of Computer Science and Eng.
University of Texas at Arlington
dicky@dali.uta.edu

Svensson, Martin
SICS, Box 1263
S-164 28 Kista, Sweden
martins@sics.se

Thies, Stefanie
University of Paderborn
thies@hni.uni-paderborn.de

Thomson, Judi R.
Department of Computer Science
University of Saskatchewan
Canada
thomson@cs.usask.ca

Tierney, Mark
Swedish Institute of Computer
Science
Human Computer Interaction and
Language Engineering Laboratory
mark@sics.se

Tozzi, G.
University of Siena
Multimedia Laboratory
Via dei Termini
61-53100 Siena
tozzi@lettere.media.unisi.it

Trafton, J.Gregory
U.S. Naval Research Laboratory
Washington, DC
USA
trafton@itd.nrl.navy.mil

Vadera, Sunil
University of Salford
UK
S.Vadera@cms.salford.ac.uk

VanLehn, Kurt
Department of Computer Science
University of Pittsburgh
USA
vanlehn@cs.pitt.edu

Vogt, Christopher C.
Dept. of Computer Science and
Engineering
University of California
San Diego CA
USA
vogt@cs.ucsd.edu

Waern, Annika
Swedish Inst. of Computer Science
Human Computer Interaction and
Language Engineering Laboratory

Waszkiewicz, Pawel
Department of Computer Science
Trinity College
Dublin
Ireland

Weber, Gerhard
Department of Psychology,
University of Education
Freiburg, Germany.

Winter, Mike
ARIES Laboratory
Department of Computer Science
University of Saskatchewan, SK
Canada

Wittig, Frank
Department of Computer Science
University of Saarbrucken
Germany
fwittig@cs.uni-sb.de

Woolf, Beverly Park
School of Education and
Computer Science Department
University of Massachusetts,
Amherst
bev@cs.umass.edu

Zukerman, I.
School of Computer Science and
Software
Engineering, Monash University
Clayton
VICTORIA 3168
AUSTRALIA
ingrid@csse.monash.edu.au

AUTHOR INDEX

Page

Printed in the United States
By Bookmasters